William Carew Hazlitt

Supplements to the third and final series of bibliographical

collections and notes,

1474-1700

William Carew Hazlitt

Supplements to the third and final series of bibliographical collections and notes, 1474-1700

ISBN/EAN: 9783337718466

Printed in Europe, USA, Canada, Australia, Japan

Cover: Foto ©Lupo / pixelio.de

More available books at **www.hansebooks.com**

PREFATORY WORDS.

THE spontaneous proposal of Mr. Gray of Cambridge to prepare, as a labour of love, a General Index to my Bibliographical Works, is answerable for the deviation which the present Supplements to my Third and Final Series of *Collections and Notes* mark from the settled purpose which I had formed of printing no more titles on a sectional plan.

The dispersion of several important libraries during the last two or three seasons had involved, almost as a necessity, an accumulation at Barnes, where I live, of much new matter of interest, as I make it my unchangeable practice to let no book, if I can help it, pass through the auction-room unexamined and uncatalogued; and in addition, the rarities in the Lists published by the Trade, both in London and the provinces, may be said almost as a constant rule to fall under my notice.

In this manner it is easy to perceive how, in the course of about two years of unusual activity among the auctioneers, some 2000 fresh items might accrue; and seeing the excessively arduous process of bringing them together, and the risk of destruction by fire, I deemed it, on the whole, advisable to go to press once more, especially as by such a course the matter constituting this Appendix would be incorporated with Mr. Gray's Index.

The principal collections which have come into the market since I issued my last volume are those of Mr. R. S. Turner, Mr. Gibson-Craig, Baron Seillières, the Earl of Aylesford, and the Earl of Hardwicke.

The opportunity afforded to me by these and other sales has fructified in a large accession of entries in the Early English, the Anglo-Gallic, and the Scotish Series, as well as to the stores of works on Great Britain and Ireland of an historical, devotional, or literary character printed abroad.

The authorities at the British Museum have continued to shew me every possible courtesy in examining books in that institution; but the curators of our university and college libraries are, I am bound to say, less attentive to the wants of workers like myself, and their organisation is, as a rule, of the most rudimentary character. Even at the Bodleian, since the regretted death of Dr. Coxe,* I find a singular and lamentable backwardness on the part of the keeper to assist a gratuitous and national undertaking like the present, although my labours ought to be viewed with exceptional indulgence, as conducive to the facilitation of research; and I cannot avoid feeling that I should have experienced greater consideration from Sir Thomas Bodley than it pleased Mr. Nicholson on a particular occasion to pay me, where the application for help was of a perfectly legitimate and very modest nature. The Rev. F. Madan is personally most obliging, where I have occasionally applied for some piece of information. *Non cuivis homini contingit adire Oxonium.* I can scarcely be expected to travel to Oxford for the verification of a few words in a title, or for the collation of a tract. After all, I hope

---

* My respected acquaintance, the late Dr. Coxe, spared no pains to satisfy my occasional inquiries; but I believe that he once good-humouredly wondered if Mr. Hazlitt thought that he was there specially to act as his assistant.

that Mr. Nicholson, as he grows older, will grow wiser. At present, he must be regarded as a novice.

Nor must I omit the obligation under which I am always lying to my good friends the London booksellers—Mr. Quaritch himself, ever most liberal in the loan of any treasures which he acquires, Messrs. Jarvis & Son, Mr. Henry Gray, Mr. Leighton of Brewer Street, and many others. Messrs. Sotheby, Wilkinson, & Hodge also continue to give me every facility for inspecting the countless rarities of which I, and through me the public, owe our common knowledge to their courtesy.

I have already dwelled on the considerable aid which I have all along derived from those gentlemen whose specialism it is to form collections on particular lines; and the notable and increasing library of my friend Mr. Henry Stopes, of Upper Norwood, in the department of books illustrative of wines and other liquors in all their stages of development and application, has proved of very essential service to me. Within the limits which Mr. Stopes has thought fit to lay down for himself, some of the most instructive literature occurs—contributions of former times to topics of social interest and to many branches of economics. We see on Mr. Stopes's shelves numerous publications, not necessarily of a costly character, which shed light on the ideas of our ancestors relative to such peculiarly human subjects as agriculture, gardening, cookery, the cultivation of the vine and hop, and a variety of suggestions, counsels, and lessons which might often be of value to ourselves.

In the later instalments of my work there have been very large additions to the division dealing with law and jurisprudence, in which I feel a rather warm interest. Our statute-book has been simplified and improved, and the members of the legal profession are no doubt, as a class, men of purer and higher character than in the old time. Yet there is an atmosphere of reverential awe enveloping passed generations of lawyers of exalted rank and repute. like Littleton, Coke, Bacon, and others, which has disappeared for ever; they lived before social barriers had been broken down, and the fallacious and destructive religion of social equality and manhood-right had obtained even a hearing, much less that firm grip on our system which is going to be the gravest problem of Great Britain's future.

With reference to entries in my pages from time to time relating to the literature of the Society of Friends, I wish it to be understood that I limit myself to such as have some interest independent of the Society, which has, as is well known, its own excellent bibliographer.

It is to be expected that, after some thirty years' researches into this subject, there should be a perceptible shrinkage in the occurrence of books and pamphlets, still deficient in my volumes. There are one or two private libraries within my actual knowledge which are very likely to contain works or editions of works not yet submitted to my inspection, and stray relics are always cropping out, often from the most improbable quarters. Nor can I be otherwise than well aware that in the British Museum itself the means exist of supplying an infinite number of *lacunæ*, if my leisure had permitted an exhaustive transcript of works deposited in that institution. My readers will agree with me that this is an inevitable incidence; and a further labour in which I find myself perpetually engaged is the rewriting of the faulty articles in my *Handbook* (1867), borrowed from sources of which I did not then, or till long after, fully appreciate the untrustworthiness. Among the matter which I have thus been diligently superseding, it is my duty to mention the musical bibliography of the late Dr. Rimbault, the miscellaneous Early English titles furnished by the late Mr. Collier, and the whole of the information which I was unwise enough to transfer to my own pages from the *Manual* of Lowndes.

Nevertheless I have, after careful consideration, thought it best to amalgamate with my alphabet such portions of the editions of Ames's *Typographical Antiquities*, by Herbert and Dibdin, as I had not already obtained in the ordinary way, and as seemed to me sufficiently authentic and satisfactory to be of value to my consulters. The number of entries owing their presence in these pages to such a resolution, in addition to a few from Maskell's *Centuries*, 1843, will be found to be extremely moderate, since so much of the earlier bibliographical work was executed on a principle of which I cannot approve.

The items thus derived at second-hand are carefully distinguished, those from Maskell by a †; those from Herbert by a *; those from Dibdin by a **. I was very unwilling to borrow from the last-named authority; but he registers the particulars of certain articles then in the possession of Heber, and of which I have so far failed to discover the present whereabouts.

One moral deducible from this extensive, yet still imperfect, accumulation of Early English literature is the vanity of human ambition in aspiring to collect, even regardless of outlay, the printed remains, if merely within certain lines, or on one or two specific topics; and again, we are able to see from this Bibliographical Series how far short of completeness such libraries as those of Lord Oxford and Mr. Heber fell, after a lifetime and a large fortune expended in each case in the acquisition of everything which was procurable by public or private purchase. It has been only by a process of combination that I have achieved the progress which is here observable; it has only been by calling into requisition the resources of the British Museum, all the provincial libraries, including those of Oxford and Cambridge, all private gatherings, and all the contents of the auctions during upwards of a quarter of a century.

The range of subjects continues to retain the same width as in my former alphabets; and I need scarcely observe that I take up articles into my pages quite irrespectively of their commercial value. A volume worth sixpence may easily be of far greater intrinsic importance than one which realises under the hammer a thousand sixpences. The professional collector will, I apprehend, be surprised, should my books fall by accident in his way, at the space accorded in them to publications of bygone days, which have become commercially waste paper. To suit his requirements, pieces of old literature must cut a respectable figure in the auction-room, and be conspicuous features in all prices-current. His shelves are filled with convertible chattels. He principally affects authors in the best morocco; for they are the safest goods to back.

[It had been anticipated by Mr. GRAY that his Index would be finished in October last, and my original SUPPLEMENT was accordingly printed in time to fall into it. But Mr. GRAY found, in the first place, that the task which he had imposed on himself was a far heavier one than he calculated, and secondly, he became, I am sorry to say, indisposed. The consequence has been that a very serious delay has occurred in the completion of the Index, and concurrently the residues of the large libraries of Mr. GIBSON-CRAIG and Mr. TURNER, as well as an important portion of that of the EARL OF HOPETOUN, have passed under the hammer. So far as the majority of our old families is concerned, they have ceased to take any pride in the possession of fine or rare books, as well as of any other negotiable effects. They leave that pursuit to the more cultivated among our own bourgeoisie and to the richer citizens of the United States, whose competition is already exercising a prodigious influence on the prices of certain classes of books, partly, no doubt, from the practice of employing commission agents, who come into conflict with the ordinary trade. But it struck me as a symptom that the ancient sentiment was not quite extinct here when Sir Charles Isham of Lamport refused £500 for his copy of a little volume containing "Venus and Adonis" and the "Passionate Pilgrim." How many noble lords of a certain type would have jumped at this offer! "Noblesse oblige" is a phrase which begins to bear a new sense.

I seemed scarcely to have any alternative but to annex from the above-mentioned and other incidental sources all that I had not so far properly and fully described. There was not very much in the concluding fortnight of TURNER's sale; the third and last part of CRAIG yielded a considerable crop of publications, previously unregistered by me, on TRADE, as well as of books written and printed by Scotchmen abroad, illustrating the intimate relationship which formerly subsisted between Scotland and the Continent.

The arduous and irksome nature of a bibliographer's labours must render it plain that the liberality of Messrs. JARVIS & SON in facilitating my examination of all their old pamphlets, chiefly belonging to the period from the Civil War to the end of the reign of William III., was a service of a highly appreciable character. The process has enabled me to fill up many a gap in the grand edifice which it has occupied me so long to build up, and of which the magnitude is perhaps rendered less conspicuous by the sectional treatment adopted, not from choice, but from necessity.

I regret the dual alphabet, which has been under these unforeseen circumstances created; but at the same time every item will be incorporated with the General Index to the entire Corpus of my Bibliographical labours.

W. C. H.

BARNES COMMON, SURREY,
   Midsummer, 1889.]

BIBLIOGRAPHICAL COLLECTIONS AND NOTES.

A. B. C.
** The A. B. C. with the Pater-noster, Aue, Crede, and Ten Commaundementes in Englysshe, newly translated and set forth at the kynges most gracyous commaundement. [London, Richard Lant, 1559.] Sm. 8°, 4 leaves. Printed only on one side, to be folded so as to admit of the blank pages being pasted together.

> It begins with five different Alphabets and *Gloria Patri*, then the Paternoster and Graces before and after meat. This is probably the "A. B. C. in englesshe" licensed to Lant in 1558-9.

ACADEMY.
The New Academy of Complements, Erected for Ladies, Gentlewomen, Courtiers, Gentlemen, Scholars, Souldiers, Citizens, Country-men, and all persons of what degree soever, of both Sexes. Stored with variety of Courtly and Civil Complements, . . . Compiled by L. B. Sir C. S. Sir W. D. and others, the most refined Wits of this Age. London : Printed for George Sawbridge, at the Bible on Ludgate-Hill. 1681. 12°, B—P in twelves, besides the title and frontispiece.

> This includes a collection of the choicest songs *a la mode*, both amorous and jovial.

ADAIR, JOHN, *Geographer for Scotland.*
The Description of the Sea-Coasts and Islands of Scotland, With Large and Exact Maps, For the Use of Seamen : . . . Edinburgh : Printed in this Year M.DCC.III. Large Folio. Title, 1 leaf : A—E, 2 leaves each, and the maps.

> The Gibson-Craig copy (part 2, No. 19, March 23, 1888) contained 15 maps, but was perhaps imperfect, as on sign. E occurred a catchword *Part II.*

ADDRESS.
An Earnest and Affectionate Address to the Common People of England. Concerning the Usual Recreations on Shrove Tuesday. London : Printed by J. Oliver, in Bartholomew-Close, near West-Smithfield. [Price 2s. 6d per Hundred to give away.] 12°, 4 leaves and the title.

ÆLIANUS, CLAUDIUS.
Clavdivs Ælianvs His Various History. London Printed for Thomas Dring . . . 1666. 8°, A—Z 4 in eights, A 1 and Z 4 blank.

> This appears to be the same as the edition of 1665, with a new title.

ÆSOP.
* Æsopi Phrygis et Vita . . . & fabellæ iucundissimæ : quarū interpretes hi sunt . . . Addite sunt his quædam iucūdæ ac honestæ, selecte ex omnibus facetijs Pogij Florentini, . . . [Col.] Londonij, Apud Winandum de Worde. Anno M.D.XXXV. 8°, M 4 in eights, besides the Life and Index.

The Fables of Æsop. Volume I. [and II.] Paraphras'd in Verse, Adorn'd with Sculpture, . . . By John Ogilby Esq. . . . The Third Edition. London, Printed by the Author, at his House in White-Friers. M.DC.LXXIII. 8°. Volume I. A, 6 leaves, including a blank before the title : B—R 2 in eights : *Annotations*, (a)—(d 6) in eights : Volume II. title and dedication, 2 leaves : *Annotations*, (*a)—(*b) in eights : *B—*S in eights, including the *Contents*, 2 leaves.

> The present copy has a cancel title for both volumes. In that to the second, it is called the third instead of the second edition, and has a publisher's name and address, with the date 1675 ; but the title to the first only varies in arrangement. In both, however, sculptures are mentioned, but they do not occur, blank spaces being left for them. Both parts are dedicated by Ogilby to Charles Fitzroy, Earl of Southampton.

AGAS, RADOLPH.
A Preparative to Platting of Landes and Tenements for Surueigh. Shewing the

A

Diversitie of sundrie instruments applyed thereunto. Patched vp as plainly together, as boldly offered to the curteous view and regard of all worthie Gentlemen, louers of skill. And published instead of his flying papers, which cannot abide the pasting to poasts. London, Printed by Thomas Scarlet. 1596. 4", A—C in fours, A 1 probably blank.

> This tract is addressed at the end by Agas to the public "from my lodging at the Flower de Luce, ouer against the Sunne without Fleetbridge." *B. M.*

**ALANUS AB INSULIS.
Parabola alani cū cōmōto. [This title is over a common cut. Col.] Impressus London per Winandum de worde in the fletestrete I signo solis cōmorante Anno dñi. M. CCCCC. VIII. die xxiii Augusti. 4", AA—BB, 4 leaves each : CC, 6.

> There was an earlier edition by Julian Notary, 4°, 1505.

**Parabola Alani, cum cōmento. [Col.] Explicit Alanus de parabolis. Londini in aedibus Winandi de Worde. Anno M.D.XXV. Calen. Augusti. 4°, 20 leaves.

ALBERTUS.
*[Questiones de modis significandi. At the end occurs :] Explicit liber modorum significandi Alberti, impressus ad villam sancti Albani, anno M. CCCC. LXXX. 8°, 46 leaves.

> Herbert cites Mr. Michael Wodhull as the owner of a copy.

ALCOCK, JOHN, *Bishop of Ely.*
An exhortacyon made to Relygyouse systers at the tyme of theyr consecracyon by the Renerende fader in god Johan Alcok bysshop of Ely. [Wynkyn de Worde, about 1500.] 4°.

> Communicated by Mr. Jacobus Weale, from a fragment found in another book belonging to the Cathedral Library at Wells. There are 28 long lines to a full page. The title given above occurs on a leaf marked A ii, A i having perhaps had the title or a large cut.

**Gallicantus Johannis Alcock epi Eliensis ad cōfratres suos curatos in sinodo apud Bernwell . xxv. die mensis Septembris. Anno millessimo. cccc. nonagesimo octauo. [London, Richard Pynson.] 4°, 26 leaves. Woodcut on title.

> Compare Dibdin, ii. 409-11.

ALEHOUSES.
Articles of direction touching Alehouses. Imprinted at London by Robert Barker, Printer to the Kings most Excellent Maiestie. Anno 1608. 4°, A—B in fours, B 4 blank. *H. Stopes, Esq.*

> This is a series of licensing regulations;

the localities in London and the outskirts enumerated make it very curious.

ALEMAN, MATTEO.
The Life of Guzman d'Alfarache : Or, The Spanish Rogue. To which is added, The Celebrated Tragi-Comedy Celestina. In Two Volumes. Written in Spanish By Mateo Aleman. Done into English from the New French Version, and compar'd with the Original. Adorn'd with Scuptures by Gaspar Bouttats. London, . . . 1708-7. 8°. . . A, 8 leaves : a, 2 leaves : B—Nn 2 in eights : with plates at pp. 59, 297, 330, 366, 388, 416, and 459, besides the frontispiece : Vol. II. A, 2 leaves : B—Ii 6 in eights : with plates at pp. 78, 128, 197, 275, 331, 348, and 368. *Celestina* has a separate title.

ALESIUS OR HALES, ALEXANDER, *Scotus.*
Alexandri Alesii Doctoris Theologiæ diligens refutatio errorum, quos sparsit nuper Andreas Osiander in libro, cui titulum fecit DE VNICO MEDIATORE CHRISTO. Edita Witebergæ ex officina Ioannis Lufftij Anno 1552. 8°, A—E in eights.

ALEXANDER DE VILLA DEI.
*Textus Alexandri cum sententiis [et] constructionibus. [This is over a pageant of master and pupils. The colophon :] Libro doctrinali Alexandri Richardus Pynson vigilanter correcto finem felicem imponere iubet anno domini M.CCCCC.V. 4°, 50 unnumbered leaves.

*Textus alexandri, cū sentētijs & constructionibus. [This title is over the same cut as in the ed. of 1505. At the end :] Libro doctrinali Alexandri Richardus Pynson vigilanter correcto finem felicem imponere iubet. Anno dñi M.CCCCC.xiij. 4°, A—Q in eights, Q 8 probably blank or with the mark.

ALFORD, *alias* **GRIFFITH,** *R.* **P**[*ater*] **MICHAEL,** *S.J.*
Britannia Illvstrata sive Lvcii Helenæ Constantini Patria et Fides. Avthore Michaele Alfordo Societ. Iesv. Antwerpiæ, Typis Christophori Iegers, Anno M DC XLI. 4°. Engraved title, dedication to Charles I., &c., 12 leaves : A—Hhh 2 in fours.

Fides Regia Britannica Sive Annales Ecclesiæ Britannicæ. Ubi potissimum Britannorvm Catholica, Romana, et Orthodoxa Fides per Quinque Prima Sæcula : . . . asseritur . . . Leodii, . . . M.DC.LXIII. . . . Folio. 4 vols.

ALGIERS.
Relazione dell'Abbreviamento delle Gal-

ere nel Porto di Algieri Fatto dal Capitano Riccardo Giffort Inglese. La Notte Del Martedi Santo. a di 13. di Aprile. 1604. In Firenze, Nella Stamperia Sermatelli l'Anno 1604. 4°, 4 leaves.

ALLEN, WILLIAM.
An Admonition to the Nobility and People of England and Ireland concerninge the present warres made for the execution of his Holines Sentence, by the highe and mightie Kinge Catholike of Spaine. By the Cardinal of England. M.D.LXXXVIII. 8°, A—C in eights : D, 6. *Grenv. Coll.*

ALLOT, WILLIAM.
Thesavrvs Bibliorvm, . . . Opera & industria Gvlielmi Allotti Angli, . . . concinnatus. . . . Lvgdvni, . . . M.D.LXXXV. 8°. *, 8 leaves : A—Iii in eights, last leaf blank.

> The colophon makes the book printed in 1584 : Vimiaci. Excudebat Ioannes Symonetus. 1584.

ALUM.
A Proclamation prohibiting the Importation of Allvme, and the buying and spending thereof in any His Maiesties Dominious. Imprinted at London by Bonham Norton, and John Bill, . . . M.DC.XXV. A broadsheet formed of three leaves.

AMERICA.
A Proclamation forbidding the disorderly trading with the Saluages in New England in America especially the furnishing of the Natiues in those and other parts of America by the English with Weapons, and Habiliments of Warre. Imprinted at London by Robert Barker, . . . 1630. A broadsheet formed of two leaves.

By the King. A Proclamation for the more effectuall Reducing and Suppressing of Pirates and Privateers in America. London, Printed by Charles Bill, Henry Hill, and Thomas Newcomb, Printers to the Kings most Excellent Majesty. 1683/4. A broadside, formed of two sheets.

AMMAN, JOHN CONRAD, M.D.
The Talking Deaf Man : Or, A Method Proposed, whereby he that is born Deaf, may Learn to Speak. By the Studious Invention and Industry of John Conrade Amman, an Helvetian of Shafhuis, D^r of Physick. . . . now done out of Latin into English, by D. F. M.D. 1693. London, Printed for Tho. Hawkins, in Georgeyards, Lumbard-street, 1694. Price Bound One Shilling. Sm. 8°, A—E in twelves, and a, 6 leaves.

> After the original dedication by the author there is a second by Daniel Fox, the translator, to his learned friends, Richard Waller and Alexander Pittfield, Esquires, of the Royal Society.

ANDREWS, MARGARET.
The Life and Death of Mrs Margaret Andrews, the only Child of Sir Henry Andrews, Baronet, And the Lady Elizabeth his wife of Lathbury in the County of Bucks. Who died May 4th 1680. In the 14th Year of her Age. . . . London, Printed for Nath. Ponder . . . 1680. Sm. 8°. A, 8 leaves : a, 4 leaves : B—H 4 in eights, H 4 blank. Dedicated by the anonymous writer to Sir Henry and Lady Andrews. With Epitaphs.

ANNE OF AUSTRIA, *Consort of Louis XIII. of France.*
Les Amours D'Anne D'Autriche Epouse de Louis XIII. Auec Monsieur le C. D. R[ichelieu] le veritable Pere de Louis XIV. aujourd'hui Roi de France. . . . Nouvelle Edition Revue & Corrigee. A Cologne . . . M.DC.LXXXIII. 12°. *, 10 leaves, besides a frontispiece : A—H in twelves, H 12 blank. Dedicated to my Lord Lovelace in an epistle, where the writer dwells on the subservience of the Court of Charles II. to that of France.

> This volume contains "Examen des pretextes de l'invasion des François pour l'iustruction des Anglois."

ANTIPHONALE.
Antiphonale ad usum ecclesie Sar . politissimis imaginibus decoratum. Venalis habetur Londini a Francisco Byrckman in cimiterio sancti Pauli. [Parisiis, per Wolffgang Hopyl pro Francisco Byrckman Coloniense. 1519-20.] Folio. 2 vols. With woodcuts and music.

> This book, of which the only complete copy known seems to be that in the British Museum, contains the *Pars Hyemalis* and the *Pars Æstivalis*. It is divided into five portions with separate signatures :— *Temporale* or *Proprium de Tempore*, a—i in eights, i 8 presumably blank : *Kalendarium*, 6 leaves under ✠ : *Psalterium*, a—z in eights, followed by 2 sheets of eight, z and & : *Commune Sanctorum*, A—E in eights, F, 10 : *Proprium Sanctorum*, A—X in eights, and AA—BB in sixes.

ANTODE.
Cviqve Svvm. Antode Contra Cathari Cantilenam.

> Meum meum :) ≡ (Meum tuum :
> Tuum meum :) ≡ (Tuum tuum .

[Col.] Cantabrigiæ : Ex celeberrimæ Academiæ Typographeo. An Dom. 1635. 4°, 4 leaves. In Latin verse.

ARCANDAM.
The Most Excellent, Profitable and Pleasant Book of the Famous Doctor, . . .

Arcandam, . . . Printed by W. W. for William Thackeray, ... 8°, A—M 4 in eights, A 1 blank. With cuts.

ARCEUS, FRANCISCUS.
A most excellent and Compendiovs Method of curing woundes in the head, and in other partes of the body, with other precepts of the same Arte, practised and written by that famous man Franciscvs Arcevs, Doctor in Phisicke & Chirurgery : and translated into English by John Read, Chirurgion. . . . Imprinted at London by Thomas East, for Thomas Cadman. 1588. 4°. A, 4 leaves : ¶—3 ¶ in fours : B—Kk in fours. Dedicated to John Bannister, William Clowes, and William Pickering, surgeons. With several copies of verses and curious scraps of poetry in the volume.

ARISTOTLE.
Here be . vij. Dialogues. The fyrst is of the sōne and of the Moone. The seconde of Saturne, and of the Clowde. The . iii. of the Sterre named Transmontana, and other sterres. The . iiij. of the euyn Sterre and the morowe Sterre. The . v. of the Raynebowe, and the sygne Cancer. The . vi. of Heauen, and of Earth. The . vij. of the Eyre, and of the wynde. By these dialogues, a man maye take to hym selfe good Counsayle. [Col.] Imprynted by me Robert Wyer. . . . Sm. 8°, A—D 2 in fours. *B. M.*
    Sotheby's, April 6, 1887, No. 101, in a volume, ending imperfectly on C 4.

The Ethiques of Aristotle, that is to saye, preceptes of good behanoure and perfighte honestie, now newly trāslated into English. [Col.] Imprinted at Londō in the parishe of Christes Church within newgate by Richard Grafton, Printer too our soueraigne lorde Kyng Edward the VI. 1547. . . . 8°, L 3 in half sheets. Dedicated by John Wilkinson, the translator from the Italian, to Edward, Earl of Derby.

ARMY.
A Petition from Severall Regiments of the Army, viz. Colonell Fleetwoods, Colonell Whalies, Colonell Barksteads, &c. Presented to his Excellency, Thomas Lord Fairfax, at St. Albans, on Saturday the '11. of this present November, 1648. Wherein is set forth their Desires for a speedy, safe, and just settlement, that thereby the Kingdom may be freed from the heavy burthens that now they lye under, especially that of Free-Quarter. Also, A Letter from his Excellency, to the Committee of the Army, concerning the said grievances. London, Printed for George Whittington, . . . 4°, 4 leaves.

ARTHUR.
Cy commence la table et registre des rubriches du premier volume du liure ou rōmāt fait & cōpose a la perpetuation de memoire des vertueux faiz & gestes de plusieurs nobles & excellēs cheualiers q̄ furēt au tēps du tresnoble & puissāt roy artę cōpaignōs de la table rōde. Specialemēt a la louāge du tresvaillāt cheualier lācelot du lac filz du roy ban de benoic es parties de gaulles q̄ sen dit a present estre la duchie de berry. [Col.] Ce present & premier volume a este Imprime a Rouen. en l'ostel de gaillard le bourgois l an de grace mil. cccc. iiii. xx. & huytte. xxiiii. iour de nouēbre. Par iehan le bourgois . . . Folio. Leaf with pagewoodcut on one side : aa, 4 leaves : a—z in eights : A—L 4 in eights. With woodcuts. In two columns.
    Sotheby's, Feb. 28, 1887 (Scillières), No. 68, the first volume only, stained and wormed.

Le preux et vaillāt cheuallier Artus de bretaigue Nouuellemēt Imprime a paris. [Col.] Cy finist le liure du vaillāt et preux cheualier Artus fiiz du duc de bretaigne. Imprime à paris par Michel le noir libraire iure . . . Le quinzeiesme iour de feurier L'an Mil cinq cens et deux. 4°. A, 8 leaves : B—Ii in sixes. With woodcuts. Long lines. Le Noir's device is on Ii 6 verso.

S Ensuit le preux cheuallier Artę de Bretagne. Traictant de merueilleux faitz Imprime nouuellēt a Paris en la rue neufue nostre dame a l enseigne de l escu de France. xxxvj. 4°. a, 6 ll. : b—d in fours : e, 8 leaves : f—i in fours : k, 8 leaves : l—o in fours : p, 8 leaves : q—v in fours : 8 leaves under an irregular signature : y—z in fours : z, 4 leaves : A—B in fours : C, 8 leaves : D—G in fours : H, 8 leaves : I—M in fours, with the imprint and mark repeated on M 4 *verso.* In two columns. With woodcuts.
    Sotheby's, Feb. 28, 1887, No. 69.

Great Britain's Glory : Being the History of King Arthur ; With the Adventures of the Knights of the Round Table. London : Printed by and for W. O. and sold by the Booksellers. 4°, A—C in fours. With cuts.
    An abridgment by J[ohn] S[hirley,] who signs the preface with his initials.

ARTICULI.
Articvli ad Narrationes Novas pertin for

mati. Londini in Ædibus Roberti Redman. Anno. M.D.XXXIX. 8°, A—D in eights.

ARUNDEL MARBLES.
Marmora Oxoniensia, Ex Arundellianis, Seldenianis, aliisque constata. Recensuit, & Perpetuo Commentario explicavit, Hvmphridvs Prideavx Ædis Christi Alumnus. Appositis ad eorum nonnulla Seldeni & Lydiati Annotationibus. Accessit Sertorii Ursati *De Notis Romanorum Commentarius.* Oxonii, E Theatro Sheldoniano. MDCLXXVI. Folio. A, 4 leaves : a, 4 leaves : b, 2 leaves : (A)—(B) in fours : (C), 2 leaves : (D)—(Y) in fours : Aa—Qqq in fours : A—I 2 in fours. With numerous engravings. Dedicated to Henry Earl of Norwich, Earl Marshal of England.

ASCHAM, ANTHONY.
A little Herball of the properties of Herbes, newly amended & corrected, wyth certayn Additions at the ende of the boke, declaring what Herbes hath influence of certain Starres and constellations, wherby maye be chosen the best and most lucky tymes / and dayes of their ministration, according to the Moone beyng in the signes of heauē the which is daily appoited in the Almanacke, made and gathered in the yeare of our Lorde God. M. D. L. the . xii. daye of February, by Anthony Aschā, Physycyon. [Col.] Imprynted at London, in Paules churcheyearde, at the signe of the Swanne, by Jhon kynge. 8°, A—K in eights, K 8 blank.

ASCHAM, ROGER.
Rogeri Aschami Epistolarum, Libri Quatuor. Accessit Johannis Sturmii, Aliorumque Ad Aschamum, Anglosque alios Eruditos Epistolarum Liber Unus. Editio Novissima, Prioribus auctior. . . . Oxoniæ, . . . MDCCIII. 8°. Frontispiece of portraits, 1 leaf : (a), 4 leaves : (a)—(b 2) in fours : (a)—(e 3) in fours : A—3 B 2 in fours. Edited by William Elstob, who dedicates it to Robert Heath, Esq.

ASHE, JOHN, M.P.
A Second Letter sent from John Ashe Esquire, a Member of the House of Commons, to the Honourable William Lenthall, Esquire, Speaker. . . Concerning divers Messages, and passages between the Marquesse Hartford, Lord Pawlet, Lord Seymour, Lord Coventry, and others his Majesties Commissioners : And the Deputy Lievetenants and other Commissioners for the County of Somerset. . . . London, Printed by A. N. for Ed. Husbands : and I. Franke, 1642. August 16. 4°, A—B in fours.

ASHE, SIMEON, AND WILLIAM GOODE.
The Continuation of the Intelligence From the Right Honourable, the Earl of Manchester's Army, Since the taking of Lincolne ; May 6th untill the first day of this instant Iune, 1644. By Sim. Ash and William Goode, Chaplains to the said Earl. Allowed of by Authoritie, and entred according to Order. London, Printed for Thomas Underhill, at the Bible in Woodstreet. 1644. 4°, 4 leaves, the last blank.

ATTWOOD, WILLIAM.
The Superiority and Direct Dominion of the Imperial Crown of England, over the Crown and Kingdom of Scotland, and the Direct Succession to both Crowns inseparable from the Civil, Asserted in Answer to Sir Thomas Craig's Treatise of Homage and Succession. . . . London, Printed for J. Hartley, next Door to the King's Head Tavern in Holbourn, 1704. 8°, A—Oo in eights. Dedicated by W. Attwood to Charles Lord Mohun, Baron of Oakhampton.

AUSTIN OF ABINGDON, ST.
*The myrrour of the chyrche. [Beneath this is a cut of Jesus Christ with irradiated head, clothed in a long dress.] ¶Here foloweth a devout treatyse cōteynynge many goostly medytacyons. . . , [Col.] Thus endeth the denoute treatyse called the myrour of the chyrche made by St. Austyn of Abyndon. Emprynted at London in Southwarke by Peter Treueris. 4°, A—F 4 in eights and fours. With the "Petycion of R. Coplande the prynter" in four 7-line stanzas on the back of the title and his Envoy at the end.

AUSTIN, WILLIAM, *of Gray's Inn Esquire.*
Triumphus Hymenaeus . . . 1662.
The separate title to the *Joyous Welcome*, which contains A in fours, besides the title, is as follows :—
A Joyous Welcome To the most Serene, and most Illustrious Queen of Brides Catherin, The Royal Spovse and Consort of Charles the Second King of Great Britain, France, and Ireland : Presented to Her Majesty upon the River of Thames, At Her first coming with the King to the City of London, August the 23. 1662, By William Austin, Esq ; —*Rex & Regina beati*—Virg. Æneid. lib. 8.

(6)

B.

*B. G., *M.A.*
Newes out of France for the Gentlemen of England. A stratagem most ventrously attempted, and valiantly atchived by the French King the 27. day of July, 1591. Wherein is deciphered, what Trust his Royal Majestie reposeth on the Valour of the English, and their dutifull seruice unto Him at all Assayes. Newes also touching Sixteen ships taken nigh the Haven of Deepe, and the discomfiture of the Popes Forces transported into France, towards the Aide of the Leaguers, both concurring on the 28. of July last past. With a Report of the Princely Meeting and Honorable Conjoyning of the whole Power of the French King, the sixth day of this present Moneth of August, consisting of English, German, and his own People. Printed for Iohn Kid. [1591.] 4°, 10 leaves. Black letter.

BACON, FRANCIS, *Viscount St. Alban, Lord Chancellor of England.*
Francisci Baconi Eqvitis Avrati, . . . De Sapientia Vetervm, Liber. Ad Inclytam Academiam Cantabrigiensem. Iam recusus. Londini, Apud Iohannem Billivm. Anno M.DC.XVII. 12°, A—F in twelves.
Instavr. Mag. P. I. Of the Advancement and Proficience of Learning or the Partitions of Sciences. IX Bookes. Written in Latin by the most Eminent Illustrious & Famous Lord Francis Bacon Baron of Verulam . . . Interpreted by Gilbert Wats. Oxford. Printed by Leon: Lichfield, Printer to the University, for Rob: Young & Ed. Forrest. CIƆ IƆC. XL. Folio. Portrait and engraved title, the latter by W. Marshall: ¶, 4 leaves: ¶¶, 2 leaves: ¶¶¶, 1 leaf: A, 2 leaves: B—C in fours: aa—gg in fours: hh, 2 leaves: †, 4 leaves: ††, 2 leaves: † (repeated), 1 leaf: A (repeated)—3 R in fours: 3 R (repeated), 2 leaves with colophon, &c. Dedicated by Wats to Prince Charles.

A Letter of Advice Written by Sr Francis Bacon to the Duke of Buckingham, when he became Favourite to King James. Never before Printed. London, Printed for R. H. and H. B. . . . 1661. 4°, A—B in fours.

BAYLY, ROBERT.
A Parallel of the Liturgy, with the Mass-Book, The Breviary, the Ceremonial, and other Romish Rituals. . . . By that Reverend and Faithful Preacher of Gods Word, Robert Bayly, Late of Glasco in Scotland. Printed in the Yeer, 1661. 4°, A—L in fours.

BANGOR.
Peter Lugg: Or, Three Tales of an Old Woman of Bangor Preaching over her Liquor. Recommended to the Perusal of Courtiers, Soldiers, Beaus, Bishops, Cits, Wits, Criticks, Priests, & Poets, or whomsoever that pleases to Buy.

—— *Plebs est pessimus Tyrannus.*
Arma tenenti, omnia dat, qui justa negat.

London: Printed for T. Warner, . . . 1718. Price 6d. 8°, A—F in fours, F 4 blank, C repeated, no pp. 17-24. In prose.

BAKER, HUMPHREY.
*The well sprynge of Sciences which teacheth the perfect worke and Practise of Arithmeticke, both in whole numbers and fractions, with such ease and compendious instruction into the sayde arts, as hath not heretofore bene by any set out nor laboured. Beawtified with moste necessarye Rules and Questions, not onely profitable for Marchauntes, but also for all Artificers, as in the table doth partlye appeare: set forthe by Humfrey Baker Citisyn of London. Printed at London by Rouland Hall, for James Rowbothum, and are to be solde at his shop in Chepeside vnder Bowe Churche, at the signe of the Rose and Pomegranet. 1562. 8°, 160 leaves, besides prefixes. Dedicated to Master John Fitzwilliam, Governor of the Society of Merchauts-Adventurers into Flanders, &c.

BARBARA, SAINT.
*Here begynneth the lyfe of the glorious vyrgyn and marter saynt Barbara. [This is over a cut representing the saint. The colophon is:] Here endeth the lyfe of saynt Barbara. Imprinted in London by me Julyan Notary dwellynge in Poules chirche yarde at the west dore besyde my lorde of Londons palayse at the signe of the thre kynges. Anno post virgineum partum. [1518.] 4°, 4 leaves.

BARLOW, WILLIAM.
The Navigators Svpply. Conteining many things of principall importance belonging to Nauigation, with the description and vse of diuerse instruments framed chiefly for that purpose; but seruing also for sundry other of Cosmo-

graphy in generall the particular Instruments are specified on the next Page. . . . Imprinted at London by G. Bishop, R. Newbery, and R. Barker. 1597. 4°, A—L 2 in fours, and a—b in fours. Dedicated to the Earl of Essex. With plates between B and C, at D 2, E 2 and 3, and H, and commendatory verses in Latin and English.

Psalmes   ⎫   ⎧ Praier
 and   ⎬ of   ⎨ and
Hymnes   ⎭   ⎩ Thanksgiuing,

Made by William Barlow, Bishop of Lincolne, For his owne Chappell and Familie onelie. *Dulcis apud Deum.* . . . Hieron. . . 1613. 4°, black letter, A—D in fours, D 4 presumably blank. Without prefixes.

Sotheby's, June 13, 1887, No. 253.

BARNES, ROBERT.
The supplication of doctour Barnes vnto the moost gracyous Kynge Henrye the eyght with the declaration of his articles condened for heresy by the byshops. [Col.] Imprinted at London in Poules chur[c]hyard at the signe of S. Augustyne by Hugh Syngelton. Cum preuilegio. . . . 8°, A—Z in eights, and 4 leaves beyond Z unsigned.

Sotheby's, June 13, 1887, No. 254.

BARRIFFE, WILLIAM.
Military Discipline : . . . . The second Edition, Newly revised and much inlarged By William Barriffe, Lieutenant. [Quot from Psalm 144, 1.] London, Printed by R. O. for Ralph Mab. 1639. 4°. A, 8 leaves, besides the portrait by Glover, A 1 occupied by a shield of arms : ¶, 4 leaves : a, 4 leaves : B—Bb in eights : Cc, 6 leaves, besides two folded leaves : Dd, 4 leaves. There are also folded leaves at pp. 90 and 98.

Mars, His Trivmph. Or, The Description of an Exercise performed the xviii. of October, 1638. in Merchant-Taylors Hall. By Certein Gentlemen of the Artillery Garden London. London, Printed by I. L. for Ralph Mab. 1639. 4°. *, 4 leaves : A—F in fours. Dedicated to Alderman Thomas Soame, President of the Artillery Garden, Captain John Ven, Vice-President, and others. With diagrams and music.

BARROUGH, PHILIP.
The Method of Physick, . . . The fifth Edition, corrected and amended. London, Imprinted by Richard Field, dwelling in great Woodstreete. 1617. 4°, A—Hh in eights : Ii, 4, the last two leaves blank.

The Method of Physick, . . . By Philip Barrough. The seventh Edition. London, Printed by George Miller, dwelling in Black-friers. 1634. 4°, A—Hh in eights : Ii, 2 leaves.

BARTHOLOMEUS DE GLANVILLE.
Hier beghinnen de titelen vz syn de namen der boeken daer men af sprekē sal eñ oec die capitelen der eerwaerdighen mans bartolomeę engelsman en een gheordent broeder van sinte franciscus oerde Ende heeft xix. boekē die sprekende sijn vande eÿgenscappen der dingen . . . [Col.] Hier eyndet dat boeck. . . . M.CCCC. eñ LXXXV . . . Ende is gheprint en . . . haerlem . . . Folio. aa, 5 leaves : bb, 4 leaves : a (repeated), 8 leaves, a i and viii. with page-woodcuts : b—c in eights, c 4 a page-woodcut : d—m in eights, m 7 a page-woodcut : n—r in eights : z, 8 leaves: s, 8 leaves : a second gathering of eight under another font of s : t—v in eights : u, 8 leaves, u 2 a page-woodcut : w—y, 8 leaves each, y 7 a page-woodcut : z, 2 gatherings of eight, the last but one of the second a page-woodcut : ρ, 6 leaves : ē, 5 leaves followed by a blank : A, 8 leaves, A1 a page-woodcut: B—Q in eights: R—Y in eights, including U and V : AA—BB in eights : CC—DD in sixes : EE, 7 leaves, the last with a page-woodcut. In two columns.

BASILIOS, *Emperor of Constantinople*.
The Sixty Sixe Admonitory Chapters of Basilius, King of the Romans, to his Sonne Leo, in Acrostick manner : That is, the first letter of euery Chapter, making vp his name and title. Translated out of Greeke by Iames Sevdamore. Printed at Paris. M.DC.XXXVIII. 8°. Title, dedication to Prince Charles, and "Of the Author," 3 leaves : A—Q in fours.

BATH, ORDER OF THE.
The Manner of Creating the Knights of the Antient and Honourable Order of the Bath, According to the Custom used in England in Time of Peace. With a List of those Honourable Persons who are to be created Knights of the Bath at his Majesties Coronation, 23 Aprill, 1661. London, Printed for Phil. Stephens at the Kings Arms over against the Middle Temple. 1661. 4°. A—B 2 in fours.

A True Relation of the Ceremonies at the Creating of the Knights of the Honourable Order of the Bath, the 18. & 19. April 1661. With a Perfect List of their Names, in the same Order as they were Knighted by His Majesty. *In uno tria juncta*. London, Printed for Philemon Stephens, at the Kings-Armes over against the Middle-Temple-Gate in Fleet-street. 4°, A—B 2 in fours.

BECANUS, MARTINUS, S.J.
Svmma Actorvm Facvltatis Theologiæ Parisiensis contra Librum inscriptum Controversia Anglicana de Potestate Regis & Pontificis &c. Londini, Excudebat Bonham Norton . . . Anno cIↃ. IↃ. XIII. 4°, A—D 2 in fours.

BECON, THOMAS.
*Newes out of heauen both pleasaunt & ioyfull, lately set forth to the great cõsolation and cõforte of all christen mẽ. By Theodore Basille. [Quot. from Romans, 10. *O how beautyfull* . . . At the end occurs:] Imprynted at London in Botulphe lane, at the sygne of the whyte Beare, by John Mayler for John Gough. Anno dãi 1541. Cum priuilegio ad imprimendum solum. Per Septennium. 8°, H in eights. With a prologue addressed " To the ryght worshipfull Maister George Pierpount."

The Pomander of Prayer, by T. Becon. [Quot. from Eccl. 14.] Imprinted at London by John Daye. Cum Priuilegio. 8°, A—Q 4 in eights. Printed within borders.

The Jewel of Joye. Philemon, Eusebius, Theophile, and Christofer, talke togither. [This forms a headline on B i. At the end occurs:] These bokes are to be solde in the shop at the litle conduit in chepeside. [London, John Day and William Seres, about 1550.] 8°, B—Y in eights: Aa, 4 leaves, and the title with other introductory matter. *B. M.*

> This copy wants all before B i, including title and (probably) dedication to the Princess Elizabeth, as in the collected edition of the Works. In that dedication Becon gives a very interesting account of his travels in certain English shires, including Warwickshire, which he found unusually rich in men of education and culture.

*A comfortable Epistle vntoo Goddes faythfull people in Englande / wherein is declared the cause of taking awaye the true Christen religion from them / & howe it maye be recouered and obtained agayne / newly made by Thomas Becon. [Quot. from Habakkuk 1.] At the end occurs: Imprynted at Strasburgh in Elsas, at the . . . goldẽ Bibal, in the moneth of August . . . M.D.Liiii. Sm. 8°.

BEDE.
Venerabilis Bedae presbyteri de temporibus siue de sex ætatibus huius seculi Liber incipit. Venditur in vico diui Iacobi Sub Leone Argenteo. [Col.] Impressus Parisius in Bellouisu Anno domini. 1507 Die. 5. Aprilis. Per Iohanne Petit Commorante in Vico Diui Iacobi. Sub Leone Argenteo. 4°. a, 8: b, 4: c, 8: d, 4: e, 6.

BEHN, APHRA.
Plays Written by the late Ingenious Mrs. Behn, Entire in Two Volumes. . . . London, Printed for Jacob Tonson, . . . M.DCC.II. 8°.

Poems upon Several Occasions; With A Voyage to the Island of Love. Also The Lover in Fashion, being an Account from Lycidus to Lysander, of his Voyage from the Island of Love. By Mrs. A. Behn. To which is added a Miscellany of New Poems and Songs, by several Hands. The Second Edition. London, Printed for Francis Saunders . . . 1697. 8°. A, 8 leaves: (a), 8 leaves: B—K in eights: Table, 1 leaf: B—I in eights; *Lycidus* . . . a—d in eights: *Miscellany*, B—M in eights: Table, 2 leaves. Dedicated to James Earl of Salisbury.

BELLOMAYUS, JOHANNES.
**[Gradus Comparationum. At the end occurs:] Emprynted by Richarde Pynson. 4°, eight leaves, or A in eights.

> Dibdin quotes the Heber copy, wanting the title, which I have not seen in any of the editions, and did not know what book he was describing. This is apparently the *editio princeps*, and is complete with a single sheet of eight.

BELLOPOLIUS, PETRUS.
Petri Bellopoelii Galli Tarnacii de Pace inter invictissimos Henricvm Galliarvm, et Edvardvm Angliae, Reges Oratio. Londini in .Edibus Guillelmi Powell. Cvm Privilegio. 1552. 4°, roman letter, A—G in fours: H, 5. Dedicated to John [Dudley] Duke of Northumberland.

BERNARD, ST.
An Epistle of sãit Bernarde / called the golden epistle / whiche he sẽt to a yõg religyous man whom he moche loued. And after the sayd epistle / foloweth four reuelations of Saint Briget. [Col.] ¶ Printed at London by Thomas Godfray. Cum priuilegio Regali. 8°, A—C in eights.

**A compẽdius & a moche fruytefull treatyse of well liuynge, cõtaynyng the hole sũme and effect of al vertue. Wrytten by S. Bernard & translated by Thomas Paynell. Cum priuilegio ad imprimendum solum. [Col.] Imprynted at London in Paules church yearde . . . by Thomas Petyt . . . 8°, 198 leaves +

prefixes and a table. Dedicated to the Princess Mary.

A Hive of Sacred Honie-Combes Contayning Most Sweet and Heavenly Covnsels: Taken ovt of the Workes of the Mellifluovs Doctor S. Bernard, Abbot of Clareval. Faithfully translated into English by the R. Fa. Antonie Batt Monke, of the holie Order of S. Bennet, of the Congregation of England. Printed at Doway by Peter Avroy, for Iohn Heigham Anno 1631. Sm. 8°. *, 8 leaves : **, 4 leaves : A—Qq in eights : Rr, 10 leaves. Dedicated to Queen Henriette Marie de Bourbon by Batt.

Prefixed is an Epigram by Brother Leander Neville, and some Verses to the Reader by Batt himself.

BERNARD, RICHARD, *of Batcombe.* The Isle of Man : . . . The seuenth Edition. London, Printed for Edward Blackmore, . . . 1630. Sm. 8°, A—N in twelves, last leaf blank.

Puttick's, July 19, 1888, No. 111, misdated 1610.

BERTHOLDUS, ANDREAS, *of Oschatz.* The Wonderfull and strange effect and vertues of a new *Terra Sigillata* lately found out in Germanie. With the right order of the applying and administring of it : being oftentimes tried and experienced by Andreas Bertholdus of Oschatz in Misnia. At London, Printed by Robert Robinson for Richard Watkins. 1587. 8°. A, 4 leaves : B—D 4 in eights. *B. M.*

Dedicated from Alvingham, 14th August, 1587, by R. G. to Doctors Maister and Baylie, in an epistle, where B. G. refers to the exertions of Mr. Hugh Morgan, her Majesty's apothecary, in introducing into England the rarest, perfectest, and best sorts of all manner of plants, fruits, juices, metals, minerals, &c., for the preserving or restoring of health.

BEZA, THEODORE.

A briefe and piththie summe of the Christian faith made in forme of a confession, with a confutation of all such superstitious errours as are contrary therevnto. Made by Theodore of Beze. Translated out of French by R. F. Printed at London by Richard Serll, dwellyng in Flete lane, at the signe of the halfe Egle and the keye. 8°. Title, dedication by R. Fylls to the Earl of Huntingdon, and first leaf of Table, 8 leaves : A—Bb in eights, A 8 blank.

BIBLE.

Sacræ Bibliæ Tomvs Primvs [et Secundus.] London, T. Berthelet, 1535. 4°.

The Vulgate version. See *Reliquiæ Hearnianæ,* 2nd ed., i. 18. Hearne quotes, under date of July 30, 1705, a letter from Wanley, keeper of the Harleian Library, to Dr. Charlett, in which he describes a copy, though imperfectly, and in a note Dr. Bliss, editor of the *Reliquiæ,* completes the account from a copy, wanting title and preface, in the Bodleian.

From these two sources we glean the following particulars :—

Sacræ Bibliæ Tomvs Primvs, in Qvo Continentvr, Quinque Libri Moysi, Libri Josuæ, et Judicum, Liber Psalmorum, Prouerbia Salomonis, Liber Sapientiæ, et Novum Testamentum Iesv Christi . . . [Col.] Londini, Excvdebat Thomas Bertheletvs Regivs Impressor. Anno MDXXXV. Mense Ivl. 4°. Title and preface (wanting in copy referred to) : *Tabela Historiarrm,* 8 leaves : the work, 304 leaves, the last blank. The *New Testament* commences on XXiii, col. b. This is Bliss's mode of conveying bibliographical information.

Wanley states that in the preface, which he supposes to have been written by the King himself, the rest of the Scriptures are promised. The announced and implied second volume probably included the Apocrypha, or it would have been more slender than the first, and, which is more singular, the New Testament would, if it had appeared, have been interposed.

Herbert, p. 425, gives the title with some literal variations. He cites the Bodleian copy, but does not say that it was titleless.

The Byble / Which is all the holy Scripture : In whych are contayned the Olde and Newe Testament truly and purely translated into Englysh by Thomas Matthew. Esaye 1. Hearcken to ye heauens . . . M, D, XXXVII. [Col.] The ende of the newe Testament / and of the whole Byble. To the honoure and prayse of God was this Byble prynted and fynesshed / in the yere of oure Lorde God a. M, D, XXXVIII. Large folio. In two columns. *, 6 leaves : **, 8 leaves : ***, 6 leaves : a z in eights : Aa—3 I in eights : 3 K, 9 leaves : *New Testament,* with separate title, A—O in eights, the colophon on O 8. With woodcuts.

The Byble in Englyshe of the largest and greatest volume, auctorysed and apoynted by the commaundemente of oure moost redoubted Prynce, and soueraygne Lorde kynge Henrye the . viii . supreme heade of this his churches and Realme of Englande : to be frequented and vsed in euery churche . . . Printed by Edwarde Whitchurch. Cum priuilegio ad imprimendum solum. 1541. Large folio. In two columns. With woodcuts and the titles enclosed within broad engraved borders. Preliminaries, 6 leaves : a—i in eights : *Second Part,*

A—O 4 in eights : *Third Part*, AA—3 H in eights : 3 L 6 leaves : *New Testament*, Aa—Kk in eights : Ll—Mm in sixes. With the following colophon on Mm 6 verso: The ende of the newe Testament and of the whole Byble. Fynyshed in Nouember. Anno. M.CCCCC. XLI. A day faithfully ended.

Y Beibl Cyssegr-Lan. Sef Yr Hen Destament, ar Newydd. 2 Timoth. 3. 14. 15. Imprinted at London by the Deputies of Christopher Barker, . . . 1588. Folio. Black letter. In two columns. Dedicated by William Morgan to Queen Elizabeth. Title and Calendar, 7 leaves : A—4 Y in sixes : 4 Z 5 leaves.

Y Bibl Cyssegr-Lan. Sef yr Hen Destament ar Newydd. 2 Tim. 3. 16. . . . Printedii Yn Llundain gan Bonham Norton a John Bill . . . 1620. Folio. Black letter. In two columns. 4 leaves : B. 4 leaves : C. 4 leaves : A—4 E in sixes : 4 E 6 blank : *New Testament*, separate title, 1 leaf : [A]—[Y 3] in sixes. But [A] should be [A 2] as the title belongs to the sheet. With a Preface by Richard, Bishop of St. Asaph, and the dedication by W. Morgan to Queen Elizabeth retained.

BICKNOLL, EDMUND.

A Sword against Swearyng, conteyning these principal poyntes. 1. That there is a lawful vse of an oth, contrary to the assertion of the Manichees & Anabaptistes. 2 How great a sinne it is to sweare falsly, vaynely, rashly, or customably : 3 That common or vsual swearing leadeth vnto periurie. 4 Examples of Gods iuste and visible punishment vpon blasphemers. . . . At London, Printed by Richarde Watkins, dwelling in Paules Churchyard. 1579. 8°. A—F in eights. B. M.

Dedicated to Mr. Alexander Nowell and two other divines.

BIGGS, NOAH. *Chymiatrophilos*.

Mataeotechnia Medicinae Praxeos. The Vanity of the Craft of Physick. Or, A New Dispensatory. Wherein is dissected the Errors, Ignorance, Impostures, and Infirmities of the Schools, in their main Pillars of Purges, Blood-letting, Fontanels or Issues, and Diet, &c. And the particular Medicines of the Shops. With an humble Motion for the Reformation of the Universities. And the whole Landscape of Physick. And discovering the *Terra Incognita* of Chymistrie. To the Parliament of England. London. Printed for Giles Calvert . . . 1651. 4°, a—d in fours : A—Gg in fours.

BISHOPS.

A very Lively Portrayture of the Most Reverend Arch-Bishops, The Right Reverend B. of the Chvrch of England : Set forth in xx. irrefragable positions, concerning their Authority, power, and practise, as they onely are our Diocesan Lord Bishops, . . . A Labour vndertaken for the peace of all Gods people, . . . Printed in the Yeare, 1640. 4°, A—H in fours, H 4 with the Contents of the *Positions*.

The Bishops Mittimvs to goe to Bedlam. Vpon their accusation of high Treason by the Parliament for making their petition and protestation to his Majesty against the proceedings of the same. Wherein is shewed the principall causes of their distraction and the evil effects of this their distemper. Anno. 1641. With a charg to the Master Warders, and Keepers of this prison for to use their best means to recover their wits againe. London, Printed for I. W. in the yeare 1641. 4°. 4 leaves.

A Rent in the Lawne Sleeves Or Episcopacy Eclypsed. By the most happy interposition of a Parliament Discoursed Dialogue-wise betweene a Bishop and a Iesuite, wherein is shewed the Ambition of the Prelacy, . . . London Printed for Iohn Thomas. 1641. 4°, 4 leaves.

A Conspiracie of the Twelve Bishops in the Tower, against Mr Calamie, Mr Burton, Mr Marshall, and many other other worthy Divines, &c. As also how they obscenely made those Articles, wherein Mr Pym and the other Parliament men were impeached . . . London, Printed for W. Bond, 1641. 4°, 4 leaves, the last page occupied by woodcuts.

BLACKWOOD, ADAM.

Adversvs Georgii Bvcanani Dialogvm. De Ivre Regni apvd Scotos, pro regibus apologia. Per Adamum Blacvodaeum Senatorem apud Pictonas. Pictauis . . . 1581. 4°. Title, dedicati on to Mary Q. of Scots and her son James, and verses, &c. 6 leaves : A—T: in fours.

Iacobi Magnae Britanniae et Hiberniae Regis. inauguratio. Parisiis, Apud P. Mettayer. . . . 1606. 8°, a—c 2 in fours. Partly in verse.

The prose introduction is subscribed : "Nexa mancipio rura. Blackvodaeva." The *Inauguratio* is in verse and in italic type.

BLAEV, WILLIAM JOHNSON.

The Sea Mirrovr Containing a Briefe Instruction in the Art of Navigation ; And A Description of the Sea and Coasts of the

Easterne, Northerne, and Westerne Navigation ; Collected and Compiled together out of the Discoveries of many Skilfull and expert Sea-men, . . . and Translated out of Dutch into English, By Richard Hynmers. Newly corrected of many faults. Amsterdam, Printed by William Iohnson Blaev, dwelling vpon the Water, by the Old Bridge, at the Signe of the Golden Sunne - Dyall. cIɔ. Iɔ cxxxv. Cum Privilegio. Folio. With numerous charts, maps, and diagrams. Divided into three Books, each of which forms distinct parts, with separate paging to the several Books.

**BODY OF POLICY.
The book which is called the body of polycye, and it speketh of Vertues and good maners. lib. III. Translated out of French. [Col.] Thus endeth the boke of the body of polycye. Imprynted at London without Newgate in S. Pulkers parysh by John Skot the yere m ccccc xxi. 4°.

The copy seen by Ames and Herbert was printed on vellum. Neither they nor Dibdin give any collation.

BOIARDO, MATTEO MARIA, *Count of Scandiano.*
Orlando Inamorato. The three first Bookes of that famous Noble Gentleman and learned Poet, Mathew Maria Boiardo Earle of Scandiano in Lombardie. Done into English Heroicall Verse, By R. T. Gentleman.

*Parendo impero
Imperando pereo.*

Printed at London by Valentine Sims, dwelling on Adling hil at the signe of the white Swanne. 1598. 4", A—I 3 in fours. In 8-line stanzas. Dedicated by Robert Tofte to the Lady Margarite Morgan, wife of Sir John Morgan, of Chilworth in the County of Surrey, Captain of Her Majesty's horsemen in that shire. *B. M.*

George Steevens's copy. At the end occurs : *Il Disgratiato.* R. T. G.

BONAVENTURA.
The Life of the Most holy Father S. Francis, Written, and in one booke compiled, by that famous and learned man S. Bonauenture a Freer Minor, Cardinall of the holy Roman Church Bishop of Alba, and the Seraphicall Doctor of the Church. Now lately translated into our English tongue. . . . Imprinted at Doway, by Martin Bogard, 1635. Sm. 8°. ã and ẽ, 8 leaves each ; A—Z in eights : leaf as to *Errata.* Dedicated by F. C., *the peruser,* to the Lady Winifred Englefield. Translated by Anthony Montague.

BOOK.
*The contents conteyned in thys boke. Fyrst a kalander. A prayer to say at your vprysynge. . . Thys Emprynteth at westmynster by me Julyan Notary. Dwellynge in kyng strete. Anno domini M. vc. ii. die mensis Aprilis. 12°.

Described by Herbert from a small fragment in the possession of John Fenn, Esq.

BOOKS.
A Proclamation to inhibite the Sale of Latine Bookes reprinted beyond the Seas, hauing been first Printed in Oxford or Cambridge. Printed at London by Bonham Norton and Iohn Bill, . . . M.DC.XXV. A broadsheet formed of two leaves.

BOURNE, WILLIAM.
*A Regiment for the Sea, containing very necessary matters for all sorts of Sea-men and Trauailers, as Masters of ships, Pilots, Marriners, and Marchants, Newly corrected and amended by the Author. Wherevnto is added a Hidrographicall discourse to go vnto Cathay, fiue seuerall wayes. Written by William Bourne. Imprinted at London by T. Este for John Wight. [At the end is added :] 1584. 4°. Dedicated to Edward Earl of Lincoln.

BOWREY, THOMAS.
A Dictionary English and Malayo, Malayo and English. To which is Added Some short Grammar Rules & Directions for the better Observation of the Propriety and Elegancy of this Language. And also Several Miscellanies, Dialogues, and Letters, in English and Malayo . . . Together with a Table of Time, . . . London : Printed by Sam. Bridge for the Author, . . . 1701. 4°, A—4 E 2 in fours : *, 4 leaves : a (between A and B), 4 leaves. With a map of the countries where the Malayo tongue is spoken. Dedicated to the Directors of the English East India Company. *B. M.*

BOYD, ZACHARY.
The Last Battell of the Sovle in Death, 1. Volume. Carefullie digested . . . Bernard in Serm. *Novissima sunt quatuor,* . . . Idem. *Senibus mors* . . . Printed at Edinburgh, by the Heires of Andro Hart. 1629.

Sotheby's, April 19, 1888, No. 89. A differing title-page only.

BOYLE, ROGER, *Earl of Orrery.*
A Treatise of the Art of War : Dedicated

to the Kings Most Excellent Majesty. And Written by the Right Honourable Roger Earl of Orrery. In the Savoy: Printed by T. N. for Henry Herringman. . . . M.DC.LXXVII. Folio. Portrait of Charles II. on horseback by De Blois, and title, 2 leaves : a—b—c, 2 leaves each : titles of chapters, &c., 1 leaf : B— 3 G, 2 leaves each, last leaf blank.

BRADFORD, JOHN.
*All the examinacions of the Constante martir of God, M. Iohn Bradforde, before the Lorde Chancellor, B. of Winchester, the B. of London, & other cōmissioners: whervnto is annexed his priuate talk & conflictes in prison after his condemnacion, with the Archb. of York, the B. of Chichester, Alphonsus, and King Philips confessour, two Spanish freers, and sundry others. With his modest learned and godly answeres. Anno Domini. 1561. Cum Priuilegio . . . [Col.] Imprinted at London in Fletestrete at the Signe of the Faucon by William Griffith, and are to be sold at the little shop in saincte Dunstones churchyard . . . The xiii. daie of Maye. 8°, 114 leaves.

BRADY, ROBERT, M.D.
An Historical Treatise of Cities, and Burghs or Boroughs. Shewing, Their Original, and whence, and from whom they received their Liberties, Privileges and Immunities; what they were, and what made and constituted a Free Burgh, & Free Burgesses. . . . London : Printed for Samuel Lowndes . . . 1690. Folio, A—L in fours : *Appendix*, A—D in fours : E, 6.

BRETON, NICHOLAS.
The Pilgrimage to Paradise, ioyned with the Countesse of Pembrookes loue, compiled in verse by Nicholas Breton Gentleman. Cœlum virtutis patria. At Oxford printed, by Ioseph Barnes, and are to be solde in Paules Church-yeard, at the signe of the Tygers head. 1592. 4°. ¶, 4 leaves: A—N in fours, N 4 with the *Errata*. B. M.

    The Corser copy. Dedicated to the Countess of Pembroke, after which comes an address by the author to the students and scholars of Oxford and a republication of a portion of the *Bower of Delights*, 1591. Both the poems in this volume are in stanzas of six lines.

BRETONNEAU, FRANÇOIS.
Abregé de la Vie de Jacques II. Roy de la Grande Bretagne, &c. Tiré d'un écrit Anglois du R. P. François Sanders, de la Compagnie de Jesus, Confesseur de Sa Majesté. Par le P. François Bretonneau de la mesme Compagnie. Avec un recueil des sentimens du mesme Roy, sur divers sujets de Pieté. A Paris, De l'Imprimerie Royale. M. DCCIII. Title and *Avertissement*, 3 leaves : A—Bb in sixes: Cc, 2 leaves. With a portrait after Kueller.

    Sotheby's, June 1888 (Turner, 1562). On the flyleaf occurs : " For ỹ English Dominicans at Louvain from ỹ Queen of England."

BREVIA.
*Natura breuium. The olde tenures. Lyttlton tenures. The new talys. The articles vppon the new talys. Diuersyte of courtes. Justyce of peace. The chartuary. Court baron. Court of hundrede. Retorna brenium. The ordynaunce for takynge of fees in the escheker. . . . Cum priuilegio. [Col.] Thus endeth these xii. bokes . . . Prentyd by w. Rastell in Fletestrete in saynt Brydys chyrche yarde, the yere of oure lorde 1534. 4°.

    Herbert says that it was also printed this year in 24mo. He gives no collation.

[Natura Brevium. The colophon is :] Here endeth the boke of Natura breuium Emprynted by Richard Pynson. Folio, a—c in eights, a 1 blank : d—e in sixes : f, 8 : g—h in sixes : i, 4, the last leaf with the mark only. There is no regular title.

Natura Breuiũ [Col.] Here endeth the boke of natura breuium. Emprynted by Richarde Pynson. Folio, A—H in sixes : I, 4 leaves. With Pynson's device on the last page. *Grenv. Coll.*

    There is no title-page, what is given above occurring as a headline on A i.

*Natura breuium newly and moost trewly corrected / with diuers additions of statutes / boke / cases / pleas in abatemētes of the sayd writtes & theyr declaracions / & barres to the same added and put in theyr places most conuenient. [Col.] Here endeth the Natures of writtes in Frenche. Imprynted by me Robert Redman / at London dwellynge in the Fletestrete by saint Dunstones churche at the syne of the George. Cũ Prinilegio a rege Indulto. Folio, A—O in sixes : P, 8.

*Natvra Brevivm Newly and moost treuly corrected. Wyth dyuers additions of statutes, boke cases, . . . Imprynted in the yeare of our Lorde God M.CCCCC.XLV. [Col.] ¶ Imprynted at London Wythout Temple barre in saint Clementes paryshe by me Henry Smyth. 8°. 179 leaves, besides the tables at end.

*Registrum omniũ breuium tam originaliũ quam iudicialium. Londini. Apud

Guilielmum Rastell. 1531. Cvm Privilegio. [Col.] Thus endyth thys boke called the Register of the wryttys orygynall and indiciall, prentyd at London by Wyllyam Rastell, and is to sell in Fletestrete at the house of the sayde Wyllyam, or in Poulys chyrch yarde, or els at temple barre at the house of Robert Redman. Cvm Privilegio. Folio.

> The writs are in Latin ; but some of the rules and notes are in French. The first part has 321 leaves, besides the table ; the second, or judicial writs, 85 leaves and the table.

**Returna Brm. [Col.] Emprynted at Lōdon in fletestrete By Rychard Pynson. The yere of oure lord god. M.CCCCC. xvi. 4°, 12 leaves.

*Returna brenium. [Col.] Explicit Returna Briuium nouiter castigatum / Impressum Londonij per me Robertum Redman Anno domini M.CCCCC.xxxii. die vero mensis Februarij. xviij. 8°, A—B 4 in eights. With Pynson's cypher.

Returna breuium. An. M.D.XLIIJ. [This title is in a compartment, and there is no colophon or other imprint.] 8°, A—B 4 in eights.

> Apparently from the press of Robert Toy, with whose edition of the *Ordinance* it is in this copy bound up. But I suspect it to be merely part of the collective impression of twelve of these pieces, of which there were one or two issues for the convenience of lawyers and students.

BREVIARIUM.
Breuiarij Aberdonēsis ad percelebris ecclie Scotorẹ potissimuẹ vsum et consuetudinē Pars hyemalis : de tp̄e et de stīs ac dauitico psalterio congruenter per ferias diuiso: cum Inuitatorijs hymnis Antiphonis capitulis Responsorijs horis feriaẹ cōmēorationibẹ p̄ āni curriculū necnō cōe scorẹ plurimaqẹ v'ginū & matronarẹ ac diuersorẹ scōrẹ legēdis : q̄ sparsim in incerto antea vagabantur : cum Kalendario et mobiliū festorum tabula ppetua varijsq ; alijs adiūctis & de nouo additis sacerdotibẹ plurimū q̄ necessarijs i Ediinburgēsi oppido walteri chepmā mercatoris īpēsis īpressa Februarijs idibus. Anno salutis n̄re & g̃re. ix M. supra et quīgētēsimū. 4°. *Calendar*, 8 leaves : *Regula perpetua*, &c., 8 leaves in eights : *Advent Sunday*, &c., A—NN· in fours : *Proprium sanctorum*, A·—DD· in fours. In two columns.

(ii.) Breuiarij Aberdonēsis . . . Pars estiualis : . . . ī Ediburgēsi oppido walterī chepmā mercatoris īpēsis impressa pridie nonas Junii. Anno salutis n̄e & g̃re . x. M. supra et quīgētēsimū. 4°. *Calendar*, 8 leaves : *Regula perpetua*, &c., 4 leaves : a—kk in fours : [no A :] B—P in fours : Q, 1 leaf : *Proprium sanctorum*. A—XX in fours, with the colophon, dated June 4, 1510, on XX 4 *recto*, and Chepman's device on the reverse.

*Breuiariū secundū vsum hereford. [This title in red is over a cut of the portcullis crowned and supported, &c. At the end occurs :] Ad benedictissimi semperq ; sacratissimi domini ac saluatoris nostri iesu christi gloriam : et ad totius celestis curie laudē : atq ; singularem illustrissimo comitis richemonten. commendationem : necnon ad totiẹ ecclesie hereford' vtilitatem et salutem : impressum est hoc breuiarium secūdum eiusdem diocesis vsum in clarissimo rathomagen . emporio : impensis et cura Inghelberti haghe dicte comitis bibliopole ac dedititii Anno salutis christi Millesimo quingentesimo quīto. ii. non. augusti. 16° or small 8°. In two parts, the second commencing with fresh signatures, AA—FF in eights, FF 8 blank. Dedicated to the Countess of Richmond and Derby.

> Herbert does not give the collation of Part I.

BRIDOUL, FATHER TOUSSAINT, *of the Society of Jesus.*
The School of the Eucharist Established upon the Miraculous Respects and Acknowledgments, which Beasts, Birds, and Insects, upon several Occasions, have rendred to the Holy Sacrament of the Altar . . . now made English, and published, With a Preface concerning the testimony of Miracles. . . . London : Printed for Randal Taylor, . . . 1687. 4°, A—I in fours, besides the title and *Imprimatur.*

BRIEGERUS, JULIUS.
Flores Calvinistici Decerpti ex Vita Roberti Dvdlei Comitis Lecestriae in Anglia ; Hollandia ac Zelandia pro Elizabetha Angliæ Regina Gubernatoris. Ioannis Calvini, Thomæ Cranmeri, Ioannis Knoxij ; aliorumque Protectorum & Apostolorum sectæ Zvvinglianæ & Caluinianæ in Anglia, Scotia, Gallia, Belgio & Germania. . . . Neapoli . . . Anno M.D.LXXXV. 8°, A—F 3 in eights.

BRINSLEY, JOHN.
Pveriles Confabulatiunculæ : Or Childrens Dialogues, Little conferences, or talkings together, or little speeches together, or Dialogues fit for children. London, Printed by H. L. for Thomas

Man. 1617. Small 8°, A—E 4 in eights.
B. M.
> With a postscript by John Brinsley, who speaks of condescending to the requests of those who had called for the translations mentioned and promised in his *Grammar-School*, 1612.

BROUN, ANDREW, M.D.
A Vindicatory Schedule, concerning the New Cure of Fevers : . . . . Edinbvrgh, Printed by John Reid, at his Printing-house in Bells Wynd, at the head of the Court of Guard. 1691. To be sold be John Mackie In the Parliament Close. 8°. Title, 1 leaf: dedications to James Viscount Stair, &c., 9 leaves : Preface, Contents, &c., 13 leaves : A—O 2 in eights.

BROWN THOMAS.
Memoirs Relating to the late Famous Mr. Tho. Brown. With a Catalogue of his Library. London, Printed, and Sold by B. Brag. . . . 1704. (Price Six Pence.) 4°, A—D, 2 leaves each, a leaf of E with verses, and title and half-title, 2 leaves more.

BROWNE, SIR THOMAS, M.D.
Pseudodoxia Epidemica : . . . . The Third Edition, Corrected and Enlarged by the Author. Together with some Marginall Observations, and a Table Alphabeticall at the end. [Quot. from Julius Scaliger.] London, Printed by R. W. for Nath. Ekins, . . . 1658. Folio. Title and other prefixes under A, 6 leaves : no B : C—Xx in fours.

BRUNUS, LUDOVICUS, *Bishop of Asti*, ob. 1508.
Cronica summaria Serenissime dñe Hispaniarum regine [Isabella of Castile] : et de eius obitũ. Londini per R. Pynson. [1504.] 4°, 12 leaves. *Huth Coll.*
> Apparently a reprint of the supposed Roman edition, of which a copy is in the Br. Museum. The chief interest of this tract is in connection with the Spanish alliance and Catharine of Arragon.

BUCHANAN, GEORGE.
Rervm Scoticarvm Historia, libris xx. descriptâ . . . 1624. Francofvrti ad Mœnvm. 8°. (:) 4 leaves : A—li 4 in eights.

Rerum Scoticarum Historia . . . Vltratrajecti . . . CIƆ IƆC. LXVIII. 8°. *, 4 leaves : a—c 2 in eights : A—3 D 2 in eights.

Rerum Scoticarum Historia . . . Trajecti ad Rhenum, . . . M.DC.XCVII. 8°, a—e in eights : A—Zz in eights.

Georgii Buchanani Scoti Franciscanus et Fratres. Elegiarum Lib. 1. . . . Quibus jam recens accedunt De Sphœra Libri V. In Bibliopolio Commeliano. CIƆ IƆ CIX. 8°, A—N 4 in eights.

Georgii Buchanani Scoti ad Viros sui Seculi clarissimos, Eorumque ad eundem, Epistolæ. Ex MSS. accurate descriptæ, Nunc primum in lucem editæ. Londini . . . 1701. 8°, A—G in eights, A 8 with *Errata*.

BUCKINGHAMSHIRE.
The Copy of a Letter from Alisbvry. Directed to Colonell Hampden, Colonell Goodwin, and read in both Houses of Parliament, May 18. 1643. Relating how his Maiesty hath but 12 or 1400 of his Forces, under the Command of the Earle of Cleveland, the Lord Shandosse, the Lord Crayford, and Sir Iohn Byron, into those parts, who amongst many other cruelties fired a Countrey Towne called Swanborne, . . . With An Ordinance concerning the Arch-Bishop of Canterbury. . . . London, May 19. Printed for Iohn Wright . . . 1643. 4°, 4 leaves.

BULLEIN, WILLIAM, M.D.
*Bulleins Bulwarke of defēce againste all Sicknes, Sornes, and woundes that doce daily assaulte mankinde, whiche Bulwarke is kepte with Hillarius the Gardiner, Health the Phisician, with their Chirurgian, to helpe the wounded soldiers. Gathered and practised frõ the moste worthie learned, both old and newe ; to the greate comforte of mankinde : Doen by Willyam Bulleyn, and ended this Marche. Anno salutis, 1562. Imprinted at London by Jhon Kyngston. Folio. Dedicated to Lord Hunsdon.

[BULLINGER, HENRY, AND THEODORE DE BEZE.]
A Confession of Fayth, made by common consent of diuers reformed Churches beyonde the Seas ; with an Exhortation to the Reformation of the Churche. Perused and allowed accordinge to the Queenes Maiesties Iniunctions. Imprinted at London by Henry Wykes, for Lucas Harrison. [1566.] Small 8°, A—F 2 in eights and A—O in eights.
B. M.
> The Preface "Vnto the Christian Reader" is signed *I. O.* The exhortation is by Theodore de Beze, and is addressed to Louis of Bourbon, Prince of Condé, from Geneva, the 10 from the Calends of March 1565. At the end occurs : "This confession of faith, was publiquely presented again to the kings Maiestie, Charles the . ix. of that name at Poissy the yeare 1561, the ninth Septemb."

*A Confesion of Faith . . . Imprinted at London by H. Bynneman, for Luke Harrison, M.D.LXXI. 8", S in eights.

BUNYAN, JOHN.
The Pilgrim's Progress. From this World to that which is to come. The Second Part. Delivered under the Similitude of a Dream. Wherein is set forth The manner of the setting out of Christian's Wife and Children, their Dangerous Journey, and Safe Arrival at the Desired Country . . . By John Bunyan. *I have used Similitudes*, Hos. 12. 1. London, Printed for Nathaniel Ponder, . . . 1684. 12°. A, 6 leaves : B—K in twelves : L, 4, besides the frontispiece and a cut between pp. 182-3.

> On the back of the title is Bunyan's appointment of N. Ponder as the publisher, and the book is introduced by a metrical interlocution by the author, in which a statement of Objects is followed by Answers. I describe Mr. Elliot Stock's copy ; in the Lenox Library at New York is a second copy with a cut between pp. 52-3, not in this, and some leaves of advertisements at end.

The Pilgrims Progress, From this World to that which is to come : The Second Part . . . London, Printed for Nath. Ponder . . . 1687. Frontispiece, 1 leaf : A, 6 leaves : B—I in twelves ; I, 6, the last leaf blank. With two page-engravings at pp. 52-3 and 160-1.

The Barren Fig-tree : Or, The Doom & Downfal of the Fruitless Professor. Shewing, That the Day of Grace may be past with him long before his Life is ended. . . . To which is added His [Bunyan's] Exhortation to Peace and Unity among all that fear God. London, Printed for J. Robinson, . . . 1688. 12°, A—H in twelves.

BURGES, C., D.D.
No Sacrilege nor Sin to Alienate or Purchase Cathedral Lands, as such : Or, A Vindication of, not onely the Late Purchasers ; but, of the Antient Nobility and Gentry ; yea, of the Crown it self, all deeply wounded by the false Charge of Sacrilege upon New Purchasers. The third Edition, Revised, and Abbreviated, for the Service of the Parliament : With a Post-script to Dr. Pearson. . . . London : Printed by James Cottrel. 1660. 4°, A—K in fours. Dedicated to the Parliament.

BURLEY, WALTER.
Incipit Pulcher tractatę collectus p venerabilem doctorē Walterū burley Anglicū.
De vita pñor. [This is a headline on the top of the leaf following the Table. At the end occurs :] Et sic tinitur perpulcher tractatus . . . [Coloniæ] Per me Arnoldū ter Hornē Anno dñi. 1472. 4°. Table, 12 leaves : the work, 85 leaves. Without signatures and catchwords.

> Sotheby's, June 1888 (Turner, 740). The figures of the date are very singular, and remind one of the mysterious Caxton monogram.

Liber de vita ac moribus ph'orum. poetarū q3 veterę ex multis libris tractus ; necnō breuiter & cōpendiose p venerabilem virum mgrm walter3 burley cōpilatus incipit feliciter. [Col.] Liber de vitz a [sic] moribus ph'orum impressę per me Conradū de lomborch. Admissus añt ac approbatus ab alma vniuersitate Coloniensi desinit feliciter. 4°, A—I in eights : m, 9.

BURTON, RICHARD.
Unparallel'd Varieties . . . . The Second Edition. London, Printed for Nath. Crouch, . . . 1685. 12°, A—H in twelves, and I, 8 leaves, besides the frontispiece and plates at B, E, F, H, and I.

Winter - Evenings' Entertainments. In Two Parts . . . By R. B. The Third Edition. London, Printed for Nath. Crouch . . . . 1705. 12°, A—H in twelves. With cuts.

BUSH, PAUL, *Priest and Bonhomme of Edingdon* [Addington].
*This lytell boke conteynethe certayne godly medycynes necessary to be vsed among weldisposed people to eschew & to auoyde the comen plage of pestilens / thus collecte and sette forth in ordre by the diligent laboure of the religyous brother syr Paule Bushe preste and bonehome in the good house Edyngdon . . . [Col.] Impryuted by me Robert Redman Cum priuilegio. 8°, A—B 4 in eights. With an addres by the author to the readers on the back of the title in three 7-line stanzas.

BUSHELL, THOMAS.
A Iust and True Remonstrance of His Maiesties Mines-Royall in the Principality of Wales. Presented by Thomas Bushell Esquire, Farmor of the said Mines-Royall to his Majestie. Printed at London by E. G. 1641. ¶ Cum privilegio. 4°, A—E 2 in fours.

BUTLER, CHARLES, *of Magdalen College, Oxford*.
*Rhetoricæ libri duo, quorum Prior de Tropis & Figuris, Posterior de Voce &

Gestu, Præcipue in vsum scholarvm accuratius editi. Oxoniæ. Excudebat Iosephvs Barnesivs. 1600. 8°, A—I 4 in eights, besides the prefixes. Dedicated to Sir Thomas Egerton, Lord Keeper.

Suggeneia. De Propinqvitatis Matrimonium impediente Regvla. Quæ vna omnes quæstionis huius difficultatis facilè expediat. Authore Carolo Bvtler, Magd. ... Oxoniæ, Excudebant Iohannes Lichfield & Gvlielmvs Tvrner, ... 1625. 4°, A—K 2 in fours.

C.

C. H., *Gent.*
The Plain Englishman's Historian : Or, A Compendious Chronicle of England, From its first being Inhabited to this present Year 1679. ... London, Printed for Langley Curtis in Goat Court on Ludgate-hill. 1679. 12°, A—G in twelves, A with *Imprimatur* and G 12 blank.

C. J.
Brief Observations Concerning Trade, and Interest of Money. By J. C. London, Printed for Elizabeth Calvert at the Black-spread Eagle in Barbican, ... 1668. 4°, A—E in fours, E 4 blank.

On C 3 occurs a separate title to a reprint of *A Tract against Usurie*, 1621.

A Short Addition to the Observations ... By the same Hand. London, Printed for Henry Mortlock, ... 1668. 4°, A—B in fours, first and last leaves blank.

C. J., *D.D.*
Contemplations on the Life & Glory of Holy Mary, The Mother of Jesus. With a Daily Office, agreeing to each Mystery thereof. ... Paris, Anno Domini, 1683. Permissa Superiorum. Sm. 8°. A, 4 leaves : (a), 4 leaves : B—N in fours.

CALVIN, JOHN.
The Mynde of the Godly and excellent learned man M. Jhon Caluyne, what a Faithfull man, which is instructe in the Worde of God ought to do, dwellinge amongest the Papistes. [Quot. from 2 Cor. 6.] Anno Domini M.D.XLVIII. [Col.] Imprinted at Ippyswiche by me Jhon Oswen. Cum priuilegio. ... 8°, A—K 4 in eights, K 4 with the colophon.

*Of the life or conuersation of a Christen man, a right godly treatise, wrytten in the latin tongue, by maister John Caluyne, a man of ryght excellente learnynge and of no lesse conuersation. Translated into English by Thomas Broke Esquier, Paymaister of Douer. An. M.D.XLIX. The first day of January. [Col.] Imprinted at London by John Daye & Wyllyam Seres dwelling in Sepulchres parishe, ... 8°, A—K 3 in eights.

*An epistle both of Godly Consolacion and also of aduertisement, written by John Caluine the pastour & preacher of Geneua, to the right noble prince Edwarde Duke of Somerset, before the tyme or knoweledge had of his trouble, but deluyered to the sayde Duke, in the time of his trouble, and so translated out of frenshe by the same Duke. Imprinted at London by Edward whitchurche, the . v. daye of Aprill. 1550. Cum priuilegio ... 8°, E 2 in eights.

*The Catechisme, or maner to teache Children the Christian Religion. Made by ... Jhon Caluin. ... Imprinted at London by Jhon Kyngston. 1582. 8°, A—K in eights.

Crvdelitatis Calvinianæ Exempla Dvo Recentissima ex Anglia. Quorum primum, continet barbarum ac sæuum Caluinianorum edictum recenter editum contra Catholicos : alterum vero, exhibet indignissimam mortem Illustrissimi viri comitis Northumbriæ in castro Londinensi occisi mense Iulio huius Anni. 1585. ... Adiectum est in fine exemplar quarundam literarum ex Anglia ... Anno Domini 1585. 8°, A—D 6 in eights.

CAMERARIUS, P., *Councillor to the Free State of Nürnberg.*
The Living Librarie, Or Meditations and Observations Historicall, Natvral, Moral, Political, and Poetical. Written in Latin ... And done into English by Iohn Molle Esquire.

Hee, of all others, fittest is to write,
That intermingleth Profit with Delight.
Horace.

London Printed by Adam Islip. 1621. Folio, A—Mm in sixes, first and last leaves blank. Dedicated to John [Williams,] Lord Bishop of Lincoln, Lord Keeper, by Richard Baddeley. The title is within an engraved compartment.

The translator appears to have died some time before the publication of his work. It is one which deals with a large variety of curious particulars, as, for instance, gypsies, beggars, devils, lycanthropy, dress, &c.

CAMPION, THOMAS.
Songs of Mourning : Bewailing the vnimely death of Prince Henry. Worded by Tho. Campion. And set forth to bee sung with one voyce to the Lute, or Violl : By John Coprario. London : Printed for Iohn Browne, and are to be sould in S. Dunstons Churchyard. 1613. Folio, A—E, 2 leaves each.

*CAPITO, WOLFGANGUS.
An Epitome of the Psalmes, or briefe meditations vpon the same, with diuerse other moste christian prayers, translated by Richard Tauerner. Cum priuilegio ad imprimendum solum. 1539. [Col.] ¶ Imprinted at London in Fletestrete at the signe of the whyte hart. 1539. Cum priuilegio . . . 8°. Dedicated to Henry VIII.

ARACCIOLI, G.
The Italian Convert, Newes from Italy of a Second Moses Or The Life of Galeacivs Caracciolvs the Noble Marquesse of Vico . . . London, Printed by A. G. for Anne More . . . 1635. 4°, A—K in fours, K 4 blank, no B.

!ARDS.
Geographical Cards made and Sold For Henry Brome at ye Gun in St. Pauls Church-yard London 1676. 12°, 52 engraved leaves and the title, on the back of which is the description of the plan. Engraved by Van Hove.

Some of the leaves are surmounted by portraits, and some refer to the English Plantations in America, Mexico, &c.

!APEL, ARTHUR, *Earl of Essex*.
An Impartial Enquiry into the Administration of Affairs in England. With Some Reflections on the Kings Declaration of July 27. 1683 . . . Printed Anno 1683. 4°, A—L in fours, besides the title and a folded frontispiece.

!ARIER, BENJAMIN.
A Copy of a Letter, written by M. Doctor Carier beyond the Seas, to some particular friends in England. Whereunto are added certaine collections found in his Closet, made by him (as is thought) of the miserable ends of such as haue impugned the Catholike Church. . . . 1615. 4°, A—F 2 in fours.

CARMICHAEL, JAMES.
*Grammatice Latinæ, de etymologia, liber secundus, ex vetustissimis artis et linguæ auctoribus depromptus, ex methodo, quam senatus literarum, regia auctoritate Sterlingi habitus, Scotiæ iuuentuti facilimam censuit. Addita sunt, sed minoribus characteribus, in prouectiorum gratiam, ex intimis artis penetralibus, pleræque a nemine prius, congesta quibus auctor pueris properantibus interdici velit. [Cambridge, Thomas Thomas, 1587.] 4°, 26 leaves + prefixes. Dedicated by Carmichael from the printer's office, the ides of September, 1587.

This was apparently designed as a sequel to Andrew Symson's *Rudimenta*, 1587. See Hazlitt's *School-Books*, 1886, p. 187.

CARMINA.
*Carminvm Proverbialivm Totius humanæ vitæ statum breuiter deliniantium, . . . Impressum Londini, 1588. [Col.] Excudebat Thomas Dawsonus ex assignatione Chr. Barker. Sm. 8°, pp. 216.

CARTA FEODI.
**Carta feodi simplicis cum littera atturnatoria. [Col.] Impressa Londoñ per wynandum de worde in vico the fletestrete in signo solis cōmorātem. Sm. 8°, 27 leaves.

*Paruus libellus continens formam multarum rerum prout patet in kalendario in fine in contento. [Col.] ¶ Impressum per me Robertum Redman. Anno domini milessimoquingentisimo. xxx. 8°, A—D in eights : E, 10. With Pynson's cypher on the last page.

*Paruus libellus continens formam multaru̅ rerum, . . . [Col.] Explicit Carta feodi. Impressum Londini per Richardum Kele, An. dñi. M. ccccc. xlvi. 8°, 50 leaves.

CARY, WALTER.
A boke of the propertyes of herbes the which is called an Herbal. [Col.] Imprynted at London by my John Skot dwellynge in Fanster lane. 12°, A—K 4 in eights. With his device below the colophon.

CARYLL, JOSEPH, *Preacher to Lincoln's Inn*.
The Saints Thankfull Acclamation at Christs Resvmption of his great power and the Initials of this Kingdome Delivered in a Sermon at Westminster before the Honourable House of Commons, upon the day of their solemne Thanksgiving unto God, for the great victorie given our Armie, under the Command of the Noble

Lord Fairfax, at Selby in Yorke-shire, and to other the Parliaments Forces in Pembrock-shire, April 23rd 1644. London, Printed by G. M. for Giles Calvert . . . 1644. 4°. A, 2 leaves: B—H in fours, and the title.

CATECHISM.
*A shorte Catechisme. A briefe and godly bringinge vp of youth / in the Knowlege and cōmaundementes of God in fayth / prayer and other articles / necessary to be knowne of all those that wilbe partakers of the kyngdom of Jesus Christ: set forth in maner of a Dialogue. . . . Imprynted the year after the creation of the worlde 5525. And after the byrthe of our Sauiour 1550. 8°, L in half-sheets. [Col.] Imprinted at London by Edwarde Whitchurche. . . .

CATHOLICS.
The Svpplication of all the Papists in England to King James, at his first comming to the Crowne, For a Tolleration of that Religion. . . . Whereunto is added, A Letter sent from Bishop Abbot Archbishop of Canterbury, to the King; against Toleration of the Popish Religion . . . London, Printed by E. Griffin, 1642. 4°, 4 leaves.

CHAMBERLAYNE, EDWARD, M.D.
Angliæ Notitia; . . . The Second Edition corrected and much augmented . . . In the Savoy, Printed by T. N. for John Martyn Printer to the Royal Society, . . . M DC LXIX. 12°. A, 6 leaves: B—X in twelves.

CHAPMAN, GEORGE, AND OTHERS.
Eastward Hoe. As It was playd in the Blackfriers. By The Children of her Maiesties Reuels. Made by Geo: Chapman. Ben: Iohnson. Joh: Marston. At London Printed for William Aspley. 1605. 4°, A—H in fours. There is no introductory matter except the Prologue on the back of the title.

> In this Chapman was assisted by Jonson and Marston. There were at least *four* editions the same year. For some obnoxious expressions touching the Scots the authors were committed, but subsequently pardoned by the King. These passages remain in one or two extant copies; but in most they were cancelled.

CHARLES STUART THE FIRST, *King of Great Britain* (1625-48).
By the King. A Proclamation signifying his Maiesties pleasure, That all men being in Office of gouernment at the decease of his most deare, and most royall Father King James, shall so continue, till his Maiesties further direction. Printed at London by Bonham Norton and Iohn Bill, . . . M.DC.XXV. A broadsheet formed of two leaves.

A Proclamation declaring the Kings Maiesties Royall pleasure touching the Inhabitants of Algier, Tunis, Sallie, and Tituan, in the parts of Africa. Imprinted at London by Bonham Norton, and Iohn Bill, . . . M.DC.XXVIII. A broadsheet.

Lawes and Ordinances of Warre, For the better Government of His Maiesties Army Royall, in the present Expedition for the Northern parts, and safety of the Kingdome. Under the Conduct of his Excellence, The Right Honourable Thomas Earle of Arundel and Surrey, Earl Marshall of England, &c. and Generall of his Majesties Forces. Imprinted at Newcastle by Robert Barker, . . . And by the Assignes of John Bill. 1639. 4°, A—D in fours, A 1 with a cut of the royal arms.

The Bloody Treatie: Or, Proceedings between the King and Prince Rupert. As also, Between P.r. Rupert and Capt. Pickering, who hath brought in 4. of the Kings Collonels, to the Parliament; with the whole proceedings of Ruperts perambulation from the King at Newark, and his return to Woodstock with 400. Horse. And how cruelly they used Captaine Pickering during the Treatie . . . With Ruperts Letter to the King about a bloody massacre . . . London, Printed for J. C. 1645. 4°, 4 leaves.

A Private Letter, From an Eminent Cavalier, To his highly honoured friend in London; Freely relating the present state of His Majesties Forces. London, Printed, Sept. 10, 1642. 4°, 4 leaves.

His Majesties Desires and Command to all the Trayned Bands and others on this side Trent, and Dominion of Wales to be in Readinesse with Horse and Arms to serve His Majesty for defence of the Kingdome, and to be in such readinesse, that they may be able to march at 24 houres warning at the furthest . . . With the Sheriffe of Yorkshires Proposition to the Gentry and Commonalty of that County. Iuly 1. 1642. Likewise, A Letter which came from Manchester, . . . Iuly 6. Printed for Iohn Norton, 1642. 4°, 4 leaves.

Sundry Observations of severall Passages and Proceedings in the North, there taken by a Subject well-affected to the Protestant Religion, His Majesties Royall

Honour and Greatness, . . . Sent unto a faithfull and intimate friend of his in London. Containing a Description of the Qualities, Conditions, Aims, and Intents of such as intend to act the fearfull Tragedie. The Destruction of His Majesty, and His Kingdoms . . . London, Printed for F. C. July 29. 1642. 4°, 4 leaves.

A true and exact Relation of the manner of his Maiesties setting up of His Standard at Nottingham, on Munday the 22. of August. 1642. . . . London, Printed for F. Coles. 1642. 4°, 4 leaves. With a cut on the title, containing a head of the King, a small view of Nottingham, &c.

An Exact Relation, Shewing how the Governour of Portsmouth Castle delivered it up in the name of the King to the Malignant Party. Whereupon he thrust out the Protestants placing ill affected persons in their Garrisons. Also A Terrible Combate Fovght in Bedfordshire between two Knigts [sic], The one sent in Commission of Array by the King, the other by the Parliament. . . . Likewise, The Lord Brooke His Resolution concerning the Lord of Northampton . . . August 5. Printed for Io. Handgats, 1642. 4°, 4 leaves.

Lawes and Ordinances of Warre, Established for the better Conduct of the Army By His Excellency the Earle of Essex Lord Generall of the Forces raised by the Authority of the Parliament, for the defence of the King and Kingdom. London, Printed for Iohn Partridge and Iohn Rothwell, September, 1642. 4°, A—D in fours.

An Abstract of some Letters, sent from Dorchester, to some friends in London, dated the 3. of Septem. 1642. Containing A True Relation of the late proceedings of Marquesse Hartford and the Cavaliers, at Sherborn Castle, with the opposition of that and other adjacent Counties to those Proceedings. London : Printed for Henry Overton, . . . 1642. 4°, 4 leaves.

A Letter written from the Right Honorable the Earle of Bedford, to a Lord of the House of Peeres, Of all the remarkable passages about Sherborn Castle. Being A full Relation of the graet overthrow given to the Cavalleers within a mile of Eivill : With the Resolution of the Earle of Bedford, to die in the cause. Desired by the Lords in Parliament, that this Letter be forthwith printed and published. London, Printed for Hugh Perry, Septemb. 15. 1642. 4°, 4 leaves.

The Fovre Petitions of Hvntington Shire, Norfolk Svffolk, and Essex. Ioyntly concerning the libertie of the Subiecte, to the Honourable Assembly of the High Court of Parliament. Vnanimously concurring to the rooting out of Papists and their Religion from our Kingdome ; . . . The Petition of Huntington-shire, particularly containing the behalfe of the Lord Kimbolton. London, Printed for Iohn Hammond, 1642. 4°, 4 leaves.

His Majesties Message to the House of Commons : Concerning an Order made by them for the borrowing of one hundred thousand pounds of the Adventurers Money for Ireland Together with the Answer of the House of Commons . . . September 6. London, Printed for John Wright, 1642. 4°, 4 leaves.

A true and exact Relation of the Proceedings of His Majesties Army in Cheshire, Shrop-Shire, and Worstershire. Together with what hath happened to the late Lord Strange now Earl of Derby, before Manchester. With the Resolution of the Town to oppose him, and the number of Men which were slain. London, Printed for M. Batt. Octob. 5. 1642. 4°, 4 leaves.

Some Observations concerning Iealousies between King and Parliament, With their causes and cures. *Raptim Scripta.* London. Printed for Iohn Rothwell 1642. 4°, 4 leaves.

The Kings Maiesties Instructions Vnto the Earle of Northampton, the Lord Dunsmore, the high Sheriff of the County of Warwick, and the rest of the Commissioners. For putting the Commission of Array in execution, in the said County of Warwick. London, Printed for A. Norton, 1642. 4°, 4 leaves.

The Proceedings in the late Treaty of Peace. Together with several Letters of his Majesty to the Queen, and of Prince Rupert to the Earle of Northampton, which were intercepted and brought to the Parliament. With A Declaration of the Lords and Commons upon those Proceedings and Letters . . . London, Printed for Edward Husbands, . . . 1643. 4°, A—M in fours.

A More full Relation of the great Battell fought betweene Sir Tho: Fairfax, and Goring, on Thursday last. 1645. Made in the House of Commons by Lieut: Col:

Lilbourne, the last Messenger that came from the Army. With the manner of the Fight, Goring cut on the Eare, the Lieutenant Generall of the Ordnance taken, and the particulars of what losse was on both sides. And the Routing of a party of Gorings Forces by the Clubmen. . . . London, Printed by T. Forcet for Peter Cole. 1645. 4°, 4 leaves.

Numb. 2. Papers of Surrendring the Kings Majesty to English Commissioners on Satturday last, and Newca-tle surrendred to Major-Generall Skippon. With an Accompt of the whole businesse, in relation to that Agreement; . . . And a List of the Lords, Knights and Gentlemen, that attend His Majesty to Holmsby, and the Convoy and Carriages . . . London : Printed by J. Coe, neer Cripplegate. Anno Dom. 1647. 4°, 4 leaves.

The Propositions of the Lords and Commons Assembled in Parliament for a safe and well grounded Peace. Presented to His Majesty at Hampton Court, the seventh of Septemb. 1647. And now to be Treated on in the Isle of Wight . . . Imprinted at London for John Wright . . . 1648. 4°, 12 leaves, or A—C in fours.

Prince Charles His Declaration, For satisfaction of all his Majesties Loyall Subjects in England, Scotland, and Ireland, July 31. 1648. Signed *Willoughby, Hopton, Culpepper*. Printed in the Yeare 1648. 4°, 4 leaves. With the Prince of Wales's feathers on title, accompanied by the motto *Mors et Vita*.

Two Great Victories : One at Dover against Sir Richard Hardreds, and 2000 Officers and Souldiers. The Block-Houses taken, with 30 piece of Ordnance, by Coll: Rich, the Castle Relieved, and the Enemy punished. Another Victory in Wales : Tenby Castle taken by Lieutenant Gen: Cromwell. And Coll: Powel, Coll: Kemish, Coll: Donell, and 30 Officers, all prisoners at mercy, 20 piece of Ordnance taken, 300 Armes, 40 Horse, 5 Coulours, and 4 Barrels of Gunpowder. Also A Letter from Bow, of Transactions between the Commissioners of Parliament and the Essex men, Sir William Hicks, and divers others taken Prisoners. Printed at London by Robert Ibbitson, in Smithfield, near the Queenes-head Tavern, 1648. 4°, 4 leaves.

His Majesties Message to both Houses of Parliament, Brought from the Isle of Wight upon Monday the fourteenth of August 1648. By the Right Honourable the Earle of Middlesex, Sir Iohn Hipsley, and Master Bunckley concerning the Personall Treaty. Printed in the Yeare. 1648. 4°, 4 leaves.

The Charges of the Commons of England, Against Charls Stuart, King of England, Of High Treason, and other High Crimes, exhibited to the High Court of Justice, By John Cook Esquire, Solicitor General, appointed by the said Court, for, and on the behalf of the People of England. As it was read to Him by the Clerk in the said Court, . . . London, Printed for Rapha Harford, at the Gilt Bible in Queens-Head-Alley in Pater noster Row. 1648. 4°, 4 leaves.

King Charles His Speech Made upon the Scaffold at Whitehall Gate, Immediately before his Execution, on Tuesday the 30. of Jan. 1648. With a Relation of the manner of his going to Execution. Published by speciall Authority. London Printed by Peter Cole, . . . 1649. 4°, 4 leaves.

CHARLES STUART THE SECOND, *King of Great Britain* (1660–85).

A Relation in form of Journal, of the Voiage and Residence which the most Excellent and most Mighty Prince Charls the II. King of Great Britain, &c. hath made in Holland, from the 25 of May, to the 2 of June, 1660. Rendered into English out of the Original French, By Sir William Lower, Knight. Hague, Printed by Adrian Vlack, Anno M, DC. LX. With Priviledge of the Estates of Holland and West - Freesland. Folio. Portrait of Charles in armour, title and The Printer to the Reader, 3 leaves : A—Ff, 2 leaves each. With plates at pp. 30, 32 (misprinted 26), 78, 88, 90, and 106, and some copies of verses signed by Sir W. Lower at end, including an acrostic poem on Charles's name and title by the same.

> In the Westmoreland copy (Sotheby's, July 13, 1887, No. 315), occurred at the end (u)–(i), 2 leaves each, a Latin poem also printed at the Hague in 1660, entitled *Anglia Triumphans*, by Robertus Keuchemus.

A Collection out of the Book called Liber Regalis, Remaining in the Treasury of the Church of Westminster. Touching the Coronation of the King and Queen together, According to the usual Form. London, Printed by R. D. for Charls Adams, at the Talbot in Fleetstreet, over again't Fetter-Lane. 1661. 4°, A—B 2 in fours.

cone : Or, some Reflections Upon
rse Called *Omnia à Belo comesta*.
ng Some Animadversions from
th, upon the Letter out of the
. . London, Printed, 1668. 4°,
in fours.

Narrative of the Old Plot. Being
Ballad. To the Tune of, Some
Papists had a Plot, &c. London,
for Charles Corbet at the Oxford-
Warwick-Lane, 1683. A folio
e, containing 18 4-line stanzas.

Treaties of Peace and Commerce
ed between the late King of
memory Deceased, and other
and States ; With Additional
i the Margin, Referring to the
Articles in each Treaty, and a
Reprinted and Published by His
s Especial Command. London,
by His Majesties Printers ; . . .
°, A—Ll in fours, Ll 4 blank,
itle and Table, 2 leaves.

on-Craig, part 2, 4983, the Harleian
i old red morocco, with the arms and
Harley stamped in gold on sides and
me stamped in gold (as usual) on fly-
side cover.

r, containing some Remarks on
Papers, writ by his late Majesty
harles the Second, concerning
[Edinburgh, 1689.] 4°, 4

:RHOUSE.
Hospitall : With the Names of
Mannors, many Thousand Acres
Meadow, Pasture, and Woods ;
Rents and Hereditaments there-
onging ; The Governours thereof,
ber of Schollers and others that
tained therewith. As Also, The
and Testament of Thomas Sut-
aire, Founder of the said Hos-
. . London, Printed by Barnard
relling in Grubstreet, 1646 [July
A—C in fours. *B. M.*

IDE CROSS.
narkable Fvneral of Cheapside-
London : With The Reeson why
ops. Jesuits, Papists, Cavaliers,
uinians, refused to bee there.
ie Order and Manner of the
, and the severall Songs for that
appointed. London. Printed
ert Hodgekinsonne. 1642. 4°,
B. M.

RE.
ty condemned, by declaring the
why the Deputy-Lieutenants in-

trusted by the Parliament for Cheshire,
cannot agree to the Treaty of Pacification
made by some of that County : At Bun-
bery, December, 23, 1642. And may
serve to prevent the like in other Counties. [Col.] London Printed for Henry
Overton, . . . December, 6. 1642. 4°, 4
leaves. Without a regular title-page.

CHETHAM, JAMES, *of Smedley, near
Manchester.*
The Angler's Vade Mecvm : Or, a Com-
pendious, yet full, Discourse of Angling.
. . . The Second Edition, Illustrated with
Sculptures : And very much Enlarged.
London, Printed for T. Basset . . . and
W. Brown . . . 1689. 8°. A, 4 leaves :
D—Y in eights. With two leaves at B
and G with cuts of fish.

The Preface is dated from Smedley, Nov.
26, 1688.

CHIDLEY, SAMUEL.
Bells Founder Confounded, Or Sabinianus
confuted : With his damnable Sect. [Quo-
tations from Jeremiah, &c.] Written by
a Lover of Musick, especially in Churches.

Barns, Durand, and Platino tells,
That Pope Sabinuian brought in bells.

Anno, 603. [London, 1658-9.] 4°, A—B
in fours, B 4 blank.

CHRISTIAN.
** ¶ How and whether a Christen man
ought to fly the horryble Plague of the
Pestilence. A Sermon out of the Psalme.
Qui habitat in adivtorio altissimi. ¶ Trans-
lated out of hie Almaine into Englishe.
¶ Imprinted at London by Leonarde
Askell. [Col.] ¶ Imprinted at London
by Leonard Askell for Thomas Purfoote
dwelling in Powles church yarde at the
signe of the Lucrece. [About 1565.] 8°,
C in eights.

At the end of the *Sermon* occurs : ¶ Translated by M[iles] C[overdale] out of hye Al-
mayne, Anno. 1537.

CHRONICLE.
A cronicle of yeres, from the begynning
of the worlde, wherin ye shal fynd the
names of al the kinges of Englãd, of ȳ
mayrs & shirifs of the citie of Londõ, &
briefly of many notable actes done, in, &
sith, the reigne of King Henry the fourth
newly augmented and corrected. Anno
domini M. v. C. xlii. [Col.] Imprynted
at London by Johñ Byddell dwelling in
Fletestrete at the sygne of the sonne
agaynste the conduith. 8°, A—D in
eights, D 7 with device and D 8 blank.

CRASHAW, RICHARD.
A Letter from Mr Crashaw to the Countess

of Denbigh. Against irresolution and Delay in matters of Religion. [London, 1653. Sept. 23.] 4°, 2 leaves. In verse. B. M.

CHURCH.
Ordinatio Ecclesiæ, Sev Ministerii Ecclesiastici, In Florentissimo Regno Angliæ, conscripta sermone patrio, & in Latinam linguam bona fide conuersa, & ad consolationem Ecclesiarum Christi ubicunque locorum ac gentium, his tristissimis temporibus, Edita, Ab Alessandro Alesio Scoto Sacræ Theologiæ Doctore. Lipsiæ ... Anno M. D. LI. 4°, A—R in fours : S, 6.

CIVILITY.
The Rules of Civility ; Or, Certain Ways of Deportment observed amongst all persons of Quality upon several Occasions. Newly revised and much Enlarged. London, Printed for J. Martyn, and J. Starkey, ... MDCLXXVIII. 12°. A, 6 leaves, A 1 with an Advertisement: B—N in twelves: O, 6.

CLOSET.
A Closet for Ladies and Gentlewomen ... Corrected, Amended, and much Enlarged, by adding a very usefull Table thereunto. London, Printed by R. H. 1656. 12°, A—H in twelves, title on A 2.
> Many of the items in this volume are copied from Platt's *Jewel-house of Art and Nature*, 1594.

CLOSSE, G.
The Parricide Papist, Or, Cut-throate Catholicke. A tragicall discourse of a murther lately committed at Padstow. ... Printed at London for Christopher Hunt, dwelling in Lonells lane in Paternoster-row. 1606. 4°, A—C in fours. A 1 apparently a blank. B. M. (Freeling's copy.)

CLUN.
An Egley [sic] upon the most Execrable Murther of Mr Clun one of the Comedians of the Theator Royal, Who was Rob'd and most inhumanely Kill'd on Tuseday-night, being the 2d of August, 1664. near Totnam-Court, as he was going to his Country-house at Kentish town. London, printed by Edward Crowch dwelling on Snow-hill. A broadside. B. M.

COACHES.
Reasons to augment the Number of Hackney Coaches, Within the Bills of Mortality, from Four Hundred to Six or Eight Hundred : Most humbly tendred to the Consideration of Both Houses of Parliament. Folio, 2 leaves.

COCHLÆUS, JOHANNES.
Pro Scotiae Regno Apologia Iohannis Cochlei. Adversvs Personatum Alexandrum Alesium Scotum, Ad Serenis. Scotorū regē. M.D.XXXIII. [Col.] Excusum Lipsiæ apud Michaëlem Blum. 4°, A—E in fours, E 4 blank.
> Dedicated to James V., King of Scotland, *Prince of Ireland*, and Lord of Iceland and the Orkneys. This is the last apparently of a series of tracts relative to the reading of the New Testament in Scotland.

COCKER, EDWARD.
Arts Glory : Or, The Pen mans Treasury: Containing Various Examples of Secretary, Text, Roman, and Italian Hands. Adorned with many curious Knots and Flourishes to render them Pleasant as well as Profitable. With Directions, Theorems, and rare Principles of Art, Comprehending very much of the Authors Knowlege. Also a Receipt for Inke ; and to Write with Gold. Wholly Invented, Written, and Engraven, by Edward Cocker, dwelling on the South-side of St. Paul's Church, right over against Pauls-Chaine : Where he teacheth the Arts of Writing and Arithmetick. Are to be sold with other of the Authors Works, by Peter Stent, ... and William Fisher, at the Postern-gate next Tower-hill, London, 1659. Obl. 4°. With a portrait by Gaywood. Title, 1 leaf : Preface and Directions, 3 leaves : plates, 26 leaves : Additional Directions, 8 leaves, the last page containing an anagram on Cocker's name by Jeremy Collier.

Cockers Arithmetick : Perused and Published by John Hawkins Writing-Master near St. George's Church in Southwark, by the Authors correct Copy, ... London, Printed by J. R. for T. P. and are to be sold by John Back, ... 1694. 12°. A, 6 leaves : B—K in twelves. Dedicated to Mainwaring Davies, Esq., of the Inner Temple, and Mr. Humphrey Davies of Newington Butts, Surrey. With a portrait of Cocker.

COINS.
By the King. A Proclamation for making currant certaine French Coyne Printed at Oxford by I. L. and W. T. for Bonham Norton, and Iohn Bill, ... M.DC.XXV. A broadside.
> By reason of the suspension of the operations of the Tower Mint during the Plague. The coin was the *quart d'ecu*. The proclamation was revoked by another of the 24th July same year.

COKE, SIR EDWARD.
A Little Treatise of Baile and Maineprize. Written by E. C. Knight, and now Published for a generall good. The Second

Edition, Corected and enlarged. London. Printed for William Cooke, ... 1637. 4°, A—E in fours, A 1 blank. Black letter.

The Fourth Part of the Institutes of the Laws of England: Concerning the Jurisdiction of Courts. Proverbs 22. 28. *Ne transgrediaris* ... Authore Edw. Coke Milite, I. C. ... MDCXLIV. Printed at London by M. Flesher, for W. Lee, and D. Pakeman. Folio. Portrait by Payne. Title, and Table, 5 leaves: B—Aaa in fours: *Epilogue*, 1 leaf.

The Fifth Part of the Reports of Sr Edward Coke Knight, the Kings Attorney Generall: Of diuers Resolutions and Judgments giuen vpon great deliberation, in matters of great importance & consequence by the reuerend Judges and Sages of the Law; ... London Printed for the Companie of Stationers. Anno Dom. 1606. Cum Priuilegio. Folio. A, 6 leaves: B—K in fours. In two columns. Lat. and Engl.

COKE, ROGER.
A Discourse of Trade. In Two Parts. The First treats of The Reason of the Decay of the Strength, Wealth, and Trade of England. The latter, Of the Growth and Increase of the Dutch Trade above the English. By Roger Coke. London, Printed for H. Brome, ... and R. Horne in the first Court entering into Gresham-Colledge next Bishopsgate-street, 1670. 4°, A—M 2 in fours. Dedicated to Sir Charles Harbord. With an interesting Preface.

[COLET, JOHN, *Dean of St. Paul's*, and WILLIAM LILY.]
**Libellus de Constructione Octo Partium Orationis. [Col.] Explicit hic Libellus ... Londini Impressus per Richardum pynson Regium impressorem. Anno incarnationis dominicæ Millesimo qūigētesimo decimōtuio. 4°, 28 leaves.

> On the back of the title is a Latin letter from Dean Colet to Lily, dated 1513, in which he speaks of St. Paul's as his only son.

COLVILL, SAMUEL.
The Grand Impostor Discovered: Or, An Historical Dispute of the Papacy and Popish Religion: 1. Demonstrating the newness of both; 2. By what artifices they are maintained: ... Part 1. Divided in two Books ... By S. C. Edinburgh, Printed by His Majesties Printers, for the Author, Anno Dom. 1673. 4°, A—Ee in fours: Book 2, A—M in fours, besides two leaves between A and A 2 in the first gathering with S. Colvill's dedication to the Duke of Lauderdale.

CONFESSION.
*The humble and vnfained confession of the belefe of certain poore banished men, grounded vpon the holy scriptures of God, and vpon the articles of that vndefyled and onlye vndoubted true christian faith, which the holy catholicke (that is to say, vniuersal) churche of God professeth, specially concerning, not only the worde of God, and the ministerye off the same, but also the church and sacraments thereof. Which we send moost humbly vnto the lords of England and all the commons of the same. [Col.] From Wittonburge, by Nicholas Dorcaster. M.D.LIIII. the xiii. of May. Sm. 8°, 33 leaves.

The Confession of Faith, Together with the Larger and Lesser Catechismes. Composed by the Reverend Assembly of Divines, Sitting at Westminster, Presented to both Houses of Parliament. Again Published with the Scriptures at large, ... To which is annexed two sheets of Church-Government with the Scriptures at large. [The second Edition.] ... London, Printed by E. M. for the Company of Stationers, ... 1658. 4°. A, 4 leaves: b—c in fours, e 4 with *Errata*: *An Ordinance*, &c., *, 6 leaves: B—Q 3 in fours: *The Humble Advice*, &c., A—Ee 2 in fours, and the title: Ff, 4 leaves.

Confessio Fidei, In Conventu Theologorum authoritate Parliamenti Anglicani indicto Elaboratus; Eidem Parliamento postmodum Exhibita; ... Unà cum Catechismo duplici, Majori Minorique; E Sermone Anglicano summa cum fide in Latinum versæ. Edinburgi, Excudebat ex Officina Societatis Stationariorum, Anno Dom. 1670. 12°, A—H in twelves.

COMMONWEALTH.
An Act Prohibiting The Importing of any Wines, Wooll or Silk from the Kingdom of France, into the Commonwealth of England or Ireland, or any the Dominions thereunto belonging. Die Martis, 28 Augusti, 1649 ... London, Printed by Edward Husband and John Field, Printers to the Parliament of England, 1650. A broadside.

Panarmonia. Or, The Agreement of the People, Revised, and Recommended to the Great Patrons of the Commonwealth, and to the Sober-minded People of the Land in general: Humbly presented, with an Apology for Christian Liberty, To the Honourable Council of the Army.

London, Printed for Livewell Chapman, . . . 1659. 4°, A—F 2 in fours.

CONTEMPLATION.
*The foundement of contemplacyon. ¶ Howe a man shall contemple / and se god in creatures. [Col.] Imprynted by me Robert Wyer in saynt Martyns parysshe. ¶ Cum priuilegio regali. 8°, A—B 4 in eights.

COOK, MOSES.
The Manner of Raising, Ordering, and Improving Forrest-trees: Also, How to Plant, Make and Keep Woods, Walks, Avenues, Lawns, Hedges, &c. With Several Figures proper for Avenues and Walks to End in, and convenient Figures for Lawns. . . . London, Printed for Peter Parker . . . 1676. 4°. A, 4 leaves: a, 4 leaves: B—Dd in fours, besides four leaves with figures between Dd and Dd 3. Dedicated to Arthur Lord Capel, Lord Lieutenant of Ireland, and the preface is dated from Cassiobury, Nov. 16, 1675.

COPE, SIR ANTHONY.
A godly meditacion vpon . xx. select and chosen Psalmes of the Prophet Dauid, as wel necessary to al them that are desirous to haue y darke wordes of the Prophet declared and made playn; as also fruitfull to suche as delyte in the contemplatiō of the spiritual meanyng of them. Compiled and set furth by Sir Anthony Cope knight. Imprynted at London in Sepulchres paryshe a lytle aboue Holborne Conduit at the sygne of the Resurrection by Jhon Daye. Anno. M. d. xlvii. Cum priuilegio . . . 4°. *, 4 leaves with title and dedication to Queen Katherine Parr: A—Bb in fours, Bb 4 blank.

>Sotheby's, June 1888 (Turner, 994), the Queen's own copy, in the original richly gilt and ornamented binding, with the royal arms on sides, £27.

COPRARIO, JOHN.
Fvneral Teares. For the death of the Right Honorable the Earle of Deuonshire. Figvred in seauen songes, whereof sixe are so set forth that the wordes may be exprest by a treble voice alone to the Lute and Base Viole, or else that the meane part may bee added, if any shall affect more fulnesse of parts. The Seauenth is made in forme of a Dialogue, and can not be sung without two voyces. Inuented by Iohn Coprario. *Pius piè.* At London Printed by Iohn Windet the Assigne of William Barley, for Iohn Browne, . . . 1606. Folio, A—E, 2 leaves each.

CORIAT, THOMAS.
Mr Thomas Coriat to his friends in England sendeth greeting: From Agra the Capitall City of the Dominion of the Great Mogoll in the Eastern India, the last of October, 1616. [A woodcut of Coryat mounted on a camel.] At London printed by I. B. 1618. 4°. ¶, 4 leaves, title on ¶ 2: A—E in fours. With woodcuts.

COTTON, CHARLES.
The Compleat Gamester: Or, Instructions how to play at Billiards, Tercks, Bowls, and Chess. Together with all manner of usual and most Gentile Games either on Cards or Dice. To which is added, The Arts and Mysteries of Riding, Racing, Archery, and Cock-Fighting. The Second Edition. London: Printed for Henry Brome . . . 1676. Small 8°, A—Q 4 in eights, Q 4 blank, A 1 with the explanation of the frontispiece, and A 2 with the engraving in five compartments.

COURT.
A Proclamation for restraint of vnnecessarie resorts to the Court. Printed at London by Bonham Norton and Iohn Bill, . . M.DC.XXV. [June 25.] A broadsheet.

A Proclamation for restraint of disorderly and vnnecessary resort to the Court. Printed at London by Bonham Norton and Iohn Bill, . . . M.DC.XXV. A broadsheet formed of two leaves.

A Proclamation for the Prices of Victuals within the Verge of the Court. Imprinted at London by Bonham Norton, and Iohn Bill, . . . M.DC.XXV. A broadsheet formed of two leaves.

COURT BARON.
**Modus tenend. Cur. Barōn. cum visu franco plegii. [Col.] Imprynted at London in Poules chyrcheyarde at the sygne of the Trynyte By Henry Pepwell. 4°, 14 leaves.

**Modus tenend Cur̄ Barōn cum visu franc̄ plegij. [Col.] Impressum per Richardum Pynson Regis impressorem. 4°, 14 leaves.

>On sign. C i, in the oath of a constable, he is required to be "buxom and obedeent to the Justices," and elsewhere he swears that "he shall presentment make of blood shedding, outcries, frays, and rescous."

*Modus tenendi Cvriam Baronis. [Col.] Explicit modus obseruandi Curiam cum nouis additionibus. Impressum Londini in vico qui vocatur Fletestrete, per me Robertum Redman. Anno Dn̄i. M. D. XXXII. Cum priuilegio. 8°, 40 leaves.

end. cur. baron cum visu [Col.] ¶ Explicit. ¶ Imles chyrche yarde by John leaves. With his device shon.

UNDRED.
li Vnum Hundredū sine ordo. [This title is over royal arms without sup-Impressum per Richardum mpressorem. 4°, 10 leaves.
as Mr. Heber noted in his as, as showing the practice of art in Edward IV.'s time.

if kepynge a court Baron vyth dyuers fourmes of tes, processes, presentether maters determinable r Imprinted and corrected. [Col.] Explicit . . . Imper me Robertum Toye. ts.

andi cūr cum leta siue visu ir hoc modo. [Col.] Imi in vico qui vocatur Flete-Robertum Redman Anno xx. Cum priuilegio. 8°, s. With Pynson's cypher e.

courtz et leur iurisdictions, ia et vtilia. ¶ Impressum io Dñi. M.CCCCC.xliii. Per Iyddylton. 8°, C 4 in half

V.
Man's Argument, against gill's, Wherein is Proved, Argument, that Death is f Life, is but Weak, Fictitious, . . . Dublin: Printed , 1702. 4°. A—D, 2 leaves nk, besides a leaf with a me Queries Concerning the roperty of an English Sub-," on the reverse of which ohn Crabb's address to the

, Minister of God's Word.
ie of the whole catechisme, Question is proponed and ew wordes, for the greater immoune people and chilprinted at Edinburgh, by ris Anno M.D.LXXXI. Cum gali. 8°, G 6 in eights.
the Professors of Christ's ew Aberdeen, from Edin-r 1581.

A Short Symme of the Whole Catechisme.
. . . Edinbvrgh Printed by Iohn Wreittonn for Io. Wood, and are to bee sold at his Shop, on the South side of the hie street, a little aboue the Crosse 1632. Sm. 8°, A—G in eights.

CRAIG, SIR THOMAS, *of Riccarton.*
Ad Sereniss. et Potentiss. Principem Iacobvm Sextum e sua Scotia decedentem Pareneticon. Excudebat Robertus Waldegraue Sereniss. Reg. Majest. Typographus. CIƆ IƆ CIIL. 4°, A—B in fours. In Latin verse.
Subscribed *T. Crayirs. I. C. Edinburgenus.*

Ad Serenissimvm Britanniarum Principem Henricum, è Scotia Discedentem Propempticon. Edinbvrgi Excudebat Robertus Charteris Typographus. An. Dom. 1603. 4°, A—B in fours.

Scotlands Sovereignty Asserted. Being A Dispute concerning Homage, against those who maintain that Scotland is a Feu, or Fee-Liege of England, and that therefore the King of Scots owes Homage to the King of England. . . . By Sir Thomas Craig, Author of the Book *de Feudis.* Translated from the Latin Manuscript, with a Preface added, with a short Account of the Learned Author, and a Confutation of that Homage said to be performed by Malcolm III. King of Scotland, to Edward the Confessor, lately found in the Archives of England, and published in a single Sheet, by Mr Rymer, the King's Historiographer. London, Printed for Andrew Bell. . . . 1695. 8°, a—c 2 in eights : A—Ee 6 in eights, besides the title-page. Dedicated to my Lord Secretary Johnston by G. Ridpath the translator.

CRAKANTHORP, RICHARD, *D.D., of Queen's College, Oxford.*
Logicæ Libri Quinque :
De { Prædicabilibus.
Prædicamentis.
Syllogismo,
ejusq; speciebus, } Demonstrativo. Probabili.
Una cum Appendice de Syllogismo Sophistico. . . . Typis & impensis Roberti Young, Anno Dom. M. DC. XLI. 4°, A—Pp 2 in eights, except that A has only 6 leaves.
The dedication to his dearest master Richard Leveson is dated 1622.

CRANMER, THOMAS, *Archbishop of Canterbury.*
*All the Svbmyssyons, and recantations of Thomas Cranmer, late Archebyshop of Canterburye, truely set forth both in

Latyn and Englysh, agreable to the Originalles, wrytten and subscribed with his owne hande... Anno, M.D.LVI. Excusum Londini in Ædibus Johannis Cawodi Typographi Regiæ Majestatis. Anno, M.D.LVI. Cum priuilegio. 4°, 6 leaves.

**CREATURE, THE DYING.
**Here begynneth a lytell treatyse of the dyenge creature enfected with sykenes vncurable with many sorowfull complayntes. [Col.] Here endeth a lytell treatyse of the dyenge creature. Enprynted at London in Fletestrete at the sygne of the Sonne by Wynkyn de Worde. Anno dñi. M.CCCCC.VII. 4°.

CREDIT.
A Description of the Office of Credit; By the use of which, none can possibbly sustain Loss, but every man may certainly receive great Gain and Wealth. With a Plain Demonstration how a man may Trade with Six times his Stock, and never be Trusted; ... With Divers other publick and private conveniences and profits: As also Objections hitherto made against it, largely and fully Answered. London, Printed by the order of the Society, for Thomas Rooks, 1665. 4°, A—D in fours.

CRICHTON, JAMES.
Iacobi Critonii Scoti Ad Amplissimvm ac Reverendissumum. Virvm Gasparem Vicecomitem, Summa omnium Ordinum voluntate, Ad præclaram Archiepiscopatus Mediolanen. Administrationem, delectum, Gratvlatio. Superiorum Consensu. Mediolani, Ex Typographia Pacifici Pontij. M.D.LXXXIIII. 4°, 4 leaves, the last blank. In verse.

Epicedivm Illvstrissimi et Reverendissimi Cardinalis Caroli Boromæi, Ab Iacobo Critonio Scoto; rogatu Clarissimi ... Ioannis Antonij Magij Mediolanen. Proximo post obitum die, exaratum. De Consensv Superiorvm. Mediolani, ... M.D.LXXXIIII. 4°, 4 leaves, the fourth blank.

Epicedivm Illvstrissimi ... Caroli Boromæi. Mediolani, Ex Typographia Pacifici Pontij. M.D. LXXXIIII. 4°, 4 leaves.

A different edition. Sotheby's, June 1888 (Turner, No. 1008), printed on vellum.

Iacobi Critonii Scoti Ad Nobilissimvm Virvm, PrvdentissimvmqveSvmmae Qvestvrae Regiae Mediolanen. Administratorem. Sfortiam Brivivm, De Musarum et Poetarum inprimis illustrium authoritate, atque præstantia, soluta et numeris Poeticis vincta oratione, ab eodem defensa, Iudicium. ... Mediolani, Ex Typographia Pacifici Pontij, ... M. D. LXXXV. 4°, A—E in fours, E 4 blank.

The leaf following the title is occupied by verses headed: *Critoniers De Scipso*.

CROMWELL, OLIVER, LORD PROTECTOR (1651-8).
By the Protector. A Proclamation for putting the Laws in execution for setting Prices on Wheat. Given at White-Hall this 20, of July 1655. Published by His Highness special Command. London, Printed by Henry Hills and John Field, Printers to his Highness, MDCLV. A broadside.

By the Protector. A Proclamation Commanding a speedy and due Execution of the Laws made against the abominable sins of Drunkenness, profane Swearing and Cursing, Adultery, Fornication, and other acts of uncleannesse; For observing the Assize of Bread, Ale, and Fewel, and touching Weights, and Measures; For setting the Poor on Work, and providing for the impotent and aged poor, and punishing Rogues and Vagabonds, taking account of Church-Wardens and Overseers of the Poor; and against disturbing of publick Preachers, and profanation of the Lords day. Published by His Highness Special Command. London: Printed by Henry Hills and John Field, Printers to His Highness. 1655. A broadside.

A Modest Vindication of Oliver Cromwell from the Unjust Accusations of Lieutenant-General Ludlow in his Memoirs. Together with some Observations on the Memoirs in general. London: Printed in the Year 1698. 4°. A, 2 leaves: B—L 2 in fours.

CULPEPER, NICHOLAS.
A Physical Directory; Or a Translation of the Dispensatory Made by the College of Physitians of London, And by them imposed upon all the Apothecaries of England to make up their Medicines by. And in this Third Edition is added A Key to Galen's Method of Physick. ... By Nich. Culpeper, Gent. Student in Physick and Astrologie. ... London: Printed by Peter Cole, ... 1651. Folio, A—3 K, 2 leaves each, besides the title and the portrait of Culpeper by Cross, with four lines of verse beneath.

The Physitians Library, Containing all the Works of these most Famous Physitians following, Viz. Dan. Semertus, Laz. Riverius, Fel. Platerus. ... All which are of Excellent use for all Rational Persons, especially for all Chyrurgeons at Sea in his Most Royal Majesties Ships, ... London : Printed by Peter Cole and Edward Cole, Printers and Booke-sellers, ... 1663. Folio, B—3 Q, 2 leaves each, besides two title-pages, the second expressing itself as "Pharmacopœia Londinensis : Or, The London Dispensatory. Further adorned by the Studies and Collections of the Fellows now living of the said Colledg" . . . and dated 1661.

This book includes additions by Abdiah Cole and others, as explained by Culpepper on the second title, or that which comes second in order.

CULPEPER, SIR THOMAS, *Senior*, *Knight.*
A Tract against the high rate of Usury Presented to the High Court of Parliament, Anno Domini 1623. ... By Sir Thomas Culpeper, Sen. Knight. The Fourth Edition, To which is added a Preface, By Sir Thomas Culpeper Jun. Knight. London, Printed by T. Leach, for Christopher Wilkinson, ... 1668. 4°, A—D in fours.

A Short Appendix To a Late Treatise Concerning Abatement of Usury. By the same Author. London, Printed by Tho. Leach, for Christopher Wilkinson, ... 1668. 4°, 4 leaves.

CULPEPER, SIR THOMAS, *Junior*, *Knight.*
The Advantages which will manifestly accrue to this Kingdom by abatement of interest from six to four per Cent. London Printed by T. L. for Christopher Wilkinson, at the Black-Boy over against St. Dunstans Church in Fleetstreet. 1668. A broadside.

The Necessity of Abating Usury Re-Asserted ; In a Reply to the Discourse of Mr Thomas Manly Entituled, *Usury at Six per Cent Examined*, &c. &c. ... By Sr Thomas Culpeper, Jun. Knight. London, Printed by T. L. for Christopher Wilkinson, ... 1670. 4°, A—H in fours.

CUNNINGHAM, JAMES.
An Essay, Upon The Inscription of Macduffs Crosse in Fyfe. By I. C. 1678. ... Edinburgh, Printed by the Heir of Andrew Anderson, ... 1678. 4°, A—C 2 in fours.

In Floidum, Asaphenscm Episcopum, Scotorum Reges, Regum Ritus Sacros, Illacessitis Calumniis & immeritis, Exprobantem, Lacerantem, Traducentem, Versiculus unus & alter Hortatorius. ... Impressus Anno Dom. 1685. 4°, A—E 1 in fours.

By Mr. James Cunninghame is written in a coeval hand on the title.

D.

D. I.
A Pvblication of Gviana's Plantation Newly undertaken by the Right Honble the Earle of Barkshire (Knight of the most Noble Order of the Garter) and Company for that most famous River of the Amazones in America. Wherein is briefly shewed the lawfulnesse of plantations in forraine Countries ; hope of the natives conversion ; nature of the river ; qvalitie of the Land, Climate, and people of Gviana ; with the provisions for mans sustenance, and commodities therein growing for the trade of Merchandise and manner of the Adventure. With an Answer to some objections touching feare of the Enemie . . . London Printed by William Iones for Thomas Paine, and are to be sold in Trinitie Lane at the signe of the Horse-shooe. 1632. 4°, A—C in fours, and a leaf of D.

This tract is addressed at the commencement "To all faithfull, and well affected Christians ;" the initials *I. D.* occur at the end. My description is taken from the Wimpole copy, sold among the Earl of Hardwicke's books at Christie's this year (1888).

DALLAS, GEORGE, *of Saint-Martins.*
System of Stiles, As now Practicable within the Kingdom of Scotland : And Reduced to a clear Method, not heretofore. Consisting of VI. Parts. ... Begun in the Year 1666, and had its Period Anno 1688. Edinbvrgh, Printed by the Heirs and Successors of Andrew Anderson, ... Anno Dom. 1697. Price, Bound and Guilded on the Back, Twenty Pound Scots. Folio. Title and dedication to John Earl of Tullibardine, 2 leaves : A—Xx, 2 leaves each : dedication of Part III. to the L. Chancellor of Scotland, 1

leaf : Yy—ZZz in twos : Aaaa—Iiiiii in fours : *Indices*, 6 leaves.

DALLINGTON, ROBERT, *afterwards Sir Robert*.
Dallington Epitomis'd : Or, Aphorisms Civil & Military, New Modell'd for the Use of the Present Age. —*brevis esse laboro*. Hor. London : Printed for Elizabeth Harris, . . . 1700. 12°, A—F in twelves. Dedicated by E. Stacy to William Duke of Gloucester.

DALRYMPLE, SIR JAMES, *of Stair, Knight and Baronet*.
The Decisions of the Lords of Council & Session, In the most Important Cases Debate before them, With the Acts of Sederunt. As also, An Alphabetical Compend of the Decisions ; With an Index of the Acts of Sederunt, and the Pursuers and Defenders Names, from June 1661. to July 1681. Edinbvrgh, Printed by the Heir of Andrew Anderson, . . . Anno Dom. 1683. Folio. Title, dedication to George Earl of Aberdeen, from Leyden, Oct. 30—Nov. 9, 1683, and Index, 4 leaves : A—3 S in fours : A—Yy in fours : Index, A—K, 2 leaves each.

The Institutions of the Law of Scotland, Deduced from its Originals, and Collated with the Civil, Canon and Feudal Laws, and with the Customs of Neighbouring Nations. In IV. Books. By James Viscount of Stair, Lord President of the Session. The Second Edition, Revised, Corrected, and much Enlarged. With an Alphabetical Index to the Whole Work. Edinbvrgh, Printed by the Heir of Andrew Anderson, . . . 1693. Folio. Title, Advertisement, and Index, 3 leaves : A—3 T in fours (ending with p. 504 and Book 3) : A (p. 521)—Kk in fours : Index, A—K, 2 leaves each.

[DALRYMPLE, SIR JOHN.]
An Account of the Affairs of Scotland, In Answer to a Letter Written upon the occasion of the Address Presented to His Majesty by some Members of that Kingdom. [London, December 1, 1689.] 4°, A—F 3 in ours. Without a title-page.

"By sʳ Jon Dalrymple" is written on the first page in a coeval hand.

DANIEL, JOHN.
Songs for the Lvte Viol and Voice : Composed by I. Danyel, Batchelar in Musicke. 1606. To Mʳⁱˢ Anne Grene. London Printed by T. E. for Thomas Adams, At the signe of the white Lyon, in Paules Church-yard. Folio. A—L, 2 leaves each. With a metrical inscription after the title to Mʳˢ Anne Grene, the worthy Daughter to Sʳ William Grene of Milton, Knight.

D'ARGENCES, M.
La Comtesse de Salisbury, Ou L'Ordre de la Jaretiere. Nouvelle Historique. Premiere [et Seconde] Partie. A Paris, Chez Claude Barbin. . . . M.DC.LXXXII. . . . 12° or sm. 8°. Title, 1 leaf : A, 8 leaves : A—S 3 in eights : *Seconde Partie*, title, 1 leaf : A—R 6 in eights. Dedicated to the Duc de Bouillon.

DARELL, JOHN.
Mʳ Courtens Catastrophe and Adieu to East-India : Or, A General and Particular Protest Framed there, at Goa in Febr. 1644. For, and against the English East-India Company. Their Governour Deputy, Court of Committees, and Adventurers in England. And their Presidents, Agents, Commanders and Factors in East-India aforesaid. With A previous, conscious, and short Introduction, and Conclusion. . . . London Printed by R. I. 1652. 4°, A—B in fours, with John Darell's initials at the end.

D'AUBRAY, MARIE MAGDALEINE, *Marquise de Brinvilliers*.
A Narrative of the Process against Madam Brinvilliers ; And of Her Condemnation and Execution, For having Poisoned her Father and Two Brothers. Translated out of French . . . London : Printed for Jonathan Edwyn, at the Sign of the Three Roses in Ludgate - Street. MDCLXXVI. 4°, A—C in fours. *B. M.*

D'AVANZATI, BERNARDO.
Scisma D'Inghilterra con altre Operette . . . In Fiorenze. . . . M.DC.xxxviij. 4°. +, 8 leaves : B—Aa in fours : Bb, 6 leaves. With a portrait of the author on the back of the title.

DAVENANT, CHARLES, L.L.D.
Essays upon Peace at home, and War Abroad. In Two Parts. By Charles D'Avenant, L.L.D. *Id agendum ne omnium* . . . Tit. Liv. lib. 2. dec. 5. London, Printed for James Knapton . . . 1704. 8°. Dedicated to the Queen.

Part 1, the only portion in the Gibson-Craig copy, which was on thick paper in old English morocco binding, has A—Ee 5 in eights, and a, 4 leaves.

DAY, ANGEL.
The English Secretorie, Or, Methode of Writing of Epistles and Letters : . . . Now newly reuised, and in many parts corrected and amended. . . . London, Imprinted by Felix Kyngston, for Wil-

liam Welby, . . . 1614. 4". A, 4 leaves: B—T in eights.

DEATH.
**The Doctrynalle of Dethe. [The above title is over a woodcut, repeated on the verso. On the recto of the following leaf occurs :] This treatyse is called the doctrynale of dethe, and is to be rede afore a man or a woman whan it semeth that they be in the artycle of deth. [Colophon:] Enprynted at westmynster. In Castons hous. By me Wynkyn de worde. 4°, 16 leaves or a—b in sixes : c, 4.

In Dublin's time a copy was in the hands of Mr. Johnes of Hafod.

DE BURGO, GIO. BATTISTA, *Vicar Apostolic in Ireland, and of the De Burgh family.*
Hydravlica, O sia Trattato Dell' Acqve Minerali del Massino, . . . In Milano, M. DC. LXXXIX. . . . 12°. †, 6 leaves : A—S 10 in twelves.

DE CAUS, ISAAC.
Wilton-Garden. Are to be sould by Thomas Rowlett att his shopp neare Temple Barre. [On the 3rd leaf is added :] Le Iardin de Vuilton Construict Par Tres noble et tres puissant Seigneur Philippe Comte de Penbrooke et Mongomeri . . . Isaac de caus Inuent. [London, about 1645.] Oblong folio, 25 leaves, including the title and following one with an engraved description.

Quaritch, February, 1887, No. 866.

DE CRESSY, HUGH-PAULIN.
Exomologesis : Or, A Faithfull Narration of the Occasion and Motives of the Conversion vnto Catholike Vnity of Hvgh-Pavlin de Cressy, lately Deane of Laghlin, &c. in Ireland, and Prebend of Windsore in England. Now a second time printed ; . . . A Paris, Chez Jean Billaine, . . . M.DC.LIII. Sm. 8°. A, 6 : a, 6 : B—Cc 4 in twelves. Dedicated by Serenus Cressy to the Hon. Walter Montagu, from Paris, 21 Oct. 1652.

DE DOMINIS, MARCUS ANTONIUS, *Archbishop of Spalatro.*
A Declaration of the Reasons which moved Marcvs Antonivs de Dominis, Archbishop of Spalatro or Salonas, Primate of Dalmatia and Croatia, to depart from the Romish Religion and his Countrey. Written by Himselfe in Latine, and now for the Populare vse translated. Edinbvrgh, Printed By Andro Hart, 1617. 4°, A—C in fours.

DEER.
A Proclamation for Fee Deere. [Imprinted at London by Bonham Norton and Iohn Bill, . . . M.DC.XXVI. A broadsheet.

DE GRANADA, LOUIS or LOIS.
*Of Prayer and Meditation. Wherein are conteyned fowertien deuoute Meditations for the seuen daies of the weeke, bothe for the morninges, and eueninges. . . . Imprinted at Paris by Thomas Brumeau, at the signe of the Oliue. Anno Domini. M.D.LXXXII. 8°, 331 leaves, besides prefixes. With copperplates.

Translated by Richard Hopkins, who dedicates the volume to the Four Inns of Court.

*A memoriall of a Christian life. Wherin are treated al such things as appertaine vnto a Christian to do from the beginning of his cōuersion, vntil the end of his perfection. Deuided into seauen Treatises . . . Written first in the Spanish tongue, by the famous Religious Father, F. Lewis de Granada, Prouinciall of the holy order of Preachers, in the Prouince of Portugall. . . . Imprinted at Rouen, by George Loyselet. Anno Domini. 1599. 8°, pp. 762, besides the contents. With a few coarse engrauings.

Translated by Richard Hopkins, and dedicated by him from Rouen, the Feast of the Conversion of St. Paul, 1599, to the Four Inns of Court.

A Memoriall of a Christian Life. Wherein are treated all such thinges, as appertaine vnto a Christian to doe, from the beginning of his conuersion, Vntill the end of his perfection. Deuided into seauen Treatises: . . . Written first in the Spanish tongue, by the famous Religious Father F. Lewis de Granada, Prouincial of the holy order of Preachers in the Prouince of Portugall. At S. Omers, For Iohn Heigham, M.DC.XXV. Cum Priuilegio. 8°, A—Qq 5 in eights. With a long dedicatory epistle by Richard Hopkins, the translator, from Rouen, the Feast of the Conversion of St. Paul, 1586, "To the Right Honorable, and Worshipfvll, of the Fovre Principal Howses of Covrte in London, professing the study of the Common Lawes of our Realme."

A spiritual doctrine conteining a rule To liue wel, with diuers Praiers and Meditations. Abridged by the reuerend father Lewis de Granada of the holie order of Preachers. And divided into sixe treatises. . . . At Lovan, Imprinted by Laurence Kellam 1599. 8°, pp. 397 + prelixes and table.

Translated by Richard Gibbons, who dedicates it to Sir William Stanley, Knight,

Colonel of the English Regiment, from the College of Jesuits at Louvain, March 19, 1599-1600.

DE GUEVARA, ANTHONIO.
Spanish Letters: Historical, Satyrical, and Moral; Of the Famous Dom Antonio de Guevara: Bishop of Mondonedo, Chief Minister of State, and Historiographer Royal to the Emperor Charles V. Written by way of Essays on different Subjects, and every where intermixt with much Raillerie and Gallantry. Recommended by Sir R. L'S. and made English from the best Original by Mr Savage. *Menos fuera.* London, Printed for F. Saunders . . . and A. Roper . . . 1697. 8°. A, 4 leaves: B—N in eights. Dedicated by John Savage to Arnold, Earl of Albemarle.

DE LA FAYETTE, LA MARQUISE.
The Princess of Mompensier. Written Originally in French, and now newly rendered into English. London, Printed Anno Dom. 1666. 8°, A—F in eights, F 8 blank. *B. M.*

Zayde. A Spanish History, Or, Romance. Originally Written in French. By Monsieur Segray. Done into English by P. Porter, Esq^e; The First [and Second] Part. London, Printed for William Cademan, . . . 1678. 8°, A—M in eights, including a frontispiece: Part 2, B—N in eights, besides the title and a blank. Dedicated to the Duke of Grafton. *B. M.*

DE LA HAYE, SIEUR.
The Policy and Government of the Venetians, Both in Civil and Military Affairs . . . Faithfully Englished. London, Printed for John Starkey, . . . 1671. 12°. Title and Contents, 3 leaves: B—I in twelves: K, 2.

DE MALYNES, GERARD, *Merchant.*
Englands View, in the Vnmasking of Two Paradoxes: With a replication vnto the answer of Maister Iohn Bodine. By Gerrard de Malynes Merchant. *Opposita iuxta se posita, magis apparent.* London, Printed by Richard Field. 1603. 8°. A—N 6 in eights. Dedicated to Sir Thomas Sackville, Baron of Buckhurst.

DE MENDOÇA, DIEGO HURTADO.
The Pleasant History of Lazarillo de Tormes a Spaniard, wherein is contained his marvellous deeds and life. . . . The Third Edition, corrected and amended. *Accuerdo Oluido.* London, Printed by E. G. for William Leake, . . . 1639. 8°, A—Aa 4 in eights, first and last leaves blank.

The *Pursuit* commences on L 6 with a separate title. This edition is dedicated by Thomas Walkley, the stationer, to Sir Charles Stanhope.

DE MEZERAY, SIEUR.
A General Chronological History of France, Beginning before the Reign of King Pharamond, and Ending with the Reign of King Henry the Fourth: Containing both the Civil and the Ecclesiastical Transactions of that Kingdom. By the Sieur De Mezeray, Historiographer of France. Translated by John Bulteel, Gent. London, Printed by T. N. for Thomas Basset, . . . 1683. Folio. Title and frontispiece by Faithorne, 2 leaves: ¶, 2 leaves: B—6 F in fours: Table, a—o, 2 leaves each. Dedicated to the Duke of York by Bulteel.

DEMPSTER, GEORGE.
The Prodigal Returned to Scotland, Or, A Letter, Writen by a Gentleman to his Friend at Montrose, Wherein he Represents, The Lover's Warfare, the Vanity of reposing Confidence in Rich Friends, a short Historic of his own Misfortunes, the desireableness of Conversation, And lastly, the true Character of Magnanimity, and a noble Ambition, and the Uncertainty and Contempt of Riches. . . . Edinburgh, Printed in June 1700 by John Reid Printer, and are to be Sold at John Vallange's, Mrs. Ogstones and Thomas Carruthers Stationers in Edinburgh, their Shops. 4°. Title and dedication, 2 leaves: A, 2 leaves: B—C in fours.

Gibson-Craig, part 2, No. 1583.

DEMPSTER, THOMAS.
Tragoedia Decemviratvs Arrogatvs, Thomæ Dempsteri, A Mvresk I. C. Scoti. Ad Illustriss. D. Iacobum Augustum Thuanum . . . Parisiis, Apud Ioannem Libert, . . . M. DC. XIII. 8°. ã, 8 leaves: A—K 4 in eights, K 3-4 blank.

Licitatio Professorvm Siue Praefatio Solennis Habita Pisis postridie Kal. Nouembris M. DC. XVI. . . . Autore Thomæ Dempstero à Muresk Scoto Pandectorum in Acad. Pisana Professore ordinario. Pisis, Apud Ioannem Fontanum, M. DC. XVI. Superiorum permissu. 4° or royal 8°. A, 4: B, 6, the last leaf blank. Dedicated to the Archbishop of Pisa.

Gibson-Craig, part 2, No. 1584.

Scotia Illvstrior, Sev Mendicabvla Repressa, Modesta Parechasi Thomæ Dempsteri I. C. à Muresck, Scoti, Bononiæ Humanitatis Professoris eminentis. Qva Libelli famosi impudentia detegitur; mendacia ridicula confutantur; Scotiæ

Sancti sui Vindicantur, ac bona fide asserantur. Lvgdvni, Apud Petrum Rousier. [1620.] 8°, A—L in fours, L 4 with *Errata*, and title and dedication to F. Barberini, 3 leaves. With some verses at the end by Willy Kynmond headed " Votum pro omnibus Hibernis," which are followed by others, signed *Archy Armstrang*, both in Latin.

Menologivm Scotorvm. In quo nullus nisi Scotus gente aut connersatione, quod ex omnium gentium, monimentis, pio studio dei Gloriæ, Sanctorvm Honori, Patriæ Ornamento, Colligit publicat & inscribit Illustriss. Principi. Moecœnati. svo D. Maphæo. S. R. E. Card. Barberino. Scotorum Protectori. Thomas Dempstervs Baro de Mvresk IC. Scotus. Profess. Eminens. . . . Bononiæ, Typis Nicolai Tebaldini. M.DC.XXII. Superiorum Permissu. 4°, a—b in fours : A—E in fours.

Scotorvm Scriptorvm Nomenclatvra. Quartum Aucta. . . . Ex suis Historiarum lib. xix. excerpsit. Thomas Dempstervs . . . Bononiæ, . . . M.DC.XXII. 4°, a in fours : A—D 2 in fours.

DE NEVILLE, FRANCIS.
The Convertion of Francis de Neville, The Popes Missionary and Capvchin Preacher. Wherein many secrets of the Romish Clergy are revealed. With A Narration of the Authors Life. London, Printed for H. B. next to the Castle Taverne in Corn-hill, 1644. 4°, A—Z in fours. *B. M.* (imperfect.)

The writer's dedication to the Parliament is dated March 28, 1642.

DENNE, HENRY.
Grace, Mercy, and Peace, Conteining
1. Gods Reconciliation to Man.
2. Mans Reconciliation to God.
. . . London, Printed for the Benefit of the City of Rochester. 8°.

This includes another piece at end dated 1643.

DE PELLETIER, LE SIEUR.
La religion catholiqve sovstenve en tovs les poincts de sa doctrine. Contre le livre adressé avx Rois Potentats & Repvbliqves de la Chrestienté par Iacqves I. Roy d'Angleterre . . . A Paris. Par Iean Iannon. 1610. 8°. *Huth Coll.*

Probably the presentation-copy to Louis XIII.

DE PEYRERE, ISAAC. *of Bordeaux.*
Men before Adam. Or A Discourse upon the twelfth, thirteenth, and fourteenth Verses of the Fifth Chapter of the Apostle Paul to the Romans. By which are prov'd, That the first Men were created before Adam. London, Printed in the Year, 1656. 8°, A—Ee in eights.

DE QUEROUAILLE, LOUISE, *Duchess of Portsmouth.*
A Dialogue between The Dutchess of Portsmouth, and Madam Gwin, at parting. London, Printed for J. S. 1682. A folio leaf of verses. *B. M.*

DESAINLIENS, *alias* HOLY-BAND, CLAUDE.
The French Littelton : . . . Imprinted at London by Richard Field dwelling in the Blacke-Friers. 1593. Sm. 8°, A—O in eights.

DE SERRES, JEAN.
A Generall Historie of France. Written by John de Serres. . . . Imprinted by George Eld. 1611. Folio. ¶, 4 leaves, first blank : A, 8 : B—5 X in sixes : Table, 14 leaves. With an engraved title and a series of woodcut portraits, &c.

DE SOTO, FERNANDO.
Virginia richly valued, By the description of the maine land of Florida, her next neighbour : Out of the foure yeres continuall trauell and discouerie, for aboue one thousand miles East and West, of Don Ferdinando de Soto, and sixe hundred able men in his companie. Wherin are truly obserued the riches and fertilitie of those parts, abounding with things necessarie, pleasant, and profitable for the life of man : with the natures and dispositions of the Inhabitants. Written by a Portugall gentleman of Elnas, emploied in all the action, and translated out of Portugese by Richard Haklvyt. At London Printed by Felix Kyngston for Matthew Lownes, and are to be sold at the signe of the Bishops Head in Pauls Churchyard. 1609. 4°, A—Aa 2 in fours. Dedicated by Hakluyt from his lodging in the College of Westminster, 15 April, 1609, to the Council and others for the plantation of Virginia. *B. M.* (2 copies.)

The Worthye and Famovs History of the Travailes, Discouery, & Conquest, of that great Continent of Terra Florida, being finely Paraleld, with that of our now Inhabited Virginia. As also The Comodities of the said Country, With diuers excellent and rich Mynes, of Golde, Siluer, and other Meittals, &c. which cannot but giue vs a great and exceeding hope of our Virginia, being so neere of our Continent. . . . London Printed for

Mathew Lownes, dwelling in Paules Church-yard, at the Signe of the Bishopshead. 1611. 4°, A—Aa 2 in fours. *B. M.*
A reissue of the edition of 1609.

DE SOTO, R. F. ANDREAS, *Councillor to the Infanta Clara Eugenia.*
The Ransome of Time being Captive. Wherein is declared how precious a thing is time, how much he looseth that looseth it, & how it may be redeemed. Translated into English by J. H. At Doway, Printed by Gerard Pinsone, at the signe of Coline, 1634. 8°. *, 8 leaves: A—M 4 in eights, M 4 with *Errata*. Dedicated by John Hawkins, the translator, to Katherine Duchess of Buckingham. *B. M.*

DEVOTIONS.
A Collection of Private Devotions: In the Practice of the Ancient Chvrch, called The Hovres of Prayer As they were much after this maner published by Authoritie of Q. Eliz. 1560. . . . London, Printed by R. Yovng. 1627. 12°, A—X 9 in twelves, besides 2 leaves after title marked (A) and (a 2).
The approbation is subscribed by the Bishop of London.

DIALOGUE.
A Dialogue between Two Young Ladies Lately Married, Concerning Management of Husbands. London: Printed in the Year 1696. [April 1]. Price Six Pence. 8°, A—E 3 in fours. *B. M.*

A Continuation of the Dialogue between Two Young Ladies Lately Married. Concerning the Management of Husbands. Part the Second. Wherein is a most Passionate Letter, Full of Wit and Affection, Writ by Eloisa . . . London, Printed in the Year, 1696. Price Six Pence. 8°, A—F 2 in fours. *B. M.*

A Dialogue between Mr Smith, Monsieur Ragouse, Menheir Dorvell, and M' Manoel Texiera, in a Walk to Newington. London: Printed in the Year of our Lord, 1701. 4°, A—E 2 in fours.

DICK, WILLIAM.
The Suffering Case of William Dick, Esq; Grand-son and Heir of Sir William Dick, with others of his Family, By the Intolerable oppression of Sir Andrew Dick, an unnaturall branch thereof, humbly tendred (for redresse) to the Honourable Members of the Parliament of England. [1648.] A broadside.

DICKINSON, EDMUND.
Delphi Phoenicizantes, sive, Tractatus, in quo Græcos, quicquid apud Delphos celebre erat, seu Pythonis & Apollinis historiam, seu Pæanica certamina, & præmia, seu priscam Templi formam . . . e Josuæ historiâ, scriptisque sacris effinxisse . . . ostenditur . . . Appenditur Diatriba de Noæ in Italiam adventu, ejusque nominibus Ethnicis: nec non de Origine Druidum. His accessit Oratiuncula pro Philosophiâ liberandâ. Authore Edmundo Dickinsono, Art: Magist: & Mertonensis Collegii Socio. Oxoniæ Excudebat H: Hall Academiæ Typographus, Impensis Ric. Davis. 1655. 8°. Title, 1 leaf: *, 4 leaves: A, 8 leaves: a, 3 leaves: B—P 4 in eights. Dedicated to Dr. Jonathan Goddard of Merton College, and physician of London.
At p. 91 there is a reference to the Quakers.

DICTIONARIOLUM.
Dictionariolvm et Colloqvia Octo Lingvarvm, Latinæ, Gallicæ, Belgicæ, Tevtonicæ, Hispanicæ, Italicæ, Anglicæ, & Portvgallicæ . . . Dictionaire . . . [the same in French.] Nouuellemēt reveûs corrigez &c. Augmentez de quatre Dialogues, tres-profitable & vtil, tout au faict de marschandise, qu'aux voyages & aultres traffiques. Antverpiæ Apud Henricvm Aertsens, Anno. M.DC.LXII. Obl. 8°, A—Bb in eights, including a finely engraved frontispiece.

DIETARY.
Here begynneth a denoute treatyse named the Dyetary of ghostly helthe. [This title is on a scroll over a common pagecut. At the end occurs:] Imprynted at London in Poules chyrchyarde at the sygne of the Trynyte by Henry Pepwell. The yere of our lorde god. M. ccccc. xxi. The . xv. day of Nouembre. 4°. A⁶: B⁴: C⁶. *B. M.*
There is a second cut on the back of the title. The printer's mark is below the colophon.

DIGBY, EVERARD.
De Arte Natandi Libri duo, quorum Prior regulas ipsius artis, posterior verò praxin demonstrationemque continet. Authore Everardo Dygbeio Anglo in artibus Magistro. Londini Excudebat Thomas Dawson. 1587. 4°, A—P 2 in fours. Dedicated to Richard Wortley, Esq. With numerous woodcuts.

DIGBY, GEORGE, *Earl of Bristol.*
Two Speeches, Of George Earl of Bristol With some observations upon them By which it may appear whether or no the said Earl deserve to be involved in the Common Calamity brought upon Roman

atholicks, by the folly and presumption some few factious Papists. London rinted in the Year, 1674. 4°, A—B in urs.

Apparently from a foreign press.

GBY, SIR KENELM.
Discovrse, Concerning Infallibility in eligion. Written by a Person of Qvality, an Eminent Lord. Printed at Amerdam in the yeare. M. DC. LII. 12°, —S in eights and fours : T, 10.

Discovrse, Concerning Infallibility in eligion. Written by Sir Kenelme igby, to the Lord George Digby, Eldest ıune of the Earle of Bristol. Printed Paris by Peter Targa, Printer of the rchbishoppricke. M. DC. LII. 12°, A— in eights and fours : T, 10.

GGES, LEONARD.
Booke called Tectonicon . . . Pubshed by Leonard Digges Gentleman, in ıe yeare of our Lord, 1556. Imprinted London by Felix Kingston, dwelling Paternoster Rowe, ouer against the gne of the Checker. 1599. 4°, A—G fours, besides folding diagrams at pp. and 18. With other cuts on the letteress.

LLON, WENTWORTH, *Earl of Roscommon.*
n Essay on Translated Verse. By the arl of Roscomon. *Cape Dona Extrema uorum.* London, Printed for Jacob onson . . . 1684. 4°. A, 4 leaves :), 3 leaves : B—D in fours.

RECTORY.
Directory for the Publique Worship of od, throughout the Three Kingdoms . . Together with an Ordinance of arliament for the taking away of the ook of Common-Prayer : And for establshing and observing of this present rectory throughout the Kingdom of ngland, and Dominion of Wales. . . . ondon : Printed for the Company of tationers. 1645. 4°. Title and *Imrimatur,* 2 leaves : Ordinance as to the rayer-Book, 2 leaves : B—M in fours, [4 with the *Contents.*

n Ordinance of the Lords and Commons . . for the more effectuall putting in cecution the Directory for publique or-hip, in all parish Churches and happells within the Kingdome of Engınd and Dominion of Wales, and for the ispersing of them in all places and arishes within this Kingdome and the ominion of Wales. . . . Printed by T. W. for Edw. Husband, . . . 1646. 4°, 4 leaves.

A View of the New Directory and A Vindication of the Ancient Liturgy of the Church of England ; In Answer to the Reasons pretended in the Ordinance and Preface, for the abolishing the one, and establishing the other. The Second Edition. Oxford, Printed by Henry Hall Printer to the University. 1646. 4°, A—P in fours.

DISCOURSES.
Two Discourses. The First, Concerning the Spirit of Martin Luther, And the Original of the Reformation. The Second, Concerning the Celibacy of the Clergy. Printed at Oxford. An. 1687. 4°, A—O in fours, and A—F 2 in fours.

DISTILLER.
The Distiller of London. Compiled and set forth by the special Licence and Command of the King's most Excellent Majesty. For the sole use of the Company of Distillers of London. And by them to be duly observed and practiced. London, Printed by Robert Paske, Stationer, at the Sign of the Stationers Armes and Ink-Botle in Westminster-Street, for the Company of Distillers, 1668. Folio, A—S, 2 leaves each. A is occupied by the title and a plate of the Distillers' Arms.

In the copy belonging to Mr. Henry Stopes the list of cyphers is explained in coeval MS.

DONNE, JOHN, *Dean of St. Paul's.*
A Sermon vpon the VIII. Verse of the I. Chapter of the Acts of the Apostles. Preach'd To the Honourable Company of the Virginian Plantation. 13° Nouemb. 1622. By Iohn Donne Deane of St. Pauls, London. London. Printed by A. Mat : for Thomas Iones, and are to [be] sold at his Shop in the Strand, at the blacke Rauen, neere vnto Saint Clements Church. 1622. 4°, A—G in fours, A 1 blank. Dedicated to the Virginia Company.

There are a few interesting historical allusions.

DORSETSHIRE.
An Abstract of Some Letters sent from Dorchester, to some friends in London, Dated the 3. of Septem. 1642. Containing A True Relation of the late proceedings of Marquesse Hartford and the Cavaliers, at Sherbon Castle, with the opposition of that and other adjacent Countries to those Proceedings. London : Printed for Henry Overton, . . . 1642. 4°, 4 leaves.

C

DRYDEN, JOHN.
Of Dramatick Poesie, An Essay . . . London, Printed by T. Warren for Henry Herringman, . . . 1693. 4°, A—G in fours.

DUDITIUS, ANDREAS, *Sbardellatus.*
Vita Reginaldi Poli, Britanni, S. R. E. Cardinalis, Et. Cantvariensis Archiepiscopi. Venetiis, M.D.LVIII. Ex Officina Dominici Guerrei, & Ioan. Baptistæ fratrum. 4°, A—M in fours.

DUDLEY, JOHN, *Duke of Northumberland.*
Qvesta e la Confessione che Giouanni Duca di Northomberlando fece, essendo egli sopra il falco per essere giustitiato. [Roma o Firenze? 1553.] 4°, italic letter, 4 leaves.

DUDLEY, ROBERT, *Earl of Leicester.*
Discovrs de la Vie Abominable, Rvses, Trahison, Mevrtres, Impostvres, empoisonnements, paillardises, Atheismes, & autres tres iniques conuersations, desquelles a vsé & vse iournellement le my Lorde de Lecestre Machiaueliste, contre l'honneur de Dieu, la Maiesté de la Royne d'Angleterre sa Princesse, & toute la Republique Chrestienne. Traduict d'Anglois en François & mis en forme de Dialogue . . . M.D.LXXXV. 8°. Title, verses to the Reader, the Queen, and Lord Leicester, and Letter to M. G. in Gracious Street, 6 leaves : A—Q in eights : R, 6.

Brevis Narratio Triumphi quo a Senatu populoque Traiectensi Illustrissimus princeps Robertus DudlAEus Comes LeicEstRIVs &c. Traiecti Batauorum exceptus est Anno restitutæ salutis 1586 quarto idus Martij. Vltratrajectj Henricus Borcolous Excudebat. Anno 1586. 4°, A—B in fours.
  A collection of addresses and verses in Latin and Dutch.

DULICHIUS, HARTMANN, *pseud.*
*A worke entytled of ȳ olde god & the newe, of the olde faythe & the newe, of the olde doctryne and ȳ newe / or oryȝynall begynnynge of Idolatrye . . . [Col.]

Here endeth ȳ^e boke . . . Imprynted at London in Fletestrete by me Johan Rydell, dwelling at ȳ sygne of our lady o pite, next to Flete brydge. M. v. C. xxxiiij ȳ xv. day of June. Cum priuilegio Regali Fyrste reade / and then iudge. 8°, R in eights.
  The Preface is dated Feb. 24, 1523.

DU - MAY, LEWIS, *Sieur de Sallettes Councillor to the Duke of Wurtemburgh*
The Estate of the Empire : Or, An Abridgement of the Laws and Government of Germany. . . . Translated into French by D'Alexis Esq ; Doctor of Laws and Advocate in Parliament. Now faithfully rendred into English. London Printed by J. Macock for Richard Royston, . . . 1676. 8°, A—Z in eights title on A 2. With a portrait of the Emperor Leopold.

DURFEY, THOMAS.
Titus and Gisippus : Or, The Power o Friendship. A Moral Story, In Heroick Verse. Done from a Hint out of the Italian Prose of the Famous Boccace Concluding with a Supplement, alluding to the Queens late Gracious Speech, . . By M^r D'urfey. *Amicus certus in re in certa cernitur.* [London, about 1704.] 8° B—E in eights, and the title.

Stories Moral and Comical. Viz.
  The Banquet of the Gods.
  Titus and Gisippus : . . .
  The Prudent Husband : . . .
  Loyalty's Glory : . . .
From Hints out of Italian, Spanish, and French Authors, . . . By T. D'urfey Gent. London, Printed by Fr. Leach and sold by Isaac Cleave, . . . 8°, A—S in eights, A 1 blank, and A 2 with half title. Dedicated to Henry, Duke o Beaufort.

Tales Tragical and Comical . . . By Tho D'Vrfey, Gent . . . London, Printed fo Bernard Lintott . . . 1704. 8°. A, leaves, first blank : a, 3 leaves : B—T in eights. Dedicated to John Duke o Argyll.

E.

e delivered By
the Peace for
The one at
Sessions of the
ι that County :
49. The other
Publick sitting
ewers, at Wood-
t. Etheldred in
dnesday, Sept.
eares the neces-
f steps and de-
1. Printed for
rays-Inne-Gate
—D 2 in fours.

URY.
variensis His-
  Sæculi Libri
pse non modò
  comes etiam
nit) sub Guil-
. Angliæ Regi-
itis MLXVI ad
exi. In lucem
emisit Ioannes
djecit & Spici-
pis & Impensis
c.XXIII. Folio.
hop of Lincoln,
, 11 leaves : B

tern Parts, Or,
ι of the strange
seen and heard
on. Distinctly
of the Townes
unds Warning-
s also, the de-
rfull Sight (or
er the famous,
e in Holland.
B. Alsop, July
I. M.

hortation vnto
. vnto all those
vnto . and rest
of God / and to
ur / hauing a
Righteousnes :
foster them vp
e Woorde and
p to Elders in

the holy and godlie Vnderstandinge of
the gratious Woorde. And in the obedience of his Requiringe. Testified and
set-fourth by Elidad / a Fellow-elder with
the Elder H: N, in the Famelie of the
Loue of Iesu Christ. Translated out of
Base-almayne. [Printed abroad about
1575.] 8", A in eights.

ELIZABETH TUDOR, *Queen of England*
(1558-1602).

Iniunctions giuen by the Queens Maiesty.
Anno domini. 1559. The first yere of the
raigne of our soueraign Lady Queene
Elizabeth. Cum priuilegio Regiæ Maiestatis. 4°, A – D in fours.

> This copy may want a leaf at end with the name of the printers, Jugge and Cawood. It has some curious MSS. notes of the time, probably by the Thomas Bankes whose autograph is on the title, and who has written at the top, " Pretiū istius libri xvj⁴."
> I have since seen a second copy, which exactly corresponds with this.

*Articles to be enquired in the visitacion,
in the first yere of the raigne of our most
dread soueraigne Ladye, Elizabeth by the
grace of God, ... Anno 1559. [Col.] Imprinted at London, in Powles Chvrch
yarde by Rycharde Jugge and John Cawood printers to the Quenes Maiestie.
Cum priuilegio Regiæ Maiestatis. 4°,
A—B in fours, B 4 blank.

Discorso della Gverra Bandita contro la
Regina D'Inghilterra, Dal Re di Scozia,
e come egli ha preso la villa di Baruich, e
bruciato gran numero di Villaggi apparte-
nenti a detta Regina. Da di 9. di Nouembre vltimo fino a oggi. In Firenze,
... 1588. 4°, 2 leaves.

A short and true discourse for satisfying
all those who not knowing the truth, speake
indiscreetly of hir most excellent Maiestie,
of the Lord Willughby Gouernour of hir
Maiesties succours in the vnited Prouinces
of the Low countries, and of all the English nation : by occasion of a strange
placeat of the 17. of April 1589 . the new
stile, put foorth by certaine particular
persons (as is said) vnder the name of
Generall States of those vnited Prouinces.
By which discourse, every one is praied
and required to speak well and Honorably
of th' actions of those Estates generall
lawfully assembled. . . . [1589.] 4°, pp.
51. Roman letter.

The Secret History of the Most Renovn'd

Q. Elizabeth, and E. of Essex. By a Person of Quality. Cologne: Printed for Will with the Wisp, at the Sign of the Moon in the Eclipticke. 12°, A—E in twelves, E 12 blank, including the rough woodcut frontispiece to each of the two parts. *B. M.*

ELLIS, JOHN, *Preacher of the Word at Cambridge.*
The Sole Path to a Sound Peace. Recommended to the Honourable House of Commons in a Sermon at their publike Fast. Feb. 22. ... London, Printed by John Raworth, for George Latham, and John Rothwell, ... 1643. 4°, A—I in fours.

ENCHIRIDION.
Enchiridion pelare ecclesie Sarum: denotissimis precationibus / ac venustissimis imaginibꝫ et ijs quidem non pancis refertum. Parisijs Ex officina libraria vidue spectabilis viri Thielmanni keruer. 1528. Small 8°, a—z in eights. *More de sacramento*, 4 leaves: A—G in eights. With woodcuts. The printer's mark and colophon are on the last page.
Sotheby's, June 9, 1888, No. 659, on vellum.

ENGLAND.
The Interest of England Maintained: The Honour of the Parliament vindicated; The Malignants Plot upon the Presbyters, to make them doe their worke Discovered. ... Printed June the 8. 1646. 4°, A—C 2 in fours.

A Brief Discovrse of the Present Miseries of the Kingdome: Declaring by what practices the people of England have been deluded, and seduced into Slavery, and how they have been continued therein, and by what meanes they may shake off that bondage, they are now enthraled under. Written by a lover of his Country, for the good of all such who are not contented to be slaves, but desire to be Free-men. Printed in the Yeare, 1648. 4°, A—D in fours.
A Royalist production. A coeval MS. note on the title-page says: "Herein is given a generall account of ẏ first rise of ẏ late civil warre betwixt ẏ King & ẏ Parliam: solidè & acutè."

England's Interest Asserted. In the Improvement of its Native Commodities; And more especially the Manufacture of Wool: Plainly shewing its Exportation Un-manufactured, amounting unto Millions of Loss to His Majesty, and Kingdom. With some Brief Observations of that worthy Author Sir Walter Rawley, touching the same. ... By a true Lover of His Majesty, and Native Country. London, Printed for Francis Smith, ... 1669. 4°. Title, 1 leaf: A, 4 leaves: B, 1 leaf: C—E in fours: C (repeated)—E in fours.
The *White Horse*, one of the signs where this tract was on sale, has been altered by a coeval hand to *White Hart*.

Angliæ Speculum Morale; The Moral State of England, with the several Aspects it beareth to Virtue and Vice. With the Life of Theodatvs, and

Three Novels, Viz.
{ The Land-Mariners
  Friendship Sublimed,
  The Friendly Rivals.

... London, Printed for Henry Herringman, ... 1670. 8°, A—N 2 in eights.

Historiæ Anglicanæ Scriptores X.

Simeon Monachus Dunelmensis.
Johannes Prior Hagustaldensis.
Ricardus ———
Ailredus Abbas Rievallensis.
Radulphus de Diceto Londoniensis.
Johannes Brompton Joruallensis.
Gervasius Monachus Doroborneusis.
Thomas Stubbs Dominicanus.
Guilielmus Thorn Cantuariensis.
Henricus Knighton Leicestrensis.

Ex Vetustis Manuscriptis, Nunc primùm in lucem editi. Adjectis Variis Lectionibus, Glossario, Indiceque copioso. Londini, Typis Jacobi Flesher, ... M DC LII. Folio.
Edited by Sir Roger Twysden.

EPISTLES AND GOSPELS.
**The Pistels and Gospels of the Sondayes and festynall holy dayes, newly corrected and amended. [Col.] ¶ Imprinted by Ihon Waylande in Fletestrete, at the signe of the blew garlande. ¶ Cum priuilegio ... 4°, 68 leaves, the last blank.

ERASMUS, DESIDERIUS, *of Rotterdam.*
*An Epistell of the famous doctor Erasmꝫ of Roterdame / vnto the reuerende father & excellent prince / Christofer bysshop of Basyle / cőcerning the forbedlynge of eatynge of flesshe / and lyke constitutyons of men ... [Col.] Printed at London by Thomas Godfray. [1522.] Small 8°, R in half-sheets.
Dated from Basle, Easter-Monday, 1522.

*Commonplaces of scripture orderly, and after a compendious forme of teachynge, set forth with no litle labour, to the great profyte and helpe of all suche studentes of Gods worde, as haue not had longe exercyse in the same, by the right excellent clerke Erasmus Sarcerius. [Col.] ¶ Im-

prynted at London by Johan Byddell, dwellynge in Fletestrete at the signe of the Sonne ouer agaynst the Cundite. In the yere of our lord god . m. ccccc.xxxviij. the xij. daye of August. Cum Priuilegio. 8º.

<small>Herbert's copy was incomplete.</small>

*Flores aliquot sententiarum ex variis collecti scriptoribus. The flowers of senceis gathered out of sundry wryters by Erasmus in Latine and Englished by Rychard Tauerner. ¶ Huic libello non male conuenient Mimi illi Publiani nuper ab eodem Richardo versi. Londini. Ex edibus Wilhelmi Copland Anno. M.D.L. [Col.] Imprynted at London in Fletestrete at the sygne of the Rose Garland by Wyllyam Copland for Rychard Kele dwellynge in Lombard strete nere vnto the Stockes market at the sygne of the Egle. 8º, 8 leaves.

*Prouerbes or Adages, gathered out of the Chiliades of Erasmus, by Richard Tauerner. With new additions, as well of Latin Prouerbes, as of English. Imprinted at London, in Fleete streete, by William How. 1569. 8º, 71 leaves.

ESSAYS.
Six Familiar Essays upon
Marriage } { Death,
Crosses in Love, } { Loyalty,
Sickness, } { and Friendship.
Written by a Lady. London : Printed for Tho. Bennet, at the Half-Moon in St. Paul's Church-yard, 1696. 8º. A, 4 leaves : B—H in eights.

ETHEREGE, SIR GEORGE.
She wou'd if She cou'd ; A Comedy. Acted at His Highness the Duke of York's Theater. Written by George Etherege Esq ; In the Savoy : Printed by T. N. for H. Herringman, ... 1671. 4º. A, 2 : B—L in fours : M, 2.

ETON SCHOOL.
Dionysii Poemation De Situ Orbis. Excusum, in Vsum Scholæ Regiæ Etonensis. Londini, Apud Iohannem Redmayne. MDCLXVIII. 8º, A—C in eights, C 8 blank.

<small>The Greek text.</small>

EURIPIDES.
Hecvba, & Iphigenia in Aulide . . . Erasmo Roterodamo interprete. Eivsdem Ode de laudibus Britanniæ, Regisq ; Henrici septimi, ae regiorum liberorum eius . . . [Col.] Venetiis In AEdibvs Aldi Mense Decembri . M . D VII. 8º. Title and prefixes, 8 leaves, last two blank : A—I in eights.

EUROPE.
Evrope a Slave, unless England break her Chains : Discovering the Grand Designs of the French-Popish Party in England for several Years past. London, Printed for W. D. . . . 1681. 12º, B—E in twelves, E 12 blank, and the title.

*EXEMPLA.
Incipiūt exēpla sacre scripture ex utroque testamēto, secund. ordinē literarū collecta. Et primo de Abstinentia. [Col.] Expliciūt exēpla . . . Inpressaq ; apud uillā sancti Albani. Anno dni M.cccc.lxxxi. 8º. a⁸ : b⁸ : c⁶ : d—f⁸ : g⁶ [no h :] i—l⁸.

<small>Printed on papers with different marks, says Herbert.</small>

EXPOSITIO.
Expositio hymnorū sed'um vsum Sarum. [The rest of the page is occupied by a woodcut, the reverse blank.] No place, printer's name, or date [but apparently printed at Cologne about 1500.] 4º, A—I 5 in sixes (I 6 having probably had the colophon).

<small>Sotheby's, June 9, 1888, No. 867. This was probably printed with the Sequences, as usual.</small>

Expositio sequentiarę sedūm vsum Sarum. No place, &c. [Cologne, about 1500.] 4º, A—K in sixes.

<small>Intended to accompany the Hymns from the same press.</small>

EXQUEMLING, J.
The History of the Bucaniers : Being an Impartial Relation of all the Battels, Sieges, and other most Eminent Assaults committed for several years upon the Coasts of the West-Indies by the Pirates of Jamaica and Tortuga. Both English, & other Nations. More especially the Unparallel'd Atchievements of Sir H. M. Made English from the Dutch Copy: . . . London, Printed for Tho. Malthus at the Sun in the Poultry. 1684. 12º, A—I in twelves. With a portrait of Sir H. Morgan facing the title and a plate with four other portraits.

<small>A popular abridgment.</small>

(38)

F.

F. N.
The Husbandmans fruitfull Orchard. Shewing diuers rare new secrets for the true Ordering of all sortes of fruite in their due seasons. Also how your encrease and profite maie bee much more then heertofore, and yet your charge and labour the same. . . . Neuer before published. At London Imprinted for Roger Iackson, and are to bee sold at his shop in Fleet-street neere the conduit. 1609. 4°, black letter. A, 2 leaues : B—E 2 in fours. *B. M.*

> The *Fruiterers' Secrets*, 1604, with a new title. Gibson-Craig, part 2, No. 925 (March, 1888).

FAIRS.
By the King. A Proclamation prohibiting the keeping of Bartholomew and Sturbridge Faire. God saue the King. Printed at Oxford by I. L. and W. T. for Bonham Norton and Iohn Bill, . . . 1625. A broadside.

> In consequence of the Plague in London.

A Proclamation prohibiting the keeping of Bartholomew Fayre, Sturbridge fayre, and our Lady Fayre in Southwarke. Imprinted at London by Robert Barker, . . . and by the Assignes of Iohn Bill M. DC. XXX. A broadsheet.

FARTHING TOKENS.
A Proclamation for the continuing of Our Farthing Tokens of Copper, and prohibiting the Counterfeiting of them, and the vse of all other. Printed at London by Bonham Norton and Iohn Bill. . . . M.DC.XXV. A broadsheet formed of two leaues.

FEAST.
A Feast of Fat Things Full of Marrow. Containing several Scripture Songs taken out of the Old and New Testament. With others, composed by the Author. Together with an Hundred of Divine Hymns, being the first Century. . . . London, Printed by B. H. 1696. 12°. Title and Table, 4 leaves : Bb, 12 leaves : A, 8 leaves : B—E 4 in twelves. *B. M.*

> Sotheby's, June 9, 1888, No. 676. Probably by Elias Keach.

FENNOR, DUDLEY, *Minister of God's Word.*
An Answere vnto the Confutation of Iohn Nichols his Recantation . . . London Imprinted by Iohn woife for Iohn Harrison & Thomas Manne, dwelling in Pater noster rowe, and are there to be solde, 1583. 4°, A—Cc in fours and the title, or 104 leaves.

FESTIVAL.
*Incipit liber qui vocatur festiualis de reueso correctus et impressus. [Col.] Finitū et completū extat hoc opusculū Jn celeberrima vrbe Parisiensi. Anno dñi M. cccc. xcv. die vero xxvi. Februarii. impensis Nicolai Comitis. Folio, 125 leaves.

> Herbert's copy had not the *Quatuor Sermones* annexed.

*Incipit liber qui vocatur festiualis. [This title is over a woodcut of Jesus and Mary, with an inscription beneath. The colophon is :] Finitum et completum per Richardum Pynson cōmorantem extra barram noui templi Londonū. Anno incarnationis dominice. MCCCC. nonagesimonono. sexto die mensis Iulii. 4°, folios 156, besides the title-page, on the back of which the cut on the *recto* is repeated. There is another on the last page. In two columns.

The festyuall. [This title is on a ribbon over a page-cut. The colophon is :] Thus endeth the festyuall. Imprynted at London in Fletestrete / at ỹ sygne of the Sonne by Wynkyn de worde The yere of our lorde god. M. ccccc. xxviij. ỹ fyfth day of Nouember. The . xx. yere of the reygne of Kynge Henry the . viij. 4°, A—Y in eights and fours : AA—LL in eights and fours, except that KK and LL have 4 leaves each.

> Sotheby's, June 9, 1888, No. 810, Maskell's copy.

***FIDELITAS.**
Fidelitas. A Distinct Declaratiō of the Requiring of the Lorde and of the godlie Testimonis of the holie Spirit of the Loue of Jesu Christ. Set-fourth by Fidelitas, a Fellowe-elder with H. N. in the Familie of the Loue. Translated out of Base-almayne. . . . [Printed abroad about 1575.] 8°, A—C in eights.

FIELD, JOHN.
A brief exhortation, fruitfull and meete to be read, in this heauy tyme of Gods visitation in London to suche as be Sicke, where the Ministers do lacke, or otherwise cannot be present to comfort them. I. F. Imprinted at London, by Jhon Day, dwelling ouer Aldersgate beneath Saint Martines. Cum priuilegio. 8°, 8 leaves. *B. M.*

FIELD, RICHARD, *D.D.*
+Of the Church, Fiue Bookes. At London, Imprinted by Humfrey Lownes, for Simon Waterson. 1606. 4°, Nn 2 in fours.

Books I.—IV. only.

FIESCHI, OTTOBONE, *Papal Legate in England, afterwards Pope Adrian V.*
**Incipiunt opera supra constitutiones prouinciales et Othonis. [Col.] . . . Londonij apud humanissimum virum winandum de worde. Anno ab incarnatione xρi M.D.XXIX. vigesimo octauo die mensis Nouēbris. Sm. 8°, A—M in eights.

Constitutions pnincialles / and of Otho / and Octhobone / Translated in to Englyshe. Cum priuilegio. [Col.] Imprynted at London in Fletestrete by me Robert Redman, Anno. M. D. xxxiiii. Cvm Privilegio. 8°. ✠, 8 leaves, the last blank : A, 4 leaves with the Table : A (repeated)—X 4 in eights. *B. M.*

King's books, from Ratcliff's collection.

FISHER, JOHN, *Bishop of Rochester.*
*A sermon had at Paulis by the comandment of the most reuerend father in god my lorde legate / and sayd by John the bysshop of Rochester / vpō qūiquagesom sonday / concernynge certayne heretickes / whiche thā were abiured for holdynge the heresies of Martyn Luther that famous heretike / and for ȳ kepyng and reteynyng of his bokes agaynst the ordinance of the bulle of pope Leo the tenthe. Cū priuilegio a rege indulto. [Col.] Imprinted at London / in fletestrete / in the house of Thomas Berthelet / nere to the Cundite / at ȳᵉ signe of Lucrece. Cum priuilegio a rege indulto. 4°, A—H in fours.

FISHER, PAYNE.
A Synopsis of Heraldry, Or, The most plain, short, and easie way for the perfect attaining of that Art, containing all necessary Directions, in order thereunto. . . . London, Printed for L. Curtis, near Fleetbridge, and T. Simmons at the Princes Arms in Ludgate street. 1682. 8°. A, 8 leaves, including a frontispiece : [a]. 4 leaves : 33 numbered plates : [a new title :] The Atchievements of the Kings of England, since King Egbert. . . . 1682 : A, 8 leaves, besides 2 plates : B—I 4 in eights, besides two plates in H.

FLEETWOOD, W., *Chaplain in ordinary to their Majesties.*
A Sermon against Clipping, Preach'd before the Right Honourable the Lord Mayor and Court of Aldermen, at Guildhall Chappel, on Decemb. 16. 1694. London, Printed by Tho. Hodgkin, and are to be sold by John Whitlock, near Stationers-Hall, 1694. 4°, B—E in fours, besides the title and a leaf of *Imprimatur,* &c.

A curious tract by the author of the *Chronicon Preciosum.*

FLEMING, ABRAHAM.
The Diamond of Deuotion : Cut and squared into six seuerall points : Namely
1. The footpath to Felicitie.
2 A guide to Godlines.
3 The Schoole of skill.
4 A swarme of Bees.
5 A plant of pleasure.
6 A Grone of Graces.
Full of many fruitfull lessons auaileable to the leading of a godly and reformed life. By Abraham Fleming. . . . At London, Printed by Peter Short, . . . 1602. 12°, A - G in twelves, G 12 blank. Printed within borders. With separate titles to each part. Dedicated to Sir George Carey, Knight Marshal of the Queen's household.

FLETCHER, JOHN.
The Bloody Brother. A Tragedy. By B. J. F. [*sic.*] London, Printed by R. Bishop, for Thomas Allott, and Iohn Crook, . . . 1639. 4°. A, 2 leaves : B—I in fours.

FORD, THOMAS.
Mvsicke of Svndrie Kindes, Set forth in two Bookes : The First whereof are, Aries [*sic*] for 4. Voices to the Lute, Orphorion, or Basse-Viol, with a Dialogue for two Voices, and two Basse Viols in parts, tunde the Lute way. The Second are Pauens, Galiards, Almaines, Toies, Iigges, Thumpes and such like, for two Basse-Viols, the Lieru way, so made as the greatest number may serue to play alone, very easie to be performde. Composed by Thomas Ford. Imprinted at London by Iohn Windet at the Assignes of William Barley and are to be sold by Iohn Browne . . . 1607. Folio, A—M, 2 leaves each. Dedicated to Sir Richard Weston.

FORTESCUE, SIR JOHN.
**Pernobilis militis, cognomento Fortescu, qui temporibus Henrici sexti floruit, de politica administratione, et legibus ciuilibus florentissimi regni Anglie commentarius. Excusum Londini tipis Edwardi Whitechurche, et veneunt in edibus Henrici Smyth Bibliopole Cum

Priuilegio ad imprimendum solum. Sm. 8°, 74 leaves.

FORTUNATUS.
The Comical and Tragical History of Fortunatus: Wherein is contained his Birth, Travels, Adventures, ... London: Printed by and for W. O. and are to be sold by C. Bates, . . . 4°, A—C in fours. With cuts.

FOWLER, CHRISTOPHER, *Minister of the Gospel at St. Mary's in Reading.*
Dæmonium Meridianum. Satan at Noon. Or, Antichristian Blasphemies, Antiscripturall Divellismes, Anti-morall Vucleanness, . . . Being, A sincere and impartiall Relation of the Proceedings of the Commissioners of the County of Berks, Authorized by the Ordinance for Ejection, against John Pordage, late Minister of Bradfield, in the same County. . . . With some Notes, and Animadversions upon a Book of the said John Pordage, intituled Innocency appearing, &c. . . . London: Printed for Francis Eglesfield, . . . 1655. 4°. ¶, 4 leaves : A, 2 leaves, A 2 with *Errata:* B—X in fours, X 4 blank. Dedicated to the Protector.

FOX, EDWARD, *Bishop of Hereford.*
**Opvs eximivm de vera differentia regiæ potestatis ac ecclesiasticae et qvae sit ipsa veritas ac virtvs vtrivsque. Londini in aedibus Thomae Bertheleti. M.D.XXXIIII. [Col.] Thomas Bertheletvs Regivs Impressor excudebat. 8°, 64 leaves, the last blank. *Althorp* (Herbert's copy on vellum).

FOX, JOHN.
Ad inclytos ac præpotentes Angliæ Proceres, Ordines, & Statvs, totamq; eius gentis Nobilitatem, pro afflictis fratribvs Svpplicatio. Autore Ioanne Foxo Anglo. Basileae, Per Ioannem Oporinum. [Col.] Basileae, Anno Salutis humanæ M.D.L.VII. Mense Martio. 8°, a—e 4 in eights. Following the title is *Libelli ad Anglos carmen* and *Avtor ipse ad Libellum,* both presumably by Fox.

FRANCE.
A Letter from the Lord of Rosny, Great Treasurer of France to the Queene Regent of France. Concerning the resignation of his Offices. Faithfully translated out of French, by E. D. London Printed by Tho. Creede, for William Wright, and are to be sold at his shop on Snow - hill, at the signe of the Harrow. 1613. 4°, A—B in fours, A 1 blank. *B. M.*

Remonstrances made by the Kings Maiesties Ambassadovr, vnto the French King, and the Queene his Mother, Iune last past, 1615. Concerning the marriages with Spaine; As also certayne Diabolicall opinions maintayned by Cardinall Perron, about the deposing and murthering of Kings. Together with the French Kings Letter to the Prince of Conde, dated the 26. of Iuly last, 1615. and the Prince his Answere thereunto. Translated according to the French Copie. London, Printed by William Stansby for Nathaniel Butter, . . . 1615. 4°, A—D in fours.

L'Histoire et Discovrs Av Vray dv Siege qvi fvt mis devant la Ville d'Orleans par les Anglois, le Mardy xii iour d'Octobre. M.CCCC XXVIII. regnant alors Charles VII. Roy de France . . . A Troyes, Chez Claude Briden, . . . M.D.C.XXI. 12mo, A—M in twelves, and N, 5 leaves. Dedicated by the publisher "A Messievrs Messievrs les Maires et Eschevins de la ville d'Orleans."

A Narration, Briefely Contayning the History of the French Massacre, especially that horrible one at Paris, which happened in the yeare 1572. In the passage of which, are handled certaine Questions both Politike and Ethike, properly fit for Courtiers and States-men. The condition also of this present time is discouered, . . . London: Printed by Thomas Snodham. 1618. 4°, A—F 2 in fours. Dedicated to Dr. N. F. "the famous Patron of Learning, and learned men." *B. M.*

The Present State of the Protestants in France. In Three Letters. Written by a Gentleman at London to his Friend in the Country . . . London, Printed for John Holford, Book-seller in the Pall-Mall over against S. Alban's-Street. 1681. 4°, A—D in fours, and a, 2 leaves.

Monsieur Colbert's Ghost, Or, France Without Bounds. Being A Particular Account by what ways it has attain'd to that Supream Grandeur, . . . A Cologn, Chez Pierre Marteau. 1684. 12mo. A, 3 leaves : B—F 3 in twelves.

An Edict of the French King, Prohibiting all Publick Exercise of the Pretended Reformed Religion in his Kingdom. Wherein he Recalls and totally Annuls the perpetual and irrevocable Edict of King Henry the IV. his Grandfather, given at Nantes ; . . . Translated out of French. The Second Edition Corrected, with Additions. Printed by G. M. Anno Dom. 1686. 4°, A—E in fours.

The Proceedings of the Parliament of Paris, Upon the Pope's Bull, Concerning the Franchises in the City of Rome, and the following Ordonnance of the 26th of December. Translated into English by Order of his Excellency Monsieur Barillon, his Most Christian Majesties Ambassadour Extraordinary to the King of Great Brittain. London, Printed for R. Bentley, ... 1688. 4°, A—E in fours, E 4 blank.

The Conquest of France, With the Life, and Glorious Actions of Edward the Black Prince. . . . Printed by A. M. for Charles Bates at the Sun and Bible in Pye-Corner. 4°, A—C in fours. With cuts.

FRANCIS, BERNARD, *Student in Divinity.*
The Christian Duty. [Quot. from 1. Cor. 14. 38.] Printed at Aire By Claude François Tulliet. M. DC. LXXXIV. With Licence of Superiors. 4°. Title, To the Reader, &c., 4 leaves : A—Pp in fours : Qq, 6 leaves.

FRENCH, JOHN.
The Art of Distillation : . . . To which is added in this Third Impression Calcination and Sublimation : In Two Books. As Also, The London Distiller Exactly and truly shewing the way (in words at length, and not in mysterious Characters and Figures) to draw all sorts of Spirits and Strong-Waters ; Together with their Virtues, and Other Excellent Waters. London : Printed by E. Cotes for T. Williams at the Bible in Little-Britain. 1664. 4°, A—3 G 2 in fours, and a, 4 leaves. Dedicated to the author's friend, Tobias Garbrand, M.D., Principal of Gloucester Hall, Oxford. With woodcuts.

FULKE, WILLIAM.
A most pleasant Prospect into the Garden of naturall Contemplation, . . . By W. Fulke Doctor of Divinitie. . . . At London Printed for William Leake, . . . 1602. 8°. ¶, 4 leaves, the first blank : A—I in eights, I 8 blank.

FULLER, THOMAS, *D.D.*
Andronicvs, Or, The Vnfortunate Politician.
Shewing { Sin ; stoutly punished.
{ Right ; surely rescued.
[Quot. from Eccl. 8. 11.] By Tho. Fuller, B.D. London, Printed by W. Wilson, for John Williams, . . . 1646. 8°, A—L in eights, L 8 blank.

G.

GALENUS.
** Galeni Pergameni de pulsuũ vsu Tho. Linacro Anglo interprete. Londini in aedibus pinsonianis, cum priuilegio a rege indulto. 1522. 4°, 16 leaves. Dedicated to Cardinal Wolsey.

GALTRUCHIUS, P., *of the Society of Jesus.*
The Poetical Histories Being a Compleat Collection of all the Stories necessary for a Perfect understanding of the Greek and Latine Poets and other Ancient Authors written Orginally in French. . . . Now Englisht and enricht with Observations. . . . By Marivs D'Assigny, B.D. London, Printed by B. G. and are to be sold by Moses Pitt, . . . 1671. 8°. A, 4 leaves : b, 8 leaves : B—Mm in eights : Index, 10 leaves. Dedicated to Sir Orlando Bridgman.

GARCIA, DON.
Lavernae, Or The Spanish Gipsy: The whole Art, Mystery, Antiquity, Company, Noblenesse, and Excellency of Theeves and Theeving. With their Statutes, Lawes, Customes, Practises, Varieties, and Differences. . . . With a pleasant Discourse hee had in Prison with a most famous Theefe. . . . Now in English by W. M. London, Printed not in Newgate, 1650. 12°. A, 6 leaves : B—M in twelves : N, 4. With a woodcut frontispiece apparently intended for the hero.

The unsold copies of 1638 with a new title.

[GARDINER, STEPHEN, *Bishop of Winchester.*]
Confvtatio Cavillationvm, Qvibvs Sacrosanctvm Evcharistiae Sacramentum, ab impiis Capernaitis, impeti solet, Authore Marco Antonio Constantio, Theologo Louaniensi. Parisiis, Apud Ioannem de Roigny, . . . 1552. Cum priuilegio Regis. 4°. ã, 4 leaves : a—z in fours : A—Kk in fours.

GAREY, SAMUEL, *Preacher of the Word at Wynfarthing, co. Norfolk.*
Great Brittans little Calendar : Or, Triple Diarie, In remembrance of three daies. Diuided into three Treatises. 1. *Britanniæ vota :* or God saue the King : for the 24. day of March, the day of his Maiesties happy proclamation. 2. *Cæsaris Hostes :* or, The Tragedy of Traytors : for the fift of August : the day of the bloody Gowries Treason, and of his Highnes blessed preseruation. 3. *Amphitheatrum Scelerum :* or, The Transcendent of Treason : the day of a most admirable deliuerance of our King, Queene, . . . from that most horrible and hellish proiect of the Gun-Powder Treason. Nouemb. 5. Whereunto is annexed a short disswasiue from Poperie. London, Printed by Iohn Beale for Henry Fetherstone, and Iohn Parker. 1618. 4°, A—Oo in fours. Dedicated to the Marquis of Buckingham.

GARTER, ORDER OF THE.
St. George for England : Or, A Relation of the Manner of the Election and Installation of the Knights of the most Noble Order of St. George, called the Garter. Which is to be Solemnized on the 15. 16. and 17. of April next, at the Castle of Windsore. London. Printed for James Thrale, and are to be sold at the sign of the Cross-keyes, at Pauls gate. 1661. 4°, A—B in fours, B 4 blank.

GAUDEN, JOHN, *D.D.*
The Case of Ministers Maintenance by Tithes, (As in England,) Plainly discussed in Conscience and Prudence. Humbly propounded to the consideration of those Gentlemen of the Committee, who are in Consultation about it. Tit. 11. 9. *That thou mayest be able* . . . . London, Printed by Thomas Maxey, for Andrew Crook, . . . 1653 [Sept. 14.] 4°, B—G 3 in fours, and the title. *B. M.*

Funerals made Cordials : In a Sermon Prepared and (in part) Preached at the solemn Interment of the Corps of the Right Honorable Robert Rich, Heire apparent to the Earldom of Warwick. (Who aged 23. died Febr. 16. at Whitehall, and was honorably buried March 5. 1657. at Felsted in Essex.) By John Gauden, D.D. of Bocking in Essex. , . London, Printed by T. C. for Andrew Crook, . . . 1658. 4°. A, 4 leaves : [*]. 2 leaves : B—R 2 in fours, besides the funeral escutcheon. With some verses at the end by Gauden and Sydney Godolphin.

GEOFFREY OF MONMOUTH.
Britãnie vtriv&sq; regũ & prïcipũ Origo & gesta insignia ab Galfrido Monemutensi ex antiquissimis Britannici sermonis monumentis in latinũ sermonẽ traducta : & ab A-censio cura & impẽdio magistri Iuoni Cauellari in lucem edita : pstant in eiusdem ædibus. [MDVIII.] 4°. Title, &c, 8 leaves : A (repeated)—M in eights : N, 6 leaves, N 6 blank.

GERSON, JOHN.
The Following of Christ. Written in Latine by Thomas A Kempis . . . Reviewed and in diuers things corrected. By M. C. Confessor to the English Nuns at Paris. Who also added the Authours life in this last edition. Printed at Paris by Mistris Blageart. Anno 1636. 8°. ã—ẽ, 8 leaves each : A—Ii in eights.

The Following of Christ, Written in Latine, by Thomas of Kempis Canon Regvlar of the Order of S. Augustin. Translated into English and in this last Edition, Reuiewed & compared with several former Editions. Printed at Roan, By Ivlian Covrant. M.DC.LXX. 8°. ã, 8 leaves, title on ã 3 : ẽ, 4 leaves : A—Qq in eights, Qq 8 blank.

GETHING, RICHARD.
Digitus Dei, Or, A miraculous Victory gained by the English, upon the Rebels in Munster : Exprest in two Letters, Written to Lievtenant Colonell St. Leger, Sonne and Heir to the Right Honourable Sir William St. Leger, Knight, late Lord President of Munster, by his Lordships late Secretary, Richard Gething. September 20, 1642. London, Printed for Thomas Bates. 1642. 4°, 4 leaves.

GIBSON, SIR ALEXANDER, *of Durie, one of the Senators of the College of Justice.*
The Decisions of the Lords of Council and Session, in Most Cases of Importance, Debated, and brought before Them ; From July 1621, to July 1642. With an Index of the Pursuers and Defenders Names . . . Corrected and Revised, by W. A. J. C. Edinbvrgh, Printed by the Heir of Andrew Anderson ; . . . Anno Dom. MDCXC. Folio. Title and dedication by Gibson to Viscount Stair, 2 leaves : A—5 X 2 in fours : Index, A—L in twos. With a portrait by White after Paton.

GILLESPIE, GEORGE.
A Dispvte against the English-Popish Ceremonies, Obtrvded vpon the Chvrch of Scotland. Wherein Not only our owne

Argvments against the same are strongly confirmed, but likewise the Answeres and Defences of our Opposites, Svch as Hooker, Mortovne, Bvrges, . . . particularly confuted. . . . Printed in the yeare of our Lord 1637. 4°, A—G in fours, and a leaf of H : Aa, 3 leaves : Bb—Gg in fours : Aaa—Zzz in fours : aaa—bbb in fours : ccc, 1 leaf : Aaaa—Ffff in fours.

Reasons For which the Service Booke, urged upon Scotland ought to bee refused. [Col.] Printed in the year of God, 1638. 4°, 2 leaves.

An Assertion of the Government of the Church of Scotland, in the points of Ruling-Elders, and of the Authority of Presbyteries and Synods. With a Postscript in answer to a Treatise lately published against Presbyteriall Government. . . . Printed in the year, 1641. 4°, A—Dd in fours, Dd 4 blank : B—F in fours with the *Postscript*.

GLANVILL, JOSEPH, *F.R.S.*
Philosophia Pia ; Or, A Discourse of the Religious Temper, and Tendencies of the Experimental Philosophy, Which is profest by the Royal Society. To which is annext A Recommendation, and Defence of Reason in the Affairs of Religion. By Jos. Glanvill Rector of Bath, and Fellow of the Royal Society. London, Printed by J. Macock for James Collins . . . 1671. 8°. A, 4 leaves, first blank : B—Q in eights, last leaf blank. Dedicated to Dr. Seth Ward, Bishop of Salisbury.

GLAUBER, JOHN RUDOLPH.
The Works of the Highly Experienced and Famous Chymist, John Rudolph Glauber : Containing a Great Variety of Choice Secrets in Medicine and Alchymy In the Working of Metallick Mines, and the Separation of Metals. Also, Various Cheap and Easie Ways of making Saltpetre, and Improving of Barren-Land, and the Fruits of the Earth. . . . Translated into English, and published for Publick Good by the Labour, Care, and Charge, of Christopher Packe, Philo-chymico-Medicus. London, Printed by Thomas Milbourn, for the Author, . . . MDCLXXXIX. Folio. Title and frontispiece, 2 leaves : A, 2 leaves : (b), 2 leaves : B—5 U, 2 leaves each, besides plates at pp. 1, 55, 67, 85, 188, and 338 : *Second and Third Parts*, A—3 K, 2 leaves each, with a plate at p. 155 : A—Cc, 2 leaves each, with a plate at p. 22. Dedicated to Edmond Dickenson, M.D., Physician to the King, by Packe.

GODFRIDUS.
*Here begynneth the dyfference of astronomy, with the gouernayle to kepe mans body in helth, all the foure seasons of the yeare. [Col.] Imprynted by me Robert Wyer in Saynt Martyns Parysshe besyde Charynge Crosse. 8°, A—E in fours.
Wyer printed two editions, differing in the title and after Giii. See Dibdin, iii. 200-1.

GODWIN, FRANCIS, *Bishop of Llandaff, afterward of Hereford.*
De Præsvlibvs Angliæ Commentarius : Omnivm Episcoporvm, Necnon et Cardinalivm eiusdem Gentis, Nomina, Tempora, Seriem, atqve actiones maximè memorabiles ab vltima antiquitate reposita complexus. Per Franciscvm Godwinvm, Episcopum Landauensem. Londini, Ex Officina Nortoniana. Apud Ioannem Billivm. M.DC.XVI. Cum Privilegio Regis. 4°, A—Vv 4 in eights : A—M 2 in eights.

GODWIN, THOMAS, *M.A.*
Romanae Historiae Anthologia Recognita et Aucta. An English Exposition of the Romane Antiquities . . . Printed for Henrie Cripps of Oxford. 1625. 4°, A—Pp in fours, Pp 4 blank, besides title, dedication and preface, 3 ll. more.
I. Preces. II. Grammaticalia Qvædam. Rhetorica Brevis. Oxoniæ, Excudebat Iosephuc Barnesius. 1616. 4°. Title and pp. 119, pp. 46-7 omitted in the numbering.
Quaritch's General Catalogue, Part xiv., No. 38,164. I was too late to see this book, which had been ordered by an American customer.

GOODE, WILLIAM.
A Particular Relation of the Severall Removes, services, and successes of the Right Honorable the Earle of Manchesters Army (drawn forth of the Associated Counties of Norfolke, Suffolke, Essex, Cambridge, &c.) since he went from Bedford, April 20. to the compleating of the great Victory at Lincolne, May the 6th. 1644. Sent by William Goode from the Earles Quarters at Lincolne, to Mr Simeon Ash (of the Assembly of Divines) both Chaplaines to the said Noble Earle . . . London, Printed for Thomas Underhill, at the Bible in Woodstreet. 1644. 4°, 4 leaves.

GORDON, JAMES, *S.T.D., S.J.*
Iacobi Gordoni Hvntlæi Scotiæ Societate Iesv Doctoris Theologi, Controversiarvm Epitomes, In qua de Quæstionibus Theologicis hac nostra ætate controuersis bre-

uiter disputatur : ... Tomus Primus ... Avgvstoriti Pictonum ... 1612. .. 4°. ă, 4 leaves : č, 2 leaves : A—Vv in fours.

De Catholica Veritate Diatriba. Pro Epithalamio. Ad Serenissimvm Valliorum Principem, Magnum Britanniarum Hæredem. ... Bvrdigalae, Apud Petrvm de la Covrm. cıɔ. cı. xxıı. 8°. ă, 8 leaves : A—R in twelves, R 12 blank.

*GREENWOOD, JOHN.
M. Some laid open in his coulers Wherein the indifferent reader may easily see, howe wretchedly and loosely he hath handeled the cause against M. Penri. Done by an Oxford man, to his friend in Cambridge. [1589.] 8°, pp. 124 + the Epistle.

GREGORIUS.
A Letter Relating the Martyrdome of Ketaban, Mother of Trimorases Prince of the Georgians, & withall A notable Imposture of the Iesuites vpon that occasion : Sent from Gregorivs Monke and Priest, Agent for the Patriarke of Antioch vnto the most holy and learned Abbot Sophronivs. Written first in Greeke, and now done in English. Oxford, Printed by John Lichfield, An. D. 1633. 4°, A—D in fours, D 4 blank.

*GREGORY XIII., *Pope of Rome*.
An Oration or Funerall Sermon vttered at Roome, at the buriall of the holy Father Gregorie the 13. who departed in Iesus Christ the 11. of Aprill. 1585. Conteyning his maners, life, deedes, and last wordes at his death concerning the affayres of this present time. Together with the lamentations of the Cardinalles and whole Clergie. Faithfully translated out of the French Copie, printed at Paris ... Otherwise to be intituled : A Sermon full of Papisticall adulation and matter sufficient to procure the wise and vertuous minded to contemne such grosse and palpable blindnesse, and all persons to laugh at their absurde and erronious follies. Imprinted, Anno 1585. Sm. 8°, pp. 23. With a preface signed *Robert Greene*, and some Latin lines on the Pope by Beza.

GREY, LADY JANE.
*Jane by the grace of God, quene of England, France, and Ireland, defender of the faith, and of the church of Englande, and also Irelande, vnder Christ supreme head. To all our most louing, faithfull, and obedient subiects ... Witnesse our self at our Towre of London, the tenth daie of Iulie, in the first yeere of our reigne. God saue the queene. Londini in aedibus Richardi Graftoni reginae typographi excusum. Anno Domini M.D.LIII. Cum priuilegio ad imprimendum solum. A broadside.

*GRIBALDI, MATTEO.
A notable and maruailous epistle of the famous Doctor Matthewe Gribaldi, professor of the law in the vniuersitie of Padua : concerning the terrible iudgement of god vpon hym, that for feare of men denyeth Christ, and the knowen veritie : with a Preface of Doctor Caluine. Translated out of Latin intoo English by E. A. [Col.] Imprinted the xx. day of Aprill. Anno Do. 1550. At Worceter by Jhon Oswen. They be also to sell at Shrewsbury. Cum priuilegio ... Sm. 8°.

GUIDO DE MONTE-ROCHERIO.
*Manipulus Curatorum. [This is over a cut of the Crucifixion, &c. At the end :] Impressum per egregium Julianum Notarium Impressorem commorātem extra temple barre sub Intersignio sanctorum trium regum ... Anno domini milesimo. ccccc. octauo. xii. die Augusti. 8°, 133 leaves and the Table.

**Manipulus Curatorum. [Col.] Celeberrimi viri dñi Guidonis de monte Rocheri. liber. qui manipulus Curator' inscribitur, vna cū Tabula eiusdem, finit feliciter. Exaratus London. Impressusq; per Richardum Pynson . eadē in vrbe cōmorantem. Anno dñi. M.ccccc.viij. quarto idus Nouembris. 4°, 126 leaves.

GUILLIM, JOHN.
A Display of Heraldry : ... The fifth Edition Corrected and much enlarged by the Author himself in his life time ; Together with his own Addition of explaining the terms of Hawking and Hunting ... London, Printed by T. R. for Richard Blome, 1664. Folio. Title, 1 leaf ; dedications by Blome to the King and the Duke of Somerset, 2 leaves ; Envoy of W. Segar to the author, in verse, and other verses, 1 leaf : To the Nobility most concerned. by Blome, 1 leaf ; b, 4 leaves : B—3 F in fours ; and between Fff and Fff 2 five extra leaves marked *, &c. : Ggg. 2 leaves : Hhh—Ooo, 2 leaves each : Ppp, 3 leaves : Qqq, 2 leaves : Qqq (repeated), 1 leaf : [A], 2 leaves with *An Exact Register*, and a dedication by Blome to Algernon, Earl of Northumberland : Rrr—Ttt, 2 leaves each ; a leaf subscribed *Fr. Nower* : [B]—[3 e], 2 leaves each : [fff] 1 leaf : [ggg]—[hhh] 2 leaves each, with additional arms, &c.

GWINNE, MATTHEW, *M.D., of St. John's College, Oxford, known as* IL CANDIDO.
Nero Tragoedia Nova. . . . Londini, Typis M. F. Prostant apud R. Mynne, . . . M.DC.XXXIX. 8" or 12°, A—Il 9 in twelves.

Orationes Dvæ Londini Habitæ in Ædibus Greshamiis, An. Dom. 1598. In laudem Dei, Ciuitatis, Fundatoris, Electorum. A Matthæo Gwinne Doct. & Medicinæ ibidem prælectore, Collegij Diui Ioannis Baptistæ apud Oxon. Socio. Londini. Excudebat Richardus Field. 1605. Sm. 8°, A—F 2 in eights, F 2 blank. *B. M.*

In Assertorem Chymicæ sed veræ Medicinæ Desertorem, Fra. Anthonivm, Matthæi Gwinn Philiatri in Medicorum Londinensium Collegio quarti Censoris Registarij succincta Aduersaria. [Quot. from Virg. Æn. l. 12. 396.] Londini, Excudebat Richardus Field. 1611. 4°. *, 2 leaves : A—Kk 2 in fours. *B. M.*

GWINNETH, JOHN.
The cōfutacyon of the fyrst parte of Frythes boke, with a dysputacyon before whether it be possyble for any heretike to know that hym selfe is one or not. And also an other / whether it be wors to denye directely more or lesse of the fayth / put forth by John Gwynneth clerke. M.CCCCC.XXXVI. [Col.] Here endeth the fyrste book. [St. Albans, by John Herford, for Richard Stevenage. 1536.] 8°. Title, prologue, and errata, 4 leaves : a—t in eights. With the device of Richard Stevenage on the last page. *B. M.*

GWYN, ELEANOR, *the Elder*.
An Elogy upon that never to be forgotten Matron, Old Maddam Gwinn, who was unfortunately Drown'd in her own Fishpond, on the 29th of July 1679. A broadside in two columns. *B. M.*

A True Account of the late most doleful, and lamentable Tragedy of Old Maddam Gwinn, Mother to Maddam Eleanor Gwinn, who was unfortunately drowned, in a Fish-Pond, at her own MansionHouse near the Neat-Houses. With an Account how that much to be deplored Accident, came to pass ; and what is expected will be the sequel of the same. With an Epitaph, composed against the Solemnity of her Pompous Funeral and many other Circumstances. [London, 1679.] Folio, 2 leaves. Without any regular title. *B. M.*

GWYN, ELEANOR, *the Younger*.
Madam Gwins Answer to the Dutches of Portsmouths Letter. London Printed for J. Johnson. A broadside. *B. M.*

H.

H. E.
Straffords Plot discovered, And the Parliament vindicated, in their justice executed upon him, By the late Discovery of certain Propositions delivered to His Majestie by the late Earl of Strafford, a little before his Trial, with this Inscription : *Propositions for the bridling of Parliaments, and for the increasing of His Majesties Revenue much more than before.* . . . As also, a Form or Model for the discipline of this Designe, . . . Printed by Authoritie ; together with the Approbation of the Speaker of the Honourable House of Commons. London, Printed by Ruth Raworth, for John Dallam, dwelling in Black-fryars, neer Carterlane. 1646. 4°, A—C in fours, C 4 blank. Dedicated by E. H. to the Parliament. *B. M.*

H. H., *D.D.*
Considerations of present Use concerning the Danger Resulting from the Change of our Church-Government. Printed in the Yeere 1646. [July 15.] 4°, A—B in fours. *B. M.*

HALE, SIR MATTHEW.
A Collection of Modern Relations of Matter of Fact, Concerning Witches & Witchcraft Upon the Persons of People to which is prefixed a Meditation concerning the Mercy of God in preserving us from the Malice and Power of Evil Angels. Written by the late Lord Chief Justice Hale. Upon Occasion of a Tryal of several Witches before him. Part 1. London. Printed for John Harris, at the Harrow in the Poultrey. MDCXCIII. Price, 1'. 4°, A—H in fours, and *, 4 leaves.
This is all that I have seen.

HAMILTON, FRANCIS, *Scotus*.
De Sanctorvm Invocatione Demonstratio Dvplex. . . . Wirceburgi. . . . Anno

M.D.XCVI. 4°, A—K in fours, and a leaf of L.

Ad Reverendiss: Et Illvstriss: Principem, Ac D. D. Ivlivm, Dei Gratia, Episcopvm Herbipolensem, . . . Oratio in Solenni Restitvtione Cœnobij S. Iacobi Scotorum Herbipoli, Anno M. D. XCV. die mensis Aprilis vltimo. Habita A. R. P. Francisco Hamiltonio Scoto, Ibidem Priore. Cvm Licentia Svperiorvm. Wircebvrgi . . . [1596.] 4°, A—C 2 in fours.

Dispvtatio Theologica De Legitimo Sanctorvm Cvltv per Sacras Imagines : . . . [Wirceburgi.] Ex officina Typographica Georgij Fleischmanni. Anno M.D.XCVII. 4°. Title and 3 following leaves : A—K 2 in fours.

HARPSFELD, JOHN, B.D.

*Concio quædam admodum elegans, . . . habita coram patribus et clero in Ecclesia Paulina Londini. 26. Octobris. 1553. Cui accedunt & sequentia, nidelicet Wilhelmi Pij Decani Cicestrensis, & Iohannis Wymslei Archidiaconi Londini, Orationes laudatoriæ. [Col.] Excusum Londini in ædibus Iohannis Cawodi typographi Regiæ Maiestatis. Anno. M. D. LIII. Mense Decembri. Sm. 8°, A—D 4 in half-sheets. Italic letter.

HARRIS, JOHN.

To the Parliament of the Common-wealth of England. The Humble Representation of Captaine John Harris. Exhibited on behalfe of the Common-wealth, against the proceedings of Sir Benjamin Rudiard, Alexander Pym Esq. Anthony Nickols Esq. (and John Cox their Agent) being some of the Trustees mentioned in an Ordinance of Parliament bearing date Ian. 5. 1645. for the payment of M. Pyms debts, and raising Portions for two younger children. . . . MDCLI. 4°, A—B in fours, B 4 blank, besides a folded leaf with Harris's Petition.

> Alexander Pym here mentioned appears to have been the son of John Pym, whose debts the Parliament had promised to pay. This is an interesting tract in connection with that distinguished man.

HARVEY, CHRISTOPHER.

The Synagogve, Or, The Shadow of the Temple. . . . The second Edition, corrected and enlarged. London, Printed by J. L. for Philemon Stephens, at the gilded Lion in Pauls Church-yard. 1647. 12°. A—B in twelves : (C), 8 leaves.

HAY, ARCHIBALD.

Ad Illustriss. Tit. S. Stephani In monte Cœlio Cardinalem, D. Dauidem Betoun, Primatem Scotiæ, Archiepiscopū S. Andreæ, Episco. Meripocensem, De fælici accessione dignitatis Cardinalitiæ, gratulatorius panegyricus Archibaldi Hayi. *Res præclara est: magni iuxta ac boni viri personam agere.* 1540. [Col.] Excusum Parisijs Anno redemptionis nostræ. 1540. Decimo tertio Calend. Iunii. 4°, A—R 2 in fours. With the title enclosed in an ornamental border, the name of the printer, Egidius Gourmont, at the foot.

> On the back of the title occurs a copy of verses to the Cardinal by Jo. Butin.

*HAY, GEORGE.

The Confutation of the Abbote of Crosraguels Masse, set forth by Maister George Hay. Matth. 15. *All plantation* . . . Imprinted at Edinburgh by Robert Lekpreuik, and are to be sauld at his hous at the nether Bow. Cum priuilegio 1563. 4°, 96 leaves. Dedicated to James, Earl of Murray.

HAY, JOHN.

Dispvtationvm Libri Dvo. . . . Avctore M. Ioanne Hayo Scoto, Societatis Iesv, . . . Lvgdvni, . . . M. D. LXXXIIII. 4°, a—δ 2 in fours : A—Yy in fours, Yy 4 with device only.

HELVETIUS, J. F.

The Golden Calf, Which the World Adores, and Desires : In which is handled The most Rare and Incomparable Wonder of Nature, in Transmuting Metals ; Viz. How the intire Substance of Lead, was in one Moment Transmuted into Gold-Obrizon, with an exceedingly small particle of the true Philosophick Stone. At the Hague. In the Year 1666. . . . faithfully Englished. London, Printed for John Starkey . . . 1670. 12°, A—E in twelves : F, 5.

HENRY VIII.

Assertio Septem Sacramentorum Aduersus Mart. Lutherum . . . Parisiis . . . 1562. 8°, a—r in eights, r 8 blank : Fisher's *Defensio*, A—lll in eights.

> Sotheby's, June 1888 (Turner), Marguerite de Valois's copy, bound by Clovis Eve, £118.

**Epistola Regia ad Illvstrissimos Saxoniae Dvces pie Admonitoria. [London, R. Pynson, about 1520.] 4°, 7 leaves. With eight lines of *Errata* on the recto of the last leaf.

Illvstrissimi ac Potentissimi Regis, Senatus, Populiq; Angliæ, sententia, &c. de eo Concilio, quod Paulus episcopus Rom. Mantuæ futurum simulauit : & de ea bulla, quæ ad calendas Nouembres id prorogarit. [Col.] Londini in Ædibvs

Thomae Bertheleti Regii Impress. An. M.D.XXXVII. Cvm Privilegio. 8°, A—C 3 in eights.

HENRY II., *King of France.*
Loves Journal : A Romance, made of the Court of Henry II. of France. Printed with License at Paris, 1670. And now made English. London, Printed by Thomas Ratcliff and Mary Daniel, and are to be sold by Booksellers in London. 1671. Sm. 8°. A, 4 leaves : B—I in eights. Interspersed with poetry. *B. M.*
> A series of tales of gallantry and adventure divided into days.

HERBERT, WILLIAM, *Earl of Pembroke.*
Poems, Written by the Right Honorable William Earl of Pembroke, Lord Steward of his Majesties Houshold. Whereof Many of which are answered by way of Repartee, By Sr Benjamin Ryddier, Knight. With several Distinct Poems, Written by them Occasionally, and Apart. London, Printed by Matthew Inman, and are to be sold by James Magnes, in Russel-street, near the Piazza, in Covent-Garden, 1660. 8°. Title and dedication to Christiana, Countess of Devonshire, by John Donne the younger, editor of the book, 3 leaves : B—I 4 in eights, I 4 blank.

HEURINGIUS, SIMON, *Salicedensis, M.D.*
*[An Almanac, with woodcuts over each of the twelve months, and before each dominical letter. ... At the end :] ¶ Imprinted at London by Michel Lobley. [1545 ?]. A broadside.
> Heuringius was at this time in practice at Hagenaw as a doctor in physic and astronomy.

HEYDON, JOHN.
The Holy Guide: Leading the Way to the Wonder of the World : (A compleat Phisitian) teaching the Knowledge of all things, Past, Present, and to Come, viz. Of Pleasure, long Life, . . . With Rosie Crucian Medicines, . . . By John Heydon Philonomos, A Servant of God, and a Secretary of Nature. . . . London, Printed by T. M. and are to be sold by Thomas Whittlesey . . . 1662. 8°, a—b in eights, a 1 blank : A—3 F 3 in eights. Dedicated to Sir Richard Temple, Bart., in an interesting epistle. With some copies of complimentary verses and a portrait of the author by Cross and diagrams.

Hampaaneah Hammegulleh : Or, The Rosie-Crucian Crown : In which is set down the Angels of the Seven Planets, . . . By Eugenius Theodidactus Philonomios, A Servant to God, and Secretary to Nature. London : Printed for the Author, . . . 1664. 8", A—C in eights.

The Wise Mans Crown : Or, The Glory of the Rosie-Cross. Shewing the Wonderful Power of Nature, with the full discovery of the true *Cœlum Terræ*, or first Matter of Metals, . . . Communicated to the World By John Heydon, Gent. A Servant of God, and Secretary to Nature. . . London : Printed for the Author, . . . 1664. 8°. Portrait (three-quarter) and title, 2 leaves : A—G in fours. With a Life of Heydon by Frederick Talbot, Esquire.

HESTER, JOHN.
The first part of the Key of Philosophie. Wherein is contained the most excellent secretes of Phisicke and Philosophie, diuided into two Bookes. In the first is shewed the true and perfect order to distill, or draw forth the Oiles, . . . In the second is shewed the true and perfect order to prepare, calcine, sublime, and dissolue al maner of Mineralles, . . . 1596. Imprinted at London, by Valentine Simmes. 8°, A—H in eights. Dedicated by Hester to Dr. John Walton, Bishop of Winchester. *H. Stopes, Esq.*
> Herbert quotes Begford's papers for this little volume, and refers on that authority to a second part, which I have not yet seen.

HICKERINGILL, EDMUND.
The Ceremony-Monger. His Character. In Six Chapters . . . With some Remarks (in the Introduction) upon the New-Star-Chamber, or late Course of the Court of King's-Bench. Of the Nature of a Libel, and *Scandalum Magnatum* . . . By E. Hickeringill, Rector of the Rectory of All-Saints in Colchester. London, Printed and are to be Sold by George Larkin . . . MDCLXXXIX. 4°, A—I 2 in fours.

HICKES, GEORGE.
Speculum Beatæ Virginis. A Discourse of the Due Praise and Honour of the Virgin Mary. By a true Catholick of the Church of England. London, Printed, and are to be Sold by Randal Taylor, . . . 1686. 4°, A—F in fours, A 1 blank or with the *Imprimatur.*
> Attributed to Dr. Hicks in a coeval hand on the title.

HIERONYMUS DE SANCTO MARCHO.
Compēdium preclarū qd parva logica

seu summule dicitur ad ītroduccionem iuuenum In facultate logices, per fratrē Hieronymū de sancto marcho ordinis minorum sacri theologie baccalaurio vnperime in amplissima Oxoniensi vniuersitate q; vtiliter compilatum ad mētem doctoris subtilis Scoti. [Col. on Dd ii:] Explicit Compendiū . . . Impressum in alma coloniensi vniuersitate In edibę Quentel. Anno incarnationis domini Millesimo quingētessimo septimo xij. die mensis octobris. 4°, A—B in sixes: C, 4 : D—Y in sixes: Z, 4 : A—Dd in sixes.

HILDANUS, GULIELMUS FABRICIUS.
His Experiments in Chyrurgerie : Concerning Combustions or Burnings, made with Gun powder, Iron shot, Hot water, Lightning, or any other fiery matter . . . Translated out of Latine by Iohn Steer, Chyrurgeon. London, Printed by Barnard Alsop, living in Grubstreet, 1643. 4°, A—H in fours. With woodcuts.

HILL, THOMAS.
*A briefe and pleasaunt treatise, entituled Naturall & Artificiall conclusions: written first by sundrie scholers of the Vniuersitie of Padua in Italie, at the instant request of one Barthelmewe, a Tuscane : And now Englished by Tho. Hill Londoner, as well for the commoditie of sundrie Artificers, as for the matters of pleasure to recreate wittes at vacant tymes. Imprinted at London by John Kyngston for Abraham Kitson, 1581. Sm. 8°, A—D in eights. With a cut on the title (and again at C 7) of a candle burning in the mouth of a bottle.

HOLBORNE, ANTHONY & WILLIAM.
The Cittharn Schoole, By Antony Holborne Gentleman, and seruant to her most excellent Maiestie. Hereunto are added sixe short Aers Neapolitan like to three voyces, without the Instrument : done by his brother William Holborne. At London. Printed by Peter Short, dwelling on Breadstreet hill at the signe of the Starre. 1597. 4°. Title, 1 leaf : dedication to Thomas Lord Burgh, Governor of the Brill, &c., and Lord Deputy of Ireland, 2 leaves subscribed ANTONY HOLBORNE. Ni mereur moriur: Preface, 2 leaves : B—R in fours, R 4 with the colophon. College of Music.
This copy wants A 4.

HOLLAND, SAMUEL.
The Phœnix Her Arrival & Welcome to England. It being an Epithalamy on the Marriage of the Kings Most Excellent Majesty with the Most Royal and Most Illustrious Donna Katharina of Portugal. London, Printed for the Author. 1663. Folio, 4 leaves.

HYLTON, WALTER.
*Here begynneth the Medled lyfe / Compyled by mayster Walter Hylton / to a deuoute man in temporall Estate / how he shulde rule hym Whiche is right expedyent for euery man / and moste in especyall for them that lyue in the Medled lyfe / And it shewyth what Medled lyfe is. [Col.] Thus endeth this lytell treatyse intituled the Medled lyfe compyled by Walter Hylton / . . . Imprynted by me Robert Wyer in saynt Martyns paryshe / besyde Charynge crosse. 8°, a—f in fours.

HOLT, JOHN.
*Paruulorum Institutio ex Stanbrigiana Collectione. [Col.] Imprynted at London by Wynkyn de Worde . . . The yere of our lorde M.CCCCC.XX. in ẏ moneth of Marche. 4°, 12 leaves.

*Paruulorum institutio ex Stansbrigiana collectione. Imprynted at London in Southwarke by my Peter Treueris. 4°, 12 leaves. Black letter.

HOLWELL, JOHN.
An Appendix to Holwell's Catastrophe Mundi, Being An Astrological Discourse of the Rise, Growth and Continuation of the Othoman Family, With the Nativities of the present French King, Emperors of Germany and Turkey, All truly Rectifyed, . . . By John Holwel Teacher of the Mathematicks and Astrology. London, Printed by J. C. for F. Smith, . . . 1683. 4°, A—F in fours.

HOMILY.
An Homilie against disobedience and wylfull rebellion. The first part. [Col.] Imprinted at London in Powles Church yarde by Richard Iugge and Iohn Cawood, printers to the Queenes Maiestie. Cum priuilegio Regiæ Maiestatis. [1573.] 4°, black letter, A—K in fours.

Printed without a title-page. There are six parts of the Homily, concluding with a Thanksgiving. This issue is not in the British Museum, which possesses, however, two others slightly differing in type and spelling.

HOOPER, JOHN, *Bishop of Gloucester*.
*An Answer vnto my lord of wynchesters booke intytlyd a detection of the deuyls sophistrye, wherwith he robbeth the vnlernyd people of the trew byleef in the

sacrament of the aulter in Hoper. [Quot. from *estigia mea* . . . Prynted Agostyne Fries. Anno X in fours.

f the x. holie commande- htie God . . . Collected ture canonicall, by Iohn taine new additions, made ster Houper. Come, and At London ; Imprinted -grane, for Thomas Wood- 1590.] 8°, A—O 4 in

'ILLIAM, *of Balcomie,*

hod of Fencing : Or, The Art of Fighting with the Sheering - Sword, Small- rd and Pistol ; freed from Schools. . . . The Second r William Hope of Bal- . . . Edinburgh : Printed son . . . MDCCXIV. 4°, A—Nn in fours, besides a nd two folded plates at p. nd.

\RLES.

Death ; Or, The Fall of sionary Pindarick-Poem, the Ever to be deplor'd ht Honourable the Lord Charles Hopkins. *Tanto to.* London : Printed by he sold by Sam. Buckley Willington . . . 1698. ts.

.N, *Sieur de Villars.*
1 : Or The Bull of Pope ing the Damnation, Ex- and Deposition of Q. With some Observations ions upon it. By Thomas Lincoln. Whereunto is ll of Pope Paul the Third, Damnation . . . of King th . . . London, Printed for Robert Clavell . . . A—Ss in fours.

s upon the Bill of Divorce ce the Duke of Norfolke ary Mordant, Viz. 1. The House of Lords, together . . . London, Printed for lower . . . 1700. Folio, each.

ES.
the Empire, and of the

Election of A King of the Romans, the greatest Businesse of Christendom now in Agitation. As also of the Colledge of Electors, Their particular interests, and who is most likely to be the next Emperor. J. *Senesco, non Seynesco* II. London, Printed by F. L. for Rich : Lowndes . . . 1658. 8°. A, 4 leaves : B—I in eights.
At p. 109 Howell dates from Holborn, January 1, 1658.

HULOET, RICHARD.
Hvloets Dictionarie, newelye corrected, amended, Set in Order and Enlarged, with many names of Men, Townes, Beastes, Foules, . . . By Iohn Higgins late student in Oxeforde . . . Londini, In ædibus Thomæ Marshij. Anno . 1572. Folio. ¶, 4 leaves, with title, To the Reader, &c.: A—Zz in sixes : Aaa, 7 leaves.

HUME, DAVID.
Apologia Basilica sev Machiavelli Ingenivm, examinatum in libro quem inscripsit Principem. Auctore Davide Hvmio Theagrio Scoto-Britanno. Parisiis, M.DC.XXVI. 4", ã in fours and A—Ii in fours, last leaf blank. Dedicated to Charles I.

HUME, J.
Traité de la Trigonometrie, Povr Resovdre tovs Triangles Rectilignes et Spheriqves. Avec les Demonstrations des deux celebres Propositions du Baron de Merchiston, non encores demonstrees. Dedié A Messire Robert Kar, Comte d'Ancrame, Gentil-homme de la Chambre du Roy de la Grand' Bretagne. A Paris, . . . M DC.XXXVI. Avec Privilege dv Roy. 8°. ã, 4 leaves : ẽ, 2 leaves : ĩ, 4 leaves : a—p 2 in fours : A—Y in fours. With diagrams and a folded table between pp. 68-9.

HUNTAR, ALEXANDER, *Burgess of Edinburgh.*
A Treatise of Weights, Mets and Measvres of Scotland. With their Qvantities, and Trve Foundatione, and sundrie profitable Observations. arising vpon everie one of them. . . . Edinbvrgh, Printed by Iohn Wreittoun, and are to bee solde at his Buith, at the Nether-Bowe. 1624. With Licence. 4°. ¶, 4 leaves : A—F in fours : G—K, 2 leaves each, besides two leaves (pp. 66-7) between K 1—2. Dedicated "to the Right Honorable and his very good Lord, Sr George Hay, of Kinfaunes, Chiefe Chancelor of Scotland."

HURTADO, LUIS.
Libro segundo del Emperador Palmerin en que se recuentan los grandes e hazañosos fechos de Primaleon e Polendus sus

D

fijos e de otros buenos caualleros estrangeros que a su corte vinieron. [Col.] Fue trasladado este segundo libro de palmerin llamado Primaleō . . . de griego en nuestro lenguaje castellano e corregido e emendado en la muy noble ciudad de Ciuda drodrigo por francisco vasquez . . . Emprimiose en . . . Salamanca a tres dias del mes de Julio d. M. d. xii. años. Folio. a, 8 leaves : b—mm in sixes, mm 6 probably blank, besides the title and dedication, 2 leaves more.

    The copy described (Quaritch, August 1888, No. 1149) wanted the title-page. No copy of the First Book, and no other of this, seems to be known.

Histoire dv Prevx, Vaillant et Tres-Victorievx Chevalier Palmerin d'Angleterre, . . . A Paris, Par Iean d'Ongoys, . . . M.D.LXXIIII. 8°. ā, 8 leaves: a—z in eights : A—X 2 in eights.

HUSBANDMAN.

The Husbandman's Jewel, Directing How to Improve Land from £10 per Annum, to £50. with small charge by Planting, Making Cyder as good as Canary, for 5d a Quart or less; To Improve Land by draining, and by Hemp, Saffron, Liquorice ; To Brew Ale and Beer, make Cyder, Meed, Mum, Metheglin, and other Liquors, . . . London, Printed for G. Conyers, at the Ring in Little Brittain, Price . 1/. 12°. A, 4 : B, 6 : C, 2 : D, 6 : E, 4. *B. M.*

**HWNNY LRAETHIR.
Yny Ihyvyr hwnnylraethir. Gwyd or kymraeg. Kalandyr . . . M.D.XLVI. [London, Edward Whitchurch]. 8°, 16 leaves.

    This book, according to Ames, and his followers Herbert and Dibdin, shews the Welsh Calendar, the Creed, the Lord's Prayer, the Commandments, and the Seven Good Properties of the Church, &c. A copy in Ames's time was in the possession of Mr. W. Jones.

I.

IMPROPRIATION.
Impropriation Purchased by the Commissioners sitting at Goldsmiths-Hall, For Compositions with Delinquents. By Ordinance of both Houses of Parliament. With a List of the Names of such Persons from whom they have purchased any Revenue for Augmentation of the Maintenance of Preaching Ministers. In several Parishes within the Kingdom. Published for the satisfaction of those whom it doth concern. London : Printed by Richard Cotes. 1648. 4°, A—D 2 in fours.

    The List is very curious from the familiar names in it.

INFORMATIO PUERORUM.
**Libellus qui Informatio Pueroꝝ appellatur . . . [Col.] Impresse in ciuitate Londōn. Per Richardum Pynson. 4°, 17 leaves.

    Described by Dibdin from a titleless copy belonging to Heber. Dibdin supposed it to be an edition of the *Vocabula* of Stanbridge; but from the extracts which he furnishes it seems to correspond with the *Informatio Puerorum*, of which it is perhaps another and unknown impression.

INFORMATION.
True Information of the Beginning and Cause of all our troubles : how they have been hatched, and how prevented. Wherein we may see the manifold contrivances and attempts of forraigne and home-bred Enemies, against the Parliament, Kingdome, and purity of Religion. And how all their Endeavours whether by Force or fraud, never prospered. A Work worthy to be kept in Record, and to bee communicated to Posterity. *The people that will not understand shall fall.* London, Printed in the Yeare 1648. 4°. A—D in fours : E, 2 leaves : F, 4. With a series of copper-plate engravings in the text.

    This was probably published by T. Jenner, or at all events it is the prototype of the illustrated tracts with his name as the stationer.

INNOCENT VIII.
*Our holy fader the Pope Innocent the viij. To the perpetual memory of this hereafter to be had / by his propre mocion without procurement of our souerayn lord the Kyng. . . . [A declaration as to the marriage of Henry VII. and Elizabeth of York. 1487 ? London, W. Caxton ?] A broadside.

    Reprinted entire by Herbert, p. 1763-4.

INSTITUTION.
The Institvtion of a Christen man, conteynynge the exposition or interpretation of the cōmune Crede, of the seuen sacramentes, of the x. cōmandementes, & of the Pater noster, and the Aue Maria, Instification and purgatorie. Londini in Ædibvs Thomae Bertheleti Regii Impressoris. Anno Do. M.D.XXXVII. Mense Octob.

Cvm Privilegio. 8". a, 4 leaves: A—P in eights.

NSTITUTUM.
*Christiani hominis institutum. [Col.] Hoc fac et viues. Explicit Christiani hominis institutum. Jmpressum Lonlon . per Henricum Pepwell, in cimiterio liui Pauli, sub intersignio sancte Trinitatis commorantem M.CCCCC.XX. 4°. [4 leaves.] With the printer's mark below the colophon.
>Described from a fragment, consisting of the last leaf only, by Herbert.

NTERPRETER.
The Interpreter Wherin three principall termes of State much mistaken by the vulgar are clearely unfolded. *Qui vult decipi, decipiatur.* Anno 1622. 8°, A in eights. In verse. *B. M.* (Jolley's copy.)
>The characters or terms are : A Puritan or Protestant, A Protestant or Formalist, and a Papist. From a Scotish press.

NTERROGATORIES.
*Interrogatories. For the Doctrine and Manners of Mynisters and for other Orders in the Churche . . . Churchwardens, Scholemaisters, Clarkes. For the People. [At the end occurs :] To these Interrogatories the Ordinarie requireth an Aunswere accordingly by the laste Daye of August, or before if they maye. Imprynted at London in Foster lane by Jhon Waley. 4°.

NTRODUCTION.
*An Introduction for to lerne to reken with the pen, and with the counters, after the true cast of aritmetyke, or awgrym, in hole numbers, and also in broken newly corrected, and certayne rules and ensamples added thereunto, in the year of our lorde. 1536. [Col.] Thus endeth the scyence of awgrym, the wiche is newly corrected out of dyners bokes, because that the people may come to the more understandynge and knowlege of the sayde arte, or scyence of Awgrym. . . . Imprented in the yere of our Lorde, MCCCCCXXXVII. 8°, S in eights, three last leaves blank.
>Attributed by Herbert to the St. Albans press.

**An introduction for to lerne to reckon with the pen . . . Anno 1539. [Col.] ¶ Imprinted in Aldersgate strete by Nycolas Bournan. 8°, A—O in eights. *Bodleian.*

**An introduction for to lerne to reckon with the pen, or with the counters, accordyng to the trewe cast of Algorisme, in hole numbers or in broken, newly corrected. And certayne notable and goodly rules of false positions, there vnto added, not before sene in our Englyshe tonge, by the which all maner of difficile questions may easely be dissolued & assoyled. Anno. 1546. 8°, A—N in eights.
>There appears to be no clue to the printers, unless, like the impression of 1537, it came from the press of John Herford at St. Albans.

IRELAND.
A Relation touching the present state and Condition of Ireland. Collected by a Committee of the House of Commons, and of severall letters, lately come from the Lords Justices of Ireland and others, and Printed by order of the said House. And also the Examination of Hubert Petit, taken the 19. of February, 1641. by the direction of the Lords Justices, and Counsell of Ireland. London, Printed by E. G. for Richard Best, . . . 1641. 4°, 4 leaves.

The Coppy of a letter sent from the Earle of Traquere in Ireland the third of October 1641. To Old Father Philips, heere in England, and now prisoner in the Tower. Which letter was intercepted, at a certaine time by Sir Robert Richardson, kept private but now disclosed. Vpon which old Father Philips was committed to the Tower. With a true relation how the number of Rebels dayly increase in the woods at Ireland. Printed at London 1641. 4°, 4 leaves.

May the 4th. Captaine Yarners Relation of the Battaile fought at Kilrush upon the 15th. day of Aprill, by my Lord of Ormond, who with 2500 Foot and 500 Horse, overthrew the Lord Mountgarrets Army, . . . Together with a Relation of the proceedings of our Army, from the Second to the later end of Aprill, 1642. London, Printed for F. Coules, and G. Badger, 1642. 4°, 4 leaves. With a rough romance cut on the title representing the fight.
>It is alleged that Mountgarret had 8000 foot and 400 horse.

A Trve Relation of the late Occurrences in Ireland in two Letters ; One brought over by a Noble Gentleman, Sir Hards Waller, of a Sharpe Skirmish there happened the 29. of Iune last, . . . The other Dated the fourth of Iulie from I. H. to his Uncle W. E. . . . . London, Printed by A. N. for Edw. Blackmore. Iuly 18. 1642. 4°, 4 leaves.
>Two accounts of victories over the Irish.

A Declaration of the Commons assembled

in Parliament ; Concerning the Rise and Progresse of the Grand Rebellion in Ireland. Together with a multitude of Examinations of Persons of quality, whereby it may easily appear to all the world, who were, and still are, the promoters of that cruell and unheard of Rebellion . . . London, Printed for Edw. Husbands, . . . Iuly, 25. 1643. 4°, A—II in fours.

The Trve Copies of Two Letters sent from Ireland : Shewing the severall Battailes and Victories obtained on the Rebels there. London, Printed for J. B. and R. Smith. 1643. 4°, 4 leaves.

The Declaration and Ingagement of the Protestant Army in the Province of Mounster. Under the Command of the Right Honourable the Lord Baron of Inchiquin. Printed at Cork, and re-Printed at London in the Year, 1648. 4°, 4 leaves.

Generall Owen Oneales Letter to Collonell Monck with the Propositions of Owen Oneale, the Lords, Gentry, and Commons of the Confederate Catholiques of Ulster : To the most Honourable, and Potent, the Parliament of England. Together with Coll. Monck his Answer. And Collonell Moncks Propositions to Owen Oneale, and the rest of the Confederate Catholiques of Ulster. London, Printed for A. H. and S. G. and are to be sold near the Royall Exchange. 1649. 4°, 4 leaves.

A Letter from the Lord Lieutenant of Ireland [Oliver Cromwell] To the Honorable William Lenthal Esq. ; Speaker of the Parliament of England : Giving an Account of the Proceedings of the Army there under his Lordships Command, . . . Together with a Relation of the taking in of Wexford. . . . As also the Propositions tendred for the Rendition of Wexford : . . . London, Printed by John Field and Edward Husband, . . . 1649. 4°, A—B in fours.

An Abstract of some few of those Barbarous, Cruell Massacres and Murthers, of the Protestants, and English in some parts of Ireland, committed since the 23. of October 1641. Collected out of the Examinations. . . . Sent over to the Parliament in a Letter from the Commissioners of Parliament in Ireland, . . . And Read in the Parliament the 19 day of May 1652. . . . London, Printed for Robert Ibbitson dwelling in Smithfield neer Hosier Lane end. 1652. Folio, A—D, 2 leaves each. Black letter.

Tyrconnel's Proceedings in Ireland. And Motion in Council, as to the Burning of Dublin : Together with a Speech the made against it. Sent to a Person of Quality in London. Dublin, the 27th of January, 1688. 4°, 2 leaves.

IRVINE, C.

Medicina Magnetica : Or, The rare and wonderful Art of Curing by Sympathy Laid open in Aphorismes ; Proved in Conclusions ; and digested into an easy Method drawn from both : . . . . Preserved and Published, As a Master-Piece in this Skill. By C. de Iryngio, Chirurgeon Medicine in the Army. *Nullum numen abest.* Printed in the Year, 1656. 8° A—II in eights, first and last leave blank. Dedicated to General George Monk, Commander in chief of all the Forces in Scotland, and one of His Highness's Council for the Government of that Nation.

IRVINE, CHRISTOPHER.

Historiæ Scoticæ Nomenclatura Latino Vernacula. . . . Christophorus Irvinus Abs Bon-Bosco, Auspice Summa Numine concinnavit. Edinbvrgi, Sumptibus quorundam Bibliopolorum Edinburgensium Typisque Jacobi Watson, . . . M.DC.XC.VI 8°, A—M in fours.

ITALY.

** A ioyfull new tidynges of the good victory, that was sent to the emperour from the noble capitayne marequis Degasto, shewing how and in what manner all the Frenchmen that were in Italy with all theyr captaynes be ouercome and destroyed of the valeant prince Salern ¶ Yet another newe tidinges, shewyng howe that Barbarossa, the great Turke lieutenant, and admirall of the see, gone out of France with a great army taking many noble lordes and galleye as ye shall heare hereafter. Translated by the printer from Doutch, for Jho Ghoughe. London, by John Mayler [about 1540.] Small 8°.

*The happy entraunce of the high born Queene of Spaine, the Lady Margarit of Austria, in the renowned Citty of Ferrara. With feastinall ceremonies vsed by Pope Clement the eight, in the holy Mariage of their Maiesties. As also in that of the high borne Archduke Albertu of Austria, with the Infanta Isabella Clara eugenia, Sister to the Catholique King of Spaine, Philip the third. First translated out of Italian after the Coppy printed at Ferrara, allowed by the Magistrates . . . London Imprinted by Iohn Woolfe, . . . 1599. 4°, 4 leaves.

J.

JACOBUS DE VORAGINE.
Here begynneth the legend named in latyn legenda aurea That is to saye in Englysshe the golden legende. ffor lyke as passeth golde in value all other metallys So this legende excelleth all other bookes. [This title is over a cut occupying the rest of the page. At the end :] Thus endeth the legende named . . . whyche werke I yde accomplysshe and fynysshe att westmynster the . viij. daye of Janeuer. The yere of oure lorde Thousande cccc.lxxxxviij. and in the xiiii. yere of the reynge of kynge Henry the vii. By me wynkyn de worde. Folio.

JAMES STUART THE FIRST, *King of Great Britain* (1603-25).
In Homines Nefarios, qui scelere, ausúq; immani, Parliamenti iampridem habendi Domum, pulvere bombardico evertere, sunt machinati, scilicet quinto Novembris, 1605. Ad Præcellentissimum Principem Iacobvm, . . . Cantabrigiæ Ex officina Iohannis Legat. MDCV. 4°, A—C in fours, ¶ 4 blank. In verse.

Apologie povr le Serment de Fidelité que le Serenissime Roy de la grand' Bretagne requiert de tous ses sujets, . . . A Londres, Chez Iean Norton, Imprimeur ordinaire du Roy, és langues estrangeres. 1609. . . . 8°, A—T in fours, besides the portrait of James by Tho. de Leu : *Trilici nodo, triplex cuneus*, . . . A—N in fours.

A Declaration of His Maiesties Royall pleasure in what sort He thinketh fit to enlarge, Or reserue Himselfe in matter of Bountie. Imprinted at London by Robert Backer, . . . Anno 1610. 4°, A—E 2 in fours, A 1 and E 2 blank.

Svpplicatio ad Imperatorem, Reges, Principes, Svper Cavsas Generalis Concilij convocandi. Contra Pavlvm Qvintvm. Londini, Excudebat Bonham Norton, . . . Anno cIɔ. Iɔ. XIII. 4°, A—E in fours, A 1 and E 4 blank.

Declaration dv Serenissime Roy Jaqves . Roy de la Grand' Bretaigne . . . Povr le droit des Rois & independance de leurs Couronnes, Contre la Harangve de l'Ilvstrissime Cardinal du Perron . . . A Londres, Par Iehan Bill Imprimeur du Roy. M. DC. XV. Auec priuilege de sa Majesté. 4°, a—b and A—Q in fours.

Nostodia. In Serenissimi, Potentissimi, . . . Iacobi . . . felicem in Scotiam reditum, Academiæ Edinburgensis Congratulatio. Edinbvrgi, Excudebat Andreas Hart. Anno 1617. 4°, A—G in fours.

JAMES STUART THE SECOND, *King of Great Britain* (1685-8).
Edwardus Confessor Redivivus. The Piety and Vertues of Holy Edward the Confessor, Reviv'd in the Sacred Majesty of King James the II. Being a Relation of the Admirable and Unexpected finding of a Sacred Relique, (viz. the Crucifix) of that Pious Prince, which was found in Westminster-Abbey, (the place of his Interment) 622 Years succeeding ; . . . . London, Printed by W. D. and are to be Sold by Randal Taylor . . . 1688. 4°, A—F 2 in fours.

His Majesties Reasons for Withdrawing Himself from Rochester, Wrote with His own Hand and Ordered by Him to be Published. Reasons why in this Conjuncture no Alteration should be made in the Government of the Church of Scotland, By a Sincere Protestant and a Lover of his Country. Printed in the Year, 1689. 4°, 4 leaves.

His Majesties Late Letter in Vindication of Himself: Dated at St. Germans en Laye, the Fourteenth of this Instant January, 168⁸⁄₉. [Col.] Re-printed in the Year, 1689. 4°, 4 leaves. Without a title-page.

JAMES IV., *King of Scots* (1488-1513).
Epistola Regis Scotorum ad Christianissimum Angliae & Franciae Regem ante conflictum. Et respōsum christianissimi Angliae & Franciae Regis. [1514.] 4°, 4 leaves. With a woodcut of the royal arms on the title. *B. M.*

Sotheby's, Feb. 5, 1887, No. 1075. This is an interesting tract relative to certain grievances between England and Scotland, including piracies. James mentions in his letter, dated from Edinburgh, July 26, 1513, the famous buccaneer Sir Andrew Barton.

La summation faicte par le Roy Descosse au Roy dangleterre. Imprime a Rouen par cōge de iustice. [The rest of the page is occupied by common cuts. About 1513.] Sm. 8°, 4 leaves. Gothic letter.

This is a similar narration of grievances

between James IV. of Scotland and Henry VIII., in which the former complains of injuries inflicted on his subjects by the English king.

JAMES VI., *King of Scots* (1566–1603).
A Declaratioun of the Kings maiesties intentioun and meaning toward the lait acts of parliament. Imprinted at Edinburgh, by Thomas Vautrouillier. 1585. Cum priuilegio regali. 4°, A—C in fours.

This is a Scotish version of the tract printed the same year in English under the title of *Treason pretended against the King of Scots*, &c. Reprinted in facsimile, 4°, 1646.

JANE, JOSEPH, *of Liskeard*.
Eikon Aklastos The Image Unbroken. A Perspective of the Impudence, Falshood, Vanitie, and Prophannes, Published in a Libell entitled Eikonoklastes against Eikon Basilike Or the Pourtraicture . . . Printed Anno Dom. 1651. 4°, A—Ll 2 in fours.

JENKINS, DAVID.
Severall Papers Lately written and published by Iudge Ienkins, Prisoner in the Tower : viz. 1. His Vindication. 2. The Armies indempnity : . . . 3. Lex Terræ. 4. A Cordiall . . . 5. A Discourse touching the inconveniences of a long continued Parliament. 6. An Apologie for the Army. Anno 1647. 4°.

A general title to the separately issued pieces, that to the *Vindication* cancelled.

JESUS CHRIST.
"The passion of owr lord iesu christe wythe the contemplacyōs. [On the second leaf occurs :] Her begynnythe ẏ passion of dar seygneur, Jesu christe front ẏ resuscytacyō of lazarus and to thende translated owte of frēche ynto englysche the yer of dar lorde. M.v.c.viij. On to the leawde of god āl of the soueräie vyrgyne marie & of al ẏ sāictes of paradys celestyall. And at the requeste of the moste puissāt redoubtye kynge Henry the . vii. be the grace of god kynge of englande and of fräce : the passiō of our sauueur Jesu chryste ys translated owth of frēche yn to ēglysche with an addicio of moralytees hystoriees / examples or fygures . . . [? Paris, 1508.] Folio, G 4 in eights.

Described by Herbert from his own copy.

JOCQUET, DE.
Les Triomphes, Entrees, Cartels, Tovrnois, Ceremonies, et Avltres Magnificences faites en Angleterre, & an Palatinat, pour le Mariage & Reception, de Monseigneur le Prince Frideric V. Comte Palatin dv Rhin, Electevr dv Sainct Empire, Duc de Baviere &c. Et de Madame Elisabeth, Fille Vniqve et Princesse de la Grande Bretagne, Electrice Palatine du Rhin &c. Son Espouse. A Heidelberg, Chez Gotard Vogvelein. cIɔ Iɔ xIII. 8°, A—S in fours. With nine folded engravings. *B. M.*

This edition entirely differs from that of Lyon, described in the *Handbook*, 1867.

JOHANNES DE BURGO.
Pupilla oculi De Septem Sacramentorū administratione: de decem preceptis decalogi: ceterisq; ecclesiasticorę . . . ollicijs: Joannis de Burgo alme quondā Cantabrigiensis Uniuersitate Cancellarij : . . 1516. [Col.] . . . sumptibų puidorū Joannis Knoblouchi / & Pauli Botz . . . sub Annū dñi. M.D.xvij. Kalꜱ Martij. 4", folioes 170, besides the Table.

JOHANNES DE GARLANDIA.
*Liber synonymorū Magistri Johannis de Garlandia / vna cū expositione magistri galfridi ā̈glici / vigiliq; diligētia orthographie stilo correctus et exaratus . cum notabilibus in marginibus īsertis / in regia quoq; Cinitate Lōdon impressus per Richardū Pynson / feliciter finit Anno incarnationis domini . M.ccccc. 4°, A—I in sixes : K, 4.

Described by Herbert from his own copy, wanting the title.

JOHANNES DE MEDIOLANO.
Regimen sanitatis Salerni. This boke techyng al people to gouerne them in helthe / is translated out of the Latyne tonge in to englishe by Thomas Paynell Whiche boke is as profitable & as nedefull to be had and redde as any can be to obserue corporall helthe. [Col.] Thus endeth the regimēt of helthe. Imprinted at London in Fletestrete / in the house of Thomas Berthelet / nere to ẏe cūdite at ẏ signe of Lucrece. Anno domini 1528. mense Augusto. Cum priuilegic a rege indulto. 4°. A, G leaves : B—Y ir fours : a—e in fours : f, G. Dedicated tc John, Earl of Bedford, by Paynell.

JOHANNES SARISBURIENSIS.
[Policraticus.] Hic liber ititulatur de nug curialiū & vestigijs phorę cuię Iohanne Salesberiensis Carnotēsis epūs fuit actor [No place, &c. Attributed to the Brother of Common Life at Brussels about 1476. Folio, 250 leaves, including three blanks Two columns.

The text is preceded by the Table and b the *Euthetiens* of the author in verse, an at the end there are six pages of verses, als in Latin, on the members and functions c the human body.

OHNSON, WILLIAM.
The Light of Navigation. Wherein are declared and liuely pourtrayed all the Coasts and Hauens of the West, North and East Seas. Collected partly out of the Books of the principall Authors which haue written of Nauigation (as of Lucas Iohnson Waghenar, and divers other) ... Divided into two Bookes. ... By William Iohnson. At Amsterdam Printed by William Iohnson, ... Anno 1622. Cum Priuilegio. Obl. Folio. A—E in fours, A 1 with engraved title and A 2 with frontispiece : F—G in sixes : H, 2 leaves: I, 6 : K, 2 : L, 4 : M—Q, 2 leaves each : R, 8 : S, 2 : T, 4 : V, 2 : X, 8 : *Second Book*, with a new title, Aa, 2 : Bb, 4 : Cc, 6 : Dd—Ff, 2 each : Gg, 6 : Hh—Ii, 2 each : Kk, 4 : Ll, 2 : Mm, 6 : Nn—Pp, 2 each : Qq, 4 : Rr, 2 : Ss, 8 : Tt—Xx, 2 each. With numerous diagrams accompanied by volvelles and maps, which count in the sheets.

ONES, JOHN, *Chancellor of Llandaff*.
The Mysteries of Opium Reveal'd, By Dr John Jones, Chancellor of Landaff, a Member of the College of Physicians in London : And formerly Fellow of Jesus-College in Oxford ... A Deo Lux. London : Printed for Richard Smith at the Angel and Bible without Temple-Bar. MDCCI. 8°. A, 6 leaves, including a letter from the College of Physicians and the *Errata* : B—Bb 2 in eights, besides a folded leaf between U 3 and U 4. *H. Stopes, Esq.*

The New Art of Spelling ... By J. Jones, M.D. London, Printed in the Year 1704. 4°. A, 3 leaves : B—T in fours.

ONES, ROBERT, *Musician*.
The First Booke of Songes or Ayres of foure parts with Tableture for the Lute. So made that all the parts together, or either of them seuerally may be song to the Lute, Orpherian or Viol de gamba. Composed by Robert Iones. *Quæ prosunt singula multa iuuant*. Printed by Peter Short with the assent of Thomas Morley, and are to be sold at the signe of the Starre on Bredstreet hill. 1600. Folio. Title and To the Reader, 2 leaves : B—G 2 in fours. Dedicated to Sir Robert Sidney, Knight, Governor of Flushing. *B. M.*

This copy wants title and dedication, which were in a second very imperfect one sold among Mr. Gibson-Craig's books in 1888.

The Second Booke of Songs and Ayres, set out to the Lute, the base Violl the playne way, or the Base by tableture after the leero fashion : Composed by Robert Iones. Printed by P. S. for Mathew Selman by the assent of Thomas Morley, and are to be sold at the Inner temple gate, 1601. Folio, A—M, 2 leaves each. Dedicated " To the Right Vertvovs and Worthy Knight, Sir Henry Leonard." *B. M.*

[Ultimum Vale, or the Third Book of Airs of 1. 2. or 4. Voyces. By Robert Jones. London, T. Este, 1608.] Folio. Title, 1 leaf : dedication to Henry Prince of Wales and Preface "To the Silent Hearer," 1 leaf : B—M, 2 leaves each. *College of Music.*

This copy wants the title. It has a MS. note on the fly-leaf by Rimbault as to the rarity of the musical works of Jones.

A Mvsicall Dreame. Or The Fovrth Booke of Ayres. The First part is for the Lute, two Voyces, and the Viole de Gamba ; The Second part is for the Lute, the Viole and foure Voices to Sing : The Third part is for one Voyce alone, or to the Lute, the Basse Viole, or to both if you please, Composed by Robert Iones. *Quæ prosunt singula, multa iuuant*. London Imprinted by the Assignes of William Barley, and are to be solde in Powles Church-yeard, at the Signe of the Crowne. 1609. Folio. A—K, two leaves each : L, 4 leaves. Dedicated to Sir John Levinthorpe, Knight. *B. M.*

The First Set of Madrigals, of 3. 4. 5. 6. 7. 8. Parts, for Viols and Voices, or for Voices alone, or as you please. Composed by Robert Iones. *Quæ prosunt singula, multa iuuant*. London Imprinted by Iohn Windet 1607. 4°. *B. M.* (Bassus only) Collation : A, 2 : B—D in fours : E, 2. Dedicated to Robert, Earl of Salisbury.

JORDEN.
*Jordans medytacyons, with other dyuers matters in Englysshe : as apperyth by a short Table in the ende / after the ordre of the. A. B. C. [Col.] ¶Imprynted by me Robert Wyer in the bysshop of Norwytche rentes ... Cum priuilegio Regali: pro spatio septem annorum. 8°, a—g in fours.

JOVIUS, PAULUS.
Descriptio Britanniae, Scotiae, Hyberniae, et Orchadvm. Ex Libro Pavli Iovii, Episcopi Nvcer. De Imperiis, et Gentibvs Cogniti Orbis. ... [Col.] Venetiis apud Michaelem Tramezinum. MDXLVIII. 4°, a—hh in fours, except that the last sheet has six leaves. a is repeated.

JOYE, GEORGE.
*The subuersion of Moris faulse founda-

tion; whereupon he sweteth to set faste and shoue vnder his shamles shoris, to vnderproppe the popis chirch, made by George Joye. More is become a vayn lyar in his owne resening and arguments; and his folysh harte is blynded. Where he beleued to haue done most wysely, there hath he shewed himself a starke foole. Rom. i. *Moros* in Greke is *stultus* in Latyn, a fool in Englysshe. Vivit Dominus, cuius inuicta veritas manet in eternum. At Emdom by Jacob Aurik. [1534.] 8°, 41 leaves.

JULIUS, ALEXANDER.
Ecphrasis Paraphraseos Georgij Bucha-nani in Psalmos Davidis: Ab Alexandro Ivlio Edinbvrgeno. In Adolescentiæ studiosæ gratiam elaborata. Londini, Excusum apud Georgium Eld. M. DC. XX. 8°, A—Z in eights: Aa, 6. Dedicated to Sir Oliver St. John, Lord Deputy of Ireland. *B. M.*

JUSTICES OF PEACE.
**The boke of iustyces of peas. [This is beneath a cut of a Kin enthroned, with his judges, &c. At the end:] Thus endeth the boke of justyces of peas. Emprynted at London in Flete-strete at the signe of the rose garland by Robert Copland in the yere of our Lorde M.CCCCC. and XV. 4°.

K.

KENT.
The Bloody Husband, And Crvell Neighbovr, Or, A True Historie of Two Mvrthers, Lately committed in Laurence Parish, in the Isle of Thanet in Kent, neer Sandwich: One Murder by the hands of Adam Sprackling Esquire, . . . The other The Murther of Richard Langly, . . . Written by one that lives neer the Place where the said Murthers were committed, and was present at Mr Sprackling's tryall; And published for the warning, and good of all. . . . London, Printed by Tho. Warren. 1653. 4°, A—B in fours.
Sprackling perpetrated the murder of his own wife and also that of Langly.

KNOX, JOHN.
An Answer to a Great Nomber of blasphemous cauillations written by an Anabaptist, and aduersarie to Gods eternal Predestination. And Confvted By Iohn Knox, minister of Gods worde in Scotland. Wherein the Author so discouereth the craft and falshode of that sect, that the godly, knowing that error, may be confirmed in the trueth by the euident Wordes of God. [Quotation from Proverbs xxx. 12. Geneva.] Printed by Iohn Crespin. M. D. LX. 8°, A—Ff 4 in eights, Ff 4 with the *Errata.*

Heir followeth the coppie of the ressoning which was betuix the Abbote of Crosragnell and John knox, in Mayboill concerning the masse, in the yeare of God, a thousand fine hundreth thre scoir and two yeares. [Quot. from Apocalypse xxii.] Imprinted at Edinburgh by Robert Lekprevik, and are to [be] solde at his hous, at the nether bow. Cum priuilegio. 1563. 4°. 12 prel. leaves and A—H in fours. Black letter.

L.

LACTANTIUS.
Anthologia Lactantii Firmiani, . . . recenter in locos digesta communes per Thomam Beconum. Lvgdvni, Apvd Clementem Bavdinvm. 1558. 8°. +, 8 leaves: *, 8 leaves, the last blank: a—q 6 in eights.

LADIES.
The Petition of the Ladies of London and Westminster to the Honourable House for Husbands. [Col.] London. Printed for Mary Want-man, the Foremaid of the Petitioners, and Sold by A. Roper in Fleetstreet, 1693. 4°, 2 leaves. *B. M.*
Compare *Petition.*

‡LAMBERT, FRANÇOIS, *of Avignon.*
†The Summe of Christianitie gatheryd out almoste of al placis of scripture by

that noble and famouse clerke Francis Lambert of Avynyon. And translatyd by Tristram Revel. The yere of our lorde 1536. Sm. 8°, B—H 4 in eights.
Attributed to the press of Robert Redman by Mr. Maskell.

The minde and iudgement of maister Frañces Lambert of the wyll of man, declarynge and prouynge howe and after what sorte it is captyue and bonde, and not free: taken out of hys commentaries vpon Osee the Prophete, wherin vpon the . iiii. Chapter of the sayd prophet, he most Godly, plainlye and learnedly, entreateth, and writeth of the same. Newelye trāslated into Englishe by N. L. Anno Do. M. D. xlviii. the xviii. day of Decēbre. [Col.] Imprinted at London, by John Day, and William Seres, . . . Cum gratia . . . 8°, A—K 2 in eights, besides the dedication by Nicholas Lesse to Anne, Duchess of Somerset, 3 leaves more.

LAMBERT, JOHN, *Lord Lambert.*
Roome for Cuckolds; Or My Lord Lamberts Entrance into Sodome and Gomorah. To the Tune of, *Is there no more Cuckolds but I.* Printed for W. R. A broadside in two cols. and in verse. *B. M.*

LANCASHIRE.
To the Kings Most Excellent Maiesty, The Humble Petition of divers Recusants and others, in the County of Lancaster, that they may be received into his Maiesties Protection, and have their Armes redelivered to them, for the defence of his Maiesties Person and their Families. Together with his Maiesties Commission . . . London, Printed for Edward Husbands and Iohn Frank, . . . 1642. 4°, 4 leaves.

The Petition of divers of His Majesties faithful Subjects, of the true Protestant Religion, in the County Palatine of Lancaster: Presented to His Majestie at York the last of May, by the high Sheriffe of that Countie, and divers other Gentlemen of Quality: . . . With His Majesties Answer, June 6. 1642. London: Printed by Robert Barker, . . . 1642. 4°, 4 leaves.

Severall Letters from the Committees in severall Counties, To the Honourable William Lenthall Esquire, Speaker . . . Read in both Houses of Parliament, Iune 27. 1642. Wherein (amongst divers other Passages very remarkable) is related how the Towne Men of Manchester, put themselves into Arms, and stood upon their defence against the Lord Strange and his Forces, who came to seize on the Magazine. . . . London, Printed for Ioseph Hunscott, and Iohn Wright. 1642. 4°, 4 leaves.

Newes from Manchester Being A Trve Relation of the Battell fought before Manchester. Wherein the Lord Strange lost 150. Men besides 100. taken Prisoners, with the losse only of 12 Men of the Town side, whereof six of them were taken Prisoners. Sent in a Letter to a private Friend. London, Printed for Richard Best. 1642. 4°, 4 leaves.

A True and Perfect Relation of the Proceedings at Manchester, From Sunday the 25. of September, to Sonday the second of October, MDCXLIJ. Wherein is Related six severall Battels fought by the Inhabitants of Manchester, with two thousand men against the Lord Strange, now Earle of Derby, and the Lord Rivers with 3000. horse and foot, . . . Declared in a Letter sent from Mr Thomas Hawkins to Mr Erbie a Member of the House of Commons, and openly read in the said House, October the 4, 1642. October 6. Printed for H. Blake, 1642. 4°, 4 leaves.

A Declaration and Symmons sent by the Earl of Newcastle, to the Town of Manchester, to lay down their Arms. With the Resolute Answer of the Commanders in chief, and Souldiers in Manchester. . . . London, Printed for Peter Cole, . . . July 15. 1643. 4°, 4 leaves.

Some Notable Observations upon the late Symmons By the Earl of Newcastle, of the Town of Manchester. Written by a Worthy Member of the House of Commons, and appointed to be printed . . . London, Printed for Edward Hvsbands, . . . 1643. August 4. 4°, 4 leaves.

Preston, Novemb. 17. 1646. The Deliberate Resolution of the Ministers of the Gospel within the County Palatine of Lancaster. With their grounds and Cautions according to which they put into execution the Presbytereall Government upon the present Ordinance of Parliament. London, Printed for Luke Fawne, . . . 1647. 4°, 4 leaves.

The Harmonious Consent of the Ministers of the Province within the County Palatine of Lancaster, With their Reverend Brethren the Ministers of the Province of London, in their late Testimonies to the Trueth of Jesus Christ, and to our Solemn League and Covenant: As also against the Errours, Heresies, and Blasphemies of these times, and the Toleration of them. London, Printed by J. Macock, for Luke Fawne, ... MDCXLVIII. 4°, A—D in fours, D 4 blank.

The Paper Called *the Agreement of the People* taken into consideration, and the Lawfulness of Subscription to it Examined, and Resolved in the Negative, by the Ministers of Christ in the Province of Lancaster . . . London, Printed for Luke Fawne, . . . 1649. 4°, B—E 2 in fours, and the title.

A Trip to Leverpoole, By Two of Fate's Children, In Search of Fortvnatvs's Purse. A Satyre. Addressed to the Honourable the Commissioners of Her Majesties Customs. [Quot. from *Hudibras.*] By a Gentleman of Lincoln's-Inn : London : Printed for Richard Croskill Bookseller in Lincoln's-Inn. 1706. Folio, A—G. 2 leaves each, A 1 blank, A 2 with title, G 1 not marked, G 2 blank. In verse. *B. M.* and *H. Stopes, Esq.*

This appears to be the earliest printed account dealing with what is now one of our most important seaports and commercial headquarters. In a MS. narrative (printed in Halliwell's *Palatine Anthology,* 1850), showing the state of the place in 1704, we get an extraordinary idea of its growth in a couple of years. In the Stopes copy of the pamphlet before me, which is uncut, and finer than the only other I have seen, that in the British Museum, Liverpool is described as already threatening to eclipse Bristol.

It concludes with "The Publican his Dream," which, like the remainder, is in verse.

LANGTON, CHRISTOPHER.
**A nery brefe treatise, ordrely declaring the prīcipal partes of phisick, that is to saye: Thynges natural. Thynges not naturall. Thynges agaynst nature. Gathered, and sette forth by Christopher Langton. Anno dñi. M.D.XLVII. [Col.] Imprinted at London in Fletestrete by Edward Whitchurch the .x. day of April . . . 8°, A—M 4 in eights. With some verses on the back of the title by W. Baldwin. Dedicated to Edward Duke of Somerset.

LATIMER, HUGH.
Fruitfull Sermons Preached by the right Reuerend Father, . . . M. Hvgh Latimer, newly Imprinted with others not heeretofore set forth in print, . . . At London, printed for the Company of Stationers. 1607 Cum Priuilegio. 4°. *, 8 leaues : A—Tt 2 in eights. With Augustin Bernher's Epistle to the Duchess of Suffolk, dated from Southam, October 2, 1570, retained.

*The Sermon that the Reuerende father in Christ, Hugh Latimer, byshop of worcester, made to the clergie, in the cōuocaciō, before the Parlyament began, the 9. day of June, the 28. yere of the reigne of our Souerayne lorde kyng Henry the viii. nowe translated out of latyne into englyshe, to the intēt, that thingis well said to a fewe, may be vnderstande of many, and do good to al thē that desyre to be better. ¶ Imprynted at London by Thomas Berthelet printer to the kinges grace. The yere from the byrthe of Christ . 1537. the 23. of Nouember. Cum priuilegio. 8°, E 4 in eights.

LAUD, WILLIAM, *Archbishop of Canterbury.*
The Copie of a Letter sent from William Lavd Archbishop of Canterbury the 28. of June MDCXLI. unto the Vniversitie of Oxford : Specifying, His willingnesse to resigne his Chancellor-ship, And withall deploring his sad Estate now in the time of his Imprisonment. Printed in the yeare, 1641. 4°, 2 leaves.

Canterbvries Amazement : Or The Ghost of the yong fellow Thomas Bensted, who was Drawne, Hang'd, and Quartered by the meanes of the Bishop of Canterburie ; who appeared to him in the Tower, since the Iesuites Execution. With a Discourse between the two Heads on London Bridge, the one being Thomas Bensteds, the other the late Iesuites. Printed for F. Cowles, in the Yeare 1641. 4°, 4 leaves. Black letter. With a large descriptive cut on title and a second on A 3 *verso.*

Canterbvry's Will. With A serious Conference betweene His Scrivener and Him. Also A loving Admonition to his Brethren the Bishops. Printed in the Yeare 1641. 4°, 4 leaves. With the common woodcut portrait on title.

LAWES, HENRY AND WILLIAM.
Choice Psalms . . . 1648.

At a sale at Puttick's in March 1887 a copy of this book was sold, divided into four volumes, and having in each an inscription as follows : " Solus Deus ptector Meus W. Fiat Volvntas tua Lavs deo. Ex dono Jhs Linn : " The last sentence is in a different hand, probably that of the giver, but the rest appears to be the autograph of Mildmay Fane, Earl of Westmoreland. On the flyleaf of the Bassus part occurs : " This Musicall Set of Bookes composed by Mr Lawes are humbly and freely presented to the Right Honourable Mildmay Earle of Westmorland, as a Small addition to his new erected Library and as a Monument of my affection to the Muses from His most

humble and most affectionate Servant Iohn Lynn."
Lord Westmoreland's inscription is partly in capitals, and the words *LA VS deo* doubtless allude to the composer.
In this copy a portrait of the King, instead of being worked, as in the Huth one, on the back of the title to *Cantus Secundus*, faces it as in the other portions.

LEICESTERSHIRE.

The Impeachment and Charge of Mr Henry Hastings, Sonne to the Earle of Huntington, concerning his manifold Misdemeanours, the dangerous insurrections, and Tumults occasioned by the said Mr Hastings in the County of Leicester, . . . Also the substance of a Speech spoken by the Earl of Pembrook before the Committee, . . . July 22. London, Printed for Iohn Warden. 4°, 4 leaves. With a common cut on the last page.

An exact and true Relation of A most cruell and horrid Murther committed by one of the Cavaliers, on A woman in Leicester, Billetted in her House: Who was shot into the back, being within five Weeks of the time of her delivrey. . . . London, Printed for E. Husbands and I. Franck, . . . Sept. 17. 1642. 4°, 4 leaves.

LESCARBOT, MARC, *Escuier, Seigneur de Vrieucourt.*
La Chasse Avx Anglois en l'Ile de Rez, et au Siege de la Rochelle, Et la Redvetion de la dite ville à l'obeissance du Roy. Av Roy. A Paris Chez François Iacqvin, . . . M.DC.XXIX. . . . 8°. *, 3 leaves: A—G in fours: H, 6. In verse. Italic letter.

LESLIE.
Laurus Leslæana Explicata, Sive Clarior Enumeratio Personarum Utriusque Sexus Cognominis Leslie, Una cum Affinibus, Titulis, Officiis, Dominiis, Gestisque Celebrioribus Breviter indicatis. Quibus A sexcentis, & amplius Annis Prosapia illa Floret, . . . Græcii, . . . 1692. Large folio. a—b, 2 leaves each: A—V, 2 leaves each. Dedicated to James Earl of Leslie. With a large portrait of the Earl and a folded genealogical table.

LE STRANGE, SIR ROGER.
Considerations and Proposals in order to the Regulation of the Press: Together with Diverse Instances of Treasonous, and Seditious Pamphlets, Proving the Necessity thereof. By Roger L'Estrange. London, Printed by A. C. June 3^d M.DC.LXIII. 4°, A—E in fours, and (a), 4 leaves.

The Dissenters Sayings, In Requital for L'Estrange's Sayings. Published in Their Own Words, for the Information of the People. By Roger L'Estrange. London, Printed for Henry Brome, . . . 1681. 4°, A—G in fours, G 4 blank.

LETTERS.
Miscellaneous Letters and Essays, on several Subjects. Philosophical, Moral, Historical, Critical, Amorous, &c. In Prose and Verse. Directed to John Dryden Esq; . . . By several Gentlemen and Ladies. London: Printed for Benjamin Bragg, . . . 1694. 8°, A—Q in eights. Dedicated by Charles Gildon to Sir John Trenchard.

LILY, WILLIAM, *Grammarian.*
*A shorte introduction of Grammar generally to be vsed . . . Imprinted at London by the assignes of Frauncis Flower, 1577. 4°, L in eights.

LINCOLN, DIOCESE OF.
An Abridgement of that Booke which the Ministers of Lincolne Diocesse delivered to his Majestie, . . . 1605. . . . Reprinted, Anno Dom. 1638. Small 8°. A, 6: B—G in sixes: H, 6.

LINDEWOOD, WILLIAM.
*Constitvtiones Angliæ Prouinciales. . . . Londini Excudebat Thomas Marshe. 1557. 8°, Gg 4 in eights. Dedicated in this edition by the printer to Cardinal Pole.

LITANY.
*The Golden Letanye in Englysshe. [This title is over a woodcut of the Almighty with the Saviour between his knees, &c. At the end:] Impryuted at London in Fauster Lane, by me Iohñ Skot, dwellynge in saynt Leonardes parysshe. Sm. 8°. *Althorp.*

†The Letanie or Suffrages. 1559. No place, &c. 8°, A in eights.

LLOYD, WILLIAM, *Bishop of St. Asaph.*
An Historical Account of Church-Government As it was in Great-Britain and Ireland, When they first received the Christian Religion. London, Printed for Charles Brome . . . 1684. 8°. A, 8 leaves: (b)—(d 2) in eights: B—N 4 in eights. Dedicated to Dr. Stillingfleet and Mr. Henry Dodwell.

LOMBARDUS, PETRUS, *Hibernus, Archbishop of Armagh* (1601-25).
De Regno Hiberniæ Sanctorvm Insvlæ Commentarivs. In Qvo, Præter ejusdem Insulæ Situm, Nominis Originem, &c. Pij Conatus & Res à Principe O-Neillo ad Fidem Catholicam propagandam fœli-

citer Gestæ continentur. Lovanii, Apud Viduam Stephani Martini. 1632. 4°. Title, dedication to Clement VIII. &c., 8 leaves : A—Qqq 2 in fours.

LONDON.
[The Apprehension, Arraignement, and execution of Elizabeth Abbot, alias Cebrooke, for a cruell and horrible murther, committed on the body of Mistris Killingworth in S. Creechurch Parish neere Aldgate in London.] As also the Arraignement, Conniction, and Execution of George Iarvis Priest after the order of Saint Benedicts both which suffered death on Munday the elenenth of Aprill. 1608. [A large cut of the execution of the woman.] Printed at London, for Henry Gosson, and are [to be sold in Pater] noster-row, at the signe of the [Sun.] 4°, black letter, A—C in fours, C 4 blank.

The top of the title in the copy used was mutilated, and that portion is copied from the headline on A 2. The imprint was also imperfect. I saw the tract at Leeds, in Yorkshire, Sept. 13, 1887.
According to Arber's *Transcript*, the woman is called Seabrook, alias Abbott, and the date of execution is given as the 8th April in the Stationers' Register, where the murdered woman is said to be of Saint Katherine Crischurch, London.

A Proclamation concerning Buildings, and inmates, within the Citie of London, and Confines of the same. Printed at London by Bonham Norton and Iohn Bill, . . . [1625.] A broadside forming four leaves.

A Trve Relation of the most wise and worthy Speech made by Captain Venn, one of the Burgesses of the Parliament : to the Apprentices of London ; who rose in Cheapside upon the Combustion at Westminster on Wednesday last at night, December the 29. 1641. As also The Randevowes they had that night at the Counter in Wood-streete. With A Description of the estate of Ireland at this present time. London : Printed for R. H. 1641. 4°, 4 leaves.

An Exact and Trve Relation of that Tumultuous behaviour of divers Citizens and others at Guild-Hall, December the 12. 1642. Wherein is related the businesse they pretend, their Conference with my Lord Major and a Court of Common Counsell, their Cruelty to the Souldiers, their breach of peace, and shamefull abuse to the Citizens, with other remarkeable Things. By a sad Spectator. Printed for B. A. & R. D. Decemb. 13. 1642. 4°, 4 leaves.

Londons Declaration, In the Defence of the Citisens now in Arms. Concerning certain Aspersions cast upon them ; some calling them Traitors and Rebels to the King. Of which, They here nobly cleere themselves, . . . London, Printed for Iohn Greensmith, 1642. 4°, 4 leaves.

Whereas at the open Generall Quarter Sessions of the Publick peace holden for the City of London, at the Guildhall of the same City on Monday the three and twentieth day of Aprill, in the year of our Lord one thousand six hundred fifty and five, before Christopher Packe Mayor . . . . [the Assize of Ale, Beer, &c.] Printed by James Flesher, Printer to the Honorable City of London. Three broadside sheets printed so as to form one document.

A Brief Collection out of the Records of the City, Touching Elections of the Sheriffs of London and the County of Middlesex. [Col.] Printed by S. Roycroft, Printer to this Honourable City. 1682. Folio, 2 leaves.

The Forfeitures of Londons Charter, Or an Impartial Account of the Several Seisures of the City Charter, Together with the Means and Methods that were used for the Recovery of the same, with the Causes by which it came forfeited, as likewise the Imprisonments, Deposing, and Fining the Lord Mayor, Aldermen, and Sheriffs, since the Reign of King Henry the Third to this present Year, 1682. Being faithfully collected out of Antient and Modern Historys, and Senerally Published for the satisfaction of the Inquisitive, upon the late Arrest made upon the said Charter by Writ of *Quo Warranto*. Printed for the Author, and are to be sold by David Brown, . . . and Thomas Benskin . . . 1682. 4°, A—D in fours, and a leaf of E.

LONDON, DIOCESE OF.
*Ininnctions geuen in the visitatiō of the Reuerende father in God Edmunde, bishop of London, begunne & continued in his Cathedrall churche and dioces of London, from the thyrd day of September, in the year of our Lorde god, a thousand fiue hundreth and fifty foure, vntil the viij. daye of October, the yeare of our Lorde a thousand fiue hundreth fifty and fiue the nexte ensuyng. Imprinted at London in Paules churcheyard, at the signe of the holy gost, by John Cawood, Printer to the Kyng & Queenes highnesses. Anno Domini, M.D.LV. 4. Octobris. 4°, 9 leaves.

Κολλύριον Or Eye Salve to anoint the Eyes of the Ministers of the Province of London; That they may see their Error (at least) in opposing the present Proceedings of the Parliament and Army, in the due Execution of Justice. By a Minister of the Gospel. London, Printed by G. Dawson for Henry Cripps and are to be sold in Popes Alley. 1649. 4", 4 leaves.

LOWE, PETER.
A Discovrse of the Whole Art of Chirvrgerie ... Compiled by Peter Lowe Scottishman, ... The third Edition; corrected, and much amended. At London, ¶ Printed by Thomas Pvrfoot. An. Dom. 1634. 4". ¶, 4 leaves : A—Ff in eights: Gg, 4 : *The Presages of Divine Hippocrates*, with a new title, A—D in fours.

> The first portion is dedicated to James Earl of Abercorn, whose arms are on the back of the title, from the author's own house in Glasgow, 20th December 1612; the second to the Archbishop of Glasgow from the same address, the 7th November 1611. With woodcuts and commendatory verses by John Norden, Physician, &c.

LUTHER, MARTIN.
*A Boke made by a certayne great clerke agaynst the Newe Idoll, and Olde Devyll, whiche of late tyme, in Misnia [Meissen] shulde haue ben canonysed for a saynt. [Col.] Imprynted by me Robert Wyer dwellynge in saynt Martyns parysshe, besyde charynge Crosse. Cum priuilegio. 8°, 40 leaves.

*The true hystorie of the Christen departynge of the renerēde mā, D. Martyne Luther, collected by Justus Jonas, Michael Celius, and Joannes Aurifaber whych were therat, & translated into Englysh by Johan Bale ... [Col.] Thus endeth the oracyō or processe. ... Anno M.D.XLVI. 8°, 21 leaves.

LYTTELTON, SIR THOMAS.
Letcltun teners newe correcte. [This title is over a large page-cut probably intended to represent Henry VII. surrounded by his councillors or judges. At the end occurs :] Tenorum Lytylton Lector iam cernito finem. Folio. A, 8 leaves : B—H in sixes : I, 8. With Pynson's device and his name on I 8 verso. Grenv. Coll.

> Herbert's copy wanted the title, on the back of which we have : Incipit tabula huius Libri.
> At the end of the Earl of Roden's copy, in a coeval hand, there is this colophon on the *recto* of last leaf : Impressum per me Richardū Pynson Anno dni M. ccccc. xvj.— which may be the origin of Herbert's citation of a dated edition of that year.

**Lytylton tenures newly and moost truly correctyd & amendyd. [This title is over the arms of England and France crowned. Colophon:] Londini in Ædibus Richardi Pynsonis ... 1525. quarto idus Octobris. Sm. 8", y in eights. Law-French.

**Les Tenvres de Lyttelton novelment imprimes, es onesq; toute diligense reuises, coriges, et amendes: et enscemnt one plusours authoriteis annotes et marques en le marge de cest lyuer ou mesme les cases sount ouertement debatus et purparles plus a large. [Col.] ¶ Imprynted at London by me Robert Redman. ¶ Cum et priuilegio Regali. Small folio, 53 leaves, including the title and a blank at end.

**Lytylton tenures. ... [This title is over the King's arms crowned. Colophon :] Expliciunt tenores Lititloni cum alterationibus eorundem et additionibus nouis necnon cum aliis non minus vtilioribus. Lōdini in Ædibus Rich. Pynsoris Anno dñi. M. ccccc. xxviij. die vero xviij. Iunii. Cum priuilegio. Sm. 8° or 12", X 6 in eights.

> Pynson printed two different editions this year ; the other contains EE in eights.

Lytyltons tenures newly and most truly correctyd & amendyd. [Beneath is the crowned Tudor rose in an enclosure of pieces. Robert Redman, 1528.] Small 8vo, A—X in eights, besides a table of the kinds of tenures after the title, 1 leaf.

*Lyttyltō tenures newly imprinted. [Col.] Londini in edibus Thome Bertheleti Reg. impressoris / in Fletestrete prope aquagium sitis / sub signo Lucrecie Romane. M.D.xxx. 8°, R in eights. In French.

Lytylton Tenvres Newly Revised, and truly corrected with a table (after the alphabete to fynde out briefely the cases desyred in the same) therto added very necessary to the readers. Cvm Privilegio Ad Imprimendvm solum per septennium. [Col.] Imprinted at London in Fletestrete at the sygne of the George by Wyllyam Powel. In the yere of our Lorde 1553. Cvm Privilegio ad imprimendum solum. 8°. Title and Table, 16 leaves, last two blank : A—T in eights.

M.

M. J.
Brief Notes Upon a late Sermon, Titl'd, The Fear of God and the King ; Preech'd, and since Publish'd, By Matthew Griffith, D.D. And Chaplain to the late King. Wherein many Notorious Wrestlings of Scripture, and other Falsities are observed by J. M. London, Printed in the Year 1660. 4°, A—B in fours.

M. P., *Mercurius Scotus Hybernicus.*
The Speech of a Fife Laird Newly come from the Grave. [Robert Sanders, ? Glasgow, about 1670.] A broadside in three columns. Black letter. In verse. *B. M.*

MACER, ÆMILIUS [or rather, ODO, *a Physician*].
Macers Herbal. Practysyd by Doctor Lynacro. Translated out of laten, into Englysshe, whiche shewynge [*sic*] theyr Operacyons & Vertues, set in the margent of this Boke, to the entent you myght knowe theyr Reasons. [Col.] Imprynted by me Robert Wyer, dwellynge in seynt Martyns Parysshe at the sygne of seynt John Euangelyst, besyde Charynge Crosse. 8°, A—W in fours. Without prefixes. *B. M.*

MACKENZIE, SIR GEORGE, *of Rosehaugh.*
Observations on the Acts of Parliament, Made by King James the First [—King Charles the Second] Wherein 1. it is Observed, if they be in Desuetude, Abrogated, Limited, or Enlarged. 2. The Decisions relating to these Acts are mentioned. 3. Some new Doubts not yet decided, are hinted at. . . . By Sir George Mackenzie of Rosehaugh, His Majesties Advocat for Scotland. Edinbvrgh, Printed by the Heir of Andrew Anderson, . . . 1687. Price Bound seven Pound ten shilling Scots. Folio. *Imprimatur, &c.,* 1 leaf : A, 4 leaves : B—6 C, 2 leaves each : Additions, 2 leaves. Dedicated to James II.

Defensio Antiquitatis Regalis Scotorum Prosapiæ, . . . Auctore Geo. Mackenzie, . . . Ex Anglica in Latinam linguam versa a P. S. Trajecti ad Rhenum, . . . CIƆ. IƆC LXXXIX. 8°, A—P 2 in eights.

MACKQUEEN, JO.
The Good Patriot Set forth in the Example of the Publick-Spirited Centurion. In a Sermon Preached in the Gray-Friar Church of Edinburgh, on the first Munday of June 1683, being the Day ordinarly Observed for the Commemoration of George Herriot, The Religious Founder of the Hospital called after his Name *Herriots Hospital* . . . Edinburgh, Printed by John Reid at his Printing-house in Bells-Wynd, 1694. 4°. A, 4 leaves : To the Reader, 4 leaves : B—G 2 in fours. Dedicated to the Right Honourable Sir John Hall, of Dunglasse, Baronet, and the other Commissioners of the Scotish Burghs.

MAGNA CHARTA.
**[Magna Charta. There is no title, the work beginning with a Calendar and Table. Colophon :] Ad laudem et gloriā cuncti potentis et beate virginis marie toteq; celestis curie Paruus codex qui Antiqua Statuta vocatur Explicit London iam solerti cura ac diligēcia per Richardum Pynsonum Regis impressorem Anno Incarnationis dñice millesimo qūigētesimo . xiiij. decimo sexto idibus marcus [*sic*]. 12°, N in twelves. Agenda form.

*Magna Carta. [Col.] ¶ Ad laudem & gloriā cuncti potentis beate virginis Marie toteq; celestis curie Paruus codex qui Antiqua Statuta et Noua vocatur Explicit. In parochia sancti Clementis sub intersignio sancti Georgij. cum solerti cura ac diligentia [honesti ?] viri Roberti Redman nuperime exaratus. Anno Incarnationis dñice. Millesimo quingentesimo. xxv. nono idus Maii. ¶ Laus deo. Agenda form. Folioes 146 + 9 leaves of Tables, concluding with a leaf probably blank, and here deficient.

MAINWARING, ROGER, D.D., *Bishop of St. David's.*
By the King. A Proclamation for the calling in, and suppressing of two Sermons, Preached and Printed by Roger Manwaring, Doctor in Diuinity, intituled, *Religion and Allegiance.* Imprinted at London by Bonham Norton and Iohn Bill, . . . M.DC.XXVIII. A broadsheet.

MALVEZZI, VIRGILIO.
Stoa Triumphans : Or, Two sober Paradoxes, viz.
    1. The Praise of Banishment.
    2. The Dispraise of Honors.
Argued in two Letters by the noble and learned Marquesse, Virgilio Malvezzi.

Now translated out of the Italian, with some Annotations annexed. . . . London, Printed by J. G. 1651. 12°. A, 4 leaves; B—E in twelves: F, 8. Dedicated by T. P., the translator, to David Gwin, Esq.

MAN.

*[A broadside with a woodcut of a man on horseback, a spear in his right hand, and a shield in his left with the arms of France.] Emprynted at Beverley in the Hyegate, by me Hewe Goes. With the printer's mark or rebus, a H and a goose.

MANDERSTON, WILLIAM, Scotus, Diocesis Sancti Andreæ.

Moralia magistri guillermi Manderston scoti philosophi Sacreq, theologie pfessoris in summa et ardua philosophia bipartita ex variis autoribus p eūde nuperrime collecta. Et pro secunda impressione cū recentibɇ additionibɇ ab eodē appositis reuisa . . . nuperrime impressum [Parisiis] Anno a natiuitate dñi Millesimo quingentesimo . xxxv. Die vero. xxiii. Nouembrii. Sm. 8°, folioes 1–200 inclusively of title. Dedicated to Cardinal Beaton from Paris under date of 1523. *Huth Coll.*

MANDEVILLE, SIR JOHN.

Johannes von Monteuilla Ritter. [This is the whole title. Col.] Getruckt zu Straszburg Johannes Prússz, Anno Domini. M.cccc.lxxxiiij. Folio, black letter, with numerous woodcuts. a—b in eights: c—d in sixes: e, 8 : f, 6 : g, 8 : h, 6 : i—k—l in eights : m, 7.

Tractato de le piu maranegliose cose e piu notabile. . . . [Col.] Inīpssus boñ. p Ugonē Rugeriū āno dñi. Mcccclxxxviij. [Beneath is the printer's mark.] 4°, a—i in eights : k, 10. In two columns. Without cuts.

MANUALE.

Manuale ad vsū ecclesie Sarisburiensis. Jam recens impressum: ab erratis et mendis emunctissime vindicatum pro Jacobo Cousin. Anno. M.ccccc.xxxvij. 4°. With the music.

The copy examined ended imperfectly on y 7.

Manvale ad vsum per celebris ecclesie Sarisburiensis. Londini noviter Impressum Anno Domini. M.D.LIIII. [Col.] Manvale ad secundum [sic] vsum ecclesie Sarisburiensis, tam in cantu q̄ȝ in littera diligentissime recognitum : & nusq̄ȝ ante hac climatus impressum. In quo ea que seruat ecclesiasticus ritus ordine congruo connectuntur. 4°, a—p in eights : q, 10 leaves. Finely printed in red and black, long lines, with the music.

Manvale ad vsum per celebris ecclesie Sarisburiensis : Londini recenter impressum necnon multis mendis tersum atqȝ emendatum. Anno Domini . 1555. 4°, a—p in eights : q, 10.

This appears to be mainly the same impression as that of 1554. Both are, I apprehend, merely the Rouen edition of 1554 with a London title-page.

MANWOOD, JOHN.

A Treatise of the Lawes of the Forest : . . . London, Printed for the Societie of Stationers. Anno Dom. 1615. Cum Priuilegio. 4°. ¶ and *, 8 leaves each : A—Kk 4 in eights, Kk 4 blank.

This edition, published after Manwood's death, contains additional pieces found among his MSS., as is stated in a short but interesting preface.

MARBECKE, JOHN.

The lynes of holy Sainctes, Prophetes, Patriarches, and others, contayned in holye Scripture, so farreforth as expresse mention of them is delyuered vnto vs in Gods worde, with the interpretacion of their names : Collected and gathered . . . By Iohn Marbecke . . . Anno. 1574. [Col.] Imprinted at London by Henry Denham, and Richarde Watkins. Anno. 1574. 4°. Title, dedication by author to Lord Burleigh, and R. M. to the Reader, 5 leaves : B—X in eights : Y, 4. Black letter.

MARDELEY, JOHN, *of the Tower Mint.*

A Ruful complaynt of the publyke weale to Englande. [Col.] Imprinted at London by Thomas Raynald. [About 1547.] 4°, 4 leaves. In 4-line stanzas.

At the foot of the sixth page occur the initials J. M., probably John Mardeley. The last stanza is—

 "God saue Edward our kyng
 And hys counsellers so worthye
 and send theym grace to help thys thinge
 For the weale of the communaltye."

The Errata occur at the bottom of the seventh page. The tract is remarkable for the paucity of stops.

MARGARET, ST.

The [Life of Saint Margaret. This title is in a scroll over a woodcut occupying the rest of the page. At the end occurs :] Thus endeth the lyfe of saynt Margarete Enprynted at London in the pultry at the stockes at the longe shoppe by saynt myldredes churche, By John Mychell. 4°, A—C in fours.

Sotheby's, Dec. 23, 1887, in Lot 3302, much mutilated. The woodcut on title is repeated on the back; it represents the Saint attended by the Lion.

MARGUERITE D'ANGOULÉME, *Queen of Navarre.*

*A Godly Medytacyon of the christen sowle, conceerninge a love towardes God and hys Christe, compyled in frenche by Ladye Margaretequene of Nauerre, aptelie translated into English by the ryght vertuouse lady Elyzabeth doughter to our late soueraynne Kynge Henry the viii. [This title is over a cut of the Princess kneeling, and receiving the Saviour's blessing. At the end occurs :] Imprented in the yeare of our lorde 1548, in Apryll. 8°, 48 leaves.

Edited by John Bale, and dedicated by him to the Princess. Included is a translation by Elizabeth of the 13th Psalm in English verse.

The History of the most Illustrious Lady Queen Margaret Daughter to Henry the second, and first Wife to Henry the last of France. Truly representing the Contrivance and prosecution of the Bloody Massacre and the growth and fury of the Civill War in that Kingdome, ... Written in French by her owne most Royall hand and faithfully translated into English. By Robert Codrington Master of Arts. And recommended to the publicke. London, Printed by R. H. 1649. 8°. Title, dedication by translator to Sir Horatio Townsend, Kt and Bart., and Advertisement, &c., 3 leaves : B—Q 4 in eights, Q 4 blank.

MARKHAM, GERVASE.

A way to get Wealth. By Approued Rules of Practice in good Husbandry and Huswiferie. Containing The foure principall Offices which support and maintaine a Familie. 1. The husbanding and inriching of all sorts of grounds, making the barren equall with the most fruitfull : with the reducing to their first perfection all grounds whether arable or pasture, spoyled by the ouerflowing of Salt water, or sea-breaches, and the inriching of the Hop-garden, & other knowledges not published before : Also the preseruation of Graine, and a computation of Men & Cattell labors. II. The ordering and curing, with the natures, breeding, vse, & feeding of all sorts of Cattell and Fowle, ... III. The office of the English Housewife in Physicke, Surgerie. ... IIII. The office of Planting and Grafting. ... The first three Bookes gathered by G. M. The last by Mr William Lawson, for the benefit of the Empire of Great Britaine. And all these newly corrected and augmented by the Authors. Printed at London for Roger Iackson, and are to bee sold at his shop neere Fleetstreet Conduit. 1625. 4°. *H. Stopes, Esq.*

This is a general title to a volume containing Markham's *Farewell to Husbandry*, 1625 ; his *Cheap and Good Husbandry*, 1623 ; his *Country Contentments*, 1623 ; and Lawson's *New Orchard and Garden*, 1623. It appears to be the earliest collected issue.

Markhams Maister-Peece. Containing all Knowledge belonging to the Smith, Farrier, or Horse-Leech, ... Imprinted at London by Nicholas and Iohn Okes, dwelling in the Well yard in little St. Bartholmews neere the Hospitall Gate. 1636. 4°. Mind of the frontispiece and frontispiece itself, title, &c., 7 leaves : B—Pp in eights : Qq, 6 leaves. With woodcuts and a folded plate.

MARSHALL, STEPHEN.

A Sacred Panegyrick, Or A Sermon of Thanks-Giving. Preached to the two Houses of Parliament, His Excellency the Earl of Essex, the Lord Major ... and Commissioners from the Church of Scotland, Vpon occasion of their Solemn Feasting, to testifie their thankfulnes to God, and union and concord one with another, after so many Designes to divide them, and thereby ruine the Kingdome, Ianuary 18. 1643. Published by Order of the Lords and Commons ... London, Printed for Stephen Bowtell. ... 1644. 4°. A, 2 leaves : B—E in fours : F, 1 leaf. Dedicated to the Parliament.

MARSHALSEY.

The Ancient Legal Course and, Fundamental Constitution of the Palace-Court or Marshalsea. Together with the several Charges of all Proceedings there : And its present Establishment : Particularly set forth and Explained. Whereby it will appear of what great Authority this Court hath been in all Times. London, Printed for Robert Crofts at the Crown in Chancery-lane. 1663. 12°. A. 8 leaves, including frontispiece (A Perpetual Almanac with the Crown and *C. R.* 2d beneath) and an Explanation of it : A, repeated, 12 leaves : B, 12 : no C : D, 4. *B. M.*

This is an interesting and most rare little volume, and appears to be the only separate account of this ancient tribunal, which had its analogues in other countries, and over which the celebrated Sir Thomas Littleton presided in the time of Henry V. I can trace only one other copy besides that in the British Museum.

†MARTIAL, JOHN, *LL.D. and Student in Divinity.*

A Treatyse of the Crosse gathered ovt of

the Scriptures, . . . Imprinted at Antwerp by John Latius, at the signe of the Rape, with Privilege. Anno. 1564. 8", Aa in eights.

ARTIN, M.
A Late Voyage to St. Kilda, The Remotest of the Hebrides, Or Western Isles of Scotland. With A History of the Island, Natural, Moral, and Topographical. Wherein is an Account of their Customs, Religion, Fish, Fowl, &c. As also a Relation of a late Impostor there, pretended to be sent to St. John Baptist. By M. Martin, Gent. London: Printed for D. Brown, and T. Goodwin: At the Black Swan and Bible without Temple-Bar; and at the Queen's Head against St. Duntan's Church in Fleet street. MDCXCVIII. 8". A, 5 leaves, including half-title: *, leaves with Contents: B—L in eights, 8 with Advertisement. With a folded map. Dedicated to the Right Hon. Charles Montague, Esq., Chancellor of the Exchequer, President of the Royal Society, &c.

A Description of the Western Islands of Scotland. . . . London, Printed for Andrew Bell, at the Cross-Keys and Bible, in Cornhill, near Stocks-Market, 1703. 8", a—b in eights: A—Bb 4 in eights. With a folded map of the Islands and a plate of the Form of the Heathen Temple. Dedicated to Prince George of Denmark.

ARTIN, WILLIAM, *Recorder of Exeter.*
The Historie and Lives, of Twentie Kings of England. With the Successions of the Dvkes, and Earles of this Realme; from the Conqvest vntill the Twelfth yeare of the Famous Raigne of the most Admired Prince King Iames the First. Together with the times of the Creations of the Barons, and Baronets, of this Kingdome. By William Martyn Esquire, Recorder of the Honorable Citie of Exeter. *Frustra t per plura, quod fi ri potest per pauciora.* London, Printed by W. Stansby for Henrie Fetherstone. 1615. Folio. ¶, 4 leaves: , 6 leaves: A—Zz in fours: Aaa, 5 leaves. Dedicated to the Gallant Gentry of England. With verses to the Author by his sons Nicholas, William, and Edward.

ARTYR, PETER.
Most Godly prayers compiled out of Dauids Psalmes by D. Peter Martyr. Translated out of Latin into English by Charles Blemhan, B. Seene and allowed according to the order appointed. Imprinted at London by William Seres. 569. Cum priuilegio. 8", A—Ll 4 in eights. *B. M.*

MARTYRS.
Actiones et Monimenta Martyrum, Qvi A Wicleffo et Hvsso ad nostram hanc ætatē in Germania, Gallia, Anglia, Flandria, Italia, & ipsa demum Hispania, veritatem Euangelicam sanguine suo constanter obsignauerunt. Joannes Crispinvs, M.D LX. 4". a—β, 8 leaves each: γ, 4 leaves: A, 4 leaves: B—Ss in eights. The epistle of Crispin to the Reader is dated Geneva, 5 Kal. March, 1560.

MARVELL, ANDREW, *M.P.*
Marvels Ghost: Being the True Copy of a Letter sent to the A. B. of C. upon his suddain Sickness, at the Prince of Orange's first Arrival into London. [London, 1688.] 4", 2 leaves. In verse.

MARY, *called the Virgin.*
**Hore Beate Marie Virginis ad usum Sarum. [Col.] Hore beate marie virginis ad vsum insignis ecclesie Sarū finiunt feliciter vnaen multis sanctorū & sanctarū suffragiis, et multis aliis diuersis orationibus nouiter supadditis. Impresse Londonii per me winandum de worde commorantem in vico nūcupato de Fletestrete ad signum solis. M.CCCCC.ii. 4", 150 leaves + the Calendar.

**Hore beate Marie virginis secundum vsum insignis ecclesie Sarum totaliter ad longum & sine requie. [This is over a cut of the Salutation, and beneath it:] Be me Julyan Notary. [Col.] Hore beate Marie virginis . . . finiunt feliciter vna cū multis sanctorū et sanctarū suffragiis et multis aliis diuersis oratiōibus nouiter superadditus cū quatuor euangelis et passione dūi et cū horis dulcissimi noīnis Iesu. Impresse London without Tempell barre in Saynt Clement parysshe be me Julyan Notary dwellynge at the sygne of the thre kynges. [1504.] 4", 307 leaves.

> On the back of the title is an Almanac for 19 years from 1503. In Herbert's time a copy on vellum was in the possession of the Rev. Mr. Masters. Dibdin notices a similar one in the Towneley Collection; and he also considers the book as evidently of foreign execution.

*[Hore beatissime virginis Marie in verum usum Sarum. At the end occurs:] Hore . . . quā plurimis Bibliæ historiis decoratæ . . . Impresse quidem Parisiis in officina industrii calcographi Nicolai Prenost Impensis vero fidelissimi Mercatoris Francisci Byrkman ciuis Coloniensis & apud eundem venundantur Londonii apud Cœmeterium Sancti Pauli. Anno Dīni. 1527. die 18 Julij. 4" or small folio, 222 leaves.

E

Herbert describes this from Dr. Lort's copy, which wanted the title.

*Hore beate marie virginis ad vsum insignis ac preclare ecclesie Sarū cū figuris passionis mysteriū representātibus recenter additis. [This title is in red and black over the printer's device, name, and a copy of verses. On the back of the title is the Table to find Easter. At the end occurs :] Impresse Parisius per Johāne bignon pro honesto viro Richardo fakes Lōdon librario / & ibidē cōmorāte cymiterio sēti Pauli sub signo A. B. C. Agenda form, L in twelves.

The Table is from 1521 to 1538.

**Hore beate virginis Marie (ad vsum sacrosancte ecclesie Sarum)iam sequuntur. [This title occurs at the head of the lunar calculations for 1533, the copy employed having lost the title. At the end occurs :] ¶ Robertus wyer me excudebat, in parochio diui Martini, moram trahenti sub intersigno sancti Joannis. [1533.] Sm. 8°, 120 leaves.

MARY I. TUDOR, *Queen of England* (1553–58).

De Exeqviis Caroli V... Item De Exeqviis Mariæ Vngariæ & Mariæ Angliæ reginarum, per eundem Imperatorem [Ferdinandum] aliquot diebus post celebratis... Avgvstæ Vindelicorvm / Anno Sal. 1559. IIII. Kal. Martij. 4°, A—Z in fours : a—f in fours: g, 6.

Sotheby's, June 1888 (Turner, No. 964).

MASSACHUSETTS.

A true Relation of the Proceedings against certain Quakers, at the generall Court of the Massachusetts holden at Boston in New-England October. 28. 1659. London Printed by A. W. 1660. [March 1, 1659–60.] A broadside. *B. M.*

The Charter Granted by Their Majesties King William and Queen Mary, to the Inhabitants of the Province of the Massachusetts-Bay in New-England. Boston in New-England : Printed by B. Green, Printer to the Honourable the Lieut. Governour & Council, for Benjamin Eliot, and Sold at his Shop, near the Town-House in King's Street. 1726. Folio. Title and Charter, A—B in fours : Table of laws, A—D, 2 leaves each, and a leaf of E. *The Acts and Laws*, with a new title, also dated 1726, A—Xx in fours.

MATTHEW OF PARIS, *Monk of St. Albans, ob.* 1259.

Matthæi Paris, Monachi Albanensis, Angli, Historia Maior, à Guilielmo Conquestore, ad vltimum annum Henrici tertij. Cum indice Completissimo. L Domini 1571. [Col.] Lon apud Reginaldum Vuol Maiest. in Latinis Typogra Domini M. D. LXX. Folio. A—5 X in sixes: 5 Y, 7 lea the colophon : *Index*, a—c Edited by Archbishop Park

At the foot of the title of here employed occurs : Li uile, ex dono Mathæj Park Archepiscopi.

Matthaei Paris, Monachi A Historia Maior, . . . Cum pletissimo. . . Tigvri In O oviana, M.D.LXXXIX. Folic sixes, last leaf blank: A— NN, 5. *B. M.*

Matthæi Paris Monachi All Historia Major. Juxta E dinense 1571, verbatim rec Rogeri Wendoveri, Williel Authorisque Majori Minor Chronicisque MSS, in Bib Collegii Corporis Christi Cottoniáque, fideliter c primūm Editioni accesse Offarum Merciorum Regn trium Abbatum S. Albani V Libro Additamentorum. Authorem. Qui & Varian Adversaria, vocūmque bar sarium adjecit : simul Nominumque, Indicibus C Londini, Excudebat Ric kinson, 1640. . . . Folio. including frontispiece by *Imprimatur :* b—c in sixe Q in sixes : 4 R, 2 leaves sixes : 4 Y, 2 leaves : *Inde* in sixes : D, 8 : *Vitæ Offi* a new title dated 1639, *, 6 in sixes : Y, 7 : y, 6 leaves yyy, 6 leaves : yyyy, 4 leaves.

Edited by William V

MAXWELL, JAMES, M.A The Golden Art, Or The Enriching. Comprised : proued and confirmed by holy Scripture, . . . Ver all such persons in Citie doe desire to get, increase vse goods with a good co London, Printed for Willi are to be sold at his shop in yard, at the signe of the 1611. 4°, A—Ee in fours leaves blank, and a, 4 lea and B. Dedicated to Sir W

of London, and Sir John
d Provost of Edinburgh.

zabeths Looking-glasse of
lory. Wherein may be seen
of the faithfull: that is to
stling, victory, and reward,
at, conquest and Crown of
en. . . . [Col.] London
, Alde, for Ed. White dwell-
little north-dore of Paules,
)f the Gun. 1612. Sm. 8°,
ights, title on A 2, besides
leaves marked A. Printed
rs. Dedicated by Maxwell
test Honovr of the Memorie
llvstriovs Lady of Samothea,
her lifetime Queene-heire of
eene-dowager of France, and
escent Princesse Apparent of
ince, and Ireland." *B. M.*

SIR THEODORE, *Knight.*
s Anglo-Gallicus: Or, Excel-
oved Receipts and Experi-
okery. Together with the
Preserving. As also, Rare
ugar-Works: According to
Mode, and English Manner.
a choice Manuscript of Sir
yerne Knight, Physician to
harles. *Magistro Artis, Edere*
inted for G. Bedell, and T.
1658. 12°. A, 4: B—F in
8.

ese particulars from the Jolley,
Turner copy.

EONARD.
h Gardener: . . . London,
J. Wright at the Crown on
l, 1683. 4°, A—T in fours,
4 plates. Dedicated to Philip
Varkworth, co. Northampton,

S.
cademicus: Communicating
nce and Affairs of Oxford to
he Passive party thorowout
. From Munday in Easter-
urday the 15. of April, Anno
leaves. Without a regular

rjttjens, Communicating In-
om the Hypocrites at West-
Sectaries in the Army, and
alves of the City. From
prill, 27. to Thursday, May 4.
leaves.
No. 3, and forms sign. C.

nwell: Or, Oliver ordering

our New State. A Tragi-Comedie. Wherein is discovered the Trayterous under-
takings and proceedings of the said Nol,
and his Levelling Crew. Written by
Mercurius Melancholicus. [4 stanzas.]
Printed in the Yeare, 1648. 4°.

Mercurius Psitacus. Or, The Parotting
Mercurie . . . From Munday June 5. to
Munday Iune, 12. 1648. [4 stanzas.]
Printed in the last year of the Reigne of
this Parliament. 1648. 4°, 4 leaves.

Mercurius Psitacus: The Parotting Mercury: Communicating the Affairs of the
Kingdome, from Westminster, London,
South-Wales, Sir Marmaduke Langdale
and the Scots Forces now joyned in the
North, the Kentish and Essexian Royal-
ists, the Isle of Wight, and the town of
Colchester. From Wednesday Iune 21.
to Munday Iuly 3. 1648. [4 stanzas of
4 lines.] Printed in the Yeer 1648. 4°,
4 leaves.

A third number from July 3 to July 17
makes another tract of 4 leaves.

Mercurius Insanus Insanissimus,

Now pretty well recover'd of his wits,
He speaks plaine truth and sense by girds and
fits.
Pro Rege & pro grege
Per fidelem scrvum Principis & Patriæ.
[1648.] 4°.

This is called No. 7, but is marked A,
while another part, marked B, is numbered
2. I have seen four parts, A—D in fours.
Each has a copy of verses on the title; in
the second part the imprint is: Printed in
the Yeere, 1648. The first has no regular
title.

METCALFE, THEOPHILUS.
Short-writing. The most Easie, Exact,
Lineal and Speedy Method that hath ever
been obtained or taught. . . . The eighth
Edition much enlarged and perfected by
the Author. Which Book is able to make
the Practitioner perfect without a Teacher.
As many hundreds in this City and els-
where, that are able to write Sermons
word for word can from their own experience testifie. London, Printed, and are
to be sold by John Hancock . . . 1652.
8°, A in eights, besides the portrait and
frontispiece by Cross and 20 leaves of
engraved characters.

MEXIA, PEDRO, *Historiographer to
Charles V.*

The Foreste or Collection of Histories, no
lesse profitable, then pleasant and necessarie, docen out of Frenche into Englishe,
by Thomas Fortescue. *Aut vtile, aut in-
cundum, aut vtrumq;* Imprinted at Lon-

don by Jhon Kyngston, for Willyam Iones. 1571. 4°. a, 4: b, 2: A—Zz in fours, followed by 7 leaves irregularly signed. Dedicated to John Fortescue, Esq., Master of the Queen's Wardrobe. with whom he does not name his exact relationship.

MIDDLESEX.
*[A pardon and absolution granted by pope Clement VIII. for the church of Woxbridge in the diocese of London by Thomas Cardinal of York.] Impressum per me Richardum Fakes. A small sheet.

MIDDLETON, THOMAS.
Honorable Entertainments, Compos'de for the Seruice of this Noble Citie. Some of which were fashion'd for the Entertainment of the Lords and his Maiesties most Honorable Priuie Councell, vpon the Occasion of their late Royall Employment. Inuented by Thomas Middleton. Imprinted at London by G. E. 1621. 8°, A—E 3 in fours, E 4 having been doubtless blank.

Sotheby's, March 19, 1888, No. 114.

MIDDLETON, SIR THOMAS.
An Exact [Copy] of Lievetenant Generall Middletons Letter: To the Honourable Sir William Waller. And by him communicated to, and Read in the Honourable House of Commons, on Saturday last, being the 24. of this instant Moneth of August. 1644. Wherein is set forth a Victory obtained against the Enemy by a Partie of Horse and Dragoones, under the Command of Captaine Findler, Quarter-Master-Generall to Sir William Waller, at Farrington. . . . [London, 1644.] 4°. 4 leaves.

In this copy the imprint was cut off.

MIEGE, GUY.
A New Cosmography, Or Survey of the Whole World; In Six Ingenious and Comprehensive Discourses. With a Previous Discourse, being a New Project for bringing up Young Men to Learning. Humbly Dedicated to the Honourable Henry Lyttelton, Esq; By Gvy Miege, Gent. London, Printed for Thomas Basset, . . . 1682. 8°. Title and Advertisement, 2 leaves: B—L 2 in eights, besides two separate diagrams between D 3-4 and L 1-2.

MILTON, JOHN.
Areopagitica; A Speech of Mr John Milton For the Liberty of Vnlicenc'd Printing To the Parliament of England. [Quot. from Euripides with an English translation.] London, Printed in the Yeare, 1644. 4°, A—E in fours, and a leaf of F.

Joannis Miltoni Defensio Secunda Pro Populo Anglicano: Contra infamem Libellum anonymum cujus Titulus, *Regii sanguinis clamor* . . . Accessit Alexandri Mori . . . Fides Publica. Contra calumnias Ioannis Miltoni Scurræ. Hagæ-Comitum, . . . M.DC.LIV. Sm. 8°. *, 8 leaves: A—F 6 in twelves.

A Treatise of Civil power in Ecclesiastical causes: Shewing That it is not lawfull for any power on earth to compell in matters of Religion. The author J. M. London, Printed by Tho. Newcomb, Anno 1659. 8°, A—D in twelves.

Paradise Lost. A Poem in Twelve Books. The Author John Milton. The Second Edition Revised and Augmented by the same Author. London, Printed by S. Simmons next door to the Golden Lion in Aldersgate-street, 1674. 8°. A, 4 leaves: B—Y in eights, Y 8 blank. With a portrait by W. Dolle.

Joannis Miltoni Angli, Artis Logicæ Ad Petri Rami Methodum concinnata. Adjecta est Praxis Analytica & Petri Rami vita. Libris duobus. Londini, Impensis Spencer Hickman, Societatis Regalis Typographi, . . . 1672. 12°. With a reduced copy by Dolle of the portrait by Faithorne. A, 10 leaves, A 1-2 blank, A 10 with *Errata*: B—L 6 in twelves.

Joannis Miltonii Angli, Epistolarum Familiarum Liber Unus: Qvibvs Accesserunt, Ejusdem, jam olim in Collegio Adolescentis, Prolusiones Quædam Oratoriæ. Londini, Impensis Brabazoni Aylmeri. . . . 1674. 8°, A—K in eights, A 1 and K 8 blank, K 7 with Advertisements. A is irregularly signed.

MINES.
An Abstract of the Present State of the Mines of Bwlchyr-Eskir-Hyr [Cardigan], and of the Material Proceedings of the Committee, appointed for the Management thereof. Published for the Information and Satisfaction of the absent Partners, and at their Request. London, Printed in the Year 1700. 8°, A—M in eights.

The Second Abstract, from Jan. 30 to April 30, 1700, begins on sign. M.

The following penalties are spoken of at p. 126, and also provision for sickness for the workmen: "for Swearing, Cursing, Quarrelling, being Drunk, or neglecting Devine Service on a Sunday, One Shilling; for absenting from their Work two hours in a day without leave of the chief Operator, or refusing to obey his lawful commands, one days Wages; for absenting one whole day without leave, a weeks Wages, &c., all which Forfeitures are put into a strong Box, as a reserve for such of them as shall fall sick, or come to any accident." The FIRST convict labour, sent out as "apprentices," was employed at these mines. Under date September 11th, the ship "Hope" arrived at Dovey, from London, "amongst other Freight, hath brought several Criminals to work at the Mines." Some of them ran away, as the following shows:— "Note, *The Men run away are since taken, and committed to Newgate, in order to their Execution.*"

The Third Abstract of the State of the Mines of Bwlchyr-Eskir-Hir in the County of Cardigan. From the Thirtieth Day of April last (inclusive) to this present Nineteenth Day of December, 1700. By Order of the Committee. London: Printed by F. Collins, in the Old Bailey. 1700. Folio, 2 leaves.

The Fourth Abstract of the State of the Mines of Bulchyr-Eskir-hir, in the County of Cardigan: From the 10th Day of December last (inclusive) to this present 5th Day of May, 1701. By Order of the Committee. [Col.] London, Printed by Freman Collins, in the Old-baily, 1701. Folio, 2 leaves.

MINISTERS.
A Defence of the godlie Ministers, against the slaunders of D. Bridges, contayned in his answere to the Preface before the discourse of Ecclesiasticall gouernement, with a Declaration of the Bishops proceeding against them. . . . 1587. 4°, A—V in fours, V 4 with the *Errata*.

The Joint-Testimonie of the Ministers of Devon, whose names are subscribed; with their Reverend Brethren the Ministers of the Province of London, unto the truth of Jesus . . . In pursuance of the solemn League, and Covenant of the three Nations . . . London, Printed by William Du-gard for Ralph Smith, . . . 1648. 4°, A—E in fours, E 4 blank.

MISSALE.
†Missale secundum vsum ecclesie sarisburiensis. [Col.] Impensa et arte māgri Martini moriu civis Rothomagensis juxta insignem prioratum sancti laudi ejusdem civitatis moram trahentis officium sacrum ad usum sarum (ut vulgo loquimur) missale dictum, sollerti correctionis lima nuper castigatum et impressum: finit feliciter. Anno Domini M. cccc. lxxxii. die XII Octobris. Folio, Aa in eights: A—D in eights: E—G in sixes.

See further in Maskell (*Selected Centuries*, 1843, pp. 9-10).

*Missale secundum vsum Sarum. [Col.] In laudem sanctissime trinitatis totiusq; milicie celestis ad honorē et decorē sēē ecclesie. Sarū anglicāne ciusq; denotissimi cleri: hoc missale diuinorum officiorum vigilanti studio emendatum Jussu et impēsis prestantissimi viri winkin de worde. Impressum London, apud westmonasteriū per Julianum notarie et Johanem barbier felici numine explicitu3 est. Anno dñi. M.cccc.lxxxxviij. xx. die mensis Decembris. Folio, 286 leaves. In two columns.

Described by Herbert from his own copy, commencing on A ii.

Fortuna opes auferre: no animā potest. Missale ad cōsuetudinē insignis ecclesie Sarum vna cum dicte ecclesie institutis cōsuetudinibusq3 nuper elamitissime ipressū: additis plurimis que in ceteris desiderantur. In alma Parisiorum academia. Anno domini virtutum / cōditorisq3 mundi: Millesimo quingentesimo decimo kalendas mensis Aprilis 1510 . . . Folio, in two columns, with fine woodcuts and the music. ✠, 8 leaves; a—t in eights: v—y in sixes: A—H in eights: I, 10: *Commune Sanctorum*, &c., A—H in eights, the last page occupied by a large romance-cut, accompanied by a shield of arms.

Missale ad vsum atq3 consuetudinē insignis ecclesie Sar. nup vna cū diue ecclesie institutis consuetudinibusq3 a varijs mēdis purgatū / & ad limā redactū Additis plurimis cōmoditatibʒ que in ceteris desiderant. In alma Parisiorū academia Impēsis Francisci Byrkmā Impressum. 1515.

Nō rudis occurro: sed lima tersq ad vnguē Nuper q̄ fueram sordidus atq3 lacer.

8°, in two columns, with small cuts and the musical notes. ✠, 8 leaves: a—z in eights, followed by two sheets of 6 and 8 with the music, *Canon*, &c.: A—L in eights: A (repeated) with the *Commune Sanctorum*, &c., H in eights: I, 4: aa, 8: bb, 4.

Missale ad vsum ecclesiē Sarisburiensis. M.D.LIIIJ. [Device of Robert Valentin of Rouen and verses *Ad sacerdotem*. At the end occurs:] Missale ad vsum Sarisburiensis [sic] explicit . . . Ex officina Richardi hamiltonis typographi. Venale habetur Rothomagi / in ædibus honesti viri Roberti valētini / bibliopolarum porticulo moram tenentis. 4°. ✠, 8 leaves: a—I in eights: K, 6: *Cōmune Sctōrum*, &c., A—V in eights: A—G in eights: II, 10.

In two volumes. With woodcuts and music.

Missale ad vsū ecclesie Sarisburiensis. M.D.lv. [The device and name of Robert Valentin of Rouen and verses *Id sacerdotem*.] 4°. ✠, 8 leaves: A—R in eights: *Proprium festivitatum*, &c., A—H in eights: A—G 7 in eights (G 8 probably with Table and colophon as in the ed. of 1554). With woodcuts and music.

Missale ad vsum insignis ecclesie Sarisburiensis nunc recens typis elegantioribus exaratum, historiij nouis, varijs ac proprijs insignatum : et a mendis quam plurimis (quibus passim scatebat) omni diligentia nuper emendatum. Londini, Anno domini. M. D. LVij. [Col.] Londini, Anno verbi incarnati. M.D.LVII. Folio. ✠, 10 leaves: .·., 1 leaf, with the *Benedictio salis et aquæ*, &c. : A ii—Kk in eights. In two columns.

From the press of John Day.

*Missale ad vsum celeberrime ecclesie Eboracensis, optimis caracteribus recēter Impressum, cum peruigili maximaq ; lucubratione mendis quam pluribus emendatum. . . . Sumptibus & expensis Johannis gachet, mercatoris librarii bene meriti, juxta prefatam ecclesiam commorantis. Anno dñi decimo sexto supra millesimum et quingētessimū. Die vero quinta Februarii, completum atq; perfectum. Folio, printed in black and red, with musical notes, woodcuts, and initial letters. A—Z in eights : &. 8 leaves: +, 8 leaves, concluding with *Cautele ad missam celebrandam*.

Described by Herbert from his own copy.

**Anno incarnationis secundo supra quingentissimum atq ; millesimum, die vicesima prima mensis Septembris, opera et industria M. Petri Olinerii et Iohannis Manditier, impressorum Rothomagi, juxta sacellum ūini apostolorum principis Petri commorantium. Impensa vero Johannis Ricardi, mercatoris : hoc nouum et egregium opus sacri Missalis ad vsum famose ac percelebris ecclesie Helforden. nuper instanti ac peruigili cura visum correctum et emendatum, necnon auctoritate reuerendi in Christo patris et domini eiusdem ecclesi episcop : meritissimi ac dominorum decani et capituli, est in propatulo venale facili precio coram cunctis productum et exhibitum. [Col.] Finis missalis . . . impressum Rothomagi . . . impensis Iohannis Ricardi. . . . Folio.

Dr. Hezekiah Bedford's copy, communicated to Ames, was printed on vellum. This volume is remarkable as containing the Form of Matrimony in English.

MOCQUET. JEAN, *Keeper of the Cabinet at the Tuilleries*.

Travels and Voyages into Africa, Asia, and America, The East and West-Indies ; Syria, Jerusalem, and the Holy-Land. . . . Divided into Six Books, and Enriched with Sculptures. Translated from the French, By Nathaniel Pullen, Gent. London : Printed for William Newton, Bookseller, in Little-Britain ; . . . 1696. 8°, B—Z in eights, and the title, besides 8 leaves under s between S and T. With a series of woodcuts copied on a reduced scale from De Bry and counting in the sheets.

MONEY.

**[A proclamation made by Henry VII. against clipped money. With six impressions of the money in the margin.] Et hoc sub periculo incumbenti nullatenus omittas. Teste me ipso, apud westmonasterium quinto die. Iulii . anno regni nostri decimo nono. [1504.] Regius impressor, within seynt Elens, Guillam [Faques.] A broadside.

Described by Ames from an original then in the possession of Martin Folkes, Esq., F.R.S.

MONIPENNIE, JOHN.

The abridgement or Summarie of the Scots Chronicles, with a short description of their originall, from the comming of Gathelvs their first Progenitor out of Graecia into Egypt. And their comming into Portingall and Spaine, and of their Kings and Gouernours in Spaine, Ireland, and Albion, now called Scotland. . . . By Iohn Monipennie. Printed at Brittaines Bursse by Iohn Budge. 1612. 4°. A, 2 leaves : B—O 2 in fours : A Short Description of the Western Iles of Scotland lying in the Deucalidon Sea, being aboue 300. Also the Iles in Orkenay, and Schetland or Hethland. A—C 2 in fours, without a regular title, with the colophon : Printed at London by Simon Stafford, and a Table of Errata to the Monipennie.

It appears as if the second part had been printed subsequently as an afterthought in a different type and from a different press, and the occasion taken to correct the mistakes in the first portion, although there is no external indication of the work to which the table refers.

MONK.

The Capuchin Or The Pharisaisme, Superstition and Fanaticisme of Popery Discovered by the (Pretended Sanctity, but) real Foolery and Knavery appearing in the Lives of the strictest Monks. By a Person of Quality. London, Printed for James Collins, ... MDCLXXV. 8°, A—K 7 and Aa—Dd 2 in eights.

This appears to be the same work as that of 1671. The person of quality translated it from the French, and dedicates it, as in the edition of 1671, to Anthony, Lord Ashley, Viscount St. Giles. The second portion, commencing with a headline on Aa, is here called "The Monk's Hood, &c."

MONTAGUE, RICHARD, *Bishop of Chichester.*
A Proclamation, for the suppressing of a Booke, intituled, *Appello Cæsarem,* or, *An Appeale to Cæsar.* Imprinted at London by Bonham Norton, and Iohn Bill, ... M.DC.XXVIII. A broadsheet.

MONTAGUE, THE HONOURABLE WALTER, *Abbot of Nanteuil.*
Miscellanea Spiritualia: Or, Devout Essayes: The Second Part. 1. Tim. 1. 16. *Ideo Misericordiam* ... London, Printed for John Crook, Gabriell Bedell, and Partners, and are to be sold at the Ship in St. Pauls Church-yard, ... 1654. [Oct. 31, 1653.] 4°. A—C 2 in fours: B—Ll in fours. Dedicated to Queen Henrietta Maria from Nanteuil, August 1, 1653. *B. M.*

MONTANUS, REGINALDUS GONSALVIUS.
De Heylighe Spanische inquisitie ... door Reynaldo Gonsalvo Montan ... uv eerst in onser Nederlanscher sprake door M. Mavlvmpertvm Taphæa, ... ouergheset ... [Col.] Ghedruct tot Londen, by Ian Day, In 't laer onssleeren. 1569. Sm. 8°. *, 8 leaves: A—Aa in eights, Aa 8 blank. With a large folding plate between B and C representing an auto da fe.

Day the printer appears to have been connected with the Dutch residents in London, more especially the congregation in Austin Friars.

MONTGOMERY, ALEXANDER.
The Cherrie and the Slae. Compyled into meeter, By Captaine Alexander Montgomerie. Edinbvrgh Printed by Iohn Wreittoun. 1636. Sm. 8°, A—D in eights. *B. M.*

The Flytting betwixt Montgomerie and Polwart. Newlie corrected and ammended. Edinbvrgh. Printed by the heirs of Thomas Finlason, for Iohn Wood, and are to be sold in his shop on the South side of the high Street, a little aboue the Croce. 1629. 4°, A—C in fours, a leaf of D, and the title-page.

In R. S. Turner's sale, June 1888, No. 1970, was a 4° MS. copy of this poem, supposed to be earlier than any known printed one. It was entitled: The Flyting against the Laird of Pollart.

MORE, GEORGE, *Esquire.*
Principles for Yong Princes: Collected out of sundry Authors, by George More Esquire. ... London, Printed by Nicholas Okes dwelling neare Holborne Bridge, 1611. 12°, A—H 9 in twelves, A 1 blank. *B. M.*

MORGAN, SIR THOMAS.
A True and Just Relation of Maj. Gen. Sir Thomas Morgan's Progress in France and Flanders, With the Six Thousand English, In the Years 1657 and 1658; At the Taking of Dunkirk and other Important Places. As it was Deliver'd by the General himself. London: Printed for J. Nutt, near Stationers-hall, 1699. 4°, 12 leaves, or 6 leaves preceded by C in fours and D, 2 leaves.

Facing the title is *An Advertisement* setting forth the circumstances which led to the publication.

MOSELLANUS, PETRUS.
Paedologia Petri Mosellani Protegensis, in puerorum usum conscripta & aucta, Dialogi 37. Dialogi Pveriles Christophori Hegendorphini XII. lepidi æque ac docti. An. 1532. [Col.] Londini apud Wynandum de Worde. An. M.D.XXXII. Mens. Iunij. 8°, A—D in eights. Italic letter. With the printer's device on D 8 *verso* and the title enclosed in a border.

The copy here employed was obligingly pointed out to me by Mr. H. Newton Stevens.

MURDER.
Murther upon Murther: Being a Full and True Account of the Barbarous and Bloody Murther of Mr Jarvis Cluff, Committed by Mr James Smith, Son to Judge Smith of the Middle Temple; ... Also, The Apprehending and Taking Thomas Withers and William Edwards, (discovered to be the Persons that Murthered the Drover and Penny-Post Man at Uxbridge) ... London, Printed for J. Johnson, near Fleet-street. 1703. 8°, 4 leaves.

N.

N. M.
The Dutch Way of Toleration, Most proper for our English Dissenters. Written at the request of a Friend ... The Second Edition. London, Printed in the Year, 1690. 4°. A, 2 leaves : B—D in fours.

N. N.
Pleydoy Gedaen by N. N. Advocaet. In saake van N. N. gedaegden, in cas van falsiteyt, ter ceure. Op ende jegens N. N. Bailjau, In Olley Eysscher, ter andere zijde. Anno 1677. 8°, 10 leaves.

NAPIER, JOHN, *Lord Napier of Merchistoun.*
A Plaine Discouery of the whole Reuelation of Saint Iohn: set doune in two treatises : ... Set foorth By Iohn Napeir L. of Marchistoun younger. Whereunto are annexed certaine Oracles of Sibylla, ... Edinbvrgh Printed by Robert Walde-graue, printer to the Kings Majestie. 1593. Cum Priuilegio Regali. 4°, A—T in fours. Dedicated to James VI. from Merchistoun, Jan. 29, 1593.

Ouvertvre de tovs les Secrets de l'Apocalypse ov Revelation de S. Iean. Par deux traités ... Par Iean Napeir (c.a.d.) Nonpareil Sieur de Merchiston, reneue par lui-mesme : Et mise en François par Georges Thomson Escossois. ... A La Rochelle, ... 1602. 4°. ă and č, 4 leaves each, ŏ 4 with a folded table : A—IIh in fours, and a leaf of Ii. With the dedication to James VI. subscribed *Iean Nonpareil*.

Mirifici Logarithmorum Canonis descriptio, Ejusque usus, in utraque Trigonometria, ... Authore ac Inventore, Ioanne Nepero, Barone Merchistonii, &c. Scoto. Edinbvrgi, Ex officinâ Andreæ Hart Bibliopolæ, cɪɔ.ɪɔc.xɪv. 4°, A—H in fours, and a leaf of I : *Tables*, a—l in fours, and a leaf of m. Dedicated to Prince Charles.

Mirifici Logarithmorvm Canonis Descriptio, Ejusque usus, in utraque Trigonometria ; vt etiam in omni Logistico Mathematica, ... explicatio. Accesservnt Opera Posthvma ... Autore ac Inventore Ioanne Nepero, Barone Merchistonii, &c. Scoto. Edinbvrgi, Excvdebat Andreas Hart. Anno 1619. 4°. General title, 1 leaf : A—H in fours : I, 1 leaf : *Tables*, a—l in fours, and m, 1 leaf : *Logarithmorvm Constrvctio*, with a new title, A—I 2 in fours.

A Description of the Admirable Table of Logarithmes. With A Declaration of the Most Plentifvl, Easy, and speedy vse thereof in both kindes of Trigonometrie, as also in all Mathematicall calculations ... translated into English by the late learned and famous Mathematician Edward Wright. With an Addition of an Instrumentall Table ... All perused and approued by the Author, and published since the death of the Translator. London, Printed by Nicholas Okes. 1616. 12°, A—I in twelves : K, 2. Dedicated by the translator's son, Samuel Wright, to the East India Company, with the original preface and dedication of Napier preserved, a preface by H. Briggs, and verses by Richard Lever in praise of the author, work, and translator. There is a folded leaf in sign. I. Sign. A 12 is not in the copy used ; it may have been blank.

A Description of the Admirable Table of Logarithmes : With A Declaration of the most Plentifull, Easie, and Speedy vse thereof in both kinds of Trigonometry, ... translated into English by the late learned and famous Mathematician, Edward Wright. With an addition of the Instrumentall Table ... by Henrie Brigs Geometry-reader at Gresham-house in London. All perused and approued by the Authour, and published since the death of the Translator ... London, Printed for Simon Waterson. 1618. 12°, A—K in twelves, A 2-10 repeated and A 1 of first alphabet blank.

NARBOROUGH, SIR JOHN.
A Particular Narrative of the Burning in the Port of Tripoli, Four Men of War, Belonging to these Corsairs. By Sir John Narbrough, Admiral of His Majesties Fleet in the Mediterranean, on the 14th of January 167⅔. Together with an Account of his Taking afterwards Five Barks Laden with Corn, And of his farther Action on that Coast. Published by Authority. In the Savoy, Printed by Tho: Newcomb. 1676. Folio, A—B, 2 leaves each, besides the map by Hollar. *B. M.*

NAUNTON, SIR ROBERT.
Fragmenta Regalia, Or Observations on the late Queen Elizabeth, Her Times and Favorits. Written by Sir Robert Naunton, Master of the Court of Wards. Printed, Anno Dom. 1641. 4°, A—F 2 in fours.

NAVY.

By the King. A Proclamation for the better furnishing of the Navy, and increase of Shipping. Imprinted at London by Bonham Norton and Iohn Bill ... M.DC.XXVI. A broadsheet formed of two leaves.

The Humble Petition and Desires of the Commanders, Masters, Mariners Younger Brothers and Sea-men of the Shipping belonging to the River of Thames (whose names are subscribed to the number of 558), presented to the Right Honourable the Lords and Commons assembled in Parliament, on Thursday the 29 of June, 1648. Together with all their Transactions concerning a Personall Treaty with His Maiesty: And their undertaking for the timely reducing of the revolted Ships, &c. John Kersey, Clerk of Trinity-House. With deliberate Answers of the Lords and Commons ... London, Printed for George Lindsey, and are to be sold at his Shop at London-Stone, 1648. 4°, 8 leaves.

NEEDHAM, MARCHAMONT.

A Rope for Pol, Or, A Hue and Cry after Marchemont Nedham. The late Scurrulous News-writer. Being a Collection of his horrid Blasphemies and Revilings against the King's Majesty, his Person, his Cause, and his Friends, published in his weekly *Politicus* ... London, Printed in the Year, 1660. 4°, A—F in fours, F 4 blank, besides the title and preface.

NETHERLANDS.

The Declaration of the Duke of Brabant [Philip III. of Spain] proffering a truce of perpetual peace with the Netherland States. London, 1607. 4°.

> I insert provisionally this entry of a tract which occurred at a sale many years ago, and which, having unfortunately omitted to take the full particulars as usual, I have been unable to trace. The piece refers to the same political transaction as the next one.

Articles of Agreement, Concerning the Cessation of Warre, betweene the Arch-duke and the States of the vnited Prouinces. Procured by a Fryar, called Iohn of Ney, Confessour to the Arch-duke and the Infanta. Whereunto is annexed the state of other things happened about the same time. With Warres Testament, or his last Will, made at his departure out of the said Netherlands. Translated out of the Dutch. Imprinted at London for Thomas Archer, ... 1607. 8°, A—C in fours, A 1 blank. *B. M.*

Following the title is "Newes to the Reader, or to whom the buyer desires to send Newes," signed "Thine W. BB." "Warres Testament" is in verse. This is the copy under the press-mark 1077. d. 59. I have an account of a second copy printed the same year in 4°, and exhibiting the same collation.

The Trivmphs of Nassav: Or, A Description and Representation of all the Victories both by Land and Sea, granted by God to the noble, high, and mightie Lords, the Estates generall of the vnited Netherland Prouinces. Vnder the Condvct and command of his Excellencie, Prince Mavrice of Nassav. Translated out of French by W. Shvte Gent. London, Printed by Adam Islip, Anno Dom. 1613. Folio, A—3 D in fours, 3 D 4 blank, besides title, dedication by Shute to the Earls of Pembroke and Montgomery, and Shute's Preface, 3 leaves.

A Justification of the Directors of the Netherlands East-India Company. As it was delivered over unto the High and Mighty Lords the States General of the Vnited Prouinces, the 22ᵈ of July, 1686. Upon the Subject and Complaint of Mr Skelton, Envoy Extraordinary from the King of Great Britain, touching the Affair of Bantam, and other Controversies at Macassar, and on the Coast of Mallabar and at Gamron, in the Gulf of Persia. Likewise a Justification in Answer to the several Memorials lately given unto the States General by the Marquess of Abbeville, ... Translated out of Dutch by a good Friend, for the Satisfaction of all such as are Impartial Judges of the Matters now in Dispute between the two Companies. ... London, Printed for Samuel Tidmarsh, near the Royal Exchange. 1688. 8°, A—H 3 in eights.

NEVILE, HENRY.

Plato Redivivus: Or, A Dialogue concerning Government, Wherein, by Observations drawn from other Kingdoms and States both Ancient and Modern, an Endeavour is used to discover the present Politick Distemper of our Own, with the Causes, and Remedies. *Non Ego sum vates,* ... London, Printed for S. I. in the Year MDCLXXXI. 8°, A—S in eights.

NEW YORK.

The Laws & Acts of the General Assembly ... 1693–4.

> The copy described by me was formerly in the famous Somers Collection, and was the most valuable item in it. It is now, I understand, in the library of the Pennsylvania Historical Society.
>
> I take this to be the earliest book yet

found from the original press of William Bradford at New York.

NICHOLS, JOSIAH, *of Eastwell, Kent.*
An Order of Hovshold Instrvction: By which euery master of a Familie, may easily and in short space, make his whole houshold to vnderstand the principles and chiefe points of Christian Religion: without the knowledge whereof, no man can be saued. ... At London Printed by the Widowe Orwin, for Thomas Man, ... 1596. 8°, A—H 4 in eights. Dedicated to the Earl of Essex from Eastwell, 26 Feb. 1596-7. *B. M.*

NICKER.
The Nicker Nicked: Or, The Cheats of Gaming Discovered. The Third Edition. *Felix quem faciunt* ... London, Printed in the Year, 1669. 4°, A—B 2 in fours. *B. M.*

NICKLAES, HENDRICK.
*Terra Pacis. A true testification of the spirituall Lande of Peace; which is the spirituall Lande of Promyse, and the Holy Citte of Peace or the heauenly Jerusalem; and of the Holy and Spirituall People that dwell therin; as also of the Walking in the Spirit / which leadeth thervnto. Set-foorth by H. N: and by Him newly perused and more-playnly declared. Translated out of Base-almayne. [Printed abroad about 1574.] 8°, 82 leaves.

*Introdvctio. An Introduction to the holy Vnderstanding of the Glasse of Righteousnes. Wherin are vttered many notable Admonitions and Exhortations to the Good-life, also sundry discreet Warnings to beware of Destruction, and of wrong-conceiuing / and misvnderstanding any Sentences. Sett-forth by H N, and by him perused a-new, and expressed more playnly. [Printed abroad about 1575.] 8°. In fiue parts or divisions.

Herbert thinks that this book was printed at different presses, the foliation frequently recommencing. Part 1 has 40 leaves, the last blank: Part 2, the same: Part 3, 26 leaves: Part 4, 18 leaves: Part 5, 20.

*Epistolae H. N. The Principall Epistles of H. N / which he hath set-foorth through the holy Spirit of Loue, and written and sent them most-cheefly, vnto the Louers of ÿ Trueth and his Acquaintance. And are by him newly perused, and more playnly declared. Translated out of Base-almaine. [Printed abroad 1575-80.] 8°, pp. 418, besides preface and title.

See Herbert, p. 1639.

The Prophecy of the Spirit of Love; Set forth by H. N. ... London, Printed for Giles Calvert, ... 1649. 8°, A—G 4 in eights, A 1 and G 4 blank.

Evangelium Regui A joyful Message of the Kingdom. ... Imprinted at London. 1652. 8°, A—O 6 in eights.

A Figvre of the true and Spiritual Tabernacle, according to the inward Temple or House of God in the Spirit ... London, Printed for Giles Calvert, ... 1655. 8°, A—P 2 in eights, besides the label, perhaps followed by a blank.

NEGRI, FRANCESCO, *of Bassano.*
A certayne Tragedie, wrytten first in Italian, by F. N. B. entituled, Freewyl, and translated into Englishe, by Henry Cheke. 4°, black letter, A—Dd 2 in fours, besides title, dedication by Cheke to Lady Cheynie of Toddington, and his Address to the Reader, 3 leaves.

NORRIS, SYLVESTER.
An Antidote Or Treatise of Thirty Controversies: With a large Discourse of the Church, in which the soueraigne truth of Catholike doctrine, is faythfully deliuered against the pestiferous writings of all English Sectaryes. ... By S. N. Doctour of Diuinity ... Permissu Superiorum, M.DC.XXII. 4°. *, 4 leaves: **, 4 leaves: ***, 2 leaves: A—Tt in fours: A—Qq 2 in fours: *Third Book*, with separate title, A—Ff in fours, besides 4 leaves marked * with a dedication to the King.

The first and second parts are inscribed to the students of Oxford and Cambridge.

NORTHUMBERLAND.
A Particular Relation of the Taking of Newcastle; Expressing the faire meanes which were used to gaine the Towne; the Summons sent vnto them, and the many Letters past betwixt his Excellency the Earl of Leven, Lord Generall of the Scottish Armies, and them, with the mannor of Storming the Towne; the rendring of the Castle, and their condition since: Together with a Letter from the Committee with the Scottish Army to the Committee of both Kingdomes here; All sent by an Expresse to the Commissioners of Scotland, Octob, 29. 1644. Published by Authority. London, Printed for Robert Bostock, and Samuel Gellibrand, dwelling in Paules Church-Yard. 1644. 4°. A, 2 leaves, A blank: B—E in fours, E 4 blank.

NORTHUMBERLAND, *Archdeaconry of.*
Articles to be Enqvired of By the Ministers and Church-wardens of every Parish

within the Arch-Deaconry of Northumberland. Which are given in Charge, in the Annual Visitation of William Turner B.D. And Arch-Deacon of that Jurisdiction. . . . York Printed by Alice Broad at the Sign of the Printers Press in Stonegate. 4", 4 leaves.

NORWICH, *Diocese of.*
Articles to be enquired of within the Dioces of Norwiche, in the Metropoliticall visitation of the most reuerend father in God, Mathew, by the prouidence of God, Arche-byshop of Canterbury, Primate of all Englande, and Metropolitan, In the yeare of our Lord God, M.D.LXVII. Imprinted at London by Reginalde Wolfe. Anno Domini. M.D.LXVII. 4", 6 leaves. Black letter.

Articles to be Inqvired of within the Dioces of Norwich, in the ordinary visitation of the reuerend Father in God, Samvel, Lord Bishop of Norwich. Anno Domino 1620. & Translationis suæ primo. Imprinted at London 1620. 4", A—B in fours. Black letter.

Articles to be Inqvired of within the Dioces of Norwich: In the first Visitation of the R. Reverend Father in God, Matthew, Lord Bishop of Norwich. Printed at London, by Richard Badger. 1636. 4", A—C 2 in fours.

Articles of Enquiry and Direction for the Diocese of Norwich, In the first Visitation of the Reverend Father in God, Richard Mountagu Bishop of that Diocese, Anno Dom. 1638. Et translationis suæ primo. ¶ This Book of Articles being extremely negligently printed at London (which Impression I disavow) I was forced to review, and have it printed again at Cambridge. *R. Norv.* [Cambridge, 1638.] 4", A—B in fours, and a leaf of C.

Articles to be Enquired of in the Diocese of Norwich in the First Visitation of the Right Reverend Father in God, Edward Lord Bishop of Norwich. London, Printed by T. R. for G. T. . . . 1662. 4", A—B in fours, and the title.

NOWELL, ALEXANDER, *Dean of St. Paul's.*
Catechismus Parvus Pueris, Primum Latine qui edificatur, Proponendus in Scholis. Londini, Typis Andrew Clark, . . . 1675. 8", A—B in eights. With Nowell's dedication to the prelates.

O.

O. D.
A Perswasion to Loyalty, Or The Subjects Dvtie: Wherein is proved that resisting or deposing of Kings (under what specious pretences soever couched) is utterly unlawfull. Collected by D. O. Dedicated to all dutifull Subjects. London, Printed. 1642. 4", A—E 2 in fours.

OLDE, JOHN.
*The acquital or purgation of the moost catholyke Christen Prince Edwarde the vi. Kyng of Englande, . . . agaynst al suche as blasphemously and traitorously infame hym or the sayd Church, of heresie or sedicion. . . . [Col.] Emprinted in Waterford the . 7. daye of Nouembre. 1555. Sm. 8", F in eights.
The imprint is doubtless fictitious, and the name, perhaps, equally so.

ORDER.
*Here followeth the ordre, or Trayne of Warre that a prynce or heed Captayne ought to take . . . [Col.] Here endeth the Trayne or Policye of warre.
Go lytell treatyse, and do thy tale tell
To me of honour, & thus worship wyl wyn,
Pray the to pardon thy rude style & consell
Youth boldly valyauntly, exceut [exort] to begyn.

Imprynted by me Robert Wyer in Seynt Martyns parysshe at Charynge Crosse. Imprynted for John Gowgh Cum priuilegio Regali ad imprimendum solum. With woodcuts.
Described by Herbert from a titleless copy in the possession of Thomas Martin of Palgrave. He gives no collation.

ORDINANCE.
Thys is a true copy of the ordynance made in the tyme of the reygne of kynge Henry the . iii. . . . [Col.] Imprynted at London by Robert Toye. 8", 8 leaves or A in eights. With the crowned Tudor arms on the title.

This is probably only the last of a series of twelve similar tracts printed together with a general title. But I have not seen a copy printed by Toye.

**ORDINARIES.
Ordynaries. [This is the running title on the *recto* of the last leaf; on the *verso* we find:] Imprynted at London in Fletestrete by me Elysabeth Pykerynge, late wyfe to Robert Redman dwellynge at the sygne of the George nexte to saynt Dunstones churche: The yere of our Lorde God. M.D.xli. The xxxi. day of Ianvary ... 8⁰.

Described by Dibdin, iii. 248, *note*, from a fragment of the last leaf only in his own possession; this is marked fol. C. lxix.

ORDINARY.
**The Ordynarye of Chrysten Men. [Col.] Emprynted in the Cyte of London in the flete strete in the sygne of the sonne by Wynkyn de Worde the yere of our lorde M.CCCCC.ij. 4⁰, tt in sixes.

ORIGEN.
**Omelia Origeīs. [Col.] Impressū in alma ciuitate london. Ad rogatū Magistri will'mi Mexynnā socij collegij Ricardi whitington. In abchirche lane. [by William Faques.] 8⁰, 10 leaves. *Althorp.*

ORINOPOLUS.
Orinopolus, Or, Dreams Interpreter. Being Several Aphorisms upon the Physiognomy of Dreams made into verse Some of which receive a general Interpretation: And others of them have respect to the Course of the Moon in the Zodiack. To which is added Several Physiognomical Characters of Persons of different Humours and Inclinations. After which follows the Praise of Ale. And lastly, The Wheel of Fortune, or Pithagoras Wheel. London. Printed by Tho. Dawks, 1680. 8⁰, A—G 5 in eights, A 1 with half title and A 2 with a frontispiece. *H. Stopes, Esq.*

OSBURNE, RICHARD.
A Trve Coppy of two severall Letters sent by Mr Richard Osburne (late Attendant on his Majestie in Carisbrooke Castle,) Touching a designe to poyson his Majesty: Which Letters were read in [the] House of Peeres June 19. 1648. Printed 21. June 1648. 4⁰, 4 leaves.

OVIDIUS NASO, PUBLIUS.
Ovid's Heroicall Epistles. Englished by W. S.

*Veniam pro laude peto.
——nunc mitibus
mutare quæro Tristia.*

London, Printed by I. D. and are to be sold by Michael Sparke Iunior in Greene Arbour. 1639. 8⁰, A—N in eights. Dedicated to "the Vertvovs Ladies and Gentlewomen of England." With a series of engravings pasted on the leaves, where blank spaces were left for them by the printer, one to each Epistle. *B. M.*

All Ovids Elegies: 3 Bookes. By C. M. Epigrams by I. D. At Middlebovrgh. [About 1640.] 8⁰, A—F in eights. *B. M.*

Notwithstanding what has been said to the contrary, this book seems to have been printed in Holland.

P.

P. H.
The Manifold Miseries of Civill Warre and Discord in a Kingdome: By the Examples of Germany, France, Ireland, and other places. With some memorable Examples of Gods Iustice, in punishing the Authors and Causers of Rebellion and Treason. By H. P. London Printed for George Lindsey, July the second. 1642. 4⁰, 4 leaves.

P. H., *of Lincoln's Inn.*
An Answer to the Poysonovs sediciovs Paper of Mr. David Jenkins. London, Printed for Robert Bostock, ... 1647. 4⁰, 4 leaves.

P. H., *Marquis de C.*
The Politicks of France. With Reflections on the 4th and 5th Chapters: Wherein he censures the Roman Clergy and the Hugonots; by the Sr. l'Orme-greguy. London, Printed, and are to be sold by Thomas Orrell. ... 1680. 12⁰. A, 5 leaves, A 1 blank: B— in twelves: A—E 6 in twelves.

The first portion ended imperfectly in the copy used on I 12.

P. J.

The Copie of a Letter Written unto Sir Edward Deering, lately put out of the House, and committed to the Tower, February 2. 1641. His Bookes censured to be burnt by the common Executioner, for his strange unadvised, and sudden differing from himselfe, and opposing the whole House. Which Letter was sent as is supposed by a Worthy Member of the House of Commons, Feb. 4. 1641. London, Printed for Iohn Thomas. 1641. 4°, 4 leaves.

> The letter is dated from Covent Garden, Feb. 4, 1641.

PACE, RICHARD.
**Oratio Richardi Pacei in Pace nuperrime composita et fœdere percusso : inter invictissimum Angliae regem, et Francorum regem christianissimum in æde diui Pavli Londini habita. [Col.] Impressa Londini anno verbi incarnati M.D.XVIII. idibus Nonembris per Richardum Pynson regium impressorem cum priuilegio a rege indulto ne quis hanc orationem intra biennium in regno Angliae imprimat aut alibi impressam et importatam in eodem regno Angliae vendat. 4°. The title is within a compartment of naked boys.

PARLIAMENT.
**The Cessyōs of Parlyamēt of the imperyall Realme of Englande, And the assemblaunce of the same. [Col.] Translated out of latyn in to Englysshe by me Antony Bustarde, felowe of Lyons Inne. Imprynted by me Robert Wyer, dwellynge in saynte Martyns parysshe, in the bysshop of Norwytche rentes. . . . Sm. 8°, A—G in fours.

> On the reverse of the title is St. John without the eagle, and four hexameters and pentameters beneath.

A Declaration of the Commons Assembled in Parliament. For bringing to condigne punishment, those that have raised false and scandalous Rumors against the House, how that they intend to assesse every Mans Pewter, and lay Excizes upon other Commodities. . . . As also further directions to his Excellence the Earle of Essex Generall of the Army, and to the Committee for his assistance in the Army, appointed by both Houses of Parliament. London, Printed for Richard Best, October, 10. 1642. 4°, 4 leaves.

Certain Propositions made by the High Covrt of Parliament, To the Trained Bands, in, and about the Citie of London, October 17. 1642. For the drawing out of fiftie in a Company to goe and ioyne with other Counties, to stop the Cavaleers for comming to London. . . . Whereunto is added diverse weightie Reasons, shewing that this present Warre cannot continue long. London : Printed for John Franke, October 21. 1642. 4°, 4 leaves.

A Declaration of the Lords and Commons . . . That no Ships, Barques, or other Vessels shal from henceforward make any Voyage to New-Castle, for the fetching of Coales, or any other Commodity, untill that Towne shall be reduced into such hands, as shall declare themselves for King and Parliament . . . Ian. 16. Printed for Lawrence Blacklocke at Temple Bar. 1642. 4°, 4 leaves.

An Ordinance of the Commons Assembled in Parliament : In Vindication of Thomas Brown, Maximillian Bard, &c. Commissaries for seizing of Horses, Mares and Geldings, for the Parliaments service . . . London, Printed for Edw. Husbands, . . . May 17. 1643. 4°, 4 leaves.

An Ordinance of the Lords and Commons Assembled in Parliament, For the speedy setting forth of certaine Ships (in all points furnished for War) to prevent the bringing over of Souldiers, Money, Ordnance, and other Ammunition from beyond the Sea, to assist the King, against the Parliament in England. . . . London, Printed for Iohn Wright in the Old Bayly. Decemb. 12. 1642. 4°, 4 leaves.

An Ordinance of Parliament, Concerning The Subsidie of Tonnage and Poundage. London, Printed by T. Badger for Lawrence Blaikelock, and are to [be] sold at [Temple] Barre in Fleet-streect, 1642. 8°, A in eights, first and last leaves blank : *A Subsidie granted to the King*, with a separate title, 9 leaves : *Ordinance for the Continuance of the Subsidy*, with a separate title, 3 leaves ;

An Order of the Lords and Commons . . . for the Regulating of Printing, and for suppressing the great late abuses and frequent disorders in Printing many false, Scandalous, Seditious, Libellous and unlicensed Pamphlets, to the great defamation of Religion and Government. Also, authorizing the Master and Wardens of the Company of Stationers to make diligent search, seize and carry away all such Books as they shall finde Printed, or reprinted by any man having no lawfull interest in them, . . . London, Printed for I. Wright in the Old-baily, Iune 16. 1643. 4°, 4 leaves.

An Ordinance of the Lords and Commons ... Whereby All Vintners are required to bring in the Money due for the half Excise of all Wines remaining in their hands, at, or before the eleventh of November last: According to two former Ordinances of Parliament, of the eleventh of September, and the first of October. London, Printed by Richard Cotes, and John Raworth. 1643. 4°, 4 leaves. *H. Stopes, Esq.*

An Ordinance of the Lords and Commons ... Concerning all Brewers and Makers of Beere, Ale, Cider, or Perry, for payment of the Excise imposed by an Ordinance of Parliament before the delivering thereof, upon paine of forfeiture of double the value of the Said Commodities ... London, Printed by Richard Cotes and John Raworth. 1643. [October 17.] 4°, 4 leaves. Black letter. *H. Stopes, Esq.*

Die Martis, 28 Novemb. 1643. Additionall Articles of the Lords and Commons in Parliament, to the Ordinance of Excise. ... London, Printed by Richard Cotes and Joh. Raworth. 4°, 4 leaves. *H. Stopes, Esq.*

An Ordinance of the Lords and Commons ... for continuance of the Subsidy of Tonnage and Poundage, together with the Book of Rates, in full force and power from the 25. of March 1645. untill the 26. of March 1647. Also for Repealing and making void the Ordinances of Parliament prohibiting the importation of Currans. [21 Feb. 1644-5.] 8°, 8 leaves, of which the earlier are numbered. Without a title.

[An Ordinance of Parliament in respect to abuses in the importation of certain goods. 14 April, 1645.] At the end occurs: London, Printed for Laurance Blaicklock, ... 1645. 8°, A in fours. Black letter.

An Ordinance of the Lords and Commons ... for the continuance of Tonnage and Poundage. [13 March 1646-7.] 8°, 4 leaves. Without a title-page.

An Ordinance of the Lords and Commons ... For the establishing of the Subsidy of Tonnage and Poundage, together with the Book of Rates, from the 26. of March 1648. untill the 26. of March, 1651. ... London. Printed for Lawrence Blaiklock, ... 1647. 8°, A—C in eights: *The Rates*, B—L 4 in eights.

The Parliament-Porter: Or, The Doorekeeper of the House of Commons. Truly informing the Kingdome of the plots and Stratagems of the headlesse thing sitting at Westminster under the name of a Parliament: With the most speciall intelligence from London, the Army, and the Navy. [4 stanzas of four lines.] Printed in the Yeer, 1648. 4°, 4 leaves.

This is called No. 4.

The Parliament-kite. Or the Tell-tale Bird, Communicating Intelligence from all parts of the Kingdome, touching all Affaires, Humours, Conditions and Designes. Especially from Westminster, Scotland, Wales, Ireland, and the Head-Quarters. From Thursday July 20. to Thursday, July 27. 1648. [4 stanzas.] Printed in the Yeer of the Saints Fear. 1648. 4°, 4 leaves.

This is No. 10.

England at her easement, Evacuating those Clods at Westminster, who depressed her stomack worse then the Night-Mare, and had almost strangled her. The names of her Doctors, the costivenesse of her body, ... ever since the Saints militant began the Siege at Colchester, that the Navy revolted from the Rebells, and Sir Marmaduke Langdale joyned with the Scots. ... Printed in the Yeare. 1648. 4°, 4 leaves.

A Declaration of the Parliament of England, Upon the marching of the Armie into Scotland. London, Printed by William Du-gard, by the Appointment of the Council of State, Anno 1650. 4°, A—D in fours, D 4 blank.

A Full Declaration of the true State of the Secluded Members Case. In Vindication of Themselves, and their Priviledges, and of the respective Counties, Cities and Boroughs for which they were elected to serve in Parliament, against the Vote of their Discharge, published in print, Jan. 5. 1659. by their Fellow Members. Compiled and published by some of the Secluded Members, who could meet with safety and conveniencie, without danger of a possible surprize by Redcoats. ... London Printed, and are to be sold by Edward Thomas, ... 1660. 4°, A—H in fours.

Some Considerations upon the Question, Whether The Parliament is Dissolved By it's Prorogation for 15 Months? The two Statutes upon which this Question depends are, 4. Edw. 3. Cap. 14. ... 36. Edw. 3. Cap. 10. ... Printed in the

Year, 1676. 4°, A—D 2 in fours, D 2 blank.

Qu. Whether the King, Lords and Commons now Assembled, be a Legal Parliament, and may Act as such? [Col.] Edinburgh, Reprinted in the Year 1689. 4°, 4 leaves.

Several Queries Relating to the present Proceedings in Parliament; More especially recommended to the Consideration of the Bishops. [1689.] 4°, 4 leaves.

PARSONS, COLONEL.

A New Book of Cyphers; More Compleat and Regular than any yet Extant: Wherein the whole Alphabet (twice over) Consisting of 600 Cyphers Is variously Changed, Inter - woven, and Revised. With the Coronets of England, By Allowance of the Earl Marshal . . . Composed by Colonel Parsons. London Printed for the Author, in the Old Palace Westminster . . . MDCCIV. Obl. 4°, 52 numbered leaves, besides title, &c., 4 leaves.

PARSONS, ROBERT.

*A brief discours contayning certayne reasons, why catholiques refuse to goe to church. Written by a learned and vertuous man, to a friend of his in England, and dedicated by I. H. to the queenes most excellent maiestie. Imprinted at Doway by John Lyon. With privilege. 8°, 88 leaves, including 15 of Preface and two blanks at end.

> Herbert says, by mistake, 70 leaves. The running title is: The 1. Part contayning Reasons of Refusal. No more seems to be known. Written under the name of John Howlett.

*A Booke of Christian Exercise . . . Imprinted at London by I. Iackson and Ed. Bollifant, for Iohn Wight, and are to be solde at the great North doore of Paules. 1586. 12°, Ee 10 in twelves. Dedicated to Edwin, Archbishop of York.

> The preface is directed from Bolton-Percy, July 9, 1584.

Leicestors Common-Wealth fully Epitomiz'd. Conceived, spoken, and published with most earnest protestation of all dutifull good-will, and affection towards this Realme, for whose good onely it is made common to many. With a pleasant discription of the first Originall of the Controversies betwixt the two Houses of Yorke, and Lancaster. Printed in the yeare, 1641. 4°, A—B in fours.

> A MS. note in an early hand says: "A most virulent invective against ye E. of Leicester."

PATERNOSTER.

*A deuout treatise vpon the Pater noster / made fyrst in latyn by the most famous doctour mayster Erasmus Rotorodamus, and tourned in to englisshe by a yong vertuous and wel lerned gentylwoman of . xix. yers of age. [Col.] ¶ Thus endeth the exposicion of the Pater noster. Imprinted at London in Fletestret / in the house of Thomas Berthelet nere to the condite / at the signe of Lucrece. Cum priuilegio a rege indulto. 4°, a—f in fours. With a preface by Richard Hyrde to the translator, Frances S., dated from Chelcheth [Chelsea], October 1, 1524.

*The Pater Noster / the Crede / & the commaundements of God in Englyshe with many other Godly lessons. Ryght necessary for youth and all other to lerne and know accordynge to the commaundement, and Iniunctions: gyuen by thauctorite of the kynges hyghnes: through this his realme. 1538. [Col.] God save the kynge. ¶ Prynted at London in Paules Churche yarde, at the sygne of the maydens heed: by me Thomas Petyt. 8°, H in eights.

PATRICK, ST.

Saint Patricks Pvrgatory. [This is a headline on B 1 of a volume, of which I have not seen any other copy hitherto. London, about 1635.] 4°, [A]—S in fours. B. M.

> The authorship is doubtful; but it seems likely that it was written by the William Stuart who subscribes a letter to Viscount Ely, Chancellor of Ireland, and the other Lords Justices, stating that he had received a letter from Lord Balfour, directed to himself and others, ordering them to seize the Cave to His Majesty's use. The Order follows, dated Sept. 13, 1632, and is succeeded by a letter from the Bishop of Clogher to Archbishop Usher, describing the place. His lordship speaks of the Cave as "a poure beggerly hole, made with some stones, layd together with mens hands without any great Art."

PAYNELL, THOMAS.

**The Piththy and moost notable sayinges of al Scripture, . . . [Col.] Imprinted at London in the Flete-strete at the signe of the Rose Garland by me Wyllyam Copland, for Rychard Iugge. Sm. 8°. In two parts. Part 1, 78 leaves + 12 leaves of Table: Part 2, 90 leaves + 12 leaves of Table.

PENKETH, THOMAS, *of Warrington.*

[Questiones Quodlibitales.] At the end, before the *Additiones*, occurs: Explicit feliciter. M.CCCC.LXXIIII. [Venetiis, N. Jenson et Socii.] Folio, 111 leaves. In two columns. Without signatures, catchwords, and foliation.

PENN, WILLIAM.
Some Fruits of Solitude, In Reflections and Maxims Relating to the Conduct of Human Life. The Second Edition. Printed at London, and Re-printed at Edinburgh, 1694. 12°, A—F in sixes.

PENRUDDOCK, JOHN.
The Triall of the honourable Colonel John Penruddock of Compton in Wiltshire, and his Speech; Which he delivered the day before he was beheaded in the Castle of Exon, being the 16. day of May 1655. to a Gent. whom he desired to publish them after his death. Together with his prayer upon the Scaffold, and the last Letter he received from his vertuous Lady, with his Answer to the same. Also the Speech of that Piously resolved Gent. Hugh Grove of Chisenbury in the parish of Enford, and County of Wilts, Esq.; beheaded there the same day. Printed by order of the Gent. intrusted. 1655. 4°. A—C 2 in fours. *B. M.*

The speech of Hugh Grove of Chisenbury or Chassenbury occupies the recto of C 2.

PERCEFOREST.
La Treselegāte Delicieuse Mellifluc et tresplaisante Histoire du tresnoble victorieux & excellentissime Roy Perceforest Roy de la grant Bretaigne / fundateur du Franc palais / et du Temple Soucrain dieu / Anecques les meruciluusses enterprinses / faitz / & aduētures / du tresbelliqueulx Tadiffer / Roy Descosse. Lesquelz L'ēpereur Alexandre le grant couronna Roys soubz son obeissance. . . . Nouellemēt Imprime a Paris. Mil. v. cēs. xxxi[—xxxii.] Folio. 6 volumes. In two columns. Without cuts, except a large one on back of title of vol. v. Vol. i.—C. 4 leaves: a—z in sixes, followed by two sheets of six and one of eight: Vol. ii.—aa, 3 leaves: A—z in sixes, followed by a sheet of six and another of eight: Vol. iii.—Title and Table, 2 leaves: aa — z[z] in sixes, followed by two sheets of six: AA, 6 leaves; BB, 3: Vol iv.—Title and Table, 2 leaves: A—Z in sixes, followed by two sheets of six, last leaf blank: Vol. v.— Title and Table, 2 leaves: A—T in sixes, T 6 blank: Vol. vi.—Title and Table, 2 leaves: A—V in sixes: X, 4.

Sotheby's, June 1888 (Turner, 2752).

†PERIN, F[RATER] WILLIAM, *Prior of the Friars Preachers of Great St. Bartholomew's in Smithfield.*
Spirituall exercyses and goostly medita-tions, and a neare waye to come to perfection and lyfe contemplative, . . . Neulye Imprynted at Caen by Peter le Chandelier. Sm. 8°, It in eights: A right fruitefull monitor, concerning the ordre of a good Christian mans life. Made by the famouse Doctour Collecte, some time Deane of Poules. 4 leaves.

PERSECUTION.
De Persecvtione Anglicana Commentariolvs, A Collegio Anglicano Romano, Hoc Anno Domini cIɔ Iɔ xxcII. in Vrbe editus, & iam denuo Ingolstadii excusus: . . . Sm. 8°, A—G 6 in twelves.

PETAVIUS, DIONISIUS.
The History of the World: Or, An Account of Time. Compiled by the Learned Dionisius Petavius. And continued by Others, To the Year of our Lord 1659. Together with A Geographicall Description of Europe, Asia, Africa, and America. London, Printed by J. Streater, and are to be sold by Luke Fawne, . . . MDCLIX. Folio, A—5 V in fours, besides title and portrait.

Apparently translated by R. P.

PETER, JOHN, *M.D.*
A Philosophical Account of this Hard Frost. . . . Written in Answer to a Letter of a Person of Quality, and at his Command made publick for the Common Good. London, Printed for Sam. Smith . . . 1684. 4°, B in fours, a leaf of C, and the title. Dated from Lewisham, Feb. 2, 1683-4.

PEYTON, SIR EDWARD, *Knight and Baronet.*
The Divine Catastrophe of the Kingly Family of the House of Stuarts: Or, A Short History of the Rise, Reign, and Ruine Thereof. . . . London, Printed for Giles Calvert . . . 1652. 8°. A, 4 leaves, A 1 blank: B—K in eights, followed by three leaves in larger type (pp. 145-9). Dedicated to the Parliament.

There are no pp. 143-4. The author calls himself on the title "a diligent observer of those times."

PEYTON, THOMAS, *of Lincoln's Inn.*
The Glasse of Time, In the Two First Ages. Diuinely handled, By Thomas Peyton of Lincolnes Inne Gent. London, Printed by Bern[a]rd Alsop. 1623. 4°. Title and dedication to King James, 2 leaves: A—L 3 in fours [L 4 blank]: M 2—Z 3 in fours. With woodcuts.

In this issue a printed title dated 1623 has been substituted for the engraved one, and the separate one to Part 2 cancelled. It is the third and last issue of the book.

Sotheby's, Jaunuary 28, 1887, No. 991.

PHAER, THOMAS.
*The boke of chyldren. The regyment of lyfe. A treatyse of the pestilence. [Col.] Imprynted at London on the south syde of Aldermary churche by Edwarde Whytchurche. 1544. Cum priuilegio ad imprimendum solum per septennium. Sm. 8°.

PHILANAX MISOPAPPUS.
Rawleigh Redivivus; Or The Life & Death of the Right Honourable Anthony Late Earl of Shaftsbury. Humbly dedicated to the Protesting Lords. By Philanax Misopappus. *Virtuti Pompeii quæ potest Par Oratio inveniri?* Cicero. London, Printed for Thomas Malthus at the Sun in the Poultrey. 1683. 8°, A—P in eights, concluding with an Elegy and Epitaph. With a portrait.

> The dedication to the Duke of Monmouth is signed *S. N.*

PHILANAX VERAX.
A Letter to the King, when Duke of York, Perswading him to return to the Protestant Religion, wherein the chief Errors of the Papists are exposed, and the Tendency of their Doctrines to promote Arbitrary Government, proved. By an Old Cavalier, and Faithful Son of the Church of England, as Establisht by Law. [Edinburgh, 1688.] 4°, 4 leaves.

PHILOLOGUS PHILOMUSUS.
A Letter from The Master of a Private School, to a Reverend Member of the General-Assembly, concerning the Education of Children, &c. [Edinburgh, 1704.] 4°, 4 leaves.

> The letter is subscribed *Philologus Philomusus.*

PHILPOT, JOHN, *Archdeacon of Winchester*.
†The examinacion of the constaunt Martir of Christ, John Philpot Archediacon of Winchestre at sondry seasons in the tyme of his sore emprisonment, conuented and bayted, as in these particular tragedies folowyng, it maye (not only to the christen instruction, but also to the mery recreacion of the indifferent reader) most manifestly appeare. [London, Henry Sutton, about 1560.] Sm. 8°, Q in eights: An Apologie of Johan Philpot written for spitting upon an Arrian, with an invective against the Arrians (the very natural chyldren of Antichrist), A—C 6 in eights.

PHIORAVANTI, LEONARDO, *Cavaliere, M.D.*
Three Exact Pieces of Leonard Phioravant Knight and Doctor in Physick, Viz. His Rationall Secrets, and Chirurgery, Reviewed and Revised. Together with a Book of Excellent Experiments and Secrets, . . . Whereunto is annexed Paracelsus his One hundred and fourteen Experiments: With certain Excellent Works of B. G. à Portu Aquitano. Also Isaac Hollandus his Secrets concerning his Vegetall and Animall work. With Quercetanus his Spagyrick Antidotary for Gun-Shot. London Printed by G. Dawson, and are to be sold by William Nealand, at his Shop at the Sign of the Crown in Duck-lane, 1652. 4°. Title, To the Reader by J. H. and W. J., and Table, 4 leaves: A—3 O 2 in fours.

PHYSICIANS, COLLEGE OF, OF LONDON.
Statuta Collegii Medicorum Londinensium. The Statutes (or By-Laws) of the Colledge of Physicians of London. 8°, A—N 6 in eights, N 6 blank. Engl. and Latin.

> A former owner has inserted at the foot of the title the date 1687 in MS. Gibson-Craig, June 1887, No. 1595, with the book-plate of John, Earl of Hyndford.

PICCOLOMINI, ÆNEAS SYLVIUS, *afterward Pope Pius II.*
The Most Excellent Historie, of Euryalus and Lucretia. London, Printed by Thomas Creede, and are to be solde by William Barley, at his shop in Gratious streete, neare Leaden Hall. 1596. 4°, A—N in fours, A wrongly marked. *B. M.*

> Dedicated to Charles Blunt, Lord Mountjoy, by William Braunche, the translator, who speaks of himself as a young man in an Address to the Reader. In a second " to his dearest Muriphilus [*sic*]" he seems to say that this gentleman was the person who put in his way the original work.

PITTILLOH, ROBERT, *Advocate*.
The Hammer of Persecution; Or, The Mysterie of Iniquity, in the Persecution of many Good People in Scotland, under the Government of Oliver Late Lord Protector, And continued by others of the same Spirit; Disclosed, with the Remedies thereof. [Quot. from Scripture.] London, Printed for L. Chapman 1658. 4°, A—B in fours.

Scotland Mourning: Or, A New Discovery of the Sad Consequences which accompanies the Delay of the setling Judicatories in that Nation . . . [Quot. from Scripture.] London, Printed in the Year 1659. 4°, A in fours: B 1.

PLAGUE.
[A Proclamation concerning the Plague.]

F

By the Maior . . . God saue the Quene. Imprinted at London by John Daye. [16 Sept. 1574.] A broadside.
> Reprinted in *Antiq. Repertory*, 2nd ed., i. 350-1.

Orders, Thought Meet by His Maiestie, and His Privy Councell, to bee executed throughout the Counties of this Realme, in such Townes, Villages, and other places, as are, or may bee heereafter, infected with the Plague, . . . Also, An Aduice, set downe by the best learned in Physick . . . London, Printed by Bonham Norton and Iohn Bill . . . 1625. 4", A—C in fours.

Morbvs Epidemius Anni 1643. Or, The New Disease With the Signes, Causes, Remedies, &c. Published by Command. Oxford, Printed by Leonard Lichfield, . . . 1643. 4", A—D 2 in fours.

Physicall Directions in Time of the Plagve. Printed by Command from the Lords of the Councell. Oxford, Printed by Leonard Lichfield, . . . 1644. 4", 4 leaves.

PLANTER AND CYDERIST.

The Compleat Planter & Cyderist: Or, Choice Collections and Observations for the Propagating all manner of Fruit-Trees, And the most Approved Ways and Methods yet known for the Making and Ordering of Cyder, And other English-Wines. By a Lover of Planting. London: Printed for Tho. Basset. . . . 1685. 8", A—S 4 in eights. *H. Stopes, Esq.*
> The Preface is dated May 24, 1683, but is not signed.

PLATT, SIR HUGH.

Delights for Ladies, To adorne their Persons, Tables, Closets, and Distillatories: With Beuties, Banquets, Perfumes and Waters. Read, Practise, and Censure. London. Printed by William Dugard. 1656. 12", A—H in twelves. *H. Stopes, Esq.*
> This, like the other editions, contains a good deal of matter common to Plat's *Jewel-House*, 1594: it is the last appearance of the *Delights*.

PLAYERS.

A Lenten Prologue Refus'd by the Players. [About 1680.] A broadside in verse.

PLUTARCH.

The gouernaūce of good helthe, by the moste excellent phylosopher Plutarche, the moste eloquent Erasmus beynge interpretoure. [Col.] Imprynted by me Robert Wyer. Cum priuilegio regali ad imprimendum solum. 8", black letter, A—D in fours. *B. M.*
> The leaf following the title, on the back of which occur two cuts and the Argument of the work, contains an inscription headed : To the excellente mau Johñ yonge, mayster of the Roles : Erasmus of Roterodame, wyssheth healthe.

**¶ The preceptes of the excellent clerke & graue philosopher Plutarche, for the preseruation of good healthe. Londini In officina Ricardi Graftoni . . . 1543. Sm. 8", a—e in eights : f, 10, besides the dedication by John Hales, the translator, to Lord Chancellor Audley.

POLE, REGINALD, *Cardinal, and Archbishop of Canterbury.*
Reginaldi Poli Cardinalis Epistola De Sacramento Evcharistiae Nvnc primvm in Lvcem Edita, opera Deodati Qnistri Cremonensis. Cremonae, Apud Christophorum Draconium, 1584. Ex Superiorum consensu. 8". *, 4 leaves : A—G 2 in eights.

Reginaldi Poli Cardinalis Britanni, Ad Henricvm Octavvm . . . Pro Ecclesiasticæ Vnitatis Defensione, Libri Qvatvor. Nunc primùm in Catholica Germaniæ Academia typis excusi. Quis & quantus vir hic Poivs fuerit, Lectorem, verbis Pavli Manvtii, Præfatio docebit. Ingoldstadii, . . . CIƆ. IƆ. LXXXVII. 8". (:), 8 leaves : A—Z in eights : a—g 4 in eights.

POLWHEELE, ELIZABETH.

The Frolick : Or The Lawyer Cheated. An new Comedy first Coppye. Written by Mrs E. P. 1671. 4". 91 leaves, including two blanks at end.
> Dedicated to Prince Rupert by the writer, who describes herself as an unfortunate young woman haunted by poetic devils. This, the original MS., has the book-plate of Arthur Hewes, Esq., doubtless a descendant of Rupert's mistress. The play is divided into acts and scenes.

POPERY.

Fiscus Papalis. Sive, Catalogus . . . A part of the Popes Exchequer, That is A Catalogue of the Indulgences and Reliques belonging to the seauen principall Churches in Rome. Laying downe the Spiritual riches and infinite treasure which (as sure as the Pope is holy & true) are to be found in the Catholike Roman Churche, whereof the poore Heretikes in England haue not one Mite. Taken out of an antient Manuscript, and translated Together with certaine notes and Comments . . . By a Catholike Diuine. London, Printed by Nicholas Okes, for George Norton, . . . 1617. 4", A—N in fours, A 1 and N 4 blank. *B. M.*

A Mittimvs to the Ivbile at Rome : Or, The Rates of the Popes Cvstom-Hovse.

Sent to the Pope, as a New-yeeres-gift from England, this Yeere of Iubile, 1625. And faithfully published out of the old Latine Copie with Obseruations vpon the Romish Text, By William Crashawe, Batchelor of Diuinity, and Pastor at White-Chappell. London : Printed by G. P. for Iohn White, and are to be sold at his Shop, at the Signe of the Holy-Lambe, in Little Brittaine, neare Aldersgate-Street, M.DC.XXV. 4°. Title, 1 leaf : A, 4 leaves : a, 4 leaves : B—Q in fours, Q 4 blank.

The title-page is followed by an address "To the English Reader, whether Protestant, or Papist, be he a true Catholique, or a Romane. An Aduertisement to helpe his Vnderstanding in the reading of this strange Booke," after which comes "A Cauuon or direction to all Readers, touching these Romane Coynes," in which there is an attempted explanation of the value of the contemporary Papal and Italian currency. A *grosso*, a *carlino*, a *julio*, a *quattrino*, a ducat, and a florin, are enumerated. A ducat and a florin are described as equivalent, the ducat as = 10 *julios*, and the *julio* = 6d. Ten *quattrini*, again, are = a *julio*, and thirty = a *carlino* or *grosso*. On a 3–4 occur some Latin lines to the Author and the Book.

The English Pope, Or, A Discourse Wherein the late mysticall Intelligence betwixt the Court of England, and the Court of Rome is in part discouered. And withall An Account given of the true Grounds of this vnnaturall, more then civill warre. Together with an Epistle to the Reverend Divines now convened by Authority of Parliament, for consultation in matters of Religion. London, Printed for Robert Bostock, . . . 1643. 4°, A—E in fours.

PORTIFORIUM.
[Portiforium seu Breuiarium ad usum Sarum. At the end occurs :] Impressuȝ Parisiis Anno dñi M.cccc. nonagesimonono. Sm. 8°. Printed in two columns. In red and black inks. *B. M.*

Collation of this copy, which is on vellum, but which is not perfect: Calendar, 6 leaves, Table of Moveable Feasts and *Benedictio Salis et Aquæ*, 2 leaves : a—o in eights : p. 6 : *In festo sc̄c̄ trinitatis* [a headline], aa—ff in eights : A—O in eights : *Festum nominis Jesu*, aa, 8 leaves : BB, 8 leaves.

Portiforiū seu Breuiariū ad vsum ecclesie Sarisburiensis : castigatū / suppletum / marginalibus quotationibus adornatū / ac nūc primum ad verissimum ordinalis exēplar in suum ordinē a peritissimis viris redactū. Vna cum directorii (quod et Pica vocant) interpositione Adiūcto etiam indice pernecessario de festiuitatum / Dominicarū / octauarū / feriarumq̃ diuisione. Pars Estiualis. 8°. *B. M.*

Collation : †, 8 leaves with title in a border, and Calendar ; A—G in eights : a—q in eights : AA—NN in eights : OO, 10. [Col.] Impressa Parisius. Annodñi. M.ccccc. decimo. secundo kal. Februarii.

Portiforium seu Breuiariū ad vsum ecclesie Sarisburiensis castigatum suppletū marginalibus quotationibus adornatum, ac nunc primum ad verissimum ordinalis exemplar in suum ordinem a peritissimis viris redactum. Paris Hyemalis. Parisiis. Apud viduam Francisci Regnault, . . . 1554. ✠, 8 leaves : A—Y 4 in eights : *Psalterium* . . . a—t 4 in eights, t 4 recto blank, the reverse with a woodcut : *Proprium sanctorum*, A—G 4 in eights. In two columns.

POVEY, CHARLES.
A Discovery of Indirect Practices in the Coal-Trade, Or A Detection of the Pernicious Maxims and unfair Dealings of a certain Combination of Men, who affirm, *It is a Cheat to be Just, and Just to Cheat.* To which are added some Proposals for the Improvement of Trade and Navigation in general, and of the Colliery-Trade of New-Castle in particular. London, Printed by and for H. Hills, . . . 1700. 4°, B—G in fours, G 4 blank, and the title.

POWELL, COLONEL.
Colonell Powell and Col. Poyers Letter to His Highnesse the Prince of Wales ; With their Declaration, for Restoring His Majesty, the Protestant Religion, the Lawes of the Land, and the Liberty of the Subject. To which is Added *An Exhortation to the People* of England and the Citty of London. By A Welwisher of His Maiesty, The Kingdomes Peace, and the Peoples Freedome. Printed Anno Dom. 1648. 4°, 4 leaves.

POWELL, THOMAS.
The Attovrneys Academy : Or, The manner and Forme of proceeding Practically, . . . The third Impression Corrected and inlarged with additions of the Verge Court and others. . . . London Printed for Benjamin Fisher, . . . 1630. 4°. *, 2 leaves : A—Pp 2 in fours.

PRAYER.
*A good and Godly Prayer to be said at all tymes, of euery Christen, both man and woman, with a prayer vpon the Pater noster or Paraphrase vpon the same. ¶ Imprynted at London by John Alde, for Mychell Lobley. Anno. 1563. 8°, 8 leaves.

Described by Herbert from his own copy.

*The Pomander of prayer. [Col.] Imprented at London in the Fletestrete / at the sygne of the Rose garlande / by Robert Coplande. The yere of our lorde. M.CCCCC.XXX. the xxxi. day of October. 4°, A—G in fours, besides four leaves unsigned before the prologue.

**The Pomander of prayer . . . [Col.] ¶ Imprynted in Fletestrete at the sygne of the George, by Robert Redman the yere of our lorde. M.D.XXXI. 8°, A—E in eights : F, 10.

PRAYER, BOOK OF COMMON.

An Accompt of all the Proceedings of the Commissioners of both Perswasions, Appointed by his Sacred Majesty, According to Letters Patents, for the Review of the Book of Common Prayer. &c. London Printed for R. H. 1661. 4°, A—F in fours and B—Q in fours.

Advice to the Readers of the Common Prayer, and to the People Attending the same. With a Preface concerning Divine Worship. Humbly offered to consideration, for promoting the greater Decency and Solemnity in performing the Offices of Gods Publick Worship, Administred according to the Order Established by Law amongst us. By a well-meaning (though unlearned) Layick of the Church of England. London ; Printed for Randal Taylor, . . . 1682. 4°. Title and to the Reader, 2 leaves : A—G 2 in fours.

PRAYERS.

*Denoute prayers in englysshe of thactes of our redemption. [This is over a cut of the Saviour with the cross, &c. At the end occurs :] ¶ Imprynted by me Roberte Redman Cum priuilegio. 8°, A—C 4 in eights.

**The manuall of prayers, or the prymer in Englyshe, set out at length, whose contentes the reader by the prologe next after the kalender shal some perceaue, and there in shal se bretly the order of the whole boke. Set forth by Ihon late bysshoppe of Rochester, at the commaundement of the ryght honourable lorde Thomas Crūwel, lorde priuie seale, vicegerent to the kynges hyghnes. *The prayer of a ryghteous man* . . . Iacob. Cum priuilegio. [Col.] Imprynted in bottol lane, at the sygne of the whyt heare by me Ihon Mayler for Ihon Waylande, and be to sell in powles churchvarde, by Andrew Hester, at the whyt horse, and also by Mychel Lobley at the sygne of saynt Mychell. Cum priuilegio. . . . 4°. Gg in fours. With an almanac for 17 years from 1540.

A Manual of Godly Praiers, and Litanies Newly Annexed, Taken out of many famous Authours, and distributed according to the daies of the weeke. With A large and ample exercise for the Morning and Evening. Newly Augmented, . . . At Roven, By Cardin Hamillon. 1614. Sm. 8°, A—Aa 2 in twelves, besides 14 leaves with title, Preface, Advertisements, Calendar, &c.

PRECES.

*Preces priuatæ, in studiosorum gratia collectæ, & Regia authoritate approbatæ. Math. 26. Vigilate & orate . . . ¶ Londini, excudebat Gulielmus Seresius. Anno. 1568. Cum privilegio. 8°, Qq in half-sheets, besides the prefixes.

Preces in Usum Antiquæ & Celebris Scholæ Juxta D. Pauli apud Londinates. Londini, Excudebat Johannes Baker, . . . 1677. 8°, A—C in fours.

PRESBYTER.

The Character of a Presbyter, or, Sr. John Anatomized. London, Printed for John Calvin at the Presbyters Head in Pauls-Church-Yard, 1660. 4°, A—B 2 in fours.

PRESERVATIVE.

*A godly and holsom preseruatyue agaynst disperacio at all times necessarye for the soule : but then chieflye to be vsed and ministred when the deuil doth assault vs most fiercely, & deth approcheth neiste. . . . [Col.] Imprynted at London in [Lothbury] by Wyllyam Copland, for Rychard Kele. 8°, A—E in eights.

PRIESTS.

Ban Wedy i Dyany . . . A Certaine Case Extracte out of the auncient Law of Hoel da, Kyng of Wales in the yere of oure Lorde, nyne hundred and fourtene passed : whereby it maye [be] gathered that priestes had lawfully maried wyues at that tyme.

i. Cor. vii.
It is better to mary, than to burne
St. Ambrosse.
The consent of the wyll, is thys burnyng.

. . . [Col.] Imprinted at London by Roberte Crowley, dwellyng in Elye rentes in Holburne. The yere of our Lord M.D.L. Cum priuilegio ad imprimen. solum. 4°, 4 leaves. Welsh and Engl.

*A Briefe Historie of the glorious Martyrdom of 12. Reuerend Priests, executed within these twelve Monthes for Confession and defence of the Catholike faith, but vnder the false pretence of Treason, with a note of sundrie things that befel them in this life & Imprisonment : and a Pre-

face declaring their Innocencie. Printed
an : 1582. 8⁰.

> Herbert gives no collation ; a copy was in one of Thorpe's Catalogues. Among the priests were Campion and Sherwin.

PRIMER.

*This prymer of Salisbery vse / bothe in Englyshe and in Laten is set out a long without any serching. And dyuerse expedient holsome exortatyons of crysten lyuynge. The matyns, Pryme and houres ⸺ the vii ⸺ salmes the lateny the salmes of the passion with the salme *Beati immaculati* ⸺ and saynt Jeroms sauter ⸺ And a confession general Also here vnto Annexed, a fruytful werck called (the paradyse of the soul) with dyuerse deuoute meditations and prayers therin ⸺ which hath not ben vsyal sayd nor redde afore & al in englyshe. Also with Jhesus matyns with pryme ⸺ and houres and euynsonge. & cetera. ¶ Cum-gratia et Priuelegio Regali. ¶ God saue our most noble kynge the . viij. Henry with his gratious quene Anne and all theyre progeny. John Gowghe the prynter. [Col.] Here endeth this prymer with the paradyse of the soule. Imprynted by Johan Gowge dwellyng in London, in cheapsyde next Paulis gate. 1536. 8⁰. With cuts.

> The Almanac for 20 years begins with 1535. Annexed to Herbert's copy was : ¶ An exposition after the maner of a contemplacyon vpon y͡u li. psalme called Miserere mei Deus ; a prayer to Jesus ; the Paternoster ; and a prayer for the king and queen. Herbert remarks that this Primer follows a good deal that by W. Marshall of 1535.

**The Primer in Englishe and Laten set oute at lengthe with the exposicion of Miserere and In te Domine Sperani, and with the Epistles and Gospels thorowe out all the whole yere. ¶ Imprinted at London by Ihon Mayler at the signe of the whyte Beare in Botulph lane. S in eights. *The Exposicion* . . . [Col.] Imprynted at London in Botulph lane by my Ihon Mayler. E in eights. *The Epistles and Gospels* . . . [Col.] ¶ Imprynted in Botolph-lane . . . by me Ihon Mayler. 83 leaves, besides the table. 8⁰.

[The Primer. At the end occurs :] Imprinted at London by Thomas Gaultier, at the costes and charges of Robert Toye, dwelling in Paules Churche-yarde, at the sygne of the Bell. Very small 8⁰, printed in red and black, probably A—U in eights.

> The copy used commenced on C ii, and wanted the whole of the Calendar.

Here after Foloweth the Prymer in Englysshe and in latin sette out alonge : after the vse of Sarum. [Robert Valentin's device.] M.D.lv. [Col.] Impressum rothomagi impensis honesti viri Roberti valentini bibliopolaru͂ porticulo mora͂ tenen͂. M.D.lv. 8⁰, A—S in eights. With woodcuts.

> The Latin is printed in the margin in small type in red and black.

The Primer in Englishe and Latine, set out a long, after the vse of Sar : with many godlie and denoute praiers : as apeareth in the table. Imprinted at London, by Jhon kyngston, and Henry Sutton. 1557. Cum priuilegio . . . 4⁰. Title and Calendar, 4 leaves : *, 4 leaves : (¡, 4 leaves : ( ), 4 leaves : (.1.), 4 leaves : A—Z in fours : ß, 4 leaves : Aa—Dd in fours, with the colophon on Dd 4 *verso :* Imprynted at London in Fletestrete at the sygne of the Sunne ouer against the Cunduite by John Wayland. Cum priuilegio per septennium.

*The Prymer in Englishe and Latine, after Salisbury vse . . . [Col.] Imprynted at London by the assignes of Jhon Wayland, forbidding all other Persones to Prynt or cause to be prynted this Prymer or any other in Englysshe or in Latyne. [1558.] 8⁰, Dd in eights.

The Primer, Or Office of the Blessed Virgin Marie, in English According to the last Edition of the Roman Breviarie. Printed at Mackline by Henry Iaey, Anno M.DC.XV. Cum Gratia & Priuilegio. 8⁰, A—Rr in sheets of 8 and 10 alternately. With a frontispiece and engravings by Wierx. *B. M.*

PRINTING.

Reasons Humbly Offered for the Liberty of Unlicens'd Printing. To which is Subjoin'd, The Just and True Character of Edmund Bohun, The Licenser of the Press. In a Letter from a Gentleman in the Country, to a Member of Parliament. London, Printed in the Year MDCXCIII. 4⁰, A—D in fours.

A Letter to a Member of Parliament, Shewing, that a Restraint on the Press is inconsistent with the Protestant Religion, and dangerous to the Liberties of the Nation. London ; Printed by J. Darby, and sold by Andr. Bell . . . MDCXCVIII. 4⁰, A—D in fours.

PROCESSIONALE.

*Processionale ad vsum insignis ac præclare ecclesie Saru͂ / nouiter ac rursus castigatu / per excellentissimum ac vigilantissimum et reuerendissimum in Christo patrem dominū nostrū dominū episcopū de vinton feliciter incipit. Antwerpie impressum per Christophorū endouie impensis honesti mercatoris petri kaetz. Anno Domini. 1525. Die vero. 6. Februarij . . . Venundantur Londonii apud petrum kaetz. 4°, 176 leaves, the last having a colophon and device.

Processionale cōpletum per totum āni circulū. Ad vsum celebris ecclesie Eboracensis. de nouo correctum & emendatum Collectis. Impēsis honesti viri Johannis Gachet librarij Eboraci cōmorantis. M.v.ccccc.xxx. [Col.] Finit processionale ad vsum Eboracē . nouiter Impressum expēsis honesti viri Johannis Gachet. 8°, A—M in eights. With the musical notes. *B. M.*

Bandinel, 1861, £86, bought for the British Museum.

PROGNOSTICATION.

**Prognostycacion & Almanacke of two Shepherdes, necessarye for all Housholders. [Col.] Thus endeth the wyse Prognostication : Imprinted by me Robert Wyer dwellynge in Seynt Martyns parysshe, in the Duke of Suffolkes rentes, besyde charynge Crosse. Sm. 8°, A—B in fours.

The last page contains, according to Dibdin, an Almanac for 1556, so that it might be one of Wyer's latest publications.

PROPHESY.

The Panther-Prophesy, Or, A Premonition to all People, of Sad Calamities and Miseries like to befal these Islands. To which is added, An Astrological Discourse Concerning That strange Apparition of an Army of Horse seen in Wales, near Montgomery, December the 20th 1661. . . . Printed in the Year, 1662. Folio, A—C, 2 leaves each.

PRYNNE, WILLIAM.

The First Part of an Historical Collection of the Ancient Parliaments of England, From the yeer of our Lord 673, till the end of King John's Reign, Anno 1216. Wherein is clearly demonstrated by Histories and Records beyond contradiction, That The Ancient Parliaments, and Great Councils of England, during all this tract of time, and many yeers after, were constituted, and consisted onely of our Kings, Princes, Dukes, Earls, . . . and those we now usually stile the House of Peers ; and that both the Legislative and Judicial Power resided onliy [sic] in them ; without any Knights, Citizens, Burgesses of Parliament, or Commons House, . . . By William Prynne, of Swanswick, Esquire. . . . London, Printed for Robert Hodges. 1649. 4°, A—D in fours.

PSALMANAZAR, GEORGE, *a native of Formosa, now in London.*

An Historical and Geographical Description of Formosa, An Island subject to the Emperor of Japan. Giving an Account of the Religion, Customs, Manners, &c. of the Inhabitants. Together with a Relation of what happen'd to the Author in his Travels, particularly his Conferences with the Jesuits, and others, in several Parts of Europe. Also the History and Reasons of his Conversion to Christianity, . . . Illustrated with several Cuts. London : Printed for Dan. Brown, . . . and W. Davis, . . . 1704. 8°, A—Y in eights, and a, 4 leaves. Dedicated to the Bishop of London. With plates at pp. 166, 173—4, 194, 207, 224—6 (4), 228, 230 (2), 233, 266, 276 (2), and 278.

PSALMS.

A Century of Select Psalms, and Portions of the Psalms of David, Especially those of Praise, Turned into Metre, and fitted to the usual Tunes in Parish-Churches. For the use of the Charter-House, London. The Fifth Edition Corrected. By John Patrick, Preacher there. London, Printed by J. H. for L. Meredith . . . 1691. 12°, A—G in twelves, title on A 2 : H, 6.

**Psalmes of Dauid drawen into English metre by Thomas Sterneholde. Cum priuilegio ad imprimendum solum. Imprinted at London by Edward Whitchurche Anno Domini 1551. Sm. 8vo, A—G in eights.

The Whole booke of Psalmes, Collected into Englishe meeter by T. Stern. I. Hopk. and others : conferred with the Hebrew, with apt notes to sing them withal . . . London. Printed by Iohn Wolfe for the assignes of Richard Day. 1587. 8°, A—Bb in eights. Black letter. With the music. The title is within a broad woodcut border.

*The Psalter or Psalmes of Dauid. Corrected and pointed as they shalbe song in Churches, after the translation of the great Byble : With certayne addicions of Collectes and other the ordinary seruice, gathered out of the booke of Common prayer, confirmed by Acte of Parliament in the fyrst yere of the raigne of our soueraigne Lady Quene Elizabeth Anno Christ. 1. 5. 6. 0. Cum priuilegio. [Col.] Imprinted at London by Richarde Jugge and John Cawood. 4°. In two parts.

Psalmæ Y Brenhinol Brophwyd Dafydh, gwedi i cynghanedhu mewn masuran cymreig. Gann Capten Wiliam Middelton. . . . Simon Stafford a Thomas Salisbury ai printodbyn Llunden. 1603. 4°. ¶, 4 leaves: A—Qq in fours, Qq 4 blank. Dedicated by Middleton to Thomas Middleton Esquire. Black letter.

PSALTERIUM.

**Psalterium cum Hymnis sed'm vsum et cōsuetudinem Sarum et Eboracen . . . [Col.] Explicit Psalterium cū amiphonis d icalibę & ferialibę suis locis insertis, vna cum hymnis eccl'ie Sarum et Eboracen. deseruientibus. Impressum Parisiis Expēsis & sumptibę honesti mercatoris Gwilhelmi Brettōn. Anno virginæi partę. M.ccccc.vi. Die vero. xxij. kalendas Aprilis. 4°. The Psalter, &c., 136 leaves: the Hymns for morning and evening, with a Table at end, 40 leaves.

**Psalterium ad decandāda in choro officia ecclesiastica accommodatissimum : cū sexpetita letānia / hymnis quoq; ac vigiliis defunctorū vna cū kalendario & tabulis ex diuersis orthodoxorū practicis patrū collectis : ad simpliciū sacerdotū clericorūq; instructionem nūc quidem impressū : et a quodā erudito castigatū et aucti. 1530.

Venundantur Londonii in cimiterio diui Pauli / apud Johannē renis / sub intersignio sancti Georgii. 16°.

After the Psalter, &c., there occurs on fol. 137: "Sequūtur hymni per totū annū dicendi . . . ad vsum Sarum & Eboraceu.," and two tables on eight leaves, the last blank.

Herbert notes that Ames recites the book with this variant addition : "Sequuntur hymni secundum vsum Eboracen. qui non sunt in vsum Sarum."

Psalterium Dauidis, ad vsum ecclesie Sarisburiensis. Impressum Londini, per Ioannem Kyngston, & Henricum Sutton, Typographos. 1555. 8°. Title and Calendar, 8 leaves : A—R in eights. The title is within an engraved border.

Sotheby's, Feb. 23, 1887, No. 751.

PURCELL, JOHN, M.D.
A Treatise of Vapours, Or, Hysterick Fits . . . London, Printed, and Sold by H. Newman . . . 1702. 8°. A, 4 leaves : B—L in eights : M, 4. Dedicated to Sir John Talbot.

PURY, THOMAS, of Gloucester.
Mr Thomas Pvry Alderman of Glocester his Speech, Upon that clause of the Bill against Episcopacy, the which Concernes Deanes, and Deanes and Chapters, at a Committee of the whole Hovse. Printed in the yeare 1641. 4°, A—B 2 in fours.

Q.

QUARLES, FRANCIS.
Enchiridion : Containing Institvtions . . . Written by Fra: Quarles. London, Printed by R. F. 1644. 12°. A, 6 leaves : B—K in twelves.

R.

RANDOLPH, JOHN.
Honour Advanced : Or, A briefe account of the long keeping, and late leaving of the Close at Liechfield, Being a full Relation of all the Passages worthy observation during the whole time of the Siege ; As also of the honourable tearmes upon which it was resigned. Together with the Names of those valiant Commanders who have done this service both for Church and State ; . . . By Captaine John Randolph, A Commander, and eye-witnesser in the said Close . . . Printed for Tho: Underhill. 1643. 4°, 4 leaves.

RECORDE, ROBERT, of Tenby, M.D.
*The Ground of Artes . . . with diuers new additions, as by the table doeth partely appeere. Made by Robert Recorde Doctor of Physicke. Imprinted at London, by Reynold Wolff. Cum Sereniss. Regis priuilegio. 8°, A—P 4 in eights.

This impression includes at the end : The art of numbering by the hand, newly added.

REDDISH, WILLIAM.
Strange News from Stratton in Cornwal: Or, A True Relation of a cruel Bloody Murther committed by one J[ohn] R[oss] upon his own Father, for lucre of enjoying his Estate; who (after he had committed the Fact, and had laid the Knife in the Bed wherein his Father lay) called in several Neighbours to witness that his Father had murthered himself. . . . Written by one William Reddish, who was in Stratton at the same time, when the Murther was committed: And written since in a letter to Mr Pearce Manaton in Wind-mill-Court, in the Butcherrow near Temple-Barr by his Brother, living within half a Mile of the said Town. With Allowance. Printed for I. Coniers, at the Sign of the Raven in Duck-Lane. 4°, 4 leaves. *B. M.*
    This was Borlase's copy. It is inlaid; but I have met with no other.

REGI, DOMENICO.
Della Vita di Tomaso Moro Gran Cancelliero D'Inghilterra Libri Due Con accrescimento di notitie in questa Impressione Del P. Domenico Regi . . . . In Bologna, 1681. . . 12°. +, 12 leaves, including half-title, frontispiece, and portrait: A—P 6 in twelves.

REGISTER.
A Seasonable Proposal to the Nation, Concerning A Register of Estates in this Kingdom, Tendred to the Consideration of the Publick-Spirited in both Houses. . . . Printed in the Year 1669. 4°, 4 leaves.

REYNARD THE FOX.
The most delectable History of Reynard the Fox Newly Corrected and purged . . . As also augmented and inlarged . . . London, Printed by J. Bell, 1650. 4°, black letter, A—V in fours. With cuts.

REYNOLDS, JOHN.
Blood for Blood: Or Murthers Revenged. Briefly, yet Lively set forth in Thirty Tragical Histories. To which are added Five more, Being the sad Product of our own Times, Viz. Charles the Martyr. Montrose and Argyle, Sonds & his two Sons, Overbury and Turner, Knight and Butler. With a short Apendix to the present age. . . . Faithfully digested for the benefit of Posterity By T. M. Esq; Oxford, Printed for the Author and are to be sold by the Booksellers in London. 1661. 8°. Frontispiece, 1 leaf: title, dedication to the Marquis of Newcastle, and Preface. 1 leaves: A—Z in eights, Z 8 with the label.

RICH, COLONEL.
The Declaration of Colonel Rich's Regiment. With the Engagement they have Entered into. Also Major Braman's Letter to Lievtenant Colonel Lagoe, upon their going into Portsmouth. To which is another Letter sent from Major Braman to a Friend of his in London. London, Printed by T. M. for Livewell Chapman, . . . 1659. 4°, 4 leaves.

RICHARDSON, ROBERT, *Canonicus, of Cambuskenneth.*
Exegesis in Canonem diui Augustini recès aedita, per Fratrē Robertum Richardinum [cele]bris Ecclesiæ Kambuskenalis canonicum. Lvtetiae, in aedibus Christiani Wechel . . . 1530. Sm. 8°. Title within a border, 1 leaf: Epistle to the Abbot Alexander Mylne of Cambuskenneth and Preface, 6 leaves: Contents, 6 leaves, followed by a blank: A, 6 leaves: B, 4: C, 4: D, 4: E, 6: F—H in fours: I, 6 leaves: K—M in fours: N, 6: O—Q, in fours: R, 6: S—Z in fours: a, 6: b—d in fours: e, 6: f—h in fours: i, 6: k—m in fours: n, 6: o—q in fours: r, 6: s—u in fours: x, 6: y—z in fours: Aa—Bb in fours, Bb 4 with colophon: AA, 6: BB—CC in fours: DD, 6: EE—HH in fours, HH 4 with colophon and mark.
    Sotheby's, April 24, 1888, No. 2248.

RICHARDSON, ROBERT, *B.D., Minister in London.*
A Briefe and Compendious exposition vpon the Psalme called *Deprofundis* which haue bene . And presentelye is horrible and detestable . Abused in the Churche of God. And nowe translated to the trew sens: to Gods glorie & to the Edification and comfort of his Church. By M. Roberte Richardson Batchelere of diuinetie and Minister in Londen. [Col.] Imprinted at London by Thomas Purfoote for William Norton. 8°, black letter, A—B in eights. *Britwell.*

RIDPATH, GEORGE.
Short-hand yet shorter: Or, The Art of Short-Writing advanced . . . By George Ridpath. . . . London, Printed by J. D. for the Author, 1687. 8°, A—C in eights, besides 2 folding plates. Dedicated to Philip, Lord Wharton.

ROBERTSON, GEORGE.
Vitæ & mortis D. Roberti Rolloci Scoti narratio. Scripta per Georgium Robertsonum. Adiectis in eundem quorundam Epitaphijs. Edinbvrgi Apud Henricum Charteris. 1599. Sm. 8°, A—C in eights. *B. M.*

ROBINSON, HENRY.

Englands Safety, in Trades Encrease. Most humbly Presented to the High Court of Parliament.

> *Mercatura si tenuis, sordida ; si magna, splendida.*
> —— *Quaerenda pecunia primum.*

By Henry Robinson, Gent. London, Printed by E. P. for Nicholas Bourne, at the South Entrance of the Royall Exchange. [1641?] 4°. A, 3 leaves: B—H in fours, H 4 with the *Errata*.

> The date in this copy has been nearly cut away.

Certain Proposalls in order to the Peoples Freedome and Accommodation in some Particulars. With the Advancement of Trade and Navigation of this Common-Wealth in generall. Humbly tendered to the view of this prosperous Parliament. ... by Henry Robinson. London, Printed by M. Simmons, in Aldersgate-streete ... 1652. 4", A—D in fours, D 4 blank.

ROBINSON, THOMAS, *Lutenist.*

In God reioyce, With instrument and voyce. The Schoole of Mvsicke: Wherein is taught, The Perfect Method of Trve Fingering of the Lute, Pandora, Orpharion, and Viol de Gamba ; with most infallible generall rules, both easie and delightfull. Also, a method, how you may be your owne instructer for Prick-song, by the help of your Lute, without any other teacher : with lessons of all sorts, for your further and better instruction. Newly composed by Thomas Robinson, Lutenist. London: Printed by Tho. Este, for Simon Waterson, ... 1603. Folio, A—O, 2 leaves each. Dedicated to the King. The title is engraved. *B. M.*

> Robinson states in his epistle to James, that he had been employed at Elsinore in Denmark to instruct Queen Anne in music.

New Citharen Lessons, With perfect Tunings of the same, From Foure course of Strings to Fourteene course, euen to trie the sharpest teeth of Ennie, with Lessons of all sortes, and methodicall Instructions for all Professors and Practitioners of the Citharen. By Thomas Robinson, Student in all the seuen liberall Sciences. London Printed by William Barley, and are to be sold at his Shop in Gracious-streete. 1609. Cum Priuilegio. Small folio, A—M in fours. Dedicated to Sir William Cecil, Viscount Cranborne, following which epistle is a preface to the Reader, subscribed " Your musicall friend Thomas Robinson." With woodcuts. *B. M.*

ROMAN HISTORY.

A New and Easie Method to Understand the Roman History ... By way of Dialogue, For the Use of the Duke of Burgundy. Done out of French, with very large Additions and Amendments by Mr Th. Brown. The Third Edition Corrected: ... London : Printed for R. Willington, ... MDCCIII. Small 8° or 12", A—N 6 in twelves.

ROMBUS.

Rombvs the Moderator : Or, The King Restor'd. From whence followes the Arraignment of seven incomparable Malefactors : with their faults, Confessions, and Astraeas severe Sentence, Rombus his qualifications : The Prisoners reprieves, and severall Punishments. A certain strange Accidentall, *alius*, his Excellenscey begeting, and a presage of his Fortune, with other remarkable Passages. [12 lines of verse.] Printed in the Year. 1648. 4", A—B in fours.

ROSARY.

**Here begynneth the Rosary of our Sauyour Iesu, gyueing thankes and prayse to his holy name, by maner of meditacion of prayer : for all the labours & great paynes that he suffred for man in this worlde, from the fyrst instant of his blessed Incarnacion, vnto his glorious Ascencion : Of the whiche is made mention in the . xxxii. chapiter of the . vi. day & thirde boke : And this treatise cōtayneth . vii. chapt's as seuyn meditacions for the vii. dayes in the weke. [This title is over a cut of Christ crowned with thorns, &c. Colophon :] Thus endeth the Rosary of our sauyour Iesu. Imprinted at London in Fletestrete by Richard Pynson priter to the kynges noble grace. Cum priuilegio. 4", A—D in fours and sixes.

*The Rosary with the articles of the lyfe & deth of Iesu Chryst, and peticiōs directe to our lady. [Col.] Thus endeth the Rosary in englysshe. Imprynted at London in Fauster-lane, by John Skot, dwellyng in saynt Leonardes parysshe. In the yere of our lorde M.ccccc.xxxvij. Sm. 8°, A—C in eights. *Althorp.*

ROSSE, ALEXANDER.

Three Decads of Divine Meditations. Whereof each one containeth three parts. 1. A History. 2. An Allegory. 3. A Prayer. With a commendation of the priuate Cōuntrey life. By Alexander Rosse his Maiesties Chaplaine in Ordinarie. London, Printed by A. M. for Francis Constable and are to be sold at the Signe of the Crane in S^t. Paules Church-yeard. 4", A—E in fours, first leaf blank. Dedicated in verse to the Lady Kinloss.

Leviathan Drawn out with A Hook : Or Animadversions upon Mr Hobbs His Leviathan. Together with some Observations upon Sr Walter Raleigh's History of the World. London, Printed by Tho. Newcomb, for Richard Royston at the Angel in Ivy-Lane. 1653. 12". General title. 1 leaf : Observations on Hobbs, A—F 6 in twelves : Observations on Raleigh, a—c in twelves, besides Table and Preface, 4 leaves.

> The first piece is inscribed to Francis Lucy, Esq.

Virgilii Triumphantis Libri III. Instante Alexandro Rosæo. Roterodami, Sumptibus Arnoldi Leers. 1661. Sm. 8°. Engraved and printed titles and dedication to Charles II., 3 leaves : A—O 8 in twelves.

ROSY CROSS.
The Fame and Confession of the Fraterternity of R : C : Commonly, of the Rosie Cross. With A Preface annexed thereto, and a short Declaration of their Physicall Work. By Eugenius Philalethes. [Quot. from Jareb. apud Philostrat:] *Veritas in Profundis.* London. Printed by J. M. for Giles Calvert, ... 1652. 8°. A, 8 leaves, title on A 2 : (a)—(d 4) in eights : B—E in eights.

> From the address of Eugenius Philalethes [Thomas Vaughan] to the Reader we collect that he was merely the publisher of a translation, he adds that the Preface, which follows, is his own. But in Crossley's copy (Part I., No. 2514) at p. 56 occurred this MS. note, apparently in the handwriting of the author : " Here ends the Fame and Confession of the Fraternitie : That which followes is my owne."—*T. Vaughan.* There is another note in the same hand and several passages marked.

ROWLANDSON, JOSEPH.
A True History of the Captivity & Restoration of Mrs Mary Rowlandson . . . 1682.

> *Revised collation:* A—G 2 in fours, the Sermon by Joseph Rowlandson, who doubtless wrote the whole, commencing on F with the following headline : A Sermon Preached at Weathersfield, Nov. 21. 1678. By Mr. Joseph Rowlandson, it being a day of Fasting and Humiliation. It is on Jeremiah xxiii. 33, and is addressed in a Preface " To the Courteous Reader, (especially the Inhabitants of the Town of Weathersfield, and Lancaster, in New-England."

RUMP.
The Rump serv'd in with a Grand Sallet. Or, A New Ballad, To the Tune of the Blacksmith. London, Printed in the Year 1660 [March 1, 1659-60.] A broadside in two columns. *B. M.*

Fortunate Rising, Or The Rump Upward. London, Printed for Henry James. A broadside in two columns in verse. *B. M.*

Bumm-Fodder Or Waste Paper Proper to wipe the Nations Rump with, or your Own. Finis, in English, The Rump. A broadside in two columns in verse. *B. M.*

Arsy Versy : Or, The Second Martyrdom of the Rump. To the Tune of *The Blind Beggar of Bednall-green.* A broadside in two columns in verse. *B. M.*

The Re-Resurrection of the Rump : Or, Rebellion and Tyranny revived. The third Edition. *To the Tune of the Blacksmith.* Finis, in English, The Rvmp. A broadside in two columns and in verse. *B. M.*

Rump Rampant : With Sweet Old Cause in sippits : Set out by Sir T. A. Perfumer of his late Highnesse. To the Tune of, *Last Parliament sat as snugg as a Cat.* A broadside in two columns and in verse. *B. M.*

The Rump Roughly, yet righteously Handled : In a New Ballad : To the tune of *Cock Lorrel.* A broad-side in two columns and in verse. *B. M.*

A Vindication of the Rump : Or, The Rump Re-Advanc'd. To the Tune of, *Vp tails all.* Rumpatur. London, Printed for Rosicleer Arsewind, the Rvmps Leather-Seller. A broadside in two columns and in verse. *B. M.*

RUTTER.
**The Rutter of the see with the hauens, rodes, soundynges, kennynges, wyndes, floodes, and ebbes, daungers and costes of dyuers regions, with the lawes of the yle of Auleron, & the iudgementes of the see. [Col.] Thus endeth the Rutter of the see, with the lawes of the yle of Auleron, lately translated out of Frenche into Englyshe. Imprinted at London in Poules chyrche yarde at the signe of ye Maidens Head by me Thomas Petyt. The yere of our lorde God M.D.XXXVI. The . XVIII. daye of Marche. Sm. 8°.

S.

S. C.
The Art of Complaisance Or The Means to oblige in Conversation . . . The Second Edition. London, Printed for John Starkey . . . 1677. 12º. A, 6 leaves : B—H in twelves : I, 6.

S. J.
Masquarade du Ciel : Presented to the Great Queene of the Little World. A Celestiall Map, representing the True Site and Motions of the Heavenly Bodies, through the yeeres 1639, 1640, &c. Shadowing the late Commotions, between Saturn and Mercury, about the Northern Thule. . . . By J. S. London, Printed by R. B. for S. C. 1640. 4º, A—F 2 in fours, besides *Imprimatur* and title. Dedicated to the Queen.

S. S., Gent.
The Secretaries Studie : Containing new familiar Epistles. Wherein Ladies, Gentlemen, and all that are ambitious to write and speak elegantly, and elaborately, in a succinct & facetious strain, are furnished with fit Phrases, . . . *Sic juvat indulgere fugacibus horis.* London, Printed by T. H. for John Harrison in S. Pauls Church-Yard, 1652. 8º, A—T 4 in eights, A 1 blank. Dedicated by S. S. to the Right Honorable, and most munificent, Francis, Lord Willoughby of Parham.

SAINTS.
The Fierie Tryall of Gods Saints ; (These Suffered for the witnes of Iesus, and for the word of God (vnder Queene Mary,) who did not worship the Beast, nor his Image, nor had taken his marke vpon their foreheads, or on their hands, or on their Garments, and these liue and raigne with Christ : Reuel. 20. 4.) As a Counterpoyze to I. W. Priest his English Martyrologe. And the Detestable Ends of Popish Traytors : . . . . At London, Printed by T. P. for Arthur Iohnson. 1611. 4º, A—I 3 in fours : *Postscript*, A—B in fours, B 4 blank. With a frontispiece representing *The Popes charge to his Bratts.*

SALISBURY, *Diocese of.*
*Iniunctions gyuen by the bysshop of Salysbury throughout his Dioces. . . . [Col.] Imprynted at the sygne of the sonne, by Johan Byddell, and are to sell at the closegate in Salysbury. [1538.] 4º, 4 leaves.
See Herbert, p. 487. Described by him from his own copy.

SALLUSTIUS, C. C.
Here begynneth the famous cronycle of the warre / which the romayns had agaynst Jugurth vsurper of the kyngdome of Numidy : whiche cronycle is compyled in latyn by the renowmed romayn Salust. And translated into englysshe by syr Alexander Barclay preest / at comaundement of the right hye and mighty prince : Thomas duke of Northfolke. [Below is a shield of arms occupying the rest of the page. At the end occurs :] Thus endeth the famous cronycle . . . imprented at London by Richarde Pynson printer vnto the kynges noble grace : with priuylege vnto hym graunted by our sayd souerayn lorde the kynge. Folio, a in sixes : A—N in sixes : O—P in fours, or 92 leaves.
The copy described has belonged to the Duke of Roxburghe, Sir Mark Sykes, and Mr. Heber, and was lent to me by Mr. T. V. Carr of C. C. Oxford. The large cut on a 4 seems to represent Barclay offering the book to the Duke of Norfolk. There was no Duke Thomas before February 1514.

SALTER, HUMPHRY.
The Genteel Companion ; Being exact Directions for the Recorder : With a Collection of the Best and Newest Tunes and Grounds Extant. Carefully Composed and Gathered by Humphry Salter. London, Printed for Richard Hunt and Humphry Salter, at the Lute in St. Paul's Church-Yard. 1683. Obl. 8º. Title and dedication to all Ingenious Lovers of Music, 2 leaves : Directions, 4 leaves : the Music, 26 leaves.

SALTONSTALL, WYE.
The Complaint of Time against the Tumultuous and Rebellious Scots. Sharpely inveighing against them (as most justly they deserue) this yeare, 1639. By W. S. London Printed by B. A. and T. F. for Richard Harper in Smithfield, at the Bible and Harpe. 1639. 4º, 4 leaves. In verse. With a large cut on the title. *B. M.*

SALTPETRE.
A Proclamation for the maintenance and encrease of the Mines of Saltpeter, and the true making of Gunpowder, and reforming abuses concerning the same. Printed at London by Bonham Norton,

and Iohn Bill, ... M.DC.XXV. A broadsheet formed of three leaves.

**SALUS.
Salvs Corporis, Salvs Anime Pius contra venereos, gliada Homeri. [This is over Richard Fawkes the printer's device. At the end :] Impressum est presens opusculum londoniis in divi pauli semiterio, sub virginei capitis signo : Anno salutis. Millesimo quingētesimo nono. Mensis vero Decembris die XII. Folio, A—D 4 in eights. *Bodleian.*

SAMPSON, RICHARD.
†Richardi Sampsonis, Regii Sacelli Decani Oratio, qua docet, hortatur, admonet omnes potissimũ anglos, regiæ dignitati eum primis ut obediant, quia uerbum dei præcipit, episcopo Romano ne sint audientes, qui nullo iure diuino, in eos quicquam potestatis habet, postquam ita iubet rex, ut illi non obediant. . . . Londini In Ædibvs Tho. Bertheleti. [Col.] Thomas Bertheletvs Regivs Impressor Excvdebat. Cvm Privilegio. 4°, 14 leaves.

SANDERS, GEORGE.
A briefe discourse of the late mnrther of master George Sanders, a worshipful Citizen of London : and of the apprehension, arraignement, and execution of the principall and accessaries of the same. Seene and allowed. Imprinted at London by Henrie Bynnyman, dwelling in Knightriders streete, at the signe of the Mermayde. Anno. 1577. 8°, A—B in eights.
Puttick's, January 31, 1888, No. 872.

SANDERS, NICHOLAS.
Les Trois Livres dv Doctevr Nicolas Sanders, Contenants l'origine & progrez du schisme d'Angleterre. . . . Augmentez par Edouard Rishton, premierement Imprimez en Latin, en Allemaigne, & depuis plus correctement à Rome. *Celuy qui celle la verité,* ... Aug. M.D.LXXXVIII. 8°. Title and Argument, 2 leaves : ā, 4 leaves : A—Oo in eights.
With an interesting preface by Rishton, who was in exile in France, on his escape or deliverance from an English prison.

SARPI, PAOLO.
The History of the Inquisition : Composed by the Reverend Father Paul Servita, who was also the Compiler of the Councell of Trent. A Pious, Learned, and Curious Worke, necessary for Councellors, Casuists, and Politicians. Translated out of the Italian Copy by Robert Gentilis. London : Printed by J. Okes, for Humphrey Mosley, ... 1639. 4°, A—M in fours, A 1 with the *Imprimatur.*
In the Address of the Printer to the Reader we are led to understand that a MS. copy of the original had fallen into the hands of Gentilis, and that the Italian had not so far been published.

The Opinion of Padre Paolo, of the Order of the Servites, Consultor of State, Given to the Lords the Inquisitors of State. In what manner the Republick of Venice ought to govern themselves, both at home and abroad, to have perpetual Dominion. Deliver'd by Publick Order, in the Year 1615. London : Printed for R. Bently, ... 1689. 12°, A—F in twelves, A 1 with *Imprimatur.* Dedicated to Henry, Viscount Sidney, in an epistle of some interest, by W. Aglionby.
The dedication copy in old red morocco was sold in the second part of Gibson-Craig's library in March–April 1888.

SAUNDERS, RICHARD, *Student in Astrology and Physic.*
Saunders Physiognomie, And Chiromancie, Metoposcopie, The Symmetrical Proportions and Signal Moles of the Body, ... The Second Edition very much Enlarged. London, Printed by H. Brugis, for Nathaniel Brook, ... 1671. Folio. With a portrait. Title and dedication. to Elias Ashmole of the Middle Temple, 3 leaves : a—c 2 in fours with verses, &c. : B—Eee in fours. With diagrams.

SAVERY, THOMAS, *Gentleman.*
The Miners Friend ; Or, An Engine to raise Water by Fire, Described. And of the manner of Fixing it in Mines. With an Account of the several other Uses it is applicable unto, and an Answer to the Objections made against it . . . London : Printed for S. Crouch at the Corner of Popes-Head-Alley in Cornhill 1702. 8°, A—F in eights, F 8 blank.

SCHOOLMASTER.
The English Schole-Master Or Certaine rules and helpes, whereby the natives of the Netherlandes, may bee, in a short time, taught to read, understand, and speake, the English tongue. By the helpe whereof, the English also may be better instructed in the knowledge of the Dutch tongue, than by any vocabulars, or other Dutch and English books, which hitherto they have had, for that purpose. Amsterdam. Printed in the Year 1646. 12°, A—K 10 in twelves including a duplicate title. Engl. and Dutch. *B. M.*
Dedicated to the true natural inhabitants, and all lovers of the peace and prosperity of the United Netherlands.

The English Schole-Master; Or, Certaine rules and helpes, . . . Amsterdam, Printed by Iohn Bouman, in the Year 1658. 12", A—K in twelves. *B. M.*

The English ⎱ ⎰ French, Latine ⎰ ⎱ Dutch, Schole-master, Or, An Introduction to teach young Gentlemen and Merchants to Travell or Trade. Being the onely helpe to attaine to those Languages. Printed in the Netherlands 25 times, and this being the first Edition in London. By A. G. for Michael Sparke, at the Signe of the blue Bible in Greene Arbour. 1637. Sm. 8°. Frontispiece, title, and M. S. to the Reader, 3 leaves: A 4 (wrongly marked A)—G 8 in eights, G 8 blank. In four columns. *B. M.* (the Bliss copy.)

This is, in fact, a tetraglot vocabulary.

SCHRODER, JOHN, *M.D.*
Zoologia: Or, The History of Animals As they are useful in Physick and Chirurgery. Divided into Four Parts; The First trenteth of the more perfect Terrestrial Creatures. The Second of Birds. Third of Fishes. Fourth of Insects. London: Printed by E. Cotes, for R. Royston at the Angel in Ivie-lane, and Rob. Clavel at the Stags-head near St. Gregories in St. Pauls-churchyard, 1659. 8°. A, 4 leaves: B—L in eights: M, 4 ll.

The translator was T. Batesonn, who, in the Address to the Reader, cites Wither's *Motto*. Under the Terrestrial Creatures in H occurs: "*Homo*, Man and Woman."

The Compleat Chymical Dispensatory, In Five Books: Treating of all Sorts of Metals, Precious Stones, and Minerals, of all Vegetables and Animals, and things that are taken from them, . . . Written in Latin, by Dr. John Schroder, That most Famous and Faithful Chymist. And Englished, By William Rowland, Dr. of Physick . . . London: Printed by John Darby, for Richard Chiswell, and Robert Clavell, . . . 1669. Folio. Title, 1 leaf: dedication by Rowland "To the Right Honourable, and others, the Merchant Adventurers of England, and to all ingenious Druggists, Chirurgions, Apothecaries, and all such as study Philosophy or Physick in their Mother-Tongue," 2 leaves: B—Yyy in fours, last leaf blank.

SCOTLAND.
Epistola Exhortatoria ad Pacem, Missa ab illustrissimo Principe Domino Protectore Angliæ, ac cæteris Regiæ Maiestatis Consiliarijs, ad Nobilitatem ac plebem, uniuersumq; populum Regni Scotiæ.

[Col.] Excusum Londini, tertio Nonas Martias per Reginaldum Wolfium, Regiæ Maiestatis in Latinis typographum. Anno Domini 1548. 4", A—D in fours.

Certeine Matters Concerning the Realme of Scotland, composed together. . . . As they were Anno Domini, 1597. London, Printed by A. Hatfield, for Iohn Flasket . . . 1603. 4°, B—M in fours: N, 1 leaf, and the title-page. *Grenv. Coll.*

Another copy in the Museum has a title differing in orthography, and a third varies in the imprint.

An Act and Ordinance Set down be the Lords of Privie Counsell and Session, anent the pryces to be taken heir-efter be the Clerks and Writters, bering publick function and office within this Kingdome. For all sic writts, acts, letters, and tracts, as concerns their office . . . Edinbvrgh. ¶ Printed be Thomas Finlason, and are to be sauld at Nidreis wynd heid 1616. With the K. M. Licence. 4", A—D 2 in fours, D 2 with the mark.

The Dissolution of the Parliament in Scotland Novemb. 19. 1641. After a sweet Sympathy, and agreement betwixt the King and his Subiects, in the setling of all Affaires, . . . with an Act of Parliament ordaining the whole subiects and Lieges of that Kingdome to obey, maintaine, and defend the conclusions, Acts and Constitutions of this last Session of Parliament, . . . Wherein is declared the illegall practices of Iohn, Earle of Traquair, . . . Together with a true Copy of the Band, as it was subscribed by the Noblemen, . . . London, Printed for John Wright. 1641. 4°, 4 leaves.

A Declaration of the Officers of the Army in Scotland to the Churches of Christ in the three Nations. Edinbvrgh, Printed by Christopher Higgins, in Harts-Close, over against the Trone-Church, Anno Dom. 1659. 4°, 4 leaves.

An Address Sign'd by the greatest part of the Members of Parliament of Scotland, and Deliver'd to His Majesty at Hampton-Court, the 15th day of October, 1689. 4", 4 leaves. Without a regular title.

A Memorial concerning the Disorders of the Highlands, Especially The Northern Parts thereof, and the Isles of Scotland, With an Account of some Means, by which the same may be Redressed and Prevented, and how Religion and Vertue may be promoted in these Parts. Edinbvrgh Printed in the Yeer M.DCC.III. 4°, 5 leaves.

A Letter from the Nobility, Barons and Commons of Scotland, in the Year 1320, yet extant under all the Seals of the Nobility, Directed to Pope John: Wherein they declare their firm Resolutions, to adhere to their King Robert the Bruce, as the Restorer of the Safety, and Liberties of the People, . . . Translated from the Original, in Latine, as it is insert by Sir George Mackenzie of Rosehaugh, in his Observations on Precedency, &c. Edinburgh, Re-printed in the Year 1703. 4°, 4 leaves.

Memorial about a Commission for Visiting Schools, Colleges and Universities. [Col.] Printed [at Edinburgh] in the Year 1704. 4°, 2 leaves.

A Dialogue between a Country-Man, and a Landwart School-Master, Concerning the Proceedings of the Parliament of England, in Relation to Scots Affairs, &c. Edinburgh, Printed by John Reid Younger in the Year 1705. 4°, 4 leaves.

The Booke of Common Prayer, . . . Edinburgh, Printed by Robert Young, . . . M.DC.XXXVII. Cvm Privilegio. Folio.
<small>Sotheby's, April 24, 1888, No. 1429. This copy included the Psalter, commencing on aa.</small>

The CL. Psalmes of David in Meeter: With CL. Praiers vpon the said Psalmes; Ilk ane following the Psalme. . . . Prented at Edinbvrgh be Henrie Charteris. 1595. Cum Privilegio Regali. 8°, A—Mm 4 in eights. With the music.

The Psalmes of David in Meeter, With Baptisme, the Lords supper, and Marriage: and certaine Psalmes and prayers. Edinbvrgh, Printed by Iohn Wreittoun, and are to be sold at his shop a little below the Salt-Trone. 1635. Small 8° or 12°. *, 12 leaves: A—Q in twelves.

The Confessioun of faith Professit, and Belevit, be the Protestantes within the Realme of Scotland, Publisched be thaim in Parliament. And be the Estatis thairof, Ratifeit and appreuit, as hailsū, & sound Doctrine groundit vpon the infallible treuth of Goddis worde. Math. 24. *And this glad tydingis* . . . [Col.] Thir Actis, and Artycles, ar Red in face of Paliarment. And ratifiit be the three Estatis of this Realme. At Edinburgh ÿ 17. day of Iuly, the ʒeir of God. Ane thowsand fyue hundreth three score ʒeris. And Imprentit be me Ihone Scott. 1561. 4°, black letter, A—E 2 in fours, besides the title. *Grenv. Coll.*

The Confession of the Faythe and Doctrine beleued and professed, by the Protestantes of the Realme of Scotlande, exhibited to the Estates of the same in parliament, and by their publicke voices authorised as a doctrine. grounded vpon the infallible Worde of God. Math. 24. *And this glad tidings* . . . Set furth and authorised according to the Queenes Maiesties Iniunctions. Imprinted at London by Rouland Hall, dwellyng in Goldyng lane at the sygne of the three arrowes. 1561. 8°, A—C in eights. *B. M.*

The Confession of Faith of the Kirk of Scotland, Svbscribed By the Kings Maiestie and his Housholde, in the yeare of God, 1580. With a Designation of such acts of Parliament, as are expedient, for justefying the Vnion, after mentioned. And subscribed by the Nobles, Barrons, Gentlemen, Burgesses, Ministers, and Commons, in the yeare of God, 1638. [Three quotations. No place, name, or date.] 4°, A—C 2 in fours.

*The Actis and Constitutionis of Parliament maid be the rycht excellent princes Marie quene of Scottis. [Col.] Imprintit at Edinburgh, be Robert Lekpreuik. 1565. Folio. Black letter.
<small>This collection embraces 25 Acts and a Table.</small>

*The actis of parliament of the maist hie, maist excellent, and michtie prince, and our souerane lord, Iames the sext, . . . begun and halden at Edinburgh, the xv day of December, the ʒeir of God, ane thousand fyue hundreth LXVII ʒeir, be our said souerane lordis derrest cousin and uncle, Iames of Murray, lord Abirnethie regent to our souerane lord his realme and leigis; togeddir with the prelatis; . . . The said actis being oppinlie red. . . . [Col.] Imprintit at Edinburgh be Robert Lekpreuik, prentar to the kingis maiestie, the VI. day of April, the ʒeir of God, ane thousand fyue hundreth thre scoir aucht ʒeiris. Folio.

*In the Parliament Haldin and begun at Edinburgh the xxiiii Day of October, the Zeir of God, ane thousand, fyue hundreth, four scoir & ane zeiris. . . . Imprintit at Edinburgh, be Henrie Charteris. Anno.

M.D.LXXXII. Cum Priuilegio Regali. Folio.

This collection embraces 37 chapters.

SECTS.
*The original & sprynge of all sectes & orders by whom, whā or were they beganne. Translated out of hye Dutch in Englysh. [Col.] ¶ Here emdeth the treatyse of all sectes, orders and religions, both of Christendom and the Jewes: translated out of hye Dutch in Englysshe. ¶ Printed in Southwarke by me James Nicolson for Jan Gough. Cum priuilegio. 8", 64 leaves + prefixes.

SEDGWICK, OBADIAH, B.D., *Pastor of Coggeshall in Essex.*
A Thanksgiving-Sermon, Preached before the honourable House of Commons at Westminster, April 9. 1644. For the happie and seasonable Victory of Sir Will. Waller and Sir Will. Balfore, &c. over Sir Ralph Hopton and his Forces raised against the Parliament. . . . London, Printed by J. R. for Samuel Gellibrand. . . . 1644. 4°. A, 2 leaves : B—E in fours.

SELDEN, JOHN.
Johannis Seldeni Jurisconsulti Opera Omnia Tam Edita quum Inedita. In Tribus Voluminibus. . . . Londini. . . . MDCCXXVI. Folio. With a portrait by Vertue.
Edited by David Wilkins, S.T.P.

SELLER, JOHN, *Senior.*
The Sea Gunner : Shewing the Practical Part of Gunnery, as it is used at Sea. And, As an Introduction thereto, there is exhibited two Compendiums, one of Vulgar, the other of Decimal Arithmetick. With necessary Tables relating to the Art. To which is added An Appendix, . . . Composed by John Seller, Senior. London : Printed by H. Clark for the Author, and are to be sold by him at the Hermitage in Wapping, 1691. 8°, A—Q in eights, besides folded leaves at pp. 36 and 156, pp. 1 and 24 of Appendix, and a frontispiece.

SEQUESTRATION.
All the severall Ordinances and Orders Made by the Lords and Commons . . . concerning Sequestring the Estates of Delinquents, Papists, Spyes and Intelligencers. Together with Instructions for such Persons as are imployed in sequestring of such Delinquents Estates. Very usefull for those whom it doth or may concern. . . . London. Printed for Edward Husbands, . . . 1644. 4°, A—E in fours, and between C and D, A 2—B 4 in fours with additional orders on the subject.

All the severall Ordinances and Orders . . . London, Printed for Lawrence Blacklock, at the Signe of the Mear-mayd at the Middle-Temple-Gate. 1645. 4°, A—F in fours.

SERMONES.
*Quatuor Sermones. [Col.] Finitum London Per Richardum Pynson Anno dñi. M.CCCC.LXXXIX. 4", A—E in sixes : F, 8. Without a regular title.
Printed to accompany Pynson's edition of the *Festival* of the same date.

SHAKESPEAR, WILLIAM.
Macbeth : A Tragedy. Acted At the Dykes-Theatre. London, Printed for William Cademan, . . . 1673. 4°. A, 2 leaves with title and Persons' Names : B—K 2 in fours.

SHEEP-KILLERS.
Strange but true News from Several parts of the Kingdome, Of certain Sneep-killers, Or a sort of New Tallow-chandlers In the Counties of Essex, Leicester-shire, Northamptonshire, and part of Warwickshire, &c. With a particular account of their proceedings, the number and manner of their killing them. Likewise, How they come to be discovered and taken by a Journey man Shoomaker, and are now in Leicester Goal, till next Assises. Published by a well-wisher to his King and Countrey. Printed for [Reuben Ruhais ?] 1675. 4°, 4 leaves.
The line of imprint has been partly cut off.

SHEPPARD, SAMUEL.
Epigrams Theological, Philosophical, and Romantick. Six Books, Also The Socratick session, Or The Arraignment and Conviction, of Julius Scaliger, with other Select Poems. By S. Sheppard. London, Printed by G. D. for Thomas Bucknell, at the Signe of the Golden Lion in Duck-Lane, 1651. Sm. 8°, A—S in eights, besides a frontispiece in compartments. *B. M.*
Dedicated to the author's friends, Christopher Clapham and James Winter, in an epistle modelled on that of Davenant before his *Madagascar*, 1638.

SHIRLEY, JOHN.
The Accomplished Ladies Rich Closet of Rarities . . . . The Fifth Edition, with Large Additions, Corrected and Amended. London, Printed by W. Wilde for N. Boddington in Duck Lane ; and J. Blare on London Bridge. 1696. 12° or sm. 8°, A—H in twelves. *H. Stopes, Esq.*

SHROPSHIRE.
A Letter from Shrewsbury; setting forth the Design which the Anabaptists and Quakers had to secure the Castle, and to have received five hundred more unto them in opposition to the Parliament. London, Printed for T. H. [March 1, 1659-60.] A broadside. *B. M.*

SIBBALD, SIR ROBERT, *M.D.*
Disputatio Medica De Variis Tabis speciebus.... Robertus Sybbaldus, Scoto-Edinburg.... Lugduni Batavorum, ... cIɔ. Iɔc. LXI. 4°, A—B in fours, B 4 blank. Dedicated to John, Earl of Lindsay.

Nuncius Scoto-Britannus, Sive Admonitio de Atlante Scotico Seu Descriptione Scotiæ Antiqvæ et Modernæ.... Cum Tabulis Geographicis in lucem publicam ilicò edendâ per Robertum Sibbaldum.... Edinburgi In Officinâ Typographicâ Davidis Lindesii, ... M.DC.LXXXIII. Folio. Title, 1 leaf: ¶, 2 leaves: A, 1 leaf: B—E, 2 leaves each: *Catalogus*, &c., 7 leaves: A—Ee, 2 leaves each: Ff, 1 leaf: Index. 3 leaves: *Pars Secunda*, with a new title, dedication, and Index, 3 leaves: A, 1 leaf: B—O, 2 leaves each: P, 1 leaf: Index and List of Plates, 2 leaves: Plates, 18 leaves.

Scotland Illustrated: Or, An Essay of Natural History, In which are Exquisitely displayed the Nature of the Country; The Dispositions and Manners of the Inhabitants, and the Various Diseases incident to them; ... And the manifold Productions of Nature in the Threefold Kingdom, (viz.) Vegetable, Animal and Mineral, ... Illustrated with near Fifty Copper Plates. Being the Work of Twenty Years. Published by the Command of ... Charles II. ... By Sir R. Sibbald M.D. Knight, Geographer to His Majesty, and Fellow of the Kings Colledge of Physicians at Edinburgh. Edinburgh, Printed by J. K. J. S. and J. C. and are to be Sold by Tho. Malthus at the Sun in the Poultry. London. 1684. Folio.

    A reissue of the *Nuncius*, 1683, with a new title.

Phalainologia Nova. Sive Observationes de Rarioribus quibusdam Balænis in Scotiæ Littus Nuper Ejectis.... Edinburgi, Typis Joannis Redi. M DC XCII. 4°. A—F 2 in fours, besides title and following leaf.

Auctarium Musæi Balfouriani, E Musæo Sibbaldiano, Sive Enumeratio & Descrip-

tio Rerum Rariorum, ... Quas Robertus Sibbaldus, M.D. Eques Auratus, Academiæ Edinburgenæ donavit. ... Edinburgi, Impressum per Academiæ Typographum, Sumptibus Academiæ, 1697. 8°, A—Ff in fours. *B. M.*

The History, Ancient and Modern, of the Sheriffdoms of Fife and Kinross; With the Description of Both, and of the Firths of Forth and Tay, And the Islands in them. In which, there is an Account of the Royal Seats and Castles; And of the Royal Burghs and the Ports; ... With an Account of the Natural Products of the Land and Waters. By Sir Robert Sibbald, Doctor of Medicin ... Edinbvrgh: Printed by James Watson, for the Author. M. DCC. X. Folio. Title and leaf of dedication to the Right Honourable the Earl of Rothess, Sheriff-principal of Fife, 2 leaves: ++, 3 leaves: B—Tt, 2 leaves each: Appendix, 2 leaves, and a folded plate between K and L.

SIMON, *of London Wall, Anchorite.*
**¶The Fruite of Redempcion: very profitable and moche necessary for euery christen man. [This title is over a cut of the Cross enclosed in a border. At the end occurs:] ¶ Imprinted by me Robert Redman ... The yere of our lorde god. M.D.xxxi. 8°, A—E 4 in eights.

SINNERS.
**The Contemplacyon of Synners. [Col.] Here endeth the treatyse called the Contemplacion of synners for every day of the weke a singular medytacyon. Emprentyd at Westmynster by Wynkyn de worde th. x. daye of Iuly. the yere of our lorde M.CCCC.LXXXIX. 4°.

    Compiled and finished at the request of Richard Fox, Bishop of Durham, and Lord Privy Seal.

SMART, PETER.
A Sermon Preached in the Cathedrall Chvrch of Dvrham. Iuly 7. 1628 ... Printed in the Yeare, 1640. 4°, A—E in fours.

SMITH, RICHARD.
Florvm Historiæ Ecclesiasticæ Gentis Anglorvm, Libri Septem.... Parisiis, ... M.DC.LIIII. ... Folio. ã, 6 leaves: A—HHh in fours, the last leaf with the *Approbatio*, &c. Dedicated to Pope Innocent X.

SNAPE, ANDREW, *Junior, Farrier to His Majesty.*
The Anatomy of An Horse. Containing An exact and full Description of the Frame, Situation and Connexion of all

his Parts, (with their Actions and Vses) exprest in Forty-nine Copper-plates. To which is added an Appendix, Containing two Discourses: The one, of the Generation of Animals; And the other, of the Motion of the Chyle, and the Circulation of the Bloud. London, Printed by M. Flesher for the Authour, and are to be sold by T. Flesher... 1683. Folio, A—Fff in fours: 3 G, 2 leaves. With a portrait of the author by White, an. æt. 38, 1682, and the plates. Dedicated to Charles II.

> Sotheby's, July 23, 1888, No. 111, large paper, old red morocco gilt, the great Duke of Ormonde's copy, £20.

SNAWSELL, ROBERT.
A Looking-Glasse for married Folkes. Wherein they may plainly see their deformities; and also how to behaue themselues one to another, and both of them towards God. Set forth Dialogue-wise for the more tastable and plainnesse sake, By R. S. ... London. Printed by N. O. for Henry Bell, and are to bee sold at his shop on Holburne Hill neere the crosse Keyes. 1610. Sm. 8°, A—H 4 in eights, first and last leaves blank. *B. M.*

SOLDIERS.
A Proclamation for restraint of disorders in Souldiers, prested for his Maiesties seruice. Printed at London by Bonham Norton, and Iohn Bill, ... M.DC.XXV. A broadsheet formed of two leaves.

SOMERSETSHIRE.
A Fvll Declaration of All Particulers concerning the March of the Forces under Collonel Fiennes to Bristoll, and their carriage upon their enemies approach. As also A Relation of the late bloody abominable conspiracy against the City of Bristoll, ... With the certaine Information, touching the death of Will: Kendall, a Trooper of Collonel Essex, who was shot by the said Collonel. From a Noble hand. Aprill, 18. London: Printed for R. D. 1643. 4°, A—C 2 in fours.

SPARKE, MICHAEL, *Stationer.*
The Crvms of Comfort with godly Prayers. Corrected and amended. 7. Edition. Ioh. 6. 12. *Gather vp the broken meat.* London. printed for Mi. Sparke. 1628. 12°, A—L in twelves, A 1 blank: *Thankfull Remembrances of Gods Wonderfull Deliuerances of this Land,* with a new title, A—C in twelves, C 12 blank, besides four folded engravings, descriptive of the Gunpowder Plot, the Spanish Armada, the restoration of Protestantism under Elizabeth, and the cessation of the Plague of 1625. *B. M.*

SPARKE, THOMAS.
A Sermon Preached at Whaddon in Buckinghamshyre the 22. of Nouember 1593. at the buriall of the Right Honorable, Arthvr Lord Grey of Wilton, Knight of the most Honorable order of the Garter, by Thomas Sparke Pastor of Blechley. At Oxford, Printed by Ioseph Barnes Printer to the Vniversitie. 1593. 8°. ¶, 4 leaves: A—F 4 in eights. Dedicated to the Countess of Bedford and the Lady Grey her daughter. With some Latin elegiac lines by John Sanford.

SPRUEL, JOHN.
An Accompt Current betwixt Scotland & England Ballanced; Together with An Essay of a Scheme of the Product of Scotland, and a few Remarks on each. As also A View of the several Products of the Ports or Nations we trade to, ... By J. S. a Lover of our protestant Queen, Country, and Trade. ... Edinburgh Printed by the Heirs and Successors of Andrew Anderson, ... 1705. 4°. Title and dedication to the Duke of Argyll, 2 leaves: A—B 2 in fours: A—G, 2 leaves each.

STAFFORD, WILLIAM, *Viscount.*
Procès de Guillaume, Vicomte de Stafford, ... Traduit sur l'Original Anglois ... A Cologne, Chez Pierre Marteau, 1681. 12°, A—Gg 6 in twelves.

STANBRIDGE, JOHN, *Grammarian.*
*Vocabula mgrī Stābrigi saltem editione edita. Imprinted at London in the Southwarke by me Peter Treueris. 4°. D in fours. Black letter.

**Vocabula magistri stābrigii. [Col.] Imprynted at London by Wynkyn de Worde dwellynge in fletestrete at the sygne of the sonne agaynst the condyth. The xvij. day of August in the yere of our lorde god M.v.C. and xxxij. 4°.

*Accidentia ex Stanbrigiana: editio nuper recognita et castigata lima Roberti Whitintoni Lichfeldiensis in florentissima Oxoniensi accademia laureati. [Col.] Imprynted at London without Bishopyes gate in saynt Botulphus parysshe by me John Skot dwelling at George alley gate. 4°.

> Herbert does not give the collation.

**Accidentia ex Stanbrigiana editione nuper recognita et castigata lima Roberti Whitintoni ... [Col.] Imprynted in London in Aldersgate strete, by Nycholas Bourman, in the yere of our lord god M.cccccc. and xxxix. 4°, 16 leaves. *Althorp.*

> The text begins on the back of the title.

*Accidētia ex stābrigiana editione nuper recognita & castigata lima Roberti whitintoni Lichfeldiēsis . . . Imprynted at London in Southwarke by Peter Treueris. 4°, D in fours. Black letter.

*Accidentia . . . Imprynted in Southwarke by me Peter Treueris. 4°, A—B⁴ : C⁶.

 The title in this other Southwark impression is over a cut of a priest seated before a reading-desk.

STANDISH, ARTHUR.
The Commons Complaint. Wherein is contained Two Speciall Grievances . . . London, Printed by William Stansby. 1612. 4°, A—H in fours, A 1 and H 4 blank, besides "The Figure of the Plot," a folded leaf.

 Following the title is the royal privilege.

STARKEY, GEORGE.
Natures Explication and Helmont's Vindication, Or, A short and sure way to a long and sound life. Being A necessary and full Apology for Chymical Medicaments, . . . By George Starkey, a Philosopher made by the fire, and a professor of that Medicine which is real and not Histrionical. London, Printed by E. Cotes for Thomas Alsop . . . 1657. 8°. A, 8 leaves : a—c in eights, c 8 with the label : B—Y in eights. Dedicated to Robert Tichborn, Lord Mayor of London.

STATUTES.
[Noua Statuta. This is a headline on the first page of the text of the Acts 1 Edw. 1. to 12 Henry 7. At the end occurs :] Emprynted by my Rycharde Pynson. Folio, black letter. Table, a, 6 leaves : b—c in eights : d, 6 : a (repeated with the commencement of text)—z in eights : two sheets of 8 irregularly marked : A—C in eights : D—F in sixes : G, 4 : Anno xi. Henrici vij. [the 8th, 9th, and 10th years wanting], D, 8 : E, 6 : F, 5 : G, 3. With the printer's mark on G 3 verso.

 Aylesford sale at Christie's, March 15, 1888, No. 1735. first leaf of Table deficient, and the 19th year Hen. 7 printed by Pynson bound up at end from another book.

In this Volume are conteined the statutes made and established from the time of kyng Henry the thirde, vnto the fyrste yere of the reigne of our most gratious and victorious lorde king Henry the . viii. Anno M.D.XLIII. [Col.] Londini in officina Thomæ Bertheleti typis impress. Cum priuilegio . . . Anno. M.D.XLIII. Folio. Title and Table, 7 leaves : A—Y in eights : A (repeated) or rather Aa—Qq in eights : Rr—Tt in sixes, Tt 6 blank : a—f in eights : g—i in sixes. *H. Stopes, Esq.*

 Puttick's, Jan. 31, 1888, No. 673.

[Statutes of the First Year of Charles II.] Anno Regni Caroli IJ. Regis Angliæ, . . . Duodecimo. At the Parliament begun at Westminster, the Five and twentieth day of April, An. Dom. 1660 . . . London : Printed by John Bill and Christopher Barker, . . . 1660. Cum Privilegio. Folio. *H. Stopes, Esq.*

 This Collection opens with the Act for removing and preventing all Questions and Disputes concerning the Assembling and Sitting of this present Parliament, and contains 26 other separate titles, mostly with separate signatures. It includes the Subsidy of Tonnage and Poundage.

A Collection of all the Statutes now in Force, Relating to the Excise upon Beer, Ale, and other Liquors ; With An Abridgment of the said Statutes, and a Table of the Rates upon the several Liquors, &c. shewing by what Acts they are Imposed. To which is added A Table of Allowances for Common Brewers, &c. London, Printed by John Baskett, . . . And by the Assigns of Thomas Newcomb, and Henry Hills, deceas'd. 1722. 8°, A—Z in twelves. *H. Stopes, Esq.*

[Magnum abbreviamentum. Col.] Explicit abbreuiamentū statutor impssum p Richardū Pynson & totaliter finitum nono die Mensis octobris. Anno dñi Mill'mo quatercentessimo Nonagesimo nono. 12° or sm. 8°. Table, 7 leaves, possibly preceded by a title here wanting : a—z in eights, followed by four leaves, of which the last has on the verso the colophon and mark.

 Puttick's, May 5, 1887, No. 596. The British Museum copy has no title.

*An Abridgment of the Statutes. [Col.] Enprynted in the chepesyde at the sygne of the meremayde next to poulys gate the xxii. day of Decēber in the xix. yere of the reygne of our souerayne lorde kinge Henry the . viii. ¶ Per me Johannem Rastell. Cum Priuilegio Regali. [1527.] 8°, folioes 264.

*The grete abregement of the statutys of Englond vntyll the . xxij. yere of kyng Henry the . viij. Cum priuilegio Regali. [Col.] Prynted by w. Rastell in Fletestrete in saynte Brydys chyrch yarde. 1533. Cum priuilegio. 8°. *The Statutes* on 293 leaves, besides the statutes expired : abridgment of the statutes of the 22nd year, 16 leaves : abridgment of the statutes of the 23rd and 24th years, C 10 in eights.

This collation is Herbert's or Ames's.

*The greate abbrydgement of all ȳ statutes of Englande / vntyll the . xxx. yere of the reygne of our moste dread soueraygne lorde kynge Henry the eyght. To whom be all honour . . . Amen. Cum priuilegio Regali. [Col.] ¶ Imprynted at London in Fletestrete / at the sygne of the George nexte to Saynt Dunstones churche by me Roberte Redman. Cum priuilegio Regali. 8°, FFF in eights, besides the prologue and table.

**Annus quadragesimus Edwardi tercii nouiter impressus et castigatus. vna cum multis aliis casibus adiectis nunquam antea impressis. [This is over a cut of the King enthroned, &c. At the end we have:] ¶ Imprime a Loūdres par moy Robert Redman le . x. iour de Marche. Lan de grace . MCCCCCXXXIIII. Cum priuilegio regali. Folio, 52 leaves.

The woodcut on the title illustrates the legal costume of the time when the volume appeared.

**Anno 28. Hen. VI. [Col.] Explicit. Imprynted by Richarde Pynson prenter vnto the Kyngs noble grace. Folio, a—b in sixes.

**A°. xxxiiii. Henr. VI. [Col.] Impressus par Richardum Pynsonum regiū impressorem. Cum priuilegio. Folio. Ends on L 6. Without running title, folioes, and catchwords.

**A°. ii°. Edw. IV. [Col.] Explicit annus sed'ns E. iiii. sed'm Townsend de nono impressus in academia, ere ac impensis honesti viri Richardi Pynson Regii īpressoris. Folio. aˣ: b—d in sixes: E⁴.

**A°. iiii. Edw. IV. [Col.] Explicit annus quartus Edwardi quarti. Imprynted at London in Fletestrete, by Rycharde Pynson, prynter to ȳ Kings noble grace. Folio. a⁶: b⁴: c⁶: d⁶: e⁴: f⁶: g⁶: h⁸. The last leaf probably had the device, the colophon occurring on h 7.

Anno I. Henrici . vii. [This occurs on A ii, A i being deficient. The colophon is :] Enprynted at London withonte Tempell Barre / in Saynt Clementys parysshe / By me Julyan Notary dwellynge at the syne of the thre kynges. In ȳ yere of our lorde a. M.CCCC.vii. 4°. A—E in sixes: F, 8.

This volume contains also the second, third, and fourth years. The printer's device is on F 8 verso. Sotheby's, July 14, 1887, No. 528.

Anno vii. Henrici . vii. [This occurs on aa, the rest of the page occupied by woodcuts. Col.] Enprynted at London withoute Tempell Barre / . . . a. M.CCCCC.vii. 4°, aa in eights.

Annexed, in the same volume, sold at Sotheby's as above mentioned, occurred the 11th year, Aa—Gg in sixes, and the 19th year, A—B in sixes : C, 4 : D, 4 : E, 4 : F, 3.

*Statuta in parliamento apud Westmonesterium vicessimo quinto die Januarii anno regni metvendis-imi regis Anglie et Francie domini Hibernie Henrici septimi decimo nono tento pro bono publico subditorum suorum inter cetera edita. [This is over a cut of the King, attended by the serjeants in their coifs, &c. Col.] Emprented at London in Fletestrete at the signe of the George by saynt Dunstones chyrche by me Richard Pynson squyer and prenter vnto the kynges noble grace. Folio.

**Anno Regni Regis Henrici . viij. Tertio Statuta. The Kynge our soueraygne lorde Henry the viij. . . . [Col.] Emprynted by the commandement of our Souereign lord the Kyng and his counsell (by Richard Pynson printer vnto his noble grace, dwellyng in London in Fletestrete at the sygne of the George besyde saynt Dunstanes churche). 4°. A⁶: B⁴: C⁶: D³: E⁴.

Anno XXIII. Henrici Octavi. The king our soueraigne lord Henry the eyght by the grace of god . . . at the sessions of his high Court of parliament after diuers prorogations, helden at westminster the . xv. daye of January / in the . XXIII. yere of his most noble reign . . . hath ordeined established and enacted certaine good statutis lawes and ordynaunces in maner and fourme folowynge. [Col.] God save the Kinge. Imprinted at London in Fletestrete by Thomas Berthelet prynter to the kynges moste noble grace. . . . [1532.] Folio, A—D in sixes.

Anno. XXIII. H. VIII. The kynge oure soueraigne lorde Henry the eight . . . at the session of his highe Courte of Parliament after diuerse prorogations, holden at westminster the . xv. day of January, . . . hath ordeyned established and enacted certayne lawes and ordinances in maner and fourme folowing. [Col.] Imprinted at London in Fletestrete by Thomas Berthelet printer to the kynges moste noble grace. Cum priuilegio. Folio, A—D in sixes. With the royal arms supported by angels below the colophon.

There is a third edition in the British

Museum, differing in certain typographical particulars from these two.

*Anno secundo & tertio, Edovardi Sexti. ¶ Actes made in the session of this present Parliament, holden vpon prorogation at Westminster, the fourth day of Nouember, in the second yeare of our most dreed soueraign Lord Edward vi. . . . and there continued and kept to the xiiij. day of Marche, in the III. yeare of our sayde Soueraygne Lorde . . . [Col.] Richardvs Graftonvs Typographus Regius excudebat Anno domini. 1552. . . . Folio, 68 leaves.

*¶ Anno Qvinto et sexto Edwardi Sexti. Actes made in the Sessiō of this present parliament holden vpon prorogation at Westminster the viii. daye of Januarye, in the fifthe yeare of the reygne of . . . Edwarde the . vi. . . . and there continued and kept till the . xv. day of Aprill, in the . vi. yeare . . . [Col.] ¶ Richardvs Graftonvs typographus Regius excudebat. Mense Junii, 1552. Cum priuilegio. . . . Folio, 33 leaves.

Anno Primo Reginae Elizabethe. At the parliament begonne at Westmynster, the xxiij. of January . . . Anno. 1559. [Col.] Imprinted at London in Powles Church yarde by Richard Iugge, and Iohn Cawood, Printers to the Quenes Maiestie. Anno. M.D.LIX. Cum priuilegio. . . . Folio, A—E in sixes : F, 8 : *Act of Subsidy,* &c., A—B in sixes : C, 4. *H. Stopes, Esq.*

Anno xiiij. Reginae Elizabethe. At the parliament begunne and holden at Westminster the eyght of Maye, . . . 1572. [Col.] Imprinted at London in Powles Churchyarde by Richard Iugge, . . . Folio, A—D in sixes, D 6 blank.

Anno xviii. Reginae Elizabethe. At this present Session of Parliament by prorogation holden at Westminster the viii. day of February, . . . 1575. [Col.] Imprinted at London by Richarde Iugge, . . . Folio, A—E in sixes : F in eights: *Act of Fifteens*, &c., A—C in sixes : *Act of General Pardon*, A in sixes, the last leaf containing a table of unprinted Acts.

Anno xxxv. Reginae Elizabethae. At the Parliament begun and holden at Westminster the xix. day of Februarie, . . . Imprinted at London by the Deputies of Christopher Barker . . . 1593. Folio, A—D in sixes : E, 4 leaves : ¶, 4 leaves : ¶¶, 4 leaves : Aa—Cc in sixes : Dd, 2 leaves : Ee, 6 leaves.

Anno xliij. Reginae Elizabethae. At the Parliament begun and holden at Westminster the xxvij. day of October, . . . Imprinted at London by Robert Barker, . . . [1601.] Folio, A—Ff in sixes, Ff 6 blank : Gg, 4 leaves.

[STEPHENS, EDWARD.]
Reflections upon the Occurrences of the Last Year. From 5. Nov. 1688. to 5. Nov. 1689. Wherein the Happy Progress of the late Revolution, and the Unhappy Progress of Affairs since, are considered ; The Original of the latter discovered, and the proper Means for Remedy proposed and recommended. [Quot. from Prov. xxvii. 5. 6.] London, Printed in the Year, 1689. 4°, A—E in fours.

STEPNEY, W.
The Spanish Schoole-master. Containing Seven Dialogues, according to euery day in the weeke, and what is necessarie euerie day to be done, wherein is also most plainly shewed the true and perfect pronunciation of the Spanish tongue, . . . Newly collected and set forth by W. Stepney, professor of the said tongue in the famous Citie of London. *Spes anchora tuta.* Imprinted at London by R. Field for Iohn Harison. 1591. 8°. A, 4 leaves : B—R in eights, R 7 with Errata and R 8 blank. Dedicated by Stepney to Robert Cecil, son of Lord Burleigh, in Spanish. *B. M.*

This volume includes Proverbs and Sentences, the Lord's Prayer, the Creed, the Ten Commandments, and a Vocabulary.

STEVENSON, MATTHEW.
Occasions Off-spring. Or Poems upon Severall Occasions : By Mathew Stevenson.

Mart. *Die mihi quid melius desidiosus agas ?*
London, Printed for John Place, and are to be sold at his shop at Furnivalls Inne Gate in Holborne 1645. 12°. A, 6 leaves : B—G 6 in twelves. With a portrait by Gaywood, having some facetious verses beneath it. Dedicated to his cousin, Mr. Benjamin Cook.

ST. GERMAIN, CHRISTOPHER.
*Here after foloweth a lyttell treatise called the newe addicions. [Col.] Thomas Bertheletus regius impressor excudebat. Anno domini. M.D.XXXI. Cum priuilegio a rege indulto. 8°, 16 leaves.

STONE.
The Warming Stone, Excellent Helps really found out, tried, and had, by a Warming Stone in his Case, which not costing much, will save much cost in fire and withall avoyd the danger of fire : And likewise is very usefull and comfortable for

the colds of aged and sicke people, and for Women with child, and in Child-bed: As also for Fluxes, . . . And likewise for the Poore. . . . These Stones with their Cases are to be sold at John Bartlets Shop in Pauls Churchyard. London, Printed by R. H. for Iohn Bartlet. . . . 1640. 4°, 4 leaves. *B. M.*

> At p. 5 the writer says: "It is also exceeding usefull for all schollars to heate their hands and feet, when they must attend their studies in cold weather. And for al persons which by their trades in such seasons must keep their shops, or for the service of God continue in the Church."

STRACHEY, WILLIAM.

For The Colony in Virginea Britannia. Lawes Diuine, Morall and Martiall, &c. *Alget qui non Ardet. Res nostræ suhinde non sunt, quales quis optaret, sed quales esse possunt.* Printed at London for Walter Burre. 1612. 4°, A—N in fours, besides two leaves in A after title with dedications to the Council of Virginia, the Lord [De] La Warr, and Sir Thomas Smith. *B. M.*

> On the flyleaf of this copy is an autograph inscription by Strachey, presenting the book to William Crashaw, Minister in the Middle Temple.
>
> These Laws, &c., are represented as having been originally framed by Sir Thomas Gates in 1610, amplified and approved by Lord De la Warr the same year, and again exemplified and enlarged by Sir Thomas Dale, Marshal and Deputy-Governor, 22d June 1611.

[STUART, SIR J., AND THE REV. J. STIRLING.]

Napthali, Or The Wrestlings of the Church of Scotland for the Kingdom of Christ; Contained in A true and short Deduction thereof, from the beginning of the Reformation of Religion, until the Year 1667. . . . Whereunto are also subjoined A Relation of the Sufferings and Death of Mr Hen. McKail, and some Instances of the sufferings of Galloway and Nithisdale . . . Printed in the Year 1667. 8°. (a)—(c) in eights: (a)—(b) in eights: A—T in eights, T 8 blank.

STUBBE, HENRY.

The Common-Wealth of Oceana Put into the Ballance, and found too light. Or An Account of the Republick of Sparta, with occasional Animadversions upon Mr James Harrington and the Oceanistical Model. By Henry Stvbbe of Ch. Ch. Oxon. . . . London, Printed for Giles Calvert, . . . 1660. 4°. Title and to the Reader, 2 leaves: B—B (repeated) in fours.

STUBBES, PHILIP.

A Chrystal Glass for Christian Women, Containing A most Excellent Discourse. . . . London, Printed for William Thackeray, at the Angel in Duck-lane. 4°, A—C in fours. Black letter. *B. M.*

SULPITIUS VERULANUS, JOHANNES.

**Stans puer ad mensam. [This title is in roman letter over the printer's blackgrounded device. At the end occurs:] Londini in edibus Wynandi de Worde xxiiij. supra sesquimillesimū nostre salutis. Pridie Kalendas Nouembris. 4°, 6 leaves.

*Grammatice Sulpitianacū textu Ascēsiano recognito & ancto: vt proximo patebit epistolio. [This title is over an ordinary woodcut. The colophon:] Auctum atq; recognitū est hoc opus opera Ascensiano. Impressumq; in ciuitate London. Per Richardum Pynson: in vico dicto the Fletestrete / In signo Georgij cōmorantem. Anno . M . ccccc . v . xi. die. Augusti. 4°. A—X in sixes: Aa—Ii in sixes.

**SUM, ES, FUI.
[A Treatise of Verbs. At the end:] Printed at London in the Olde bayly by Thomas Godfray. 4°, 8 leaves. *Althorp.*

> This seems to be the only work by this printer with his place of business mentioned.

SURREY.

A most strange and rare example of the iust iudgement of God executed vpon a lewde and wicked Coniurer [Simon Pembroke]. The . xvij. day of Januarie . M.D.LXXVIJ. In the parish church of S. Marie Ouerie in Southwark, in the presence of diuers credible & honest persons. Imprinted at London, by Henrie Bennyman. 8°, black letter, 6 leaves. With a cut on the title. *B. M.*

> Following the title is a leaf of verses of a religious cast; the rest of the tract is prose.

A Brief Narrative of the Proceedings of Doctor Parr, And some of the Parishioners of Mary Magdalen - Bermonsey in the County of Surrey. Against certain People called Quakers, Inhabitants of the said Parish for not Paying and Complying with an Illegal Tax, laid under pretence of Repairing their Church. . . . Also an Exhortory Reprehension upon the whole . . . Printed in the Year 1677. 4°, A—K, 2 leaves each.

A Charge given at the General Quarter-Sessions of the Peace for the County of

Surrey, Holden at Dorking on Tuesday the 5th day of April, 1692 . . . By the Honourable Hugh Hare, Esq; . . . The Second Edition Corrected. London, Printed for John Newton . . . 1696. 4°, A—E in fours.

> Hare, one of the County Magistrates, dates from Betchworth.

SYLVESTER, BERNARD.
*Here begynneth a shorte monycyon, or counsayle of the cure & gouernaunce of a housholde / accordynge vnto policy : taken out of a pystle of a great learned man, called Bernard sylvestre. [Col.] Here endeth the boke Intituled the gouernaunce of housholde Imprynted by me Robert Wyer in the bysshop of Norwytche rentes besyde charynge crosse. 8vo, a—b in fours.

SYLVESTER, JOSHUA, Merchant-Adventurer.
Poems . . . . 1614-15. Small 8vo. 2 vols.

> On the flyleaf of a copy of this book in the hands of Messrs. Jarvis & Son, January 27, 1888, occurred the following memorandum, apparently in the autograph of Sylvester :—
> "1617. In Middlebourgh. 19°. Septembrs. To my worthy ffrind Mr. George Morgan Marchant-Adventurr.
> Accept wth this poore Mite a minde
> That honnours worth in euerie kinde."

T.

T. A.
A Rich Store-house or Treasury for the Diseased. Wherein, are many approued Medicines for diuers and sundry diseases, which haue been long hidden, and not come to light before this time. Now set foorth for the great benefit and comfort of the poorer sort of people, that are not of abilitie to go to the Physitions. By A. T. Rebus aduersis constans. At London, Printed for Thomas Purfoot, and Raph Blower, Ann. 1596. 4°. A, 2 leaves: B—V 2 in fours. Dedicated by Blower the stationer to the Right Honourable Thomas Skinner, Lord Mayor of London.

TABLES.
*[Writing Tables. At the end occurs :] Made at London by Robert Triplet, Stationer or Bookebinder, dwelling in Distaffe lane, at the signe of the Aqua vite Still, neere olde fishstreete, and are there to be solde. [1587.] Oblong 8°. [A]—D in eights.

> Described by Herbert, p. 1762, from an imperfect copy then belonging to Douce.

TANNER, THOMAS, Bishop of St. Asaph.
Notitia Monastica Or A Short History of the Religious Houses in England and Wales. By Thomas Tanner B.A. Oxford, Printed at the Theater, and are to be sold by A. and J. Churchill at the sign of the Black Swan in Pater-noster-row, London. 1695. 8°, a—f 2 in eights : plates of arms, 5 leaves : A—X 3 in eights. Dedicated to Dr. Leopold-William Finch, Warden of All Souls College.

TARBAT, GEORGE, Viscount, Clerk to H. M. Councils, Registry, and Rolls.
A Vindication of Robert III. King of Scotland, From the Imputation of Bastardy, by the clear Proof of Elizabeth Mure (Daughter of Sir Adam Mure of Rowallan) her being the first Lawful Wife of Robert the II. then Stewart of Scotland and Earl of Strathern. To be Sold at Thomas Carruther's Shop in the Parliament-Closs. Edinbvrgh, Printed by the Heirs and Successors of Andrew Anderson, . . . Anno Dom. 1695. 4°. A, 2 leaves : B—G in fours, G 4 with the Descent of Charles II. from Fergus I.

TAVERNER, JOHN.
Certaine Experiments concerning Fish and Frvite : Practised by John Taverner Gentleman, and by him published for the benefit of others. London, Printed for William Ponsonby. 1600. 4°, A—F in fours, first and last leaves blank.

> In the dedication to Sir Edmond Anderson, Chief Justice of the Common Pleas, the author states that he had been induced to print these remarks by the translation of Dubravius. He refers to this again in the Preface, where he seems to speak of himself as a person of leisure, who hereby sought to occupy his time.

TAYLOR, JOHN, the Water-Poet.
Verbum Sempiternum. London: Printed by F. Collins for T. Hive, at the Nags Head in Jewen-Street, 1693. The Old Testament, A—K in eights, A 1 with Imprimatur and A 2 with half-title : The

New, a—h in eights, h 7-8 blank. Dedicated to Queen Mary.
> The copy employed was obligingly lent to me by Messrs. Pearson & Co. of Pall Mall.

TENURES.
[The Old Tenures.] Tenir per ceruice de chiualer : est a tente p homage foialte & escuage & tret a luy garde mariage & relfʒ. [This is a headline on A 1.] No place, &c. [London, R. Pynson.] Folio, A in sixes.
> Bound up with the *Natura Brevium* and Lyttelton's *Tenures* by Pynson, from the Earl of Roden's library, sold at Sawbridgeworth in April or May 1888. A second copy is at Lambeth.

Tenir per seruice de chiualer : . . . [Col.] Impressum per Richardum Pynson. Folio, 8 leaves, the first occupied by a shield of arms. There is no title-page. *Grenv. Coll.*
> The colophon in this probably later impression occurs below the line beginning *Suite seruice*, in place of the word *Finis* in the other copy.

[The Old Tenures. Tenir per service . . . At the end :] This Booke with the Natura Breuium was Empryntyd by me Rychard Pynson at the Instaunce of my maysters of the cōpany of Stronde Inne with oute tempyll Barre. off London. Folio, a in eights, a 1 with the shield of arms only, as in the Grenville copy.
> Bound up with the *Natura Brevium* among Addington's books, and doubtless intended to accompany it, yet nevertheless a distinct publication.

Olde teners newly corrected. [Col.] Finis vetustarę legis tenurarum . . . Lōdini in edibnę Roberti Redmā Anno salut' nostre M.ccccc.xxviii. die vero xx. Januarii. Cum gratia & priuilegio. Sm. 8°, A—B in eights, B 8 blank. With the crowned Tudor rose on the title.

*The olde tenures. [Col.] Hunc libellum excudebat Thomas Bertheletus regius impressor. Anno domini Millesimo quingentesimo tricesimo. 8°, 12 leaves.

TERENTIUS AFER, PUBLIUS.
**[The Flowers and Eloquent phrases. At the end occurs :] Londini in AEdibvs Thomæ Bertheleti Regii Impressoris excvs. Anno. M.D.XXXVIII. 8°, 192 leaves + title and other prefixes.
> Herbert's copy wanted the preliminary matter.

TESTAMENT.
The New Testament of ovr Lord Iesvs Christ, translated out of Greeke by Theod. Beza. And Englished by L. T. Lvke

11. x. *Beholde, I bring you glad tidings . . .* At Dort Printed, by Isaac Canin. 1601. at the expensis of the aires of Henrie Charteris, and Andrew Hart, in Edinburgh. Cum Priuilegio Regali. Title, Calendar, &c., 8 leaves : A—Xx 3 in eights. A pocket volume. *B. M.*

*THOMAS DE CAMPIS.
Here ben cōteyned tiue notable Chapytres : moche profytable for euery man, dylygently to recorde. And after do folowe thyrteue degrees of Mortyfycacyon. [Col.] ¶Imprynted by me Robert wyer in the bysshop of Norwytche rentes. ¶Cum priuilegio regali. 8°, A—C 6 in eights.

THOMAS, WILLIAM.
[Pelegrine's Defence of Henry VIII. against the calumnies of Clement VII. in connection with the divorce from Anne Boleyn.] 4°, 64 leaves.
> An apparently unpublished MS. on paper. At the end, on the last leaf, otherwise blank, occurs :
> "Castigans castigauit me Dominus & morti non tradidit me.
>   W Thomas."
> The only title is the word PELEGRINE, beneath which, perhaps in a different hand, are two lines of verse. This leaf is followed by "Pelegrine vnto the Reader." The text commences on fol. 2 with an account of the origin of the treatise, the composition of which is laid at Bologna.
> Sotheby's, June 1888 (Turner), No. 1495.

THOMPSON, SIR JOHN, *Baronet.*
The Earl of Anglesey's State of the Government & Kingdom : Prepared and intended for His Majesty, King Charles II. In the Year 1682. but the Storm Impending growing so high prevented it then. With a short Vindication of His Lordship from several Aspersions cast upon Him, in a pretended Letter that carries the Title of His Memoirs. London : Printed for Samuel Crouch at the Corner of Pope's-Head-Alley in Cornhill. 1694. 4°, A—E in fours. Dedicated to the King and Queen.

*THORPE, WILLIAM.
The examinacion of Master William Thorpe prest accused of heresye before Thomas Arundell / Archbishop of Cāturbury / the yere of owre Lorde. M.cccc. and seuen. ¶ The examinacion of the honorable knight syr Jhon Oldcastell Lorde Cobham, burnt bi the said Archebishop in the fyrste yere of Kynge Henry the fyfth : ¶ be no more ashamed to heare it / then ye were and be / to do it. [About 1535.] 8°, I 4 in eights.

THOUGHTS.
Regular and Irregular Thoughts on Poets and Orators : London : Printed for John Hartley . . . 1697. 4°, A—E 2 in fours and the title.

THROCMORTON, JOB.
*The Defence of Iob Throkmorton against the slaunders of Maister Sutcliffe, taken out of a Copye of his owne hande as it was written to an honorable personage. Prouerbes 20. 6. *The taulke of the vngodly* . . . 1594. 4°, E in fours.

TITUS, SILAS, *Colonel.*
Traicte Politique Composé par William Allen Anglois, Et traduit nouvellement en François, ou il est prouvé par l'exemple de Moyse, & par d' autres, tirés hors de l' escriture, que Tuer un Tyran Titulo vel exercitio, n'est pas un meurtre. Lugduni, Anno. M.DC.LVIII. 12°, A—D in twelves, D 12 blank.

TOBACCO.
By the King. A Proclamation touching Tobacco. Printed at London by Bonham Norton and Iohn Bill, . . . M.DC.XXV. A broadsheet.

By the King. A Proclamation touching Tobacco. Imprinted at London by Bonham Norton and Iohn Bill, . . . M.DC.XXVI. A large broadsheet formed of three leaves.

A Proclamation for the ordering of Tobacco. Imprinted at London by Bonham Norton and Iohn Bill, . . . M.DC.XXVII. A broadsheet formed of two leaves.

TOBIAS.
*Mirabilia opera Dei : Certaine wonderfull Works of God which hapned to H. N. euen from his youth : and how the God of Heauen hath united himselfe with him, and raised up his gracious Word in him, and how he hath chosen and sent him to be a Minister of his gracious Word. Published by Tobias a Fellow Elder with H. N. in the Houshold of Love. Translated out of Base Almain. [Printed abroad about 1575.] 4°, pp. 137, besides the preface.

TREASURE.
†This Booke is called the Treasure of gladnese, and seemeth by the Copie, beying a very little Mannall, and written in Velam, to be made aboue . cc . yeres past at the least. Whereby it appereth howe God in olde tyme, and not of late only, hath ben truly confessed and honoured. The copie hereof is for the antiquitie of it, preserved, and to be seene in the Printers Hall. Set forth and allowed according to the Queenes Iniunctions.

Anno 1563. Imprinted at London by W. Williamson for Iohn Charlwood dwelling in Barbican. Small 8°.

**Here begynneth a newe boke of medecynes intytuled or callyd ỹ Treasure of pore men, whiche sheweth many dyuerse good medicines for dyuerse certayne dysseases as in ỹᵉ Table of ỹ present boke more playnly shall appere. The Boke of medicines. [Col.] Thus endeth y boke of Medycynes. Imprinted at London in ỹ pultre at ỹᵉ longe shoppe by saynt Myldredys churche dore by me Rycherd Bankes. Cum priuilegio . . . 4°, M in fours. With a cut on the title of a physician writing at his desk, &c.

Here begynneth a good Booke of Medecines called, the treasure of pore men. [Col.] Imprinted at London in Fletestrete, beneth the Conduit : at the Signe of Saynt John Euangeliste, by Thomas Colwell. 1575. 8°, A—K in eights, besides the title and Table, 4 leaves.

TREATISE.
Here begynneth a lytell necessarye Treatyse / the whiche speketh of the estate of the Comoualte and of the people / and how they ought to gouerne them in good maners. [Col.] ¶ Laus deo. ¶ Here endeth the boke Intituled good maners. Imprinted by me Robert Wyer in seynt Martyns parysshe besyde Charynge crosse. 8°, a—k in fours.

A Treatise concerning Adultery and Divorce . . . London : Printed by R. Roberts. 1700. 4°, A—E in fours.

TRIBULATION.
**Here begynnethe a lytyll treatyse which is called the XII. profytes of trybulacyon. [This title is over a cut, which Dibdin describes as "neatly executed and rare." The colophon is :] Emprynted at Westmynster in Caxtons hous. By me Wynkyn the Worde. 4°, A—D in sixes.

In Dibdin's time a copy was in the possession of Mr. Johnes of Hafod. He absurdly places it after the edition of 1530.

TRIUMPH.
The Hermetical Triumph : Or, The Victorious Philosophical Stone A Treatise More compleat and more intelligible than any extant, concerning The Hermetical Mystery. Translated from the French. To which is added, The Ancient War of the Knights ; Being an Alchymistical Dialogue betwixt our Sunne, Gold and Mercury ; . . . Translated from the German. London : Printed for Thomas Harris, at the Looking-Glass and Bible,

on London-Bridge. 8°. A, 8 leaves, including a frontispiece : (a), 4 leaves : (b), 2 leaves : B—L 2 in eights : [*], 8 leaves : [**], 2 leaves : [***], 8 leaves : [****], 2 leaves.

The Triumph of Friendship : And the Force of Love. Two New Novels from the French. London : Printed for D. Brown, . . . and J. Walthoe, . . . MDCLXXXV. Sm. 8°. A, 4 leaves : B—H in eights : I, 4 leaves. Dedicated by T. T. to Lord Lansdowne.

TURKEY.

*The tryumphant victory of the Imperyall mageste agaynst the turkes : The xxvi day of Septembre the yere of our lorde . M.CCCCC.XXXII in Steinmarke by a capytayne named Michael Meschsner. Cum priuilegio. [Col.] Deo gracias. Translated and Emprynted out of frenche into englysshe by Robert Copland dwelling in Flete strete by Flete brydge at the sygne of the Rose garland, for Rychard bankes Bookseller Anno dñi. MCCCCC. and xxxii. 4°, 4 leaves.

Reprinted entire by Dibdin (ii. 116-18) from a copy lent to him by Bindley.

**The order of the greate turckes courte, of hys menne of warre, and of all hys conquestes, with the somme of Maheometes doctrine. Translated oute of Frenche 1542. Richardus Grafton excudebat. Sm. 8°, A—H 4 in eights.

A Brief Accompt of the Turks Late Expedition. Against the Kingdome of Hungary, Transylvania, and the Hereditary Countries of the Emperour : Together with An Exact Narrative of the Remarquable Occurrences at the Siege of Newhausel. Translated out of Dutch. Printed with Privilege. London, Printed by Richard Hodgkinson, and Thomas Mab, MDCLXIII. 4°, A—F in fours.

TURNER, JAMES.

The Triumph of Truth : In an Exact and Impartial Relation of the Life and Conversation of Collonel James Turner ; which he imparted to an Intimate Friend, a little before his Execution. [1663.] 4°, B—E in fours.

The copy employed had no title or sign. A.

TURNER, RICHARD.

Yovth Know Thy Selfe.

Disce puer virtutem ex me, verumque laborem,
Fortunam ex alijs.

London, Printed by Avgvstine Mathewes and Iohn Norton, and are to be sold at the great South doore of Pauls. 1624. 4°, A—C 3 in fours. In verse. *B. M.* (Corser's copy.)

TURNER, ROBERT, *of Barnstaple.*

Roberti Tvrneri Devonii Oratoris et Philosophi Ingoldstadiensis Orationes XIV. . . . Commentationes in Loca Scriptvræ, . . . Panegyrici Dvo, . . . Ingoldstadii, . . . M.D.LXXXIIII. 8°.)(, 8 leaves : A—Q in eights : *Panegyrici*, &c., a—p in eights, p 7 with *Errata* and p 8 blank.

Roberti Tvrneri Devonii Oratoris et Philosophi Ingolstadiensis Orationes XIV. Accessit Oratio Fvnebris In Exeqviis Illvstriss. Princ. Eystensis, & Epistola ad Alanum Cardinalem. Antwerpiæ, . . . 1597 . . . 8°, a in eights : A—M 6 in eights.

TYNDALE, WILLIAM.

*A compendious introduccion / prologe or preface to the pistle of Paul to the Romayns. [After the *Introduction* occurs :] Here foloweth a treates (to fill vpp the leafe with all) of the pater noster / very necessary and profitable / . . . 8°, a—c 6 in eights.

Supposed by Herbert, whose copy had the last leaf mutilated, to have appeared between the first and second editions of Tyndale's New Testament.

TYRANTS.

The English Tyrants, Or, A brief Historie of the Lives and Actions of the high and mighty States, the Lords of Westminster, and now (by usurpation) Kings of England. Containing all their Rebellious and Traiterous Proceedings and Transactions in Parliament. With their levying of War, . . . Continued from the first Convention of this Parliament, 1640. untill the Kings Death, Jan. 30. 1648. . . . London, Printed in the Year, 1649. 4°, A—B in fours.

U.

UDALL, JOHN.
The Key of the Holy Tongve: Wherein is conteineid, first the Hebrue Grammar (in a manner) woord for woord out of P. Martinivs. Secondly, a practize... Thirdly, A short Dictionary... All Englished... By Iohn Udall. Imprinted at Leyden. By Francis Raphelengivs, cIɔ. Iɔ. xcIII. 8", A—Gg 4 in eights.

URINES.
*Here begynneth the seynge of Vrines of all coloures that Vrynes be of / with the medycines annexed to euery Vryne / & euery Vryne his Vrynal much profitable for euery man to knowe. [Col.] Here endeth the boke of seynge of waters Imprynted at London in Fletestrete / by me Elyzabeth late wyfe vnto Robert Redman, dwellyng... 8", A—F in eights.
**¶ Here beginneth the seinge of Vrynes... [Col.] Imprynted at London in Fletestrete at the sygne of the Rose Garland, by me Wyllyā Copland for Abraham Vele. In the yere of our Lord. M.D.L.II. The . xii. day of August. Sm. 8°, F in eights.

USHER, JAMES, *Archbishop of Armagh.*
Britannicarum Ecclesiarvm Antiqvitates. Quibus inserta est pestiferæ adversus Dei gratiam a Pelagio Britanno in Ecclesiam inductæ Hæreseos Historia. Collectore Jacobo Vsserio Archi-episcopo Armachano, totius Hiberniæ Primate. Dublinii, Ex Officinâ Typographicâ Societatis Bibliopolarum. Anno cIɔ Iɔc xxxIx. 4°. ¶, 4 leaves: A, 2 leaves: (a), 4 leaves: A—7 M in fours, the last leaf blank. Dedicated to the King.

The last sheet has the *Errata* only.

Prophecys Concerning the Return of Popery into England, Scotland, and Ireland. By Arch-bishop Vsher,... London, Printed for A. Bancks, MDCLXXXII. 4°, A—E in fours, E 4 blank.

V.

V. R.
The Manner of the Proceedings in the Courts of the Great Sessions in the Counties of Montgomery, Denbigh, and Flint; within North-Wales, as it is now is. Published by R. V. London, Printed, 1653. 4°, 4 leaves.

VALENCIUS.
[Expositiones super Psalterium. Col.] Expliciunt Reverendissimi doctoris Valerii sup. psalteriũ hucusq; expones. Impresse in civitate Londoniensi ad expensas Wilhelmi Wilcok per me Johannem Ietton. Anno Xp̃ı M.CCCC.LXXXI. Folio, 291 leaves + 55 more of Index. Without title, catchwords, and numerals. *Bodleian.*

VALENTINE AND ORSON.
The History of Valentine and Orson:... Belfast:... M.DCC.LXXXII. 4°, pp. 94 and the title. In two columns. With cuts.

VANDER LEYDEN HERMANNUS, *of Ghent, Physician.*
Speedy Help for Rich and Poor. Or, Certain Physicall Discourses touching the Vertue of Whey, in the Cure of the Griping Flux of the Belly, and of the Dysentery. Of Cold Water, in the Cure of the Gout, and Green-wounds. Of Wine-Vineger, in the Preservation from, and Cure of the Plague.... London, Printed by James Young, for O. P. and are to be sold by John Saywell.... 1653. 12°. A, 12 leaves, A, 1 blank : *, 6 leaves ; B—K in twelves, K 12 blank. *H. Stopes, Esq.*

The name of the English translator from the Latin does not appear.

VANE, THOMAS.
A Lost Sheep Returned Home : Or, The Motives of the Conversion to the Catholike Faith of Thomas Vane,... The Fourth Edition.... Printed at Paris, 1649. 12°, A—Ee 6 in twelves.

VAUGHAN, HENRY, *the Silurist.*
Olor Iscanvs. A Collection of some Select Poems, Together with these Translations following, &c. All Englished by H. Vaughan, Silurist. London : Printed,

and are to be sold by Peter Parker, . . . 1679. 8°, A—L in eights, title on A 3 and L 8 with the *Errata*.

A reissue of the unsold copies of 1651.

VAVASOR, FRANCIS, *of the Society of Jesus*.
Francisci Vavassoris Societ. Jesu De Epigrammate Liber et Epigrammatvm Libri Quatuor. Aucta libro editio. Parisiis, . . . M.DC.LXXVIII. 8°, A—Y in fours, Y 4 with the *Permission*, and the title.

VENICE.
Aggravii Venetiani, &c. Or The Venetian and other Grievances Together, With a Proposal for raising the Price of Tin in the Counties of Cornwall and Devon, according to the Policy of the Venetians, when they regained the Western Trade, which they had once almost lost. Most humbly presented to the King's most Excellent Majesty, . . . The First Part. London, Printed for Sam. Crouch in Cornhill, Abel Roper in Fleet-street, and Joseph Fox in Westminster-Hall, 1697. 4°, A—E 2 in fours : *The Proposal*, B—C in fours.

VERON, JOHN.
*The godly saiyngs of the old auncient faithful fathers / vpon the sacrament . . . Newlye compyled and translated oute of Latin intoo English. By Jhon Veron Senonoys. 1 Cor. xi. *As often as ye eate* . . . Imprinted the xj. day of October, Anno Do. 1550. At Worcester by Jhon Oswen. They be also to sell at Shrewesburye. Cum priuilegio. . . . 8°, H in eights.

Veron's preliminary Exhortation is dated from Hackney, 31 Oct. 1548. Dedicated to Sir John Yorke, Knight, Treasurer of the King's Mint in Southwark. Master of the Woods this side Trent, and Sheriff of London.

VERGIL, POLYDORE, *of Urbino*.
Polydori Vergilii Vrbinatis Anglicæ Historiæ Libri Vigintiseptem. . . . Basileæ, Apvd Mich. Isnigrinivm. Anno M.D.LV. Folio, a—z in sixes : A—Pp in sixes, Pp 6 with the device.

Polydori Vergilii . . . Anglicae Historiae Libri Vigintiseptem. . . . Basileae, Anno M.D.LXX. Folio, a—z in sixes : A—Ll in sixes : Mm, 4 : a—β in sixes and γ in eights, last leaf with colophon and device.

*An Abridgement of the notable woorke of Polidore Vergile. . . . Imprinted at London within the precincte of the late dissolued house of the Grey Friers, by Richard Grafton Printer to the Princes Grace, the . xvi. daie of Aprill, the yere of our lorde M.D.xlvi. Cum priuilegio. . . . 8°. 156 leaves, besides dedication and table. Dedicated to Sir Anthony Denny.

VICARS, JOHN.
Decapla in Psalmos siue Commentarivs ex decem Linguis, antiquis Patribus, . . . Londini Apud Octauianū Pulleyn : . . . CIƆ. IƆ. C. L V. Folio, A—3 G in fours, besides the frontispiece by Hollar.

VILLIERS, GEORGE, *Duke of Buckingham* (ob. 1628).
A Continued Iovrnall of all the Proceedings of the Duke of Buckingham, in the Isle of Ree. Containing these particulars. The manner of releeuing the Fort by sixe Skallops about a moneth since . . . Published by Authority. London : Printed by A. M. for Thomas Walkley, . . . 1627. [October 2.] 4°, A—B in fours, A 1 occupied by woodcuts and B 4 apparently blank.

B 3 contains verses on the death of Sir John Burrowes.

VILLIERS, GEORGE, *second Duke of Buckingham*.
The Duke of Buckinghams Speech in a late Conference. London : Printed for M. I. 1668. 4°, 4 leaves.

VINES, RICHARD.
The Impostvres of Seducing Teachers Discovered ; In a Sermon before the . . . Lord Major and Court of Aldermen of the City of London, at their Anniversary meeting on Tuesday in Easter weeke, April 23, 1644. at Christ-Church. By Richard Vines, Minister of Gods Word at Weddington in the County of Warwick, . . . London, Printed by G. M. for Abel Roper . . . 1644. 4°. A, 2 leaves : B—F in fours.

VIOLET, THOMAS.
The Advancement of Merchandize : Or, Certain Propositions for the Improvement of the Trade of this Commonwealth, humbly presented to the Right Honorable the Council of State. And also, Against the Transporting of Gold and Silver. By Tho. Violet of London Goldsmith London, Printed by William Du-Gard Printer to the Council of State. Anno Dom. 1651. Folio. A, 2 leaves with title and dedication to Lord President Bradshaw : (a)—(d), 2 leaves each : B—l, 2 leaves each. *A True Discoverie to the Commons of England, How they have been Cheated of almost all the Gold and Silver Coin of this Nation* . . . 1651, M—Rr, 2 leaves each : Ss, 1 leaf : Index, 4 leaves.

VIRGINIA.
By his Maiesties Councell for Virginia. God saue the King. [A Proclamation permitting settlers to return from Virginia by asking leave of the Governor. About 1620.] A broadside in black letter.

A Proclamation for setling the Plantation of Virginia. Printed at London by Bonham Norton, and Iohn Bill, . . . M.DC.XXV. A sheet, forming 2 leaves.

Further Reasons for Inlarging the Trade to Russia, Humbly offer'd by the Merchants and Planters Trading to, and Interested in the Plantations of Virginia and Maryland. [About 1695.] A broadside. *B. M.*

Under the same press-mark (816. m. 11) will be found a profusion of broadsides of a similar character, relating to the East India Company, St. Helena, &c.

VIRUNNIUS, PONTICUS.
Pontici Virunij dialogues ad illu. principem Rambertum Malatestam in dedicatione praesentis historiæ britanniae, in quo loca Iuvenalis deperdita, & aliorum declarantur. [On d i occurs as a headline:] Pontici Virunii historiae britannicae Liber primus incipit. [Col.] Ex Rhegio ligustico Ponticus Virunius impensa, et torcularibus suis. M. D. VIII. VI. Cal. Apryllis. 4º, b—f in fours. first and last leaves blank. Small italic letter. *B. M.*

Another copy, Sotheby's, June 1888 (Turner, 2248), with the blanks, wanting in the Museum copy, formerly Heber's.

VOCABULARY.
Den grooten Vocabulaer . . . The Great Vocabvler, in English and Dutch : That is to say common speaches of all sorts, also Lettres and Obligations to write. With a Dictionarie and the Conjugation . . . Tot Rotterdam, By Pieter van Waesberghe, . . . Anno 1644. 8º, A—II in eights. Engl. and Dutch. Without prefixes. *B. M.*

VON DER NOOT, JAN.
*The Gouernaunce and preseruation of them that feare the Plage Set forth by John Vandernote Phisicion & Surgion, admitted by the Kynge his hyghnesse. Now newly set forth at the request of William Barnard, of London Draper. 1569. Imprinted at London by Wyllyam How, for Abraham Veale. 8º, A—C 4 in eights.

W.

W. E., *Gent.*
The Whole Pleasures of Matrimony : Interwoven with sundry Delightful and Comical Stories ; . . . Written by E. W. Gent. To which is added, The Distructive Miseries of Whoring and Debauchery. With all its Dreadful Concomitants. London : Printed by T. Norris, . . . 1718. 12º, A—G in twelves, including the frontispiece.

The *Miseries of Whoring* is in verse. I find it stated that the first edition of this book appeared in 1688.

WALLIS, JOHN.
Mechanica : Sive, De Motu, Tractatus Geometricus. Authore Johanne Wallis, SS. Th. D. . . . Pars Prima . . . Londini, Typis Gulielmi Godbid ; Impensis Mosis Pitt, . . . M.DC.LXX. 4º. A, 3 leaves, A 4 having perhaps been blank ; B—P in fours, P 4 blank. With two folded leaves of diagrams at end and a portrait of Wallis by Faithorne, dated 1668. Dedicated to William, Viscount Bromeker.

Johannis Wallis, S.T.D. Geometriæ Professoris Saviliani, in Celeberrima Academia Oxoniensi Grammatica Linguae Anglicanae. . . . Editio Tertia, Prioribus Auctior. Hamburgi, . . . 1672. 8º. ß , 8 leaves :)(, 4 leaves : A—I in eights.

WARWICKSHIRE.
A True and perfect Relation of the first and victorious Skirmish between the Army under the Conduct of the Right Honourable the Lord Brooks, the Lord Grey, Collonel Hampden, Collonell Hollis, Collonell Cholmley, and others . . . And the Army under the command of the Earle of Northampton, Lord Savill, Lord Paget, Captain Legg, and Captain Clark . . . in Southam field, ten miles from Coventry in Warwickshire, on Tuesday the 23. of this instant August . . . To prevent false Relations of Dunsmoore Battaile there being no such thing. London, Printed for Matthew Walbanck, August 27. 1642. 4º, 4 leaves.

WEBB, JOHN.
John Webb, alias Hop-hodee-hoodys Last Will and Testament Who departed this

Life at his Nurses House in Turn-Mill-street, in the 85th year of his Age. With his Pretty Exploits, Character, Sayings, and Epitaph. Printed for Richard Rosse, in the Year, 1674. 4°, 4 leaves. With a large cut on the title. *B. M.*

WECKHERLIN, G. RUDOLF, *Secretary to the Duke of Wirtemburgh.*
Trivmphall Shews Set forth lately at Stutgart. Written First in German, and now in English By G. Rodolfe Weckherlin, Secretarie to the Duke of Wirtemberg. Stvtgart. Printed by Iohn-Wyrich-Resslin. M.DC.XVI. 8°.)(, 4 leaves: A—K in fours: L, 4. Dedicated to Elizabeth of Bohemia by Weckherlin, to whom we ought probably to ascribe also the verses which follow: "To Her Most-Excellent Highnesse." *B. M.*

> Translated by the author himself, who, in a Preface, states that he was requested to undertake the task by the Duke, and apologises for any imperfections in his English. These are of the kind usually found in such attempts.

*WEDDINGTON, JOHN, *Citizen of London.*
A Breffe Instruction and manner howe to kepe Merchantes Bokes of accomptes. After the order of Debitor and Creditor, as well for proper accompts, partable, Factory and other . . . Very needfull to be knowen, and vsed of all men, in the feattes of merchandize. Now of late newly set forthe, and practisyd, by Iohan Weddington, Cyttizen of London. M.D. LXVII. *The treweth seketh corners.* Prentyd in Andwarpe, by Peter van Keerberghen dwelling by owre lady Charche, at the signe of the golden Sonne. Cum gratia & Privilegio. Folio.

> Herbert, or rather Ames, gives no collation.

WELSH, JOHN.
The History of Mr John Welsh Minister of the Gospel at Aire. [Quot. from Revel. 2. 4. 5.] Edinburgh, Printed by George Mosman, . . . 1703. 4°, A—E 1 in fours.

> S^t *to be done by Mr James Kirktonne* is written in a coeval hand on the title.

WESTMINSTER SCHOOL.
Graecæ Grammatices Rudimenta in Usum Scholæ Westmonasteriensis. Londini, Ex Officina Eliz. Redmayne. MDCLXXXIII. 8°, A—V 4 in eights, V 4 blank.

Onomastikon Braku. Sive Nomenclatura Brevis, Reformata: Adjecto cum Syllabo Verborum ac Adjectivorum: . . . In Usum Scholæ Regiæ Westmonasteriensis. Londini, Ex Officina Elizabethæ Redmayne, MDCLXXXIV. 8°, A—F in eights. Engl., Greek, and Latin.

WEST NEW JERSEY.
In the General Joint-Stock and Lands of the Society of Merchants of London, Proprietors of West New Jersey in America, the 25th of March, 1696. Whereof those Marked with a * are not Capable (by their Adventure) to be Chosen Committees. [London, 1696.] A broadside.

> The example employed was mutilated, having been used as lining for another publication.

WHARTON, GEORGE.
Ephemeris: Or, A Diary
    Astronomicall,
    Meteorologicall,
    Chronologicall,
For the year of Christ 1655. By George Wharton Esq. *His ad Æthera.* London, Printed for Tho. Vere at the Angel without New-gate, and Nath. Brook at the Angel in Cornhill. 1655. 8°, A—L in fours. Dedicated to John Wroth, Esq.

> Prefixed is a curious Computation of historical events in rhyming couplets.

WHETCOMBE, TRISTRAM.
A True Relation of all the Proceedings in Ireland, From the end of April last, to this present: Sent from Tristram Whetcombe, Mayor of Kinsale, to his Brother Benjamine Whetcombe, Merchant in London. With A Certificate under the Hand and Seal of Sir William Saint-Leger, Lord President of Munster. . . . London, Printed for Ioseph Hunscott. 1642. 4°, A—B in fours.

*WHITE, FRANCIS.
Francisci Vietæi Opera Mathematica, in quibus tractatur canon mathematicus, seu ad triangula. canonicon triangulorum laterum rationalium: . . . Londini. Apud Franciscum Bouuier. M.D.LXXXIX. Folio, 79 leaves. *Bodl.*

WHITE, JOHN.
The First Centvry of Scandalous, Malignant Priests, Made and admitted into Benefices by the Prelates, in whose hands the Ordination of Ministers and government of the Church hath been. Or, A Narration of the Causes for which the Parliament hath Ordered the Sequestration of the Benefices of severall Ministers complained of before them, for viciousnesse of Life, errors in Doctrine, contrary to the Articles of our Religion, and for practising and pressing superstitious Innovations against Law, and for Malignancy against the Parliament. [Parlia-

mentary Imprimatur signed by John White in favour of George Miller.] London, Printed by George Miller, dwelling in the Black-Friers. M.DC.XLIII. 4°, A–H 2 in fours.

WHITE, ROBERT.
Cvpids Banishment A Maske Presented to Her Maiesty By younge Gentlewomen of the Ladies Hall In Deptford at Greenwich the 4th of May 1617. 4°, 19 leaves.

Unpublished MS. sold at Sotheby's, June 1888 (Turner), No. 2938. Dedicated by White to Lucy, Countess of Bedford. Preceding the leaf of Dedication is "A note of all the Maskers names," among which two boys, George Lippett and Paul Harbart, are given as representing Bacchus and Mercury. From the Evelyn Collection.

WHITEHALL, ROBERT.
Hexastichon Ieron, Sive Jeonum Quarundam extranearum (numero 258) Explicatio . . . Being an Epigrammatical Explanation of the most Remarkable Stories throughout the Old & New Testament after each Sculpture or Cut. . . . Dat. Cal. Jan. Anno Salutis M.D.C. LXXVII. Oxford, Printed by Leonard Lichfield, Printer to the University. Folio. With the 258 plates (from Vischer's edition of *Bible Cuts*) pasted on to blank spaces in the middle of each leaf, the remainder of the obverse occupied by Whitehall's verses and the description, and the reverse blank. 258 leaves + title, engraved title to Vischer, 1 leaf, Whitehall's Preface, *Imprimatur*, and Contents, 7 leaves.

The impressions seem to have been specially taken off on thin paper for insertion in this book.

WHITFORD, RICHARD.
**¶A dayly exercise and experience of deathe, gathered, and set forthe by a brother of Syon Rycharde Whytforde. [This is over a cut of Death and a young man, &c. At the end occurs:] Imprynted at London in Fletestrete by me Robert Redman next to sainct Dūstones Churche. 8°, A–D in eights.

Written twenty years before at the request of the reverend mother Dame Elizabeth Gibs.

**A werke for Housholders . . . [Col.] ¶Imprynted at London in Fletestrete, at the sygne of the George, by me Robert Redman. The yere of our lorde God. M.D.xxxvii. 8°, A–E in eights: F, G: G, 4.

The edition of 1531 by Redman forms part of a volume. See *Collections*, 3rd Series, p. 21.

WHITTINTON, ROBERT, *Grammarian*.
Whittyntoni Editio cum interpretamento Frācisci Nigri diomedes de accētū in pedestri oratiōe potius q̄ soluta observando. [Col.] Explicit whittyntoni editio: nuper Impressa Londoñ. per me Richardum pynson in vico anglice nuncupato (the Flete strete) in intersignio Georgii commorantem. Anno domini. M.CCCCC.VX. [*sic* for 1515.] 4°. A⁸: B⁶: C⁸. *B. M.*

Printed without any regular title. This seems to have been printed to accompany the treatises *De Syllabarum Quantitate* and *De Magistratibus*; but perhaps it was sold separately.

Whittyntoni Editio de consinitate grāmatices et Constructione nouiter impressa. Eborȝ Per me Vrsyā Mylner in vrbe parrochia Sancte Helene in vico (Blaake strete.) Moram traheotis [*sic*]. At the end occurs: Explicit Whittyntoni Editio de consinitate grammatices et Constructione: nouiter impresse. Eborȝ / per me Vrsyā Mylner in vico vulgariter nūcupato (blake strete) Anno domini Millesimo quingentesimo decimo sexto ./ die vero . xx. mensis Decembris. 4°, A–D in eights and fours. With a large cut on the title and the printer's mark on the last leaf. *B. M.* (Tutet's copy.)

**Roberti whitintoni Lichfeldiensis. . . . Opusculū De Consinnitate Grāmatices et cōstructione recognitum anno dñi. xix. supra sesquimilesimum. [Col.] Explicit Roberti whitintoni editio de cōcinnitate grāmatices et constructione: impressa Londoñ per wynandū de worde in eo vico q̄ dicitur vulgariter (flete strete) cōmorāte: Sub Solis intersignio. Anno dñi. M.CCCCC.xix. Idibus Iunij. 4°.

**Roberti Whitintoni Editio de Consinnitate. . . . [Col.] Londini in Ædibus Richardi Pynsonis: Christi ab incarnatione Anno. 23. supra sesquimillessimum. 16 die Iunij. 4°, 30 leaves.

**Vulgaria Roberti Whi·intoni Lichfeldiensis Laureati de institutione grāmaticulorū opusculū libello suo de cōcinnitate grāmatices accommodatū et in quattuor partes digestum. [Col.] Londini in edibus Winandi de Worde vicesimo supra sesquimillesimū nostre salutis anno. 4°, A–H in eights.

Vulgaria Roberti Whittintoni Lichfeldiensis et de institutione grammaticulorum Opusculum: libello suo de concinnitate Grammatices accommodatū & in quatuor partes digestum. [Col.] Londini ī edibus Winandi de Worde xxi. supra sesquimillesimum nostri salutis anno. 4°, A—H in fours and eights. *B. M.* (Dr. Bliss's copy.)

**Vulgaria. . . . [Col.] Londini in edibus Winandi de Worde . xxiiij. supra sesquimillesimum nostre salutis anno. 4°, 48 leaves.

**Vulgaria. . . . [Col.] Londini in edibus Winandi de Worde. xxxiij. supra sesquimillesimum nostre salutis anno. 4°, A—M in fours.

Vvlgaria Roberti whitintoni. . . . Apud inclytam Londini urbem. M. D. XXV. [Col.] Ex calcographia Richardi Pynsonis regii Impressoris. Anno verbi incarnati. M.D.XXXI. 4°, A—M in fours. *B. M.*

> The title is within an engraved border, as in the edition of 1520. This copy appears to have been made up at the time of two issues.

**Roberti Whitintoni Lauricomi Lichfeldiensis De Syllibarū Quantitatibus Opusculū recognitū Anno dñi. xix. supra sesquimillesimum. [Col.] Explicit Whitintoni Laureati Editio nuperrime recognita diligenterq; nostre salutis anno. M.CCCCC.XIX. impressa Lōdini per winādū de worde. kal. Noue. 4°.

> This includes the Editio Whitintoni with the gloss of F. Niger. Dibdin used Heber's copy, but gives no collation. The next edition, published in March 1519-20, is of course later.

De syllabarū quantitate . . . Whitintoni editio cum interpretamēto Francisci nigri. . . . [Col.] Londini in ædibus Winādi de Worden vicesimo primo supra . . . anno. 4°, A—M in fours and sixes: the Niger, &c., A⁴: B—C⁶. *B. M.*

Roberti Whittintoni. L. secunda grāmaticæ pars de syllabarū quantitate. . . . Whitintoni æditio cū interpretamēto Fracisci nigri Diomedes de accētu. . . . [Col.] Exucussum [sic] Londini in officina Petri Treueris. 4°. A⁴: B⁶: C⁴: D—I⁴: K⁶: L⁴: M⁶: N⁴: O⁶: the second portion with Niger, &c., A⁶: B—D⁴. *B. M.*

**Roberti Whitintoni De Syllabarum Quantitate. . . . [Col.] Londini in ædibus Richardi Pynson Regis impressoris vigesimo secundo supra sesquimillesimum nostre salutis anno. xxiiij. mensis Iulij. 4°, A—M 6.

Roberti Whittintoni . . . de octo partibɔ orationis opusculū : de nouo recognitum. . . . [Col.] Expliciunt Roberti whittintoni octo orationis partes fideliter : Londini per Wynādum de worde / eo in vico

quō vulgi (fletestrete) dicūt impresse : Solis sub intersignio incarnati verbi Anno M.CCCCC.XIX. Octauo Idus Aprilis. 4°. A⁴: B⁶: C⁴. *B. M.*

> After the date occur the initials *H. C.*

Roberti Whitintoni . . . de octo partibus orationis æditio. [Col.] Londini in ædibus Winandi de Worde vicesimo tertio supra sesquimillesimum nostræ salutis anno. Mense Decembri. 4°. A, 4 : B, 6 : C, 4. With the printer's large device on C 4 verso.

De octo partibus whitintoni, æditio nouissima . . . Cum priuilegio. [Col.] Londini in ædibus Winandi de Worde trigesimo tertio supra sesquimilesimum nostre salutis anno. Die vero mēsis Septembris. iij. 4°. A⁴: B⁶: C⁴. *B. M.* (the Bliss copy.)

Roberti Whittintoni . . . de octo partibus orationis . . . [Col.] Explicit Libellus octo partiū . . . Lōdini impressus p me wynādū de worde in vico anglice nūcupato (the fletestrete) in intersignio solis cōmorantem. 4°, A—C in fours and sixes. *B. M.*

Editio roberti Whittintoni . . . Declinationes nōīm tā latinorū q̃ grecorū patronymicorū & barbarorū e Prisciano Sipontino Sulpitio et Ascensio anussatim collecte cū cōmentariolo interliniari . . . [Col.] Explicit whittintoni editio de declinatione nōīm . . . Impressa Londoñ. per wynandū de worde in vico vulgariter nuncupato (the fletestrete) ad signū Solis commorantē. Anno dñi. M.CCCCC.XVII. 4°. A⁸: B⁶. *B. M.*

Editio Roberti Whittintoni [de declinatione nominum. Col.] Explicit Whitintoni editio de declinatione nōīm . . . Impressa Londini per wynandū de worde in vico (fletestrete) nūcupato; sub Solis intersigniocommorantē. Annodñi. M.CCCCC.XIX. 4°. A⁸: B⁶. *B. M.*

Declinationes nōīm . . . [Col.] Explicit . . . Impressa Londini per Wynādum de Worde in vico (fletestrete) nūcupato : sub Solis intersignio cōmorantem. Anno dñi. M.CCCCC.XXI. 4°. A⁸: B⁶. *B. M.*

Grammaticæ Whittintonianæ Liber secūdus de noīm declinatione . . . [Col.] Londini in ædibus Winandi de Worde. Anno virginei partus vicesimo quarto, supra sesquimillesimum. 4°. A, 4 : B, 6 : C, 4. With the printer's large device on C 4 *verso.*

Grammaticæ Whittintonianæ liber Secundus de nominum declinatione. [Col.] Londini in ædibus Richardi Pynsonis :

Christi ab incarnatione, anno. 25. supra sesquimilesimum. 30. Die. Iulij. 4°. A⁴: B⁶: C⁴. *B. M.*

Editio Roberti Whitintoni . . . Declinationes nominum . . . [Col.] Impressum diligenterq3 correctum per me Petrum Treueris. 4°, A—E in fours, with the printer's full-page device on E 4 *verso*. *B. M.* (Dr. Bliss's copy.)

Grammatices Primæ partis Liber primus Roberti W. L.L. nuperrime recognitus, De nominum generibus. . . . [Col.] Ex typis Winandi Wordensis vigesimo primo verbi incarnati supra sesquimilesimum anno. Pridie Nonas Feb[r]ua. 4°. A, 4 : B, 6 : C, 3 (but C 4 probably had the mark). *B. M.*

Roberti Whitintoni Editio secunda. Opusculum affabre recognitum . . . De Nominum Generibus . . . Apud inclytam Londini urbem. M.D.XX. [Col.] . . . Ex officina Richardi Pynsonis regij impressoris. Nonis Septembris. 4°, 16 leaves. *Althorp.*

Grammatices Prime partis, Liber primus Roberti W. L.L. nuperrime recognitus. De nominum generibus. . . . [Col.] Impressum per me Petrum Treueris. 4°. A, 4 : B, 6 : C, 4. With the printer's mark on C 4 *verso*.

De nominum generibus. . . . [Col.] Expliciunt genera nominũ reuisa recognitaq3; summa cum diligentia Impressum per me Petrum Treueris in Suburbio Londoniensi vulgariter (Southwarke) nuncupato∴ 4°, A—D in fours, D 4 with the full-page device. *B. M.* (the Bliss copy.)

De nominum generibus [This is a headline on A iii, A i—ii being deficient. At the end occurs:] Ex typis Winandi Wordensis, trigesimo quarto verbi incarnati supra sesquimillesimum anno. die vero mensis Octobris . xvj. 4°. A—D in fours, D 4 with the full-page device only. *B. M.*

Grammaticae Prima Pars . . . nuperrime recensita. Liber quitę De verborum Præteritis et supinis. cum commento . . . [Col.] Lõdini in ędibus Winãdi de Worde . xxi. supra sesquimilesimũ nostre redemptionis anno. 4°. A⁴: B⁶: C⁴: D⁶. *B. M.*

**Verborũ Præterita et Supina. Grammaticæ prima pars Roberti Whitintoni L. L. nuperrime recensita. Liber quintus. De verborum præteritis et supinis cũ cõmento nec non interlineari dictionum interpretatione. [Col.] Londini in edibus Winãdi de Worde . xxiiii. supra sesquimillesimũ nostre redēptiois anno. 4°.

**Verborum præterita et supina . . .

[Col.] Lõdoni in ædibę Winãdi de Worde . xxv. supra sesquimillesimum nostræ redemptionis anno. 4°, A—D in fours and sixes.

Verborũ præterita & supina. . . . [Col.] Lõdini in ędibę Winãdi de Worde . xxvj. supra sesquimillesimũ nostrę redēptiõis anno. Ad idus septēbres. 4°, A—D in fours and sixes. *B. M.*

**Verborum præterita et supina. Grammaticae prima pars Roberti Whitintoni L.L. nuperrime recensita liber quintus . . . [Col.] Londini in ædibus pynsonianis . xxii. supra sesquimillesimum nostre redemptionis anno. 4°. A⁴: B⁶: C, 4: D, 8. *Althorp.*

Syntaxis. Roberti Whitintoni Lichfeldiensis . . . Opusculũ de Syntaxi / siue constructione recensitũ . xxi. supra . . . Idi. Februa. . . . [Col.] Londini. in ędibus Winãdi Wordensis Christi ab incarnatione anno . xx. supra sesquimillesimũ. Idibę Marcij. 4°. A⁴: B⁶: C⁴: D⁶: E⁴: F⁶: G⁴. *B. M.*

> This copy, in which the date on the title and that at the end differ, is bound up in a volume formerly belonging to the old Royal Library, with the Tudor arms on sides.

**Syntaxis . . . Londonij, in ædibus Winandi Wordensis Christi ab incarnatione, anno xxiiij. supra sesquimillesimũ. 4°, 23 leaves, or A—E in fours and sixes.

Syntaxis. Roberti Vuhitintoni . . . [Col.] Londini in ęditous Winandi de Worde Christi ab incarnatione, anno . xxv. supra sesquimilesimũ. Idibus Aprilę. 4°, A—G in fours and sixes, G 4 with the large device only. *B. M.*

Syntaxis. . . . [Col.] Londonii, in ædibus Winandi Wordensis Christi ab incarnatione, xxvij. supra sesquimilesimũ pridie Cal. Nouē. 4°, A—G in fours and sixes. G 4 probably with the device, but wanting in B. M. copy.

**Syntaxis . . . Londini, in ædibus Winãdi Wordensis Christi ab incarnatione, anno . xxvij. supra sesquimillesimum, pridie No. Marti. 4°, A—G in fours and sixes. The title is within a border of pieces.

Syntaxis. . . . Cum priuilegio. [Col.] Lõdini in ædibus Winandi Wordensis Christi ab incarnatione / anno. xxxiij. supra sesquimillesimum. 4°, A—F in fours : G, 6 : H, 4, with the full-page device only on H 4 *verso*. *B. M.* (the Bliss copy.)

> The date on the title-page is 1532—a very common discrepancy.

**Roberti Whitintoni opusculum de Syntaxi . . . [Col.] Explicit Whytyntoni Editio de declinatiōe nominum . . . Impress. London. per Richardū Pynson Regis impressorē ī vico vulgariter uñcupato (the Fletestrete) ad intersigniū dīni Georgii commorantē. 4º, 16 leaves. *Althorp.*

Sintaxis. Roberti Whitintoni Lichfeldiensis in florentissima Oxoniensi academia lauriati opusculū, de Syntaxi, siue constructione recensitū . xxij supra sesquimillesimū nr̄æ salutis anno. Idi: Februa . . . [Col.] Impressum per me Petrum Treueris. 4º, A—I in fours, the printer's mark on I 4 *verso.*

> The title is in one of W. de Worde's borders.

Roberti Whittintoni . . . lucubrationes. De noīm appellatiuorū / deorū / dearū / heroū / heroinarū / locorumq3 synonimis. De epithetis deorū. . . . [Col.] Expliciunt synonima. Lōdoñ. per wynandū de worde impressa : [A fresh headline :] De magistratibͬ . . . [Col.] Anno post virgineū partū . xvii. supra Millesimū quingentesimū anno kalēdas Augusti. 4º. A 8 : B 4 : C 8 : D 6 : AA 4 (with the treatise on Magistrates.) *B. M.*

Roberti Whitintoni lichfeldiensis . . . . lucubrationes. [Col.] Londini in edibus Winādi de Worde. Anno post virgineum partum . xxi. supra sesquimillesimum. 4º. A 8 : B 4 : C 8 : D 6 : E 4. *B. M.*

Roberti Whittintoni Lichfeldiensis lucubrationes. [Col.] Londini in edibus Winandi de Worde, anno domini. M.CCCCC. XXIII. Mense Augusto. 4º. A 8 : B 4 : C 8 : D—E 4. *B. M.*

*De Heteroclytis Nominibus. Editio Roberti Whitintoni lichfeldiēsis prouatis Angliæ . . . : de heteroclytis nominibus et gradibus cōparationis. [Col.] Impressa Londini per wynādū de worde Solis sub intersignio : et in vico quō dicunt (fletestrete) commorantē Annodn̄i. M.CCCCC.XIX. Septimo Idus Iulij. 4º, 10 leaves.

De heteroclytis nominibus . . . [Col.] Londini apud wynādū de worde sub Solis intersignio ī vico (fletestrete) appellato. Anno. M.CCCCC.XX. 4º. A 6 : B 4. *B. M.*

**De Heteroclytis nominibus. . . . [Col.] Londini apud winandū de worde sub solis intersignio ī vico (fletestrete) appellato. Anno. M.CCCCC.XXI. 4º, 10 leaves. With the common cut of master and pupils on title.

**De heteroclitis Nominibus . . . [Col.] Londini in edibus Winandi de Worde, sub solis intersignio . . . Anno dn̄i. M.CCCCC.XXIIJ. 4º. 8 leaves.

De heteroclitis Nominibus. Grammaticæ Whitintonianæ Liber tertius de nominum heterocliti. . . . [Col.] Londini in ædibus Winandi de Worde : sub Solis intersignio. Anno dn̄i. M.CCCCC.XXIIIJ. Die vero Decembris. xix. 4", A—B in fours.

**De heteroclitis Nominibus . . . [Col.] Londini prælum humanissimi viri Winquin de Worde sub solari iudicio nuper ad purum restituit Idem Valesius a natu virgineo M.D.XXVI. ad idus Iulij. 4º, 10 leaves.

De Heteroclitis nominibus. [Col.] Impress. Londini per me Richardum Pynson (Impressorem nobilissime Regis gratiæ) Commorantem in uico appellato the Flete strete. Anno dn̄i. M.D.XXVII. 4º. A 6 : B 4. *B. M.*

De Heteroclitis Nominibus . . . Anno ab incarnatione domini. M.D.XXXIII. Cum priuilegio. [Col.] Impressum per me Winandum de Worde, Anno ab incarnatione domini . M.D.XXXIII. 4º, A—E in fours. *B. M.*

> Dr. Bliss's copy ; he notes on flyleaf : "This is the enlarged edition (from 8 or 10 to 20 leaves), and contains the verses at the back of the title complaining of Peter Treveris for printing the grammatical Treatises of Whitington, and spoiling them 'inuiso cum paraphraste suo.'" This is the first date at which I have noticed a book printed by De Worde *with privilege.*

De Heteroclitis Nominibus. . . . [Col.] Impressum per me Petrum Treueris. 4", A—E in fours. *B. M.*

> There are two impressions by Treveris without date, each making A—E in fours, in the Museum.

De Heteroclitis Nominibus. . . . [Col.] Impressum per me Petrum Treueris. 4º, A—B in fours. *B. M.*

> The abridged edition.

WHORING.

God's Judgments against Whoring. Being an Essay towards A General History of it, From the Creation of the World, to the Reign of Augustulus, . . . and from thence down to the present Year 1697. . . . Vol. 1. London, Printed for Richard Baldwin, . . . 1697. 8º. A, 4 : a, 8 : B—X in eights, X 8 blank.

> I have seen no more.

WICLIFFE, JOHN.

Io. Wicleti Viri Vndiqvaque pijs, dialogorū libri q̄ttuor quorū primus diuinitatē &

Ideas tractat. Secŭdus uniuersarū creatione cōplectitur. Tertius de uirtutib, uitijsq; ipsis cōtrarijs copiosissime loqtur. Quartus Ro. ecclesię sacramētā, ... graphica p̄stringit. ... M.D.XXV. [Col.] Excusum Anno a Christo nato. MDXXV. Die VII Martij. 4°. A, 6 : B, 8 : C—Xx in fours, last leaf blank.

WILBEE, AMON.
Prima Pars de Comparatis Comparandis : ... Or the first part of things compared : or of the iustification of King Charles comparitively against the Parliament ... Oxford, Printed in the Yeare, 1647. 4°, A—F in fours.

Secvnda Pars, De Comparatis Comparandis : ... Or the second part of Things compared, &c. Wherein (according to the Author's promise in his first part of this subject) is at large declared the egregious injustice and oppression, arbytrarie and violent acts and practises, and the palpable violation of the Laws and Liberties of this Nation, by certain unfaithful, wicked men in this present Parliament, ... Printed at Oxford, 1647. 4°, A—D in fours.

Comparatis Comparandis : The Second Part. Or, A Parallell of the former, and later Force, upon the two Houses of Parliament ... Printed in the Yeere 1647. 4°, A—D in fours.

A different tract on the same side.

WILLIAM III. *of Orange, King of Great Britain* (1688–1702).
The Necessity of Setling the Crown of England. [Col.] Printed in the Year 1689. 4°, 4 leaves. Without a title-page.

The Prince of Orange His Declaration : Shewing the Reasons why he Invades England, With a Short Preface, And some Modest Remarks on it. London : Published by Randal Taylor, ... MDCLXXXVIII. 4°, A—D in fours.

Four Questions Debated.
Q. 1. Whether the Exercise of the Government of England be totally subverted ? Affirm.
Q. 2. Admitting the Exercise of Government dissolved, whether the power of Settling is in the People ? Affirm.
Q. 3. Whether as the Case stands, it is best to settle the Exercise of the Government in the Person, who would be next by Lineal Descent, if King James the Second was actually dead ? Neg.
Q. 4. Whether it is consistent with the Prince's Honor to accept of the Government, especially considering his Declaration was to Redress Matters by a Free Parliament ? Affirm.
With an Answer to the Objection that the Convention will not have the Power of a Parliament. Reprinted in the Yeer, 1689. 4°, A—D in fours, D 4 blank..

Allegiance and Prerogative Considered in a Letter from a Gentleman in the Country to his Friend Upon his being chosen a Member of the Meeting of States in Scotland. Printed in the Year MDCLXXXIX. 4°. A, 4 : B, 5.

A Letter from a Clergy-man in the Country, to a Minister in the City, Concerning Ministers Intermedling with State-Affairs in their Sermons and Discourses. [Col.] Edinburgh. Re-Printed in the Year, 1689. 4°, 4 leaves.

The Addres of the University of St. Andrews to the King By the Rector, Vice-Chancellor. Heads of the Colledges, Deans of Faculties, ... Also, A Letter from the Arch-Bishops, and Bishops, to the Kings most Excellent Majesty. London, Printed by J: R: to be sold be A: L: 1689. 4°, A—C 2 in fours. With a slip of *Errata* on the back of the title.

Reflections upon Our Late and Present Proceedings in England. Edinburgh, Re-printed in the Year 1689. 4°, 4 leaves.

Obedience Due to the Present Knig [sic] Notwithstanding our Oaths to the Former. Written by a Divine of the Church of England. [1689.] 4°, 4 leaves.

A Speech of a Fellow Communer of England to His Fellow Communers of the Convention. [Edinburgh] Printed in the Year MDCLXXXIX. 4°, 4 leaves.

A Letter to a Bishop concerning the Present Settlement, and the New Oaths. [Edinburgh, 1689.] 4°, A—B in fours.

The Character of a Prince. [Col.] Edinburgh, Re-printed in the Year, 1689. 4°, 4 leaves.

Salus Populi Suprema Lex. Or, The Free Thoughts of a Well-Wisher, For a good Settlement. In a Letter to a Friend. [Edinburgh] Printed in the Year 1689. 4°, 4 leaves.

An Enquiry into the Present State of Affairs : ... [Col.] Edinburgh, Re-printed in the Year 1689. 4°, A—B 2 in fours.

A Transient View of a Curats Letter sent to a Pretended Presbyterian Minister. Dated 4. March 1689. [Edinburgh, 1690.] A folio leaf.

A Description of the most Glorious and most Magnificent Arches Erected at the Hague, For the Reception of William III. King of Great Britain. With all the Motto's and Latin Inscriptions that were Written upon every one of the said Arches. Translated into English from the Dutch. London : Printed for F. S. and are to be sold by Richard Baldwin . . . M.DC.XCI. Folio, 4 leaves.

The Pretences of the French Invasion Examined. For the Information of the People of England. London, Printed for R. Clavel at the Peacock in St. Paul's Church-Yard, 1692. 4°, A—B in fours, besides title and half-title.

The Debate at large, between the House of Lords and House of Commons, at the Free conference, held in the Painted Chamber, in the Session of the Convention, Anno 1688. Relating to the Word, Abdicated, and the Vacancy of the Throne, in the Common's Vote. Printed for J. Wickins ; And to be Sold by the Booksellers of London and Westminster, 1695. 8°, A—B in fours : C—P in eights : Q, 4.

WILLIAMS, JOHN, *Bishop of Lincoln, afterwards Archbishop of York.*
The Holy Table Name and Thing More Antiently, properly, and literally used under the New Testament, then that of an Altar : Written long agoe by a Minister in Lincolnshire, in answer to D. Coal, a judicious Divine of Queene Maries days. *Illa Sacramenti donatrix Mensa.*—Aurel. Pruden, in Peristaph. Hymno 11. Printed for the Dioecsse of Lincoln. 1637. 4°, A—Ff in fours, and a leaf of Gg.

WILLIAMS, ROGER, *of Providence, N. E.*
Mr. Cottons Letter Lately Printed, Examined and Answered : By Roger Williams of Providence in New-England. London, Imprinted in the yeere 1644. 4°. A, 2 leaves : B—G in fours.

WILLYMOTT, WILLIAM, *M.A., of King's College, Cambridge.*
English Particles Exemplify'd in Sentences Design'd for Latin Exercises : With the Proper Rendring of Each Particle Inserted in the Sentence. For the Vse of Eton School. London : Printed for Sam. Smith, . . . 1703. 8°. Title and leaf with arms of the school : B—U in eights : X, 6.

WILMOT, JOHN, *Earl of Rochester.*
Poems and Translations. Written upon several Occasions, and To several Persons. By a late Scholer of Eaton. [Quot. from Juvenal and Cicero.] London : Printed for Henry Bonwicke, at the Red Lion in St. Paul's Church-Yard. 1689. 8°. Title and Table, 4 leaves : B—L in eights : M, 4.

WILSON, JOHN, *Minister of the Episcopalian Church of Scotland.*
An Essay on Enthusiasm ; Teaching to distinguish between Inspirations Warrantable and Unwarrantable. Written at Kirkwall in Orkney, May 1699. Now Published for the Authors Vindication. To which is added, a Poem on the descent of the Holy Ghost, for Pentecost. Edinburgh. Printed in the Year, M. DCC. VJ. 4°, A—B in fours. Dedicated to the Earl of Cromarty, the death of whose wife Wilson mentions.

Three Poems, Mahanaim, Or, Strivings with a Saviour, Containing a Dialogue betwixt Jesus and an Afflicted Soul ; Peniel, Or The Combatant Triumphing, Expressing Comfort under Clouds. And the Triumph Consummat, at the State of Glory. By an Experienced Admirer of Sanctified Afflictions. . . . Printed in the Year 1706. 4°, A—D, 2 leaves each. Dedicated by J. W. to Viscountess Stormont and the Lady Æmilia Murray, her sister-in-law. *B. M.*

WINDMILL.
A New Wind-Mill, A New. At Oxford, Printed by Leonard Lichfield, 1643. 4°, 4 leaves.

This is an address or epistle directed by Abednego Canne from Boston, Januar. 2, 1642-3, "To my dearely beloved Brother Mr Jonadas Trash, at his house in Soper-lane, at the signe of the Shuttle."

WING, JOHN.
The Crowne Conivgall Or, the Spovse Royall. A Discovery of the true honor and happines of Christian Matrimony Published for their consolation who are married, and their encouragment who are not, intending the benefit of both. By Iohn Wing, Pastor to the English Congregation, resident at Vlisshing in Zeeland. Printed at Middelbvrgh, By Iohn Hellenius dwelling in the market place, at the signe of the Galley, Anno 1620. 4°. Title, Dedication to Mathew Peke, Esq., Mayor of Sandwich, and *Errata*, 4 leaves : A—T 2 in fours, T 2 blank.

WING, VINCENT.
Astronomia Britannica : In Qua Per Novum Concinnioremq; Methodum, hi quinq; Trectatus traduntur, . . . Authore Vincentio Wing, Mathem. Londoni, Typis

Johannis Macock, ... 1669. Folio. Dedicated to Sir Robert Markham, Baronet. With a large portrait by Cross, with the Inscription: *Vincentius Wing Luffenhamiensis Rutlandiæ Natus Anno. 1619. Die. 9. Aprilis.*

WINGATE, NINIAN, *of Renfrew.*
Flagellum Sectariorum, Qvi Religionis Prætextv Seditionem in Cæsarem, Avt in alios Orthodoxos Principes excitare student; ... Accessit Velitatio in Georgivm Bvchananvm circa Dialogum, quem scripsit de iure regni apud Scotos. ... Ingolstadii, ... Anno. M.D.LXXXII. 4°. a, 4 leaves: A—Z in fours; a—o in fours. Dedicated to William, Count Palatine of the Rhine, from Ratisbon.

WORCESTERSHIRE.
A Letter sent from Mr. Sergeant Wilde, and Humphrey Salwey Esq; Both Members of the House of Commons, To the Honorable, William Lenthall, Esquior, Speaker of the House of Commons; Concerning divers Passages at the Quarter Sessions in Worcester, about the execution of the Commission of Array, and the Ordinance of the Militia: At which Sessions was the greatest Assembly that hath been seen for many yeers past. Together with the humble Petition of the Grand-Jury-men ... London, Printed by Luke Norton and John Field ... July 18. 1642. 4°, 4 leaves.

WORLDS.
A Discovery of New Worlds. From the French. Made English By Mrs. A. Behn. To which is prefixed a Preface by way of Essay on Translated Prose; ... London, Printed for William Canning, ... 1688. 8°, A—L in eights, besides a, 8: b, 4: c, 2. Dedicated to William, Earl of Drumlangrig.

WORLIDGE, JOHN, *Gentleman.*
The Compleat Bee-Master; Or, A Discourse of Bees: Shewing the best Way of Improving them, and Discovering the Fallacies that are imposed by some, for private Lucre, on the credulous Lovers and Admirers of these Insects. London: Printed for, and Sold by G. Conyers, at the Ring in Little-Britain 1698. Price 8t. 6d. Small 8°. A, 4 leaves, besides the frontispiece: B—C in eights. *B. M.*

WORSOP, EDWARD, *Londoner.*
A Discoverie of sundrie errours and faults daily committed by Lande-meaters, ignorant of Arithmeticke and Geometrie, to the damage, and preiudice of many her Maiesties subiects, with manifest proofe that none ought to be admitted to that function but the learned practicioners of those Sciences: Written Dialoguewise, according to a certaine communication had of that matter. ... At London, Printed by Henrie Middleton for Gregorie Seton. Anno 1584. 4°, A—K 2 in fours. Black letter. With diagrams. Dedicated to Lord Burleigh.

WYER, ROBERT, *Printer.*
Prognosticacion Drawen out of the Bookes of Ipocras, Auicen, and other notable Auctours of Physycke, shewynge the daunger of dyuers syckenesses, that is to say, whether peryll of death be in them or not, the pleasure of almyghtye God reserued. [Col.] Finis q. R. W. Imprynted by me Robert Wyer. Cum priuilegio ad imprimendum solum. Sm. 8°, A—D in fours. With two woodcut figures of Hippocrates and Avicenna on back of title and Wyer's device on D 4 verso.

Y.

YOLANDA OF SICILY.
The Chaste Seraglian: Or, Yolanda of Sicily. A Novel. In Two Parts. Done out of French by T. H. Gent. London, Printed for R. Bentley and S. Magnes. ... MDCLXXXV. 12°. Title and frontispiece, 2 leaves: B—G in twelves: H, 10. Dedicated by Thomas Hayes to Sir William Kenricke, Baronet.

Y-WORTH, W., *Spagiric Doctor.*
Introitus Apertus ad Artem Distillationis; Or, The Whole Art of Distillation Practically Stated, And Adorned with all the New Modes of Working now in Use. ... To which is Added, The True and Genuin Way of preparing Powers by three noble Menstruums, ... Illustrated with Copper Sculptures. By W. Y-worth, Medi-

ciuæ Professor in Doctrinis Spagyriis & per ignem Philosophus. London, Printed for Ioh. Taylor . . . MDCXCII. 8°, A—N in eights, N 8 blank. With the Preface dated from St. Paul's, Shadwell, and plates at pp. 11, 31, 59, and 139. *H. Stopes, Esq.*

Chymicvs Rationalis: Or, The Fundamental Grounds of the Chymical Art Rationally Stated and Demonstrated, By Various Examples in Distillation, Rectification, and Exaltation of Vinor Spirits, Tinctures, Oyls, Salts, Powers, and Oleosums; in such a Manner as to retain the Specifick Virtue of Concrets in the greatest Power and Force. . . . In which is contained A Philosophical Description of the *Astrum, Lunare, Microcrosmicum*, or *Phospheros*. Recommended to all that desire to improve and advance profitable Truths, such as are Real and not Hystorical. By W. Y-Worth, Spagirick Physician in both Medicines, and Philosopher by Fire. London: Printed for Thomas Salusbury, . . . 1692. 8°, A—L in eights, A 8 with Advertisements. Dedicated to the Honourable Robert Boyle, Esquire. *H. Stopes, Esq.*

Z.

ZWINGLIUS, HULDRICH.
*A short pathwaye to the ryghte and true vnderstanding of the holye and sacred Scriptures: . . . now translated out of Laten into Englysshe by John Veron, Senonois. James. i. Chap. *He that wanteth wisedome* . . . Imprinted the xxiiii. daie of Maie. Anno Do. 1550. At worcester by John Oswen. Cum priuilegio. . . . Sm. 8°, n in eights. Dedicated to Sir Arthur Darcy, Knight.

SECOND SUPPLEMENT.

ADAM AND EVE.
Adam and Eve Stript of their Furbelows: Or, The Fashionable Virtues and Vices of both Sexes expos'd to publick View. . . . The Second Edition. . . . London, Printed for A. Bettesworth. . . . Price Bound 3/. 8°. A, 4 leaves : a, 2 leaves : B—P in eights. In prose and verse.

A collection of Characters.

AINSWORTH, R.
The Most Natural and Easie Way of Institution : Containing Proposals for making a Domestic Education less Chargeable to Parents, and More Easie and Beneficial to Children. By which Method, Youth may not only make a very considerable Progress in Languages, but also in Arts and Sciences, in Two Years . . . London, Printed for Christopher Hussey, at the Flower-de-Luce in Little-Britain. 1698. 4°, A—D in fours. Dedicated to Sir William Hustler. M.P.

AINSWORTH, W.
Triplex Memoriale: the substance of three Commemoration Sermons, preached at Halifax in remembrance of Mr. Nathaneel Waterhouse, with an extract out of his last Will and Testament. York, . . . 1650. 8°.

> This book occurred in the Crossley sale. No. 13; but I failed to take a note of it, and have not been able to trace it since. Crossley's had on the title the autograph of Thomas Lister. The present makeshift account is from the auctioneer's catalogue. Unknown to Mr. Davies. Mr. Crossley says, "It is by far the rarest book connected with Halifax."

ALCHEMY.
A New Light of Alchymie : Taken out of the fountaine of Nature, and Manuall Experience. To which is added a Treatise of Sylphur: Written by Micheel Sandivogius : i.e. Anagrammatical ly, *Divi Leschi Genus Amo.* Also Nine Books of the Nature of Things, Written by Paracelsus, . . . Also a Chymicall Dictionary explaining hard places and words . . . All which are faithfully translated out of the Latin into the English tongue, By J. F. M.D. London, Printed by Richard Cotes, for Thomas Williams, at the Bible in Little-Britain, 1650. 4°, A—Ff in fours, besides a second sheet of A, 4 leaves, with the Preface.

ALEXANDER, JOHN.
God's Covenant Displayed, By John Alexander A Converted Jew. With A Proæmial Discourse of the Reasons of this Conversion. London, Printed for Walter Kettilby, . . . 1689. 4°. Dedicated by Alexander to Sir John Maynard, Chief Lord Commissioner for the Great Seal of England.

The copy used ended imperfectly on E 4.

ANDERSON, ALEXANDER, *of Aberdeen.*
Alexandri Andersoni Aberdonensis Svpplementvm Apollonii Redivivi. sive, Analysis problematis hactenus desiderati ad Apollonij Pergæi doctrinam . . . non ita pridem restitutum . . . Parisiis, Apud Hadrianvm Beys, . . . Anno cIɔ. Iɔc. xII. 4°, A—M in fours, A 1 blank. With diagrams.

ANTIDOTE.
The Cabinet of Mirth : Or The Antidote against Melancholy. Compounded of Merry Tales, Jests, and Bulls. London, Printed for John Playford at his Shop in the Temple, 1674. 8°, A—G 3 in eights, sign. B omitted. With the same engraving on title as in the editions of 1661, 1669, and 1682.

> The Preface is subscribed *Tho. Jordan* in this issue. In the others the work is anonymous ; yet it was published by the same person as the editions of 1669 and 1682, so that it can scarcely have been one of Jordan's begging productions ; nor, if the book had been his, was he the man to have withheld his name when it appeared before.

ARCANA.
Curiosa Arcana : Being Curious Secrets, Artificial and Natural. In Three Parts. . . . From the last Edition in French ; which contains near as much more as any other former Edition. To which is added, A Supplement of Divers Curiosities by the Translator. The Whole Illustrated with Copper Plates, adapted to the several Subjects. London : Printed for T. N.

and Sold at the Ring in Little-Britain; where may be had Hartmans Preserver of Health. . . . Price Five Shillings. [About 1700.] 8°, A—Aa in eights, besides 6 leaves marked *F between Z and Aa, headed *Notable Things*, and printed on different paper in a smaller type. With plates at pp. 36, 77, 82, 85, 87, 107, 125, and 138. In two columns.

> Probably translated and compiled by Thomas Tryon. A very curious volume, lent to me by Mr. John Addison, of Fulham. It embraces Cookery, Medicine, Gardening, Wines, the Mechanical Arts, &c.

ARMIN, ROBERT.
Foole Vpon Foole, or Six Sortes of Sottes, shewing their liues, humours and behauiours, with their want of wit in their shew of wisdome. Not so strange as true. Written by one seeming to haue his mothers witte, when some say he is fild with his fathers fopperie, and hopes he liues not without companie. Clonnico del Curtanio Snuffe. London Printed for William Ferbrand, dwelling neere Guildhall gate ouer against the Maidenhead. 1600. 4°.

> See Halliwell-Phillipps' *Outlines of the Life of Shakespeare*, 6th ed., i. 295-6. My very old acquaintance the author, shortly before his death, afforded me an opportunity of examining for bibliographical purposes all his early English books at Brighton and Brompton; but I overlooked the present volume, taking it to be the impression of 1605.
> It differs materially from the latter in the title itself, which describes Armin as taking the part of the clown at the Curtain in 1600, whereas the copy of 1605 mentions him as thus engaged at the Globe. *A Calendar of Shakespearean Rarities*, by J. O. H. Phillipps, 1887, No. 751.
> Armin, doubtless, also wrote the *Quips vpon Questions*, 1600, which I incautiously followed Mr. Collier in my *Handbook*, 1867, in giving to John Singer the actor.

ARMY.
Physician Cure thy Self: Or, An Answer To a Seditious Pamphlet, Entituled Eye-Salve for the English Army, &c. Written and Publish'd for the Information and Benefit of the Souldjery: and to them Directed. April 23. 1660. London, Printed for H. B. at the Gun in Ivy-lane, 1660. 4°, 4 leaves.

ASSHETON, W.
An Account of Dr Assheton's Proposal (as Improved and Managed by the Worshipful Company of Mercers, London) for the Benefit of Widows of Clergymen and Others; By Settling Joyntures and Annuities at the rate of Thirty per Cent. . . .
London: Printed for B. Aylmer, . . . 1699. Sm. 8°, 10 leaves. *E. M.*

A Full Account of the Rise, Progress, & Advantages of Dr. Assheton's Proposal. London: Printed by J. R. Given Gratis at Mercers-Hall, and by J. Baker in Mercers-Chappel Porch, 1710. 12°, A—B in twelves.

ATKYNS, SIR ROBERT, *K.B., late one of the Judges of the Common Pleas.*
An Enquiry into the Power of Dispensing with Penal Statutes. Together with Some Animadversions upon A Book writ by Sir Edw. Herbert, Lord Chief Justice of the Common Pleas, Entituled, A short Account of the Authorities in Law, upon which Judgment was given in Sir Edward Hales's Case. . . . London: Printed for Timothy Goodwin, . . . 1689. Folio, A—P, 2 leaves each, A 1 with Advertisement as to publication.

ATTWOOD, WILLIAM, *Esquire.*
The Case of William Attwood, Esq; By the Late King William of Glorious Memory, Constituted Chief Justice of the Province of New York in America, and Judge of the Admiralty there, and in Neighbouring Colonies. With a True Account of the Government and People of that Province; particularly of Bayard's Faction, and the Treason for which he and Hutchins stand Attainted; but Reprieved before the Lord Cornbury's Arrival, upon acknowledging their Offences, and begging Pardon. London; Printed in the Year MDCCIII. Folio, A—F, 2 leaves each.

B. W.
A Seasonable Discourse: Shewing how that the Oaths of Allegiance & Supremacy, (As our Laws interpret them) Contain Nothing which any Good Christian ought to Boggle at. [Quotations.] Printed in the Year, 1679. 4°, A—E in fours.

BANKS.
Corporation-Credit, Or, A Bank of Credit made Currant, by Common Consent in London. More Useful and Safe than Money. London, Printed by John Gain, for the Office. Anno, M.DC.LXXXII. 4°, 4 leaves.

Englands Interest Or The Great Benefit to Trade By Banks or Offices of Credit in London, &c. As it hath been Considered and Agreed upon by a Committee of Aldermen and Commons, thereunto Appointed, by the Right Honourable, the Lord Major, Aldermen, and Commons, in Common-Council Assembled. . . . London, Printed by John Gain, for the Office, M.DC.LXXXII. 4°, 6 leaves, the last blank, the 5th with a form for subscriptions.

A Discourse concerning Banks. [Col.] London, Printed for James Knapton at the Crown in St. Paul's Church-Yard. MDCXCVII. 4°, 4 leaves.

Some Considerations Offered against the Continuance of the Bank of England, In a Letter to a Member of the present Parliament. 4°, A—C, 2 leaves each.

BARLOW, WILLIAM.
Magneticall Aduertisements: Or Divers Pertinent obseruations, and approued experiments, concerning the nature and properties of the Load-stone. . . . The second Edition. London, Printed by Edward Griffin for Timothy Barlow, and are to be sold at his shop in Pauls Church-yard, at the signe of Time. 1618. 4°, A—N in fours: *A Briefe Discovery of the Idle Animadversions of Marke Ridley*, with a new title, A—B in fours, besides a leaf of *Errata*. With woodcuts. Dedicated to Sir Dudley Digges, Knight. *B. M.*

On N 4 of the first portion occurs an interesting letter from W. Gilbert of Colchester to Mr. William Barlow, respecting his own book on the magnet, his appreciation of Barlow's labours, desire to see him, and the interest taken at Venice in the subject.

BARONETS.
Three Patents Concerning the Honourable Degree and Dignitie of Baronets.

The first containing the Creation and Grant.

The second a decree with addition of other Priuiledges.

The thirde a confirmation and explanation.

¶ Imprinted at London by Robert Barker, . . . Anno 1617. 4°, A—E in fours, A 1 blank. *B. M.*

A second copy before me has the autograph on title of Humphrey Dyson.

BARTON, DAVID, *M.A.*, *Rector of St. Margaret's, New Fish Street, London.*
Mercy In the midst of Judgment: By a gracious discovery of a certain Remedy for London's Languishing Trade. In a Sermon Preached before the Right Honourable the Lord Mayor and the Citizens of London, on September 12. 1669. at the new repaired Chappel at Guild-Hall. London, Printed for James Allestry, . . . 1670. 4°, A—H in fours, A 1 with the Mayor's invitation to Barton to publish his discourse.

A worthless performance.

BASIL, WILLIAM.
Two Letters from William Basil Esq: At-

torney General of Ireland . . . . of a Great Victory Obtained by the Parliaments Forces in the North of Ireland, on the plains of Lisnegarvy, against the Enemy there : . . . With a Relation of the taking of Dumcree; and of the Surrender of Carrickfergus upon Articles. . . . London, Printed by John Field for Edward Husband, Printer to the Parliament of England. 1649. 4°, 4 leaves.

One of these was to the Speaker, the other to the Council, on the same subject.

BASSET.
The Disorders of Bassett, A Novel. Done out of French. London, Printed for John Newton at the Three Pidgeons over against the Inner Temple Gate, in Fleet-street. 1688. 12°, A—E 10 in twelves. *B. M.*

Written to illustrate the mischief occasioned in France by the game of basset.

BAXTER, RICHARD.
The Quakers Catechism, Or, The Quakers questioned, Their Questions Answered, And Both Published, For the Sake of those of them that have not yet sinned unto Death; . . . London, Printed by A. N. for Thomas Underhill . . . and Francis Tyton . . . 1655. 4°, A—H 2 in fours, A 1 blank and H 2 with *Errata*.

BEAUMONT, JOHN. *Junior.*
The Present State of the Universe, Or an Account of I. The Rise, Births, Names, . . . of the present Chief Princes of the World. II. Their Coats of Arms, . . . III. Their Chief Towns, . . . IV. Their Revenues. To which are added some other Curious Remarks. . . . London : Printed, and are to be Sold by Randall Taylor, near Stationers-Hall. 1694. 4°. A, 2 leaves : B—O 2 in fours. Dedicated to the Honourable Charles Cottington, Esquire.

BEDE.
Venerabilis Bedae presbyteri de temporibus sine de sex aetatibus huius seculi Liber incipit. . . . Cum priuilegio. [Col.] Impressum Vene. p Ioan. de Tridino alias Tacuino anno domini . M.D.V. die . xxyiii. Mai. 4°, A—L in fours : M, 6. *B. M.*

BELL, THOMAS, *Philologus, Scotus, of Edinburgh.*
Roma Restituta, Sive Antiquitatum Romanarum Compendium Absolutum . . . Glasguae, Excudebat Robertus Sanders, . . . M.DC.LXXII. Sm. 8°. †, 6 leaves : ††, 8 leaves, last blank : A—T in eights.

This volume contains a poem on the Spanish Armada.

BELLARMINE.
A Defence of the Confuter of Bellarmin's

Second Note of the Churchs Antiquity, Against the Cavils of the Adviser. London : Printed for Ric. Chiswell, . . . MDCLXXXVII. 4", A—C in fours.

BETHELL, COLONEL.
Col: Bethels Letter to His Excellence the Lord Fairfax, Concerning the surrender of Scarbrough Castle, on Tuesday, Decemb. 19. 1648. Together, With a true Copy of the Articles . . . . London. Printed for J. Playford at his Shop in the Inner-Temple. Decemb. 25. 1648. 4°, 4 leaves.

BIBLE.
The Byble in Englyshe, that is to saye the contet of al the holy scrypture, both of ye olde, and newe testamēt, with a prologe therinto, made by the reuerende father in God, Thomas archbysshop of Cantorbury, ¶ This is the Byble apoynted to the vse of the churches. ¶ Prynted by Edward whytchurche, Cum priuilegio ad imprimendum solum. M. D. XL. [Col.] The ende of the newe Testament : and of the whole Byble, Fynisshed in Apryll, Anno M.CCCCC.XL. A dño factū est istud. Large folio. In two columns. With woodcuts. Title within a broad engraved border, Calendar, &c., 6 leaves : Prologue and Names of the Books, 4 leaves : a—l 4 in eights : *The seconde parte* . . . with a new title, A—Q 2 in eights, followed by a blank, and possibly should be by a second to complete the half-sheet. *The thirde parte* . . . with a new title, AA—3 K in eights : *The newe Testamēt* . . . with a new title, AA—NN in eights.

Sotheby's, March 29, 1889, No. 634, with autograph of "Thomas Walleys of Trowbridge, 1540." and on fly-leaf memoranda of the death of Henry Wallis of Healing, aged 85, May 4, 1775, and of Elizabeth Farr, his daughter, who was mother of fifteen children, whose names and birthsare all recorded. She died, aged 42 years, April 28, 1794.

BISHOPE, GEORGE.
New-England Judged, By the Spirit of the Lord. In Two Parts. . . . Formerly Published by Georges Bishop, and now somewhat Abreviated. With an Appendix, Containing the Writings of several of the Sufferers ; . . . Also, An Answer to Cotton Mather's Abuses of the said People, . . . London, Printed and Sold by T. Sowle, . . . 1703. 8°. *, 4 leaves : title to Part 1 : A—Xx in eights : Yy, 2 leaves : Zz, 4 leaves.
With a preface by Joseph Grover.

BLAKE, WILLIAM, *Housekeeper to the Ladies' School at Highgate.*
[Silver Drops, Or Serious Things. London, about 1680.] 8°, A—T 3 in eights, T 3 occupied by a notice, besides four plates, consisting of figures of Charity and Time, a view of Highgate Ladies' School, and a frontispiece with butterflies and verses. *B. M.*

The text begins on p. 79, the matter preceding being a series of letters addressed by Blake to various ladies of rank, who were patronesses of the Ladies' School at Highgate, where he was housekeeper. There is no regular title. The present copy appears to have belonged to the author, who has filled up in MS. the names of the benefactresses to the institution, including the Dowager - Countess of Northumberland, Lady Falkland, Lady Clayton, &c.
The leaf at end begs donors to take a receipt on the back of the plate of *Time* or *Charity*, sealed with the seals of the Treasurer, Housekeeper, and Registrar ; which may account for the scarcity of the volume in a complete state.

BLAND, PETER, *of Gray's-Inn, Gentleman.*
A Royall Position, Whereby 'tis proved, that 'tis against the Common Laws of England to depose a King : Or, An Addition to a Book, Intituled, Resolved on the Question : Or, A Question Resolved. . . . London, Printed for John Field. 1642. 4°, A—B in fours. Dedicated by Bland to his ever Honoured Uncle, Henry Shelly, Esquire, M.P.

BODIN, J.
The Sixe Bookes of a Common Weale. Written by I. Bodin a famous Lawyer, and a man of great Experience in matters of State. Out of the French and Latine Copies, done into English, by Richard Knolles. London Impensis G. Bishop. 1606. *Rex & Lex.* Folio, A—3 V in sixes : 3 X, 8 leaves. The first and last leaves are blank. [Col.] Imprinted at London by Adam Islip. 1606. Dedicated by Knolles to his especial good friend, Sir Peter Manwood, K.B.

BOHUN, R., *of New College, Oxford.*
A Discourse Concerning the Origin and Properties of Wind. With An Historicall Account of Hurricanes, and other Tempestuous Winds. Oxford, Printed by W. Hall for Tho. Bowman Anno Dom. 1671. 8°, Title, 1 leaf : *, 8 leaves : A—T in eights, T 8 blank. *B. M.*

BOOTH, HENRY, *afterwards Lord Delamere and Earl of Warrington.*
The Speech of the Honourable Henry Booth Esq; Spoken in Chester March 2. 168⁹. At his being Elected one of the Knights of the Shire for that County, to serve in the Parliament Summon'd to

Meeting-House the 7th of the third Month called May, 1682. 4°, 2 leaves.

Without a title-page.

The Devouring Informers of Bristol, &c. Being an Additional Account of some late Proceedings of those Ravenous Beasts of Prey, against Dissenting - Protestants, Bristol, April 22. 1682. 4°, 2 leaves.

Without a title page.

BRITAIN.
Britannia Triumphalis ; A Brief History of the Warres and other State-Affairs of Great Britain. From the Death of the late King, to the Dissolution of the last Parliament. *Vide quam repentè tempus res mutat humanas.* . . . London, Printed for Samuel Howes, and are to be sold at his Shop in Popes-head-Alley, 1654 [April 28]. 8°. A, 4 leaves : B—O in eights. B. M.

BROOKE, SIR ROBERT, *Knight*.
Ascvns Nouell cases de les ans et temps le Roy, H. S. Ed. 6. et la Roygne Mary, escrie en la graunal Abridgement, compose per Sir Robert Brooke Chiualer &c. la disperse en les Titles, & es icy collect sub ans. Anno Do. 1578. ¶ In ædibus Richardi Tottelli. Cum priuilegio. 8°, A—P in eights. [Col.] ¶ Imprinted at London in Fleetestreete within Temple Barre at the signe of the Hand and Starre by Richard Tottyl. the xv. of October. 1578.

BROWNE, JOHN, *Sworn Chirurgeon in Ordinary to His Majesty*.
A Compleat Treatise of the Muscles, As they appear in Humane Body, and arise in Dissection ; With Diverse Anatomical Observations Not yet Discover'd. Illustrated by near Fourty Copper Plates Accurately Delineated and Engraven. *Non Nobis Nati*. In the Savoy. Printed by Tho. Newcombe for the Author, 1681. Folio. Title and dedication to the King, 2 leaves ; Privilege and a second dedication to Christopher, Duke of Albemarle, 2 leaves ; a—c, 2 leaves each ; d, 1 leaf ; A—N, 2 leaves each ; O, 3 leaves ; P, 3 leaves ; no Q ; R, 2 leaves ; S, 2 leaves ; T, 3 leaves ; V—X, 2 leaves each ; Y, 3 leaves ; Z—Bb, 3 leaves each ; Cc, 2 leaves ; Dd, 3 ; Ee, 2 ; Ff, 3 ; Gg—Gg, 2 leaves each ; 3 H, 1 leaf. With 37 numbered plates.

BRYAN, JOHN, *Parson of Barford*.
The Vertvovs Daughter. A Sermon Preached at Saint Maries in Warwick, at the Funerall of the most vertuous and truely religious yong Gentlewoman, Mistris Ceely Puckering, Daughter and Coheire to the right Worshipfull, Sir Thomas Puckering, Knight and Baronet, April. the 14th 1636. . . . London, Printed by E. G. for Lawrence Chapman, . . . 1640. 4°. A—C in fours, C 4 occupied by an Epitaph by the Author. Dedicated to Sir T. Puckering.

BUCHANAN, GEORGE.
Georgii Bvchanani Scoti Franciscanvs et Fratres. Elegiarvm Liber I. Silvarvm Liber I. Endeca-Syllabon Liber I. Epigrammaton Libri III. De Sphæra Fragmentvm. Anno cIɔ.Iɔ.xxcIv. 8°. A—O in eights.

Georgii Buchanani Scoti Franciscanvs et Fratres. . . . In Bibliopolio Commelniano. cIɔ Iɔ cIx. 8°. A—R in eights : *Operum Poeticorum Pars Altera [Iephes, &c.]*: A—N I in eights.

Baptistes, Sive Calvmnia, Tragœdia. Avctore Georgio Bvchanano Scoto. Londini. Et prostant Antuerpiæ apud Iacobum Henricium. M.D.LXXVIII. 8°, A—D in eights. Italic letter.

Baptistes, Sive Calvmnia, Tragœdia. Avctore Georgio Bvchanano Scoto. Francofvrti. Apud Andream Wechelum. M.D.LXXIX. 8°, A—D in eights. Italic letter.

In this edition occurs a Latin epigram by Daniel Rogers, addressed to the author on his poems.

BURNABY, A., *of the Middle Temple*.
Two Proposals, Humbly Offer'd to the Honourable House of Commons, . . . I. That a Duty be laid on Malt, in the stead of the present Duty on Beer and Ale ; and likewise, that the several Engagements that Revenue lies under, be Transferr'd on that of Malt. II. That a Duty be laid on Malt, and the present Duty on Beer and Ale be continued. To which is Annex'd An Accompt, what in all Probability the Frauds of Brewers do amount to, . . . London, Printed in the Year, 1696. 4°, A—C in fours, a leaf of D, and the title.

BURNET, GILBERT, *Bishop of Salisbury*.
A Discourse on the Memory of that Rare and truely Vertuous Person Sir Robert Fletcher of Saltoun ; Who died the 13. of January last, in the thirty ninth year of his Age. Written by a Gentleman of his Acquaintance . . . Edinburgh, Printed by a Society of Stationers, Anno Dom. 1665. 8°, A—Z in fours, Z 4 blank.

A Vindication of the Authority, Constitution, and Laws of the Church and

State of Scotland. In Four Conferences. Wherein the Answer to the Dialogues betwixt the Conformist and the Non-Conformist, is examined. By Gilbert Burnet. Professor of Theologie in Glasgow. Glasgow, By Robert Sanders, Printer to the City, and University, 1673. 8°, A—Kk 4 in eights, Kk 4 blank. Dedicated to the Duke of Lauderdale.

Some Passages of the Life & Death of . . . John Earl of Rochester . . . . Dvblin, Reprinted by Joseph Ray at College-Green, for William Winter at the Wandering Jew in Castle-street, . . . MDCLXXVI. 4°, A—II in fours.

BUSHNELL, WALTER, *Vicar of Box, co. Wilts.*
A Narrative of the Proceedings of the Commissioners Appointed by O. Cromwell, For Ejecting Scandalous and Ignorant Ministers. In the Case of Walter Bushnell Clerk, Vicar of Box in the County of Wilts. Wherein is shewed That both Commissioners, Ministers, Clerk, Witnesses have acted as unjustly even as was possible for men to do by such a Power: and all under the pretence of Godliness and Reformation. [Quotations.] Printed for R. Clavell at the Stags-head in S. Pauls church yard, 1660 [August]. 8°, A—R in eights, R 8 blank. Dedicated by Bushnell to Sir Anthony Ashley Cooper, Knight and Baronet, and John Earnly, Esq., Knights of the Shire for the County of Wilts. *B. M.*

See Hazlitt's *Schools, Schoolbooks, and Schoolmasters*, 1888, p. 191.

BUTLER, JOHN, *B.D., and Chaplain to the Duke of Ormonde; Rector of Lichborrow in the Diocese of Peterborough.*
Christologia. Or A Brief (but True) Account of the certain Year, Moneth, Day and Minute of the Birth of Jesus Christ. . . . London. Printed by Joseph Moxon, . . . And by Hen. Broom, . . . 1671. 8°, A—X in eights, besides a folded plan before Part II. Dedicated to the Duke of Ormonde. With astrological diagrams.

C. C.
Treason's Master-piece: Or, A Conference Held at Whitehall between Oliver The late Usurper, And A Committee of the then pretended Parliament; Who desired him to take upon him the Title of King of England &c. with an intent to exclude the Royal Line. . . . Collected by a faithful hand. London: Printed for Daniel Major, . . . 1680. 8°, A—H in eights.

The writer subscribes himself at the end of the preface: "A hearty lover of his King and Country, C. C.—*forsan* Charles Cotton.

CALAMY, EDMUND, *B.D., Preacher at Aldermanbury, London.*
Englands Looking-Glasse, Presented in A Sermon, Preached before the Honourable House of Commons, at their late solemne Fast, December 22. 1641. . . . Published by Order of the House. London, Printed for Cadwallader Greene, and are to bee sold by Stationers, Anno 1642. 4°, A—E in fours.

CAMBRIDGE, UNIVERSITY OF.
Musæ Cantabrigienses, Serenissimis Principibus Wilhelmo et Mariæ Angliæ . . . Regi ac Reginæ, Publicæ Salutis ac Libertatis, Vindicibus, Hæc Officii & Pietatis ergò D.D. Cantabrigiæ. Ex Officina Joannis Hayes, . . . 1689. 4°, A—M in fours: a—e 2 in fours.

The second portion contains the English poems. The copy employed was on large paper in velvet.

CAMPION, EDMUND.
Rationes Decem Qvibvs Fretvs, Certamen Adversariis Obtvlit in causa Fidei, Edmundus Campianus E Societate Nominis Iesv Presbyter: Allegatæ Ad Clarissimos viros nostrates Academicos. Permissv Svperiorvm. Romæ Apud Franciscum Zanettum. 1582. 8° or 12°, A—D 6 in twelves, D 5-6 blank.

There are several editions of this work in Latin, and it was translated into German and French. It was originally printed at the Stonor press for private circulation.

CARTWRIGHT, THOMAS, *Dean of Ripon and Chaplain-in-Ordinary to His Majesty.*
A Sermon Preached to the Gentlemen of Yorkshire, at Bow-Church in London, The 24th of June. 1684. Being the Day of their Yearly Feast. London, Printed for Tho. Flesher, . . . 1684. 4°, A—E in fours. Dedicated "To my very much Honoured Friends, the respective Natives of the County of York . . . ," more especially to twelve persons named, including Sir Robert Legard, Sir Thomas Yarburgh, Abstrupas Danby, &c.

CASTELLI, GIOSEPPE.
Itinerario et sincero racconto del Viaggio fatto Dall' Altezza Serenissima Del Signor Prencipe di Parma Alessandro Farnese Per la Francia, Inghilterra, Olanda, Fiandra, e Spagna . . . In Venetia, . . . MDCLXVI. 4°, A—Cc in fours. With a portrait and frontispiece. *B. M.*

CATHOLICS.
To the Honourable The Knights, Citizens, and Burgesses of the Commons House in Parliament now assembled, In answere to the humble Petition of the Lay-Catholikes of England. London, Printed. 1641. 4°, 4 leaves.

CHAMBERLAYNE, EDWARD, LL.D., F.R.S.
England's Wants : Or Several Proposals Probably beneficial for England, . . . By a true lover of his Country. The second Edition with considerable Additions. London, Printed for Jo. Martyn, 1668. 4°, A—F in fours. *B. M.* and *H. Stopes, Esq.*

> This is a very enlightened and interesting pamphlet, proposing numerous reforms in our social, political, and juridical customs. Although published without his name, it is known to be Dr. Chamberlayne's from having been buried with him, agreeably to his instructions, with a copy of each of his other books, in his tomb at Chelsea Church. We thus become aware that he is the author of at least five pieces, to which we might otherwise have had no clue.

CHAMBERLEN, PETER.
The Poore Mans Advocate, Or, Englands Samaritan. Powring Oyle and Wyne into the wounds of the Nation. By making present Provision for the Souldier and the Poor, by reconciling all Parties. By repaying all Arrears to the Parliament Army. All publique Debts, and all the late Kings, Queenes, and Princes Debts due before this Session. *Banum quo Communius eo melius.* Truth needes no Corners, . . . London, Printed for Giles Calvert, [April, 1649.] 4°, A—F in fours: G, 6.

> Chamberlen, in his Epistle to the House of Commons, addresses it as " Ye choyce men of England."

CHARLES STUART THE FIRST [1625-48.]
[A Proclamation announcing the death of James I. and the accession of Charles I.] Imprinted at London by Bonham Norton, and John Bill, Printers to the Kings Most Excellent Maiestie. 1625. A broadside. *B. M.*

An Answer to the New Motions : Or, A serious and briefe Discussion of certaine Motions now in question. London, Printed for Robert Bostock. 1641. 4°, A—C in fours.

His Maiesties Proclamation and Declaration to all His loving Subjects, occasioned by a False and Scandalous Imputation laid upon his Maiesty, of an Intention of Raising or Leavying war against his Parliament: and of having raised Force to that end. Published at His Court at York, the 16. day of Iune 1642. With His Maiesties Declaration and Profession, disavowing any Preparations or Intentions . . . And the Declaration and Profession of the Lords, and other, of His Majesties most Honourable Privy-Counsell, now at York, disavowing any apparance of the same. Reprinted by His Maiesties Command. Oxford, Printed by Leonard Lichfield, . . . 1642. 4°, A—D in fours.

A Vindication of the King. With some Observations upon the Two Houses. By a true Sonne of the Church of England, and a Lover of his Countryes Liberty. London, Printed Anno Domini, 1642. 4°, 4 leaves.

A Few Propositions shewing the Lawfulnesse of Defence against the injurious attempts of outragious violence. [The Parliamentary Imprimatur signed *John White*, June 8, 1643.] London Printed for Samuel Gellibrand, at the Brazen Serpent in Pauls churchya[r]d, 1643. 4°, A—B 2 in fours.

His Majesties Late Protestation before His Receiving of the Sacrament. Printed in the Yeere of our Lord, 1643. [July 12.] A small broadsheet. *B. M.*

[A Proclamation by Charles I. testifying his sense of the loyalty and services of the County of Cornwall. From the Court at Sudeley Castle, Sept. 10, 1643.] Printed at Oxford, by Leonard Lichfield, Printer to the Vniversity 1643. A broadside. *B. M.*

By the King A Proclamation forbidding any of His Majesties Subjects to assist the Rebells with Men, Money, Armes, Victualls, or Intelligence, to stop any of His Majesties Messengers, or Pacquets, or to offer violence to any of His Majesties Souldiers. Printed at Oxford by Leonard Lichfield, Printer to the University. 1643. A broadside. *B. M.*

A Copie of Verses, said to be Composed by His Majestie, upon His first Imprisonment in the Isle of Wight. [29 Sept. 1648.] A small broadsheet. *B. M.*

His Majesties Paper Containing severall Questions propounded to the Commissioners Divines Touching Episcopacy. With an humble Answer returned to his Majesty by Mr. Marshall, Mr. Vines, Mr. Carill, and Mr. Seaman 4. October 1648.

Published by Authority. London printed by Moses Bell, 9 Octob. 1648. 4°, A—B 2 in fours.

    An introductory letter, signed *W. M.*, is dated from Newport, Isle of Wight, 4 Oct. 1648.

His Majesties Reasons against the pretended Iurisdiction of the high Court of Iustice, which he intended to deliver in writing on Munday Iannary 22. 1648. Faithfully transcribed out of the Originall Copie under the Kings own Hand. Printed in the Yeer 1648. A broadside. *B. M.*

A List of the Names of the Judges of the High Court of Justice, for Tryall of the King Appointed by An Act of the Commons in England in Parliament Assembled. And a List of the Officers of the said Court by them Elected. Printed at London for R. I. 1649. A broadside. *B. M.*

Munday 29th January 1648. A True Relation of the Kings Speech, to the Lady Elizabeth, and the Duke of Gloucester, the day before his Death. Another Relation from the Lady Elizabeths own hand. Printed in the Yeare, 1648 [March 24]. A broadside. *B. M.*

The Charge against the King discharged: Or, The King cleared by the people of England, from the severall Accusations in the Charge, delivered in against him at Westminster-Hall Saturday last, Jan. 20. by that high Court of Justice erected by the Army-Parliament, which is here fully answered in every particular thereof.... Printed in the first Yeere of Englands Thraledome. [1649.] 4°, A—E 2 in fours.

A True Copy of the Journal of the High Court of Justice, For the Tryal of K. Charles I. As it was Read in the House of Commons, And Attested under the hand of Phelps, Clerk to that Infamous Court. Taken by J. Nalson, L.L.D. Jan. 4. 1689. With a Large Introduction. London, Printed by H. C. for Thomas Dring, ... 1684. Folio, A—Hh, 2 leaves each, besides the portrait of the King by R. White, the title, and an address to the Reader, 3 leaves more.

A View of the Reign of King Charles the First. Wherein The True Causes of the Civil War are Impartially Delineated, By Strokes borrow'd from Lord Clarendon, Sir Philip Warwick, H. L'Estrange, and other most Authentick and Approved Historians. In Answer to the Libels lately Publish'd against a Sermon Preach'd by the Reverend White Kennet, D.D. Archdeacon of Huntingdon, &c. London: Printed for A. and J. Churchill in Paternoster-Row, 1704. 4°, A—D in fours.

CHARLES STUART THE SECOND
[1660-85.]

By the King. [A Proclamation offering a free pardon to all English officers and soldiers going over to the royal cause from that of the Parliament. Court at Stirling. 27 July 1650. Edinburgh, 1650.] A broadside. *B. M.*

A Proclamation [announcing the accession of Charles II. and the vacancy of the Crown from the death of Charles I.] Dublin Printed by William Bladen, by special Order, Anno Dom. 1660. A broadside. *B. M.*

The Form of His Majesties Coronation-Feast, to be Solemnized and kept at Westminster-Hall Upon the 23 of April 1661. London Printed for R. Crofts at the Crown in Chancery-lane, 1661. A broadside. *B. M.*

The Kings Psalter. Containing Psalms and Hymns, With Easie and Delightful Directions to all Learners, whether Children, Youths, or others, for their better reading of the English Tongue. Also Prayers for every Day of the Week, beginning with the Letters of the name of our Soveraign Lord King Charles; And Other observable Varieties, fit either for the School, or for the Closet, all which are profitable, plain, and pleasant. London, Printed for S. S. and sold by Tho. Harlley at the Black-Boy behinde St. Albans Church in Wood street. 1671. 8°, partly black letter, A—M in eights, including the frontispiece. With woodcuts. *B. M.*

    The title is followed by the following dedication: "To the Tallest Top-Branch of the Second Cedar in the Royal Lebanon of Great Britain, His Royal Grace, Edgar, Baron Dauntzey, in the County of Wilts, Earl and Duke of Cambridge, Son and Heir Apparent to the Thrice Illustrious Prince, the Most Highly Magnanimous James, Duke of York and Albany, &c. The Publisher in all prostrate humility Devotes and Dedicates this his ENCHYRIDION."
    On the back of this edifying effusion occurs a statement that the present work was intended to supersede the King's Primer, and that it was published by special authority of the Crown.

Treason, Popery, &c. Brought to a Publique Test: With regard to the Grounds of his Majesties late Declaration Concerning the Succession to the Crown.—*Fàgere Pudor, Verumque, fidesque* ... London,

Printed in the Year 1680. 4°, B—F in fours and the title.

A Relation of Two Free Conferences between Father L'Chese, and Four Considerable Jesuits, touching the Present State of the Affair of the Romanists in England. In order to the Carrying out their Great Design. Sent in a Letter from Paris, to a Considerable Popish Lord in England. Printed, in the Year, 1680. 4°. A, 2 leaves: B—F in fours.

CHARRON, PIERRE.

Of Wisdome. Three Bookes Written in French by Peter Charrō Doct' of Lawe in Paris. Translated by Samson Lennard. At London Printed for Edward Blount & Will. Aspley. 4°. ¶, 8 leaves. besides one following the title with "The subiect and order of these three Books:" A—Mm in eights: Nn, 4 leaves: Oo, 2 leaves, Oo 2 with the *Errata*. Dedicated "to the Most High and Mighty Prince, Henry, Prince of Great Britaine, Sonne and Heire apparent to our Soucreigne Lord the King." The title is engraved by W. Hole. *B. M.*

> In the dedication Lennard enters into some interesting particulars about himself, and flatters both Henry and his father very freely. He served under Sydney at Zutphen, and died, it appears, in 1630.
> Puttick's, Dec. 7, 1888, No. 896, King James the First's copy, in old calf, with the Royal Arms impressed in gold on either side of the cover.

CHIO.

An Account of Monsieur De Quesnes Late Expedition to Chio; Together with the Negotiation of Monsieur Guilleragues the French Ambassadour at the Port. In a Letter written by an Officer of the Grand Vizir's to a Pacha. Translated into English. London, Printed for Richard Tonson ... and Jacob Tonson ... 1683. 4°, B—G in fours, a leaf of H, and title, dedication to George, Marquis of Halifax, by the anonymous translator, and Preface, 3 leaves more. *B. M.*

CHURCH.

The Religion of the Church of England, The Surest Establishment of the Royal Throne; With the Unreasonable Latitude which the Romanists allow in point of Obedience to Princes. Rom. 13. 5. *Wherefore ye must needs be subject, not only for wrath, but also for Conscience sake.* London, Printed for R. P. in the Year 1678. 4°. A—F in fours.

> In the headline on A 2 this purports to be "a Letter occasioned by some late Discourse with a Person of Quality."

CLARKE, SAMUEL, *late Minister of Bennet-Finck, London*.

The Life & Death of William, Surnamed The Conqueror: King of England, and Duke of Normandy. ... London, Printed for Simon Miller, .. 1671. 4°, B—G 2 in fours and the title.

[CLEMENT, ———].

A Discourse of the General Notions of Money, Trade, & Exchanges, As they stand in Relation to each other. Attempted by way of Aphorism: With a Letter to a Minister of State . . . Wherein also some Thoughts are Suggested for the Remedying the Abuses of our Money. By a Merchant [Mr. Clement.] London. Printed in the Year, 1695. 4°. A—E in fours.

> The words between brackets are in a coeval hand in the Gibson-Craig copy, here used.

CLOTHING-TRADE.

Reasons of the Decay of the Clothing-Trade, Humbly offered to the Parliament: With some Short Proposals of Redress. By a Well-wisher to the Trade, and the true English Interest. London, Printed for Randal Taylor . . . 1691. 4°, A—B in fours.

COCKER, EDWARD.

Cocker's Decimal Arithmetick, . . . Perused, Corrected, and Published by John Hawkins . . . London, Printed for George Sawbridge . . . and Richard Wellington . . . . MDCXCV. 8°, A—Ff in eights. Dedicated by Hawkins to Sir Peter Daniel, Kt., and Peter Rich, Esq., Alderman of London, and James Reading, Esq., J.P. for Surrey.

COGAN, THOMAS.

The Haven of Health, . . . The fourth Edition corrected and amended. London, Printed by Anne Griffin, for Roger Ball, and are to be sold at his shop without Temple-barre, at the Golden Anchor next the Nags-head Taverne. 1636. 4°. ¶, 4 leaves: B, 4 leaves: A—v[v] in fours.

COIN.

The Proposal for the Raising of the Silver Coin of England, From 60 Pence the Ounce to 75 Pence, Considered; With the Consequences thereof. London: Printed for Richard Cumberland, at the Angel in St. Paul's Church-yard. MDCXCVI. 4°, A—C, 2 leaves each.

COKE, SIR EDWARD, *afterwards Lord Coke, and Chief Justice of England*.

Les Reports de Edward Coke Lattorney generall le Roigne, de diuers Resolutions,

& Iudgements donnes auec graund deliberation. per les tres-reuerends Iudges, & sages de la ley, de causes & matters en les queux ne furront vnques resolue, ou aiuges par deuant, & les raisons. & causes des dits resolutions & Iudgements, durant le tresheureux regiment de tresillustre & renomies Roigne Elizabeth, le founteine de tout Iustice, & la vie de la ley. *Lex est certa ratio* . . . Cicero. Londini in Ædibus Thomæ Wight. Cum Priuilegio. Primo Ianuarij 1600. Folio. Title and Prefaces, 4 leaves : A—Uu in fours : Xx, 6 leaves. *B. M.*

This, though not so stated on the title-page, is the first of a series of volumes published between 1600 and 1615, containing the eleven parts of Coke's *Reports*. A complete set is in the Museum.

Collation : Le Second Part des Reportes, 1602, 6 prel. leaves and A—Aa 2 in fours : Le Tierce Part, 1602, 4 prel. leaves and B—Aa in fours : Le Qvart Part, 1604, A, 4 : B, 6 : A (repeated)—Ii in fours : Qvinta Part 1606 (described in *C. & N*. 3rd S. Suppl. p. 23) : La Size Part, 1607, 11 prel. leaves : A—O in sixes : La Sept Part, 1608, a—e in sixes : f, 4 : B—H in sixes : I, 3 : La Hviet Part, 1611, ¶ and ¶¶ in sixes : A, 4 leaves : B—Gg in sixes : La Nevf^me Part, 1613, a—c in sixes and A—Aa in sixes : La Dix^me Part, 1618. a–c in sixes. d, 8, A—Z in sixes, Aa, 7 : La Vnz^me Part, 1615, A, 8 leaves, B—S in sixes.

Though I have not yet seen it, the 10th Part was doubtless printed before 1618. The 11th was reprinted in 1619. The whole is a rich treasury of information on all questions connected with early jurisprudence, and is of considerable archæological value.

The Reports of Sir Edward Coke Kt. Late Lord Chief-Justice of England, And one of His Majesties Covncil of State, of Divers Resolutions and Judgements given upon solemn Arguments, and with great Deliberation, and Conference of the most Reverend Judges, and Sages of the Law ; of Cases in Law which never were Resolved or Adjudged before ; And the Reasons and Causes of the said Resolutions and Judgements. Faithfully rendered into English. London, Printed for W. Lee, M. Walbanck. . . . 1658. Folio. Title and Preface, 2 leaves : Table, 3 leaves : A—3 A in sixes : 3 B—6 D in fours. [A new title :] The Declarations and other Pleadings contained in the Eleven Parts of the Reports . . . 1659 : B—Kk in fours : Ll—3 Z, 2 leaves each : Tables, 5 leaves. *B. M.*

Hæc Epitome Undecim Librorum Relationum Honoratissimi et Docti Viri Edvardi Coke Mil. defuncti, . . . prælo commissa fuit : . . . Londini Excus. per assignat. T. More Armigeri. 1640. 8°. A, 6 leaves : B—Oo in eights : Pp, 2 leaves. Dedicated by Edward Trotman of the Inner Temple, the Editor, to that Society. *B. M.*

A Perfect Abridgment of the Eleven Bookes of Reports, of the Reverend, and Learned K^t S^r. Edw. Coke, Sometimes Chiefe Justice of the vpper Bench. Originally Written in French, by Sr John Davis . . . London, Printed by I. G. for W. Lee, . . . 1652. 12°, A and a, 4 leaves each : B—N in twelves : O, 8. *B. M.*

The Twelfth Part of the Reports of Sir Edward Coke, Kt. Of Divers Resolutions and Judgments Given . . . in Cases of Law, The most of them very Famous, being of the Kings especiall Reference, from the Councel Table, Concerning the Prerogative, As for the digging of Saltpeter, Forfeitures, Forrests. Proclamations, &c. And the Jurisdictions of the Admiralty, . . . Also the Forms and Proceedings of Parliaments, both in England, & Ireland : With an Exposition of Poynings Law. . . . With Alphabeticall Tables, . . . London, Printed by T. R. for Henry Twyford, and Thomas Dring, . . . 1658. Folio. Title and Preface, 2 leaves : Table, 2 leaves : B—Nn, 2 leaves each. *B. M.*

On the flyleaf of this copy occurs in an old hand, the initial being somewhat indistinct. "Deus providebit. T. Rokeby ;" and at the foot of the preface, which is signed Edward Bulstrod, there is the following memorandum in a coeval hand : "Mr Bulstrode, in a Preface to ÿ 1st part of his reports makes an apology for his name being put to this book, & taxes this book as Erronious & unfitt for ÿ Press."

An Exact Abridgement of the Two last Volumes of Reports of Sr. Edw. Coke, Knight. . . . By Thomas Manley, of the Middle-Temple. . . . Printed at London : and are to be sold by Henry Twyford and Timothy Twyford. 1670. 8°, B—D 4 in eights, besides title and preface, 3 leaves more. *B. M.*

Manley states that he followed in his plan that of Edward Trotman, the abridger of Bookes 1—11.

A General Table to all the Severall Books of the Reports of the late most Reverend Judge, Sir Edward Coke, . . . With Two Alphabeticall Catalogues. . . . Composed by Tho: Ashe of Graies-Inne. London, Printed by J. Flesher, for W. Lee, . . . 1652. 8°. A, 8 leaves : a, 4 leaves : B—Gg in eights : Hh, 4. *B. M.*

The Reports of Sir Edward Coke, K\t In Verse. Wherein The Name of each Case, and the Principal Points, are contained in Two Lines. To which are added, References in the Margin to all the Editions of the said Reports, ... In the Savoy: Printed by Henry Lintot (Assignee of Edw. Sayer, Esq:) for J. Worrall at the Dove in Bell-yard near Lincoln's Inn. MDCCXLII. 8°. A, 4 leaves: a, 4 leaves: B—K in fours. *B. M.*

Le Necessarie vse & Fruit de les Pleadings, conteine en le lieur de le tresreuerend Edward Coke Lattorney general la Roigne. Quesque vn Collection de comemorable buy cases sparsim cite en les Arguments de mesmes les Reports. ... Londini In ædibus Thomæ Wight. An. Dom. 1601. Cum Priuilegio. 8°, A—N in eights. Dedicated by Richard Cary to Sir Edmund Anderson, Chief Justice of the Common Pleas. *B. M.*

The First Part of the Institvtes of the Lawes of England. Or A Commentarie vpon Littleton, not the name of a Lawyer onely, but of the Law it self. [Quot. from Martial and Cicero.] *Hæc ego grandæuus posui tibi candide lector.* Authore Edw. Coke Milite. London, Printed for the Societie of Stationers. Anno 1628. Folio. ¶ and ¶¶, 4 leaves each, ¶ 1 occupied by a portrait of Coke by Payne, dated 1629; a portrait of Littleton; A—5 G in fours: Table, with a separate title, dated 1630, A—Q, 2 leaves each. With a folded Table of Consanguinity at fol. 20. *B. M.*

The Second Part of the Institutes of the Laws of England. Containing the Expositions of many ancient, and other Statutes; ... *Quod non lego, non credo.* August. ... Authore Edw. Coke, Milite, I. C. ... London, Printed by M. Flesher, and R. Young, for E. D. ... 1642. Folio. A, 6 leaves, including the portrait by Payne (1629); B—5 A in fours: 5 B, 6 leaves. *B. M.*

At the top of the title in this copy occurs: Iohn Morris MDCXLII.

The Third Part of the Institutes of the Laws of England: Concerning High Treason, and other Pleas of the Crown and Criminall causes. [Quot.] Authore Edw. Coke Milite, I.C. ... MDCXLIV. Printed at London by M. Flesher, for W. Lee, and D. Pakeman. Folio, A—Ii in fours, and a leaf of Epilogue marked Kk. The portrait of Coke occupies A 1. *B. M.*

Synopsis Or, An Exact Abridgement of the Lord Cokes Commentaries upon Littleton: Being A briefe explanation of the Grounds of the Common Law. Composed by that Famous and Learned Lawyer Sir Humphrey Davenport Knight, heretofore Reader of that Honorable Society of Graye's Inne, ... London, Printed by E. G. for Matthew Walbancke, ... 1652. 8°. Title and R. M. Barr[ister] to the Reader, 3 leaves: B—Gg 4 in eights. *B. M.*

An Abridgement of the Lord Coke's Commentary on Littleton: Collected by an unknown Author; yet by a late Edition pretended to be Sir Humphrey Davenport Kt. And in this Second Impression purged from very many gross Errors committed in the said former Edition. ... London: Printed for W. Lee, ... 1651. 8°, B—Ff in eights, Ff 7-8 blank, besides title and To the Reader and portraits of Littleton and Coke. *B. M.*

An Exact Abridgment in English, ... The Third Impression. London, Printed by F. Leach, for Matthew Walbancke, ... 1657. 8°, A—Hh in eights, A 1 and Hh 8 blank. With a portrait of Coke. *B. M.*

A Little Treatise of Baile and Maineprize. Written by E. C. Knight, and now Published for a generall good. London: Printed for William Cooke, 1635. 4°, A—E in fours, first and last leaves blank. *B. M.*

The Compleate Copy-Holder. Wherein is contained a Learned Discourse of the Antiquity and Nature of Manors and Copy-Holds. With all things thereto incident, As. ⎧ Presentments.
⎪ Admittances.
⎨ Surrenders.
⎪ Forfeitures.
⎩ Customes, &c.
Necessary, both for the Lord and Tenant. Together, with the forme of keeping a Copy-hold Court, and Court Baron. By Sir Edward Coke, Knight. London, Printed by T. Cotes, for W. Cooke, ... 1641. 4°, A—Z in fours: Aa, 2 leaves. *B. M.*

The Compleat Copy-Holder, ... Whereunto is newly added The Relation between the Lord of a Mannor and the Copy-holder his Tenant: By that Worthy Lawyer Charles Calthrop of Lincolnes-Inne Esquire ... London, Printed for W. Lee, and D. Pakeman, 1650. 4°. A—Aa 2 in fours: A—K in fours, and the separate title to the *Relation*, &c. *B. M.*

COLE, WILLIAM.
Legal and other Reasons (With all Humility) Presented to His Most Excellent Majesty, King Charles II. And to Both His Honourable Houses of Parliament, why the Subjects of England, Should not be Imprisoned for Debt or Damages, Or any thing thereunto relating. London, Printed in the year M DC LXXV. 4º, 6 leaves.

COLLINS, DR.
Epphata to F. T. Or, The Defence of the Right Reuerend Father in God, the Lord Bishop of Elie, Lord High Amoner and Priuie Counsellour to the Kings Most Excellent Maiestie. Concerning His Answer to Cardinale Bellarmines Apologie : . . . Printed by Cantrell Legge, Printer to the Vniuersitie of Cambridge. 1617. 4º. Title, 1 leaf : ¶ 4 leaves : (a)—(e 2) in fours : A—4 C in fours.

COLLINS, HERCULES, *of Wapping.*
Three Books : Viz.
I. The Scribe instructed unto the Kingdom of Heaven.
II. Mountains of Brass : or, A Discourse upon the Secrets of God.
III. A Poem on the Birth, Life, Death, Resurrection, and Ascension of our Lord and Saviour Jesus Christ. By Hercules Collins, an unworthy Servant of Jesus Christ, and his Church in Wapping. London : Printed and sold by the Author at Wapping, and R. Mount at the Postern on Tower-Hill. 1696. 12º. A—E 2 in twelves : The Third Book, with separate signatures, A—E 4 in twelves. *B. M.*

The concluding portion is in verse; all have separate titles. Collins produced other works.

COLOM, ARNOLD.
The Lightning Colomne, Or Sea-Mirrour, Contayning The Sea-Coasts of the Northern, Eastern and Western Navigation : Setting forth in divers necessarie Sea-Cards all the Ports, Rivers, Bayes, Roads, Depths, and Sands ; very curiously placed on its due Polus-heighth furnished. With the Discoveries of the chief Countries, and on what cours and distance they lay one from another : Never theretofore so clearly laid open, and here and there very diligently bettered and augmented, for the use of all Sea-Men. As also The Situation of the Northernly Countries, . . . At Amsterdam. Printed by Jacob and Casparus Loots-Man, Booksellers upon the Water, in the Loots-Man, 1670. Large folio, A—D in fours : E, 1 leaf. (∵) 2, 1 leaf : folded maps of Europe and of the North and Zuyder Seas : (a —(e) in fours, besides the 10 maps : (A*), 4 leaves : (B*), 2 leaves, besides the 5 maps : h (at p. 53 with *The First Part of the Lightning Sea-Columne,* &c.)—n 2 in fours, besides the 15 maps : *The Second Part,* &c. A—L in fours, besides the 27 maps.

The Lightningh [*sic*] Columne, Or Sea-Mirrour, . . . At Amsterdam, Printed by Casparus Loots-Man Bookseller In the Loots-man, upon the Water. Anno 1699. Cum Privilegio. Large folio. With a frontispiece and maps.

The Privilege is dated 1680.

Lightning Colom of the Midland-Sea, Containing A Description of all the knowne Coasts, Islants, Sands, Depthes and Roads, beginning from the Narowest of the Streat, unto Alexandrette in the Levant. At Amsterdam, Printed by Jacob and Casparus Loots-Man, Booksellers upon te Water, in the Loots-Man, 1674. Folio, A—Q in fours, besides the 19 maps. The title is engraved.

COMBACHE, LOUIS, *Physician to the French King.*
Sal, Lumen, & Spiritus Mundi Philosophici : Or, The dawning of the Day, Discovered By the Beams of Light : Shewing, The true Salt and Secret of the Philosophers. The first and universal Spirit of the World. Written Originally in French, afterwards turned into Latin, By the Illustrious Doctor, Lodovicus Combachius, Ordinary Physician to the King, and publik Professor of Physick in the University of Mompelier. And now transplanted into Albyons Garden, By R. T. philomath. Printed at London, by J. C. for Martha Harrison, at the Lamb at the East-end of S. Pauls. 1657. 8º, A—P in eights, first and last leaves blank, and a, 8 leaves. Dedicated by Robert Turner of Holshot to William Pitt of Hartly-Westpol in Hampshire, Esquire.

COLVILL, WILLIAM, *Moderator of King James's College.*
Philosophia Moralis Christiana . . . Edinburgi, Excudebat Georgius Swintoun, & Jacobus Glen. Anno Dom. 1670. 8º, A—Cc 4 in eights. Dedicated to William Hay of Drumhall and John Hope of Hopetoun.

CONSTITUTIONES.
Constitutiones legitime seu legatine regionis Anglicane : cũ subtilissima interpretatione dñi Johannis de Athon : tripliciq̃s tabella. Necnon et *constitutiones*

prouinciales ab archiepiscopis Cantuarensibus edite : et sūma accuratione recognite : annotate et Parisijs coimpresse. [Col.] Clauduntur itaq5 . . . Ad laudem et gloriam optimi maximi domini nostri Jesu christi : eiusq5 plentissime matris / et totius celestis curie / necnon ad cōsernationem libertatis ecclesie anglicane. Et ad salutem atq5 eruditionem totius cleri omniumq5 christi fidelium inclytissimi anglorum regni. Anno domini Millesimo quingentessimo quarto : ad idus Semptembris. Folio. Table, A—B in eights : a—v 5 in eights.

COOKE, JOHN, *of Gray's Inn.*
Vnum Necessarium: Or, The Poore Mans Case : Being An Expedient to make Provision for all poore People in the Kingdome. Humbly presented to the higher Powers : Begging some Angelicall Ordinance, for the speedy abating of the prises of Corne, without which, the ruine of many thousands (in humane judgment) is inevitable. In all humility propounding, that the readiest way is a suppression or regulation of Innes and Ale-houses, where halfe the Barley is wasted in excesse : Proving them by Law to be all in a Præmunire, and the grand concernment, that none which have been notoriously disaffected, and enemies to common honesty and civility, should sell any Wines, strong Ale, or Beere, but others to be licensed by a Committee in every County, upon recommendation of the Minister, and such of the Inhabitants in every Parish, where need requires, that have been faithful to the Publike. Wherein there is a Hue-and-Cry against Drunkards, as the most dangerous Antinomians : And against Ingrossers, to make a dearth, and cruell Misers, which are the Caterpillars and Bane of this Kingdome. By John Cooke, of Graies Inne, Barrester. Prov. 11, 26. *He that withholdeth corne,* . . . London, Printed for Matthew Walbancke at Grayes Inne Gate. 1648. 4°, A—K 2 in fours. *H. Stopes, Esq.*

Redintegratio Amoris, Or A Union of Hearts, Between The Kings Most Excellent Majesty, the Right Honorable the Lords and Commons in Parliament, His Excellency Sir Thomas Fairfax, and the Army Under his Command : The Assembly, and every honest man that desires a sound and durable Peace, accompanied with speedy Justice and Piety. By way of respective Apologie, so far as Scripture and Reason may be Judges. *The falling out of lovers is the renewing of love.* London, Printed for Giles Calvert, and are to be sold at his shop at the black spread-Eagle near the West-end of Pauls. [1648.] 4°, A—M in fours, first and last leaves blank.

COOT, SIR CHARLES, *Lord President of Connaught.*
A true Relation of the Transactions of Sir Charles Coot, Kt. Lord President of Connaught in Ireland, and Owen-Roe-O-Neal ; As it was Reported to the Parliament from the Councel of State. Together with the Votes of the House thereupon. . . . London, Printed for Edward Husband, . . . August 28, 1649. 4°, A—C 2 in fours.

CORNWALL.
Newes from Perin [Penryn] in Cornwall : Of A most Bloody and vn-exampled Murther very lately committed by a Father on his owne Sonne (who was lately returned from the Indyes) at the Instigation of a mercilesse Step-mother. Together with their seuerall most wretched endes, being all performed in the month of September last. Anno. 1618. London Printed by E. A. and are to be sold at Christ-Church gate. 1618. 4°, black letter, A—C 2 in fours, title on A 2. With woodcuts, including a large one on the title. *B. M.*

George Daniel's copy. This narrative formed the plot for Lillo's play of *Fatal Curiosity.*

CORYAT, THOMAS.
Thomas Coryate, Travailer for the English wits, and the good of this Kingdom : To all his inferiour Countrymen, Greeting : Especially to the Sirenicall Gentlemen, that meet the first Friday of euerie Moneth, at the Mermaide in Breadstreet. From the Court of the great Mogul, resident at the Towne of Asmere, in the Easterne India. Printed by W. Iaggard, and Henry Fetherston. 4°, A—H in fours, A 4 with a woodcut. With a cut on title and others in the volume.

This issue varies, and very curiously, in the title from that already described. It appears to be textually identical.

COTTON, SIR ROBERT, *Knight and Baronet.*
A Treatise, Shewing That the Soveraignes Person is required in the great Councells or Assemblies of the State, as well at the Consultations as at the Conclusions. Written by Sir Robert Cotton, Knight and Baronet. Printed in the Yeare 1641. 4°, A—B in fours.

A Discourse of Foreign War : With an

Account of all the Taxations upon this Kingdom, from the Conquest to the End of the Reign of Queen Elizabeth. Also a List of the Confederates from Henry I. to the End of the Reign of the said Queen; shewing which have prov'd most Beneficial to England. Formerly Written by Sir Robert Cotton Baronet, and now Published by Sir John Cotton Baronet. London; Printed for Henry Mortlock ... 1690. 8°, B—K in eights, K 2 and 8 blank, besides title and preface by Sir John Cotton, and portrait of the author by T. Cross.

COVEL, WILLIAM, *D.D.*
A Ivst and Temperate Defence of the Five Books of Ecclesiastical Policie: Written by M. Richard Hooker: Against an vncharitable Letter of certein English Protestants ... At London Printed by P. Short for Clement Knight, dwelling at the signe of the holy Lambe in Paules church-yard. 1603. 4°, A—V in fours, A 1 blank. Dedicated to the Archbishop of Canterbury.

CROMWELL, OLIVER, *Lord Protector* [1653-58.]
A Letter from the Right Honorable, The Lord Lieutenant of Ireland, to The Honorable William Lenthall, Esq; ... Concerning The Taking in and Surrendring of Enistery. Carrick Town and Castle. Passage-Fort. Bandon-Bridge. Kingsale, and the Fort there. ... London, Printed by John Field for Edward Husband ... 1649. 4°, 4 leaves.

A Letter from the Right Honorable, the Lord Lieutenant of Ireland, Concerning the Surrender of the Town of Ross. and the Artillery, Arms and Ammunition there. ... London, Printed by John Field for Edward Husband. ... 1649. 4°, A—B 2 in fours.

A Letter from the Lord Lieutenant of Ireland, To The Honorable William Lenthall Esq; ... Relating the several Successes it hath pleased God lately to give the Parliaments Forces there. Together with the several Transactions about the Surrender of Kilkenny, And the Articles agreed thereupon. ... London, Printed by Edward Husband and John Field, ... 1650. 4°, A—C in fours, C 4 blank.

The Articles of the Expected Peace, Concluded between His Highnesse Oliver Lord Protector of the Common-wealth of England, Scotland, and Ireland, &c. on the one Part, And the High and Mighty Lords, the States-General ... on the other Part. Faithfully Translated out of the Dutch Copie, Printed there, and now Reprinted at London May 2, 1654. 4°, A—C 2 in fours.

Oliver's Pocket Looking-Glass, New Fram'd and Clean'd, To give a clear View of the Great Modern Colossus. Begun by K. C ——; Carry'd on by K. J ——; Augmented by K. W ——; And now Finish'd, in order to be thrown down in the Glorious R —— of Q. A ——. *So may the Man of ignominious Might* ... Printed in the Year 1711. 8°, A—K in fours, first and last leaves blank. *B. M.*

Q. D. B. V! Characteres Tyranni in Oliverio Cromwello, Angliæ Qvondam, Scotiæ et Hiberniæ Protectore, ... Dissertatione Politica ... Exponens Praeses Martinus Hassen, ... Respondens Joh. Godofredus Ulbrechtvs, ... Vitembergae ... [MDCCXII.] 4°, A—G 2 in fours, besides title and dedication.
The date in the copy used was cut off.

A True and Faithful Narrative of Oliver Cromwell's Compact with the Devil for Seven Years, on the Day in which he gain'd the Battle at Worcester; and on which, at the Expiration of the said Term, he afterwards died. As it was Related by Colonel Lindsey, who was an Eye Witness of that Diabolical Conference, Related in Mr. Arch-Deacon Eachard's History of England. With A Letter from the Lady Claypole, Oliver Cromwell's beloved Daughter, to her Sister the Vice Countess of Falconbridge, copied from the Original, and found in the Lord Falconbridge's Study after his Death, at Brussels, which in a great Measure confirms the same, also some Minutes from Secretary Thurloe's Pocket-Book, which corroborate the Truth of this Fact, never before printed. To which is added. The Earl of Clarendon's Character of the Usurper, and an Account of his Death.

*Aude aliquid brevibus Gyaris & carcere dignum
Si vis esse aliquis* ———————— Juv.

London: Printed, and sold by W. Boreham at the Angel in Pater-noster-Row 1720. Reprinted at Edinburgh. Price Three Pence. N.B. The Price of the London Copy is Six Pence. 8°, A—C in fours. *B. M.*

CROSFEILD, ROBERT.
Justice Perverted, And Innocence & Loyalty Oppressed. Or, A Detection of the Corruptions of some Persons in Places

of Great Trust in the Government; which would have been laid open the Last Session of Parliament, according to the Intention of both Houses, had it not been prevented. London, Printed in the Year MDCXCV. 4°, A—D in fours. *B. M.*

CROUCH, NATHANIEL, *alias* RICHARD BURTON.
The History of Oliver Cromwel: Being an Impartial Account of all the Battles, Sieges, and other Military Atchievements, wherein he was Ingaged, in England, Scotland, and Ireland. And likewise, Of his Civil Administrations while he had the Supream Government of these Three Kingdoms, till his Death. Relating only Matters of Fact without Reflection or Observation. By R. B. Licensed and Entred. London, Printed for Nath. Crouch, at the Bell in the Poultrey, near Cheapside. 1692. Sm. 8°, A—H 6 in twelves. With a small three-quarter portrait of the Protector.

CURWEN, ALICE.
A Relation of the Labour, Travail and Suffering of that faithful Servant of the Lord Alice Curwen. Who departed this Life the 1st Day of the 6th Moneth, 1679, and resteth in Peace with the Lord. . . . Printed in the Year 1680. 4°. A, 4 leaves: a, 2: b, 4: B—H in fours.

> Many of the documents printed here are dated from Rhode Island and other places in America or the West Indies.

D. I. H.
Mariæ Scotorvm Reginæ Epitaphivm. Londini Excudebat Johannes Charlewood, pro Roberto Wallie. [1587.] A small broad-sheet, printed within a border. *B. M.*

DALECHAMP, CALEB, *M.A., of Trinity College, Cambridge.*
Christian Hospitalitie Handled Commonplace-wise in the Chappel of Trinity Colledge, Cambridge: Whereunto is added, A short but honourable Narration of the life and death of Mr. Harrison, the late hospital Vice-master of that Royal and Magnificent Societie: . . . Printed by Th. Buck, printer to the Universitie of Cambridge. 1632. 4°, A—V in fours, title on A 2. Dedicated to John, Lord Bishop of Lincoln.

> *Harrisonus Honoratus* has a separate title.

DAUBENY, H.
Historie & Policie Re-Viewed, In the Heroick Transactions of his Most Serene Highnesse, Oliver, Late Lord Protector; From his Cradle to his Tomb: Declaring his steps to Princely Perfections, as they are drawn in lively Parallels to the Ascents of the Great Patriarch Moses, in thirty Degrees, to the Height of Honour. By H. D. Esq. Claud. de Theodos. *Solus meruit regnare rogatus.* London, Printed for Nathaniel Brook, at the Angel in Cornhill. 1659. [April.] 8°, A—X 4 in eights, A 1 and X 4 blank, and a, 8 leaves. Dedicated to the Protector Richard Cromwell. *B. M.*

D'AUNOIS, MADAME.
Memoires de la Cour D'Angleterre. Tome I. [et II.] A Paris, Chez Claude Barbin, . . . M.DC.XCV. . . . Sm. 8°. Vol. i. pp. 416 + iv ; vol. ii. pp. 352.

DAVANZATI, BERNARDO, *of Florence*.
A Discourse upon Coins, By Signor Bernardo Davanzati, A Gentleman of Florence; Being publickly spoken in the Academy there, Anno 1588. Translated out of Italian, By John Toland. London ; Printed by J D. for Awnsham and John Churchill, . . . 1696. 4°, A—D 2 in fours.

DAVIES, JAMES.
The History of His SaCRed Majesty Charles the II. . . . By a Person of Quality. . . . Cork, Reprinted by William Smith, Anno Dom : 1660. 8°, A—Z and a—e in fours, except that Z has 5 leaves.

The Civil warres of Great Britain and Ireland. Containing an Exact History of their Occasion, Originall, Progress, and Happy End. By an Impartiall Pen. London, Printed by R. W. for Philip Chetwind, and are to be sold by Booksellers, 1661. Folio, A—3 D in fours, besides the title and dedication to Charles, Duke of Richmond and Lenox. *Grenv. Coll.*

> The writer in the dedication describe himself as the Duke's most humble servans and vassal, and refers to his father and two uncles having sacrificed their lives in the royal cause.

The Civil Warres of Great Britain and Ireland. Containing an Exact History of their Occasion, Originall, Progress, and Happy End. By an Impartiall Pen. Glasgow, Printed by Robert Sanders Town-Printer, and are to be sold at his Shop, Anno Dom. 1664. Cum Privilegio. 4°. *, 4 leaves : **, 4 leaves : ***, with Proem, 1 leaf : A—Fff in fours : Ggg, 1 leaf. *B. M.*

DAVISON, WILLIAM, *Nobilis Scotus, M.D.*
Philosophia Pyrotechnica. Sev Cvrsvs Chymiaticvs, nobilissima illa & exoptatissima Medicinæ parte pyrotechnica instructus. . . . Parisiis, . . . M.DC.XL. . . . 8°. Title. *Approbatio*, Privilege, and an engraved leaf with an Emblem, 4 leaves : Dedication to James Stuart, Duke of Lenox, 2 leaves : A—Hh 4 in eights, except A, which has 10 leaves : *Pars Tertia* [et Quarta,] aa—rr in eights. With Diagrams, a folded leaf in T of first portion, and after title of Part 3, and plates at cc and mm of the second alphabet.
> The second division of the work, or Parts iii.-iv., is dedicated to Henry Percy, Earl of Northumberland.

DE BURGO, GIO. BATTISTA.
Viaggio di Cinqve Anni in Asia, Africa, & Europa Di D. Gio. Battista de Bvrgo Abbate Clarense, e Vicario Apostolico per gli Sommi Pontefici Clemente X. & Innocenzo XI. nel Regno sempre Cattolico d'Irlanda. . . . In Milano, . . . [1686.] Sm. 8°. 3 vols. Part I. A—B 4 in twelves : pp. 548. Part II. ✠, 6 leaves : pp. 503. Part III. a—b in twelves : pp. 576. With a frontispiece and plates. *B. M.*
> The first and second parts are dedicated to Mary Beatrice, Queen of England.

DE CRESSY, HUGH-PAULLIN.
Exomologesis : Or, A Faithfull Narration of the Occasion and Motives of the Conversion . . . Now a second time printed. With Additions and Explications, . . . A Paris, Chez Jean Billain, . . . MDCLIII. 12°. A, 6 leaves : a, G leaves : B—Bb in twelves : Cc, 4. Dedicated by Serenus Cressy to the Hon. Walter Montagu, Esquire.

DE FONSECA, CHRISTOPHER.
Theion Exoticon, A Discourse of Holy Love, By which the Soul is united unto God. . . . Done into English with some Variations and much Addition, By Sr. George Strode Knight. London, Printed by J. Flesher, for Richard Royston . . . 1652. Sm. 8°. A, 4 leaves, besides frontispiece and engraved title containing a small portrait of the translator : B—N 2 in twelves. Dedicated to his children by Sir G. Strode.

DE LA PRIMAUDAYE, PIERRE.
The French Academie. Fvlly Discovrsed and finished in fovre Bookes. . . . London, Printed for Thomas Adams. 1618. Folio. ¶, 6 leaves : *, 6 leaves : A—4 T in sixes, first and last leaves blank. Dedicated by the translator to his singular good friend Mr. John Barne.

DESAINLIENS, CLAUDE, *alias* HOLYBAND.
The French Littelton : A Most Easy, Perfect, and Absolvte Way to learne the French tongue : . . . Imprinted at London by Richard Field, dwelling in the Blacke Friers. 1597. Sm. 8°, A—H in twelves.

DES CARTES, RENÉ.
The Passions of the Soule In three Books . . . translated out of French into English. London, Printed for A. C. and are to be sold by J. Martin, and J. Ridley, . . . 1650. 12°, A—H in twelves : 1, 6.

DIGBY, SIR KENELM.
Demonstratio Immortalitatis Animæ Rationalis, Sive Tractatvs Dvo Philosophici, In Qvorvm Priori Natura et Operationes Corporvm, In Posteriori Vero, Natvra Animæ . . . Explicantvr . . . Ex Anglico in Latinum versa operâ & studio I. L. . . . Parisiis, . . . M.DC.LI. . . . Folio, ã—ñ in fours (thrice repeated) : A—3 K in fours : *Institvtionvm Peripateticarvm* . . . *Pars Theoretica. Item Appendix Theologica De Origine Mendi.* Authore *Thoma Anglo, ex Albis East Saxonum* [Thomas White]. a—o in fours : A—D in fours.
> The Turner copy was a presentation one on large paper, with the author's autograph inscription to the Cavr. Abbate dal Pozzo.

DIGGES, THOMAS. *Esquire, of Wotton, co. Kent, Muster-Master General of all her Majesty's Forces in the Low Countries.*
England's Defence. A Treatise concerning Invasion : Or, A brief Discourse of what Orders were best for repulsing of Foreign Forces, if at any time they should invade us by Sea in Kent, or elsewhere. Exhibited in writing to the Right Honourable Robert Dudley Earl of Leicester, a little before the Spanish Invasion, in the year 1588. To which is now added, An Account of such Stores of War, and other Materials as are requisite for the Defence of a Fort, a Train of Artillery, and for a Magazine belonging to a Field Army. And also a List of the Ships of War, and the Charge of them, and the Land-Forces designed by the Parliament against France, Anno 1678. Also a List of the present Governors of the Garrisons of England, and of all the Lord Lieutenants, and High Sheriffs of all those Counties adjacent to the Coasts. Lastly, the Wages of Officers and Seamen serving in his Majesty's Fleet at Sea per Month. Collected

by Thomas Adamson, Master-Gunner of his Majesty's Train of Artillery, Anno 1673. And now thought fit to be published for the use of the Protestant Subjects of his Majesty's Kingdoms and Plantations. London, Printed for F. Haley, in the year 1680. Folio, A—E, 2 leaves each. *B. M.*

DIRECTORIUM.

Pica sive Directorium Sacerdotum [Col.] ¶ In laudem Sanctissime Trinitatis, totiusque Milicie celestis, ad honorem & decorem S. ecclesie Eboracensis Anglicane, ejusque devotissimi cleri, hoc opus, quod Pica, sive Directorium sacerdotum nuncupatur, vigilanti studio emendatum et revisum. [Col.] Impressum Eboraci, per me Hugonem Goes, in vico, qui appellatur Steengate, anno Domini MDIX. 18 die mensis Februarii. 8°, 114 leaves. *Minster Library York* and *Sydney Sussex Coll. Camb.*

With a preface by Thomas Hannibal, Doctor of Laws. Compare Davies (*Memoir of the York Press*, 1868, p. 17) with Herbert's *Ames*, p. 437. Both copies mentioned above have now lost the leaf of colophon, which was apparently in the latter in Ames's time.

DISCIPLINE.

The First and Second Booke of Discipline. Together with some Acts of the Generall Assemblie, Clearing and confirming the same: And An Act of Parliament. [Quot. from *Exodus*, 25. 9.] Printed Anno 1621. 4°, A—O 2 in fours.

The First and Second Booke of Discipline . . . London Printed in the yeare, 1641. 4°, A—B 2 in fours: C—P 2 in fours.

DISCOVERIES.

Strange and Wonderful Discoveries of several Plots, Contrivances, and Wicked Conspiracies Laid to Ruin and Undoe some Thousands of honest and well-meaning People, found out and detected: With the Ways to avoid and prevent the danger they Threaten to this and other Kingdoms and States. Or, A Seasonable Warning to Travellers and House-Keepers, &c. Being A Discovery of the Ways and Devices High-way men take to Way-lay and Set upon such as Travel the Road: with Instructions to avoid them. As also the Foot Pad, Pick-pocket, Budge, Millken, Bubber, Shop-lift and other Thieves; with the many Pollicies and Stratagems they use, to commit Robberies of sundry Kinds, and bring their unlawful purposes about: with means to prevent or detect them. Highly necessary to be known, and now made publick at the Request of a Penitent Thief, for the good of all Honest People. Licensed according to Order. Printed for J. Conyers at the Black Raven near St Andrews-Church in Holborn. 1688. 4°, 4 leaves. *B. M.*

DISNEY, DANIEL.

Some Remarkable Passages in the Holy Life and Death of Gervase Disney Esq; To which are added Several Letters and Poems. —— *Being dead, yet speaketh.* Heb. 11, 4. London, Printed by J. D. for Jonathan Robinson . . . MDCXCII. 8°. A, 8 leaves: a, 4 leaves: B—V 4 in eights. *B. M.*

Dedicated by D. Disney "To my Honoured Mother Mrs. Barbara Disney, my Dear Sister Mrs. Mary Disney, with other near Relations, for whose use this Book was mainly intended." This is followed by a Preface by Samuel Slater.

DISNEY, WILLIAM, *Esquire*.

Nil dictum quod non dictum prius Or The Case of the Government of England Established by Law. Impartially Stated and faithfully Collected from the best Historians, President of former Ages, and Authority of Records. By W. D. Esquire. . . . London, Printed by A. B. for F. T. and are to be sold by Thomas Fox in Westminster-hall. 1681. 8°, A—N 2 in eights + prefixes, 4 leaves. *B. M.*

The True Account of the Behaviour and Confession of William Disney, Esq; Who was Tryed for High Treason by the King's Especial Commission of Oyer and Terminer, Held at the Marshalsea in Southwark, on Thursday the 25th of June, 1685. Together, with his last Dying Words. . . . [Col.] London, Printed by George Croom, . . . 1685. Folio, 2 leaves. *B. M.*

DISTILLER.

The Distiller of London. Compiled and set forth by the speciall License and Command of the Kings most Excellent Majesty: For the sole use of the Company of Distillers of London. And by them to bee duly observed and practized. London, Printed by Richard Bishop. MDCXXXIX. Folio, A—S, 2 leaves each, besides the leaf of the Company's Arms on a larger scale than in the edit. of 1668, and the Oath to be taken by Freemen, 2 leaves more. Dedicated by Sir Theodore de Mayerne and Thomas Cademan to the Distillers' Company. *B. M.*

In the dedication Mayerne and Cademan refer to the recent incorporation of the

Company, and state that they had examined the Rules, &c. The secret characters have a contemporary MS. Key, as in Mr. Stopes's copy of 1668; Dr. French, in annexing the work to his *Art of Distillation*, 1653, substituted ordinary terms for these cyphers. The Imprimatur is dated Nov. 16, 1639.

DUDITIUS, ANDREAS.

Vita Reginaldi Poli, Britanni, S. R. E. Cardinalis, Et Cantvariensis Archiepiscopi. Venetiis, M.D.LXIII. . . . 4°, A—M in fours.

DU MOULIN, PIERRE, *the Younger*.

A Letter of a French Protestant to A Scottishman of the Covenant. Wherein one of their chiefe pretences is removed, which is their conformitie with the French Churches in points of Discipline and Obedience. London, Printed by R. Young, and R. Badger. 1640. 4°, A—G in fours, A 1 blank.

Dated from Chester, March $\frac{7}{11}$, 1639-40.

A Short and True Account of the Several Advances the Church of England hath made towards Rome: Or, A Model of the Grounds upon which the Papists for three Hundred years have built their Hopes and Expectations, that England would erelong return to Popery. By Dr. Du Moulin, sometime History-Professor of Oxford. *Veritas Odium parit*. London: Printed in the Year, 1680. 4°, A—P in fours. With separate titles to the respective portions.

[DUNNING, RICHARD.]

Bread for the Poor: Or, A Method shewing How the Poor may be Maintained, and duly Provided for, in a far more Plentiful, and yet Cheaper manner than now they are, without Waste or Want. [Quot. from Mantuan.] Exeter, Printed by Samuel Darker, for Charles Yeo, John Pearce, and Philip Bishop. 1698. 4°, A—H, 2 leaves each.

ELDERTON, EDWARD.

The Hog Man's Vindication. From some Aspersions lately cast upon Him; Relating to Matters in Difference, touching the Relief of the Poor of Mile-end Old-town, in the Parish of Stepney. As also Some Arguments to shew how the Poor are Increased, and the Means to prevent it for the Future. Together with His Letter sent to the Gentlemen of that Town, at the Time of their Assessment. London: Printed for the Author, who finding but little Difference between the Charges of a Large Number and a Small, hath reserved a small quantity for Himself and Friends, and given the Rest Gratis, to Sam. Drury, Bookseller, at the Lion and [a small hole in leaf] White-Chappel, over against the Hay-Market. 1702. 4°, A—E in fours.

ELIOT, JOHN.

Ortho-Epia Gallica. Eliots Frvits for the French: Enterlaced with a double new Inuention, which teacheth to speake truely, speedily and volubly the French-tongue. Pend for the practise, pleasure and profit of all English Gentlemen, who will endeuour by their owne paine, studie, and diligence, to attaine the naturall Accent, the true Pronounciation, the swift and glib Grace of this Noble, Famous and Courtly Language. *Naturâ & Arte*. London, Printed by Iohn Wolfe. 1593. 4°, A—C 2 in fours: D—L 2 in fours: *The Parlement of Pratlers*, c—y in fours. Dedicated to Robert Dudley and in other addresses to the London professors of French and the Gentlemen Readers. *B. M.*

ENGLAND.

Englands Complaint to Iesvs Christ, Against the Bishops Canons. Of the late Sinfull Synod, A Seditious Conventicle, A Packe of Hypocrites, a Sworne Confederacy, a Traiterous Conspiracy against the true Religion of Christ . . . Printed Anno Dom. 1640. 4°, A—G 2 in fours.

Rights of the Kingdom: Or, Customs of our Ancestours: Touching the Duty, Power, Election, or Succession, of our Kings and Parliament, our True liberty, Due Allegiance, Three Estates, . . . Freely Discussed through the British, Saxon, Norman Lawes and Histories. With an Occasionall Discourse of Great Changes yet expected in the World. London, Printed by Richard Bishop. 1649. 4°, Aa—Mm in fours: F—Z in fours: a—c in fours. With a Notice and the *Errata* on back of title.

> The writer explains in the Notice in question that the matter under the double alphabet had been intended to follow the rest, and that its transposition has occasioned some mistakes in the references from one portion to the other.

A familiar Discourse, Between George, A true-hearted English Gentleman: And Hans A Dutch Merchant: Concerning the present Affairs of England. London, Printed by T. N. for Samuel Lowndes, . . . 1672. 4°, A—E in fours.

A New History of the Succession of the Crown of England, And more particularly, From the time of King Egbert, till King

Henry the Eighth. Collected Generally from those Historians who wrote of their own Times, and who consequently were the best Witnesses and Relaters of the Actions done therein. [Quot. from Nicetas Choniates and Camden.] London, Printed for Ric. Chiswell . . . MDCXC. 4°, A—I in fours.

A Brief Historical Account of Several of the most remarkable Years of War, Drought, Famine, and Pestilence in England, And the time when they happened. Together, with an Additional discourse of God's Judgments, . . . As also of the Prediction of the late excellent Mathematician and modest Astrologer Mr. Vincent Wing, as to this present Year 1699. By a Gent. . . . London, Printed for John Wells in London-house-yard, near St. Pauls. 1699. Small 8°, A in eights.

England's Glory, Begun in

I. Restoring our Religion.
I. Rectifying our Coin.

To be Compleat in

III. Reforming our Manners.

Tit. II. 14. . . . London : Printed for Rich. Baldwin, . . . 1698. 4°. A, 2 leaves : a, 2 leaves : B—D, 2 leaves each.

ENGLISHMEN.
The Rights and Liberties of Englishmen Asserted. With a Collection of Statutes and Records of Parliament against Foreigners. Shewing, . . . With other useful Observations. Humbly offered to the Consideration of the Honourable House of Commons. London, Printed for A. Baldwin in Warwick lane. 1701. 4°, A—D 2 in fours, D 2 with Advertisements.

> This tract points out the disqualifications of aliens from holding any office in England or Ireland, filling a see, following a trade, and carrying on the business of a broker.

ERSKINE, MARGARET.
An Exact and Faithful Relation of the Process Pursued by Dame Margaret Areskine, Lady Castlehaven, Relict of the Deceased Sir James Foulis of Collingtoun ; against Sir James Foulis now of Collingtoun, before the Lords of Council and Session. . . . Edinburgh, Printed at the Society of Stationers Printing-house in Harts-Close, over-against the Trone-Church, 1690. 4°, B—I in fours, and the title.

ETIENNE, HENRI.
Ane Mernellons discours Vpon the lyfe, deides, and behauiours of Katherine de Medicis, Queue Mother : wherein are displayed the meanes which scho hath practised to atteyne vnto the vsurping of the Kingdome of France, and to the bringing of the state of the same vnto vtter ruyne. Printed at Cracow. 1576. 8°, A—I 5 in eights. *B. M.*

> Sotheby's, December 11, 1888, No. 341.

EUROPE.
The Dangers of Europe, From the Growing Power of France. With Some Free Thoughts on Remedies. And Particularly on the Cure of our Divisions at Home. In Order to a Successful War Abroad against the French King and his Allies. . . . By the Author of, *The Duke of Anjou's Succession considered*. London ; Printed, and Sold by A. Baldwin, in Warwick-Lane. 1702. 4°. Title and Preface, 2 leaves : B—K 2 in fours.

EVANS, KATHERINE.
A Brief Discovery of God's Eternal Truth : And, A Way opened to the simple hearted, whereby they may come to know Christ. . . . Written in the Inquisition of Malta, by a Servant of the most High, called Katherine Evans. London, Printed for R. Wilson, 1663. Sm. 8°. A—D 4 in eights. With some short poems at the end.

F. C.
Essaies of Coniecture vpon Certaine Negotiations touchinge peace, Between the Archduke and the States, in Anno salutis 1607 By C. F. *Veritate et Reverentia*. 4°, 37 leaves.

> Puttick's, Dec. 6, 1888, No. 648j, in the original vellum. Not known to have been printed.

F. N.
The Frviterers Secrets : Containing directions for the due time, and manner, of gathering al kindes of fruite, as well stonefruit as other : and how they are to be afterwards ordered in packing, carrying and conueighing them by land or by water. . . . At London, Printed by R. B. and are to be solde by Roger Iackson. 1604. 4°, black letter. A, 2 leaves : B—E 2 in fours.

> Sotheby's, Feb. 4, 1889, in Lot 216, from W. Forsyth's collection.

FAIRFAX, SIR THOMAS.
The Displaying of the Life-Guards Colours, Or A true Narrative of the late actings of his Excellencies Life-Guard, since their Order for Marching upon London to be Disbanded : . . . With a Vindication of

divers Gentlemen imployed by them. And divers other things giving Light to each of them. Now Published to give satisfaction, and to prevent mis-apprehensions concerning the proceedings of the Life-Guard of His Excellency Sir Thomas Fairfax. *Magna est veritas & prævalebit.* London, Printed in the Year, 1648. 4°, A—B in fours.

A Warrant of the Lord General Fairfax to the Marshall Generall of the Army [Captain Richard Lawrence], To put in Execution the former Ordinance & Orders of Parliament, and Act of Common Councell, Concerning the Regulating of Printing, and disposing of scandalous Pamphlets. Whereunto is annexed the said Ordinance and Orders. London, Printed by John Macock, for John Partridge. MDCXLIX. 4°, A—B in fours.

FARTHING, JOHN.
The Excise Rectify'd: Or, A Plain Demonstration, That The Revenue now rais'd thereby is capable of being Improved at least Four or Five Hundred Thousand Pounds *per Annum*, which is now paid by the Subject, but diverted from its proper Channel into private Hands. London, Printed, 169⅝. 4°, A—B in fours.

FENTON, ROGER, *B.D.*
A Treatise of Vsvrie, ... At London Imprinted by Felix Kyngston, for William Aspley. 1612. 4°, A—Y 2 in fours.

FIENNES, WILLIAM, *Lord Say and Sele.*
The Scots Designe Discovered. Relating their dangerous attempts lately practised against the English Nation, with the sad consequence of the same. Wherein divers matters of Publick concernment are disclosed. And the Book called *Truths Manifest,* is made apparent to be *Lyes Manifest.* [By W^m ffienns Ld Say & Seale.] *Simulata pietas duplex iniquitas.* London, Printed, and are to be sold at the Marygold in S. Pauls Church-yard. 1654. 4°, A—U in fours: Aa—Ll 2 in fours.

 The attributed authorship between brackets is in a coeval hand on the title of the copy employed.

FINCH, HENRY.
A True Relation of the Twenty weeks Siege of London derry, By the Scotch, Irish, and Dis-affected English, with the Daily Proceeding Passages thereof: As also the number of men kill'd, and taken Prisoners on both sides. Related in two Letters from Captaine Henry Finch, one of the Captains of London derry, and one of the Aldermen of the City. To His Friend in London. London, Printed by R. I. for S. G. and A. W. . . . 1649. 4°, A—B in fours.

FITZHERBERT, A.
The booke of Husbandrye verye profitable & necessary . . . . Anno do. M. D. L. V. [Col.] Imprinted at London in Fletestrete at the signe of the Sunne ouer agaynst the Conduit by John Waylande. 8°, black letter, A—H in eights.

 Puttick & Simpson, May 15, 1889, in Lot 933, much mutilated.

FLEETWOOD, WILLIAM, *of King's College, Cambridge.*
Inscriptionum Antiquarum Sylloge in Duas Partes Distributa. Quarum Prior Inscriptiones Ethnicas. . . . Altera Christiana Monumenta . . . complectitur. In Usum Juventutis Rerum Antiquarum Studiosæ Edita, . . . Londini, Impensis Guil. Graves. Bibliopolæ Cantabrigiensis, M DC XCI. 8°, A—Nn 2 in eights, besides 4 leaves marked [*] between Z 2-3. Dedicated to his pupils at King's.

FLETCHER, J.
The Differences, Cavses, and Ivdgements of Vrine: According to the Best Writers thereof, Both Old and new, summarily collected. London, Printed by John Legatt. 1641. 8°. ¶, 8 leaves: A—K 4 in eights, K 4 blank. With a few cuts.

FORBES, JOHN, *of Corse.*
Genethliaca Celsissimi Principis, Ser^{morum} ac Dominorum Dn. Friderici V. Comitis Palatini Rheni. S. R. Imp. Archidapiferi et Electoris, Ducis Bavariæ, &c. Patris. Et Dn. Elizabethæ, Potentissimi Iacobi Magnæ Britanniæ . . . Regis. Filiæ Unicæ. . . . Matris: Primogeniti Filij Ecclesiæ & reipublicæ bono nascentis Cal. Jan. sub horam 12. noctis Heidelbergæ. Autore Joanno Forbesio Scoto-Britanno. Heidelbergæ, Typis Johannis Lancelotti, Acad-Typog. Anno M DC XIV. 4°, A—C in fours. In Latin verse. *B. M.*

[An Answere to M. I. Forbes of Corse His peaceable Warning. [Quotations.] Printed, Anno Dom. 1638. 4°, A—S in fours.]

FORBES, WILLIAM, *Advocate.*
The Duty and Powers of Justices of Peace in this Part of Great-Britain called Scotland. With an Appendix concerning Weights and Measures. Edinburgh, Printed by the Heirs and Successors of Andrew Anderson, . . . 1707. 8°, A—N

in eights, N 8 blank, besides title and dedication to the Right Honourable Sir David Dalrymple of Hales, Her Majesty's Solicitor.

OX, JOHN.
De Christo crucifixo concio. Ioan. Foxi. Londini, apud Iohãnem Dayum Typographum. An. Domini. 1571. Octob. 1. 4°, A—Y in fours: Aa— Ee in fours.

RANCE.
A Relation of the French Kings Late Expedition into the Spanish-Netherlands, In the years 1667, and 1668. With an Introduction discoursing his Title thereunto: And an account of the Peace between the two Crowns, made the second of May 1668. Englished by G. H. Gent. London, Printed for John Starkey, . . . 1669. 12°. A, 13 leaves, besides the title: B—I 10 in twelves.

A Compendious History of the Taxes of France, and of the Oppressive Methods of raising of them. London: Printed by J. M. and B. B. for Richard Baldwin . . . MDCXCIV. 4°. Title and anonymous dedication to Thomas, Earl of Stamford, Lord Gray of Grooby, 2 leaves: B—E in fours, and an extra leaf after E 4.

The Nativity of the Most Valiant and Puissant Monarch Lewis the Fourteenth, King of France and Navarre, Astronomically and Astrologically Handled . . . London, Printed in the Year, 1680. 4°, A—E 2 in fours.

ULBECKE, WILLIAM.
A Direction or Preparative to t e Study of the Law. . . . . At London Printed for the Company of Stationers. Anno Dom. 1620. 8°. A, 4 leaves: B—N in eights, N 8 blank.

ULLER, WILLIAM.
Right to those that Suffer Wrong: Or, a Full Confutation of the Assertions of that Grand Imposter Fuller, al' Fullee, al' Fouler, al' Elleson, al' ——— &c. Concerning the Birth of the Pretended Prince of Wales. Printed and Sold by the Booksellers of London and Westminster. 1701. 5°, A—E in fours.

UR.
Fur Praedestinatus: Siue, Dialogismus Inter quendam Ordinis Praedicantium Calvinistam & Furem ad laqueum damnatum habitus. In Quo ad vivum representatur non tantum quomodo Calvinistarum Dogmata ex se ipsis ansam praebent sceleri. . . Londini, Impensis F. G. Typis G. D. Anno Dom. 1651. 12°, A—D 6 in twelves, D 6 blank.

G. S.
An Historical Account of the Antiquity and Unity of the Britanick Churches. Continued from the Conversion of these Islands to the Christian Faith, by St. Augustine, to this present Time. By a Presbyter of the Church of England. . . London, Printed for W. Whitwood, at the Angel and Bible in Little Britain, MDCXCII. 4°, A—O in fours, O 4 with Advertisements.

G. W., Gent.
The Case of Succession to the Crown of England Stated, In a Letter to a Member of the Honorable House of Commons. Being an Answer to that Pamphlet that pretends to prove the Parliament hath no Power to alter Succession. Printed, 1679. 4°, A—B in fours. B. M.

GADBURY, JOHN.
The Nativity of the late King Charls Astrologically and Faithfully performed; With Reasons and Art, Of the Various Success, and Mis-fortune of His whole Life. Being [occasionally] a brief History of our late unhappy Wars. Unto which is added (by way of Appendix) the Genitures of the late Queen, Prince, &c. And their Sympathy, or antipathy with this illustrious Nativity compared. By John Gadbury, Philomathematikos. Fatis animur . . . Martial. London, Printed by James Cottrel. 1659 [August.] 8°, A—I in eights. Dedicated by the author to Mr. Thomas Barton, of London, Merchant. B. M.

Nuncius Astrologicus. Or The Astrological Legate: Demonstrating to the World The Success that may probably (by the Influences of the Stars) be expected from the present unhappy Controversies between the two Northern Kings: Deduced from the Nativity of His Royal Majesty of Denmark . . . London: Printed by J. Cottrel, for F. Cossinet; and are to be sold at the Anchor and Mariner in Tower-Street. 1666. 8°, A—D in eights, A 1 and D 8 blank. Dedicated to his most highly valued friend Sir Richard Hutchinson. B. M.

Natura Prodigiorum: Or, A Discourse touching the Nature of Prodigies. Together with the Kindes, Causes, and Effects, of Comets (or Blazing-stars) Eclipses and Earthquakes; . . . . With an Appendix touching the Imposturism of the Commonly-received Doctrine of Prophecies . . . By John Gadbury Philomathematikos. Non est muta rerum Natura sed undiq; loquas. Erasm. London,

Printed for Fr. Cossinet, at the Anchor and Mariner in Tower-street, 1665. 8°, A—O 4 in eights. Dedicated to Sir George Monk.

> Two editions the same year. Both are in the British Museum.

GALLEN, T., *Philomathematikos.*
Gallen 1642. An Almanack and Prognostication for the yeare of God 1642. Being the second after Leap-yeare. The most usefull now extant, and so ordered that it will serve for any part of England. *Peruse, and then censure.* London, Printed by Rob. Young for the Companie of Stationers. 12°, A, 12: B—C in sixes.

> Puttick & Simpson, May 15, 1889, in Lot 523, interleaved and annotated by some University graduate, who watched with apparent interest and curiosity the progress of the Civil War. He also gives particulars of his own life and occupation The King, the Lord General, the Earl of Essex, Sir Thomas and Lady Richardson, &c., are mentioned.

GELL, JOHN, *M.D., of Edinburgh.*
Epithalamivm et Gratvlatio, Svper Avgvssissimis Ivxtāqve felicissimis Nuptiis Sereniss. Principum, Friderici V. Comitis Palatini . . . Et Elisabethæ Iacobi, Magnæ Britanniæ, . . . Regis . . . Filiæ Vnicæ: Et Fausto Eorundem Heidelbergam adventu . . . Heidelbergæ M.DC.XIII. 4°, A—D in fours. In Latin verse. *B. M.*

GERARD, FRIAR, *of the Order of Observants.*
The interpretacyon / and sygnyfycacyon of the Masse. ¶ Here begynneth a good denoute Boke to the honoure of God / of our lady his mother / & of all sayntes / and ryght profytable to al good Catholyke persones / to knowe howe they shall deuontly here Masse. And how salutaryly they shal Confesse them. And how reuerently and honourably they shall go to the holy Sacrament or table of our sauyour Jhesu chryste / With dyuerse other profytable documente and oraysons or prayers here conteyned / Composed and ordeyned by frere Gararde frere mynoure of the ordre of the Obseruauntes. [Col.] ¶ Imprynted By me Robert Wyer / dwellynge at the sygne of saynt Johñ Euāgelyste in saynt Martyns parysshe in the felde / in the Bysshop of Northwytche rentes / besyde Charynge crosse. ¶ In the yere of our Lorde God a. M.CCCCC. xxxii. The xiii. daye of the moneth of Octobre. ¶ Cum priuilegio Regali pro spatio septem annorum. 8°, ✠, 4 leaves: a—z in fours: &, 4 leaves: A—E in fours, E 4 with the device. *B. M.*

Sotheby's, Feb. 4, 1889, No. 23, Herbert's copy.

GERSON, JOHN, or THOMAS À KEMPIS.
Colloquium Animæ: The sole-talke of the Soule: Or, A spirituall and heauenly Dialogue, betwixt the soule of Man and God. Which, for the great allinitie it hath with other bookes of the Author published heretofore in our natiue tongue, is now entituled The fourth booke of the Imitation of Christ. Translated and corrected by Thomas Rogers. At London Printed by Humfrey Lownes. 1616. Sm. 8° or 12°. A, 6 leaves: B—H in twelves: I, 6.

GILBY, ANTHONY.
A Briefe Treatise of Election and Reprobacion wythe certane answers to the obiections of the aduersaries of this doctryne written by Anthony Gvlbie. . . . Imprinted [at Geneva] by James Poullain, and Reny Houdouyn. M. D. LVI. Sm. 8°, A—D in eights.

Turner, at Sotheby's, Nov.-Dec. 1888, No. 1933, damaged.

GLOUCESTERSHIRE.
An Account of the late Hardships and Violence Inflicted upon certain Persons called Quakers for their Peaceable Religious Meetings in the City and County of Gloucester. London, Printed by Benjamin Clark in George-yard in Lombardstreet Bookseller, 1682. 4°, 4 leaves.

The Speech of Charles Trinder, Esq; Recorder of Gloucester, at his Entrance upon that Office, Janvary the 18th, 168⅞. London: Printed, and are to be Sold by Randal Taylor, . . 168⅞. Folio, A—E, 2 leaves each, A 1 with Imprimatur.

GOODWIN, JOHN.
Moses made Angry: Or, A Letter written and sent to Dr. Hill, Master of Trinity Colledg in Cambridg, Upon occasion of some hard Passages that fell from him in a Sermon preached at Pauls, May 4. 1651. By John Goodwin. . . . London, Printed by J. M. for Henry Cripps and Lodowick Lloyd, . . . 1651. 4°, A—B 2 in fours.
Dated from Coleman Street, May 9, 1651.

GORDON, PATRICK.
The First booke of the famous Historye of Penardo and Laissa, other ways call'd the warres, of Love and Ambitione. Wherein is described Penardo his most admirable deeds of arms, his ambition of glore his contempt of lvcre, with loves mightie assalts & ammorus temptations: Laissas fearful inchantment hir relief hir trauells and lastly loves admirabel

force, In hir releiving Penardo from ye fire. Doone in Heroik verse, by Patrik Gordon. Printed at Dort By George waters. 1615. 8°. Title, dedication to George, Earl of Enye, Lord Gordon, and preliminary verses, 10 leaves : A—R 2 in eights. In stanzas of 6 lines. *B. M.*
> Among the writers of encomiastic verses are W. Drummond, Alexander Gardyne, and Robert Gordon.

GORING, GEORGE.
The Declaration of Colonell Goring Vpon his Examination, touching the late intended Conspiracie against the Scots. With the Report of that worthy Gentleman Mr. Fynes to the House of Commons . . . Iune 1641. Printed in the yeare 1641. 4°, A—B 2 in fours.

GOUGE, THOMAS, *Minister of the Gospel.*
The Surest and Safest Way of Thriving. Or A Conviction of the Grand Mistake in many, That what is given to the Poor, is a loss to their Estate ; . . . . London : Printed by S. and B. G. for Nevil Simmons . . . 1676. Sm. 8°, A—F 6 in eights.
> A mere clerical performance.

GOVERNMENTS.
An Account of a Conversation Concerning a Right Regulation of Governments, For the Common Good of Mankind. In A Letter to the Marquess of Montrose, the Earls of Rothes, Roxburgh, and Haddington, from London the 1st of December 1703. London : Printed for A. Baldwin, 1704. 8°, A—D in eights.

GRANTHAM, THOMAS, *M.A., Curate of Eston, near Tocester, co. Northampton.*
A Motion against Imprisonment, wherein is proved that Imprisonment for debt is against the Gospel, against the good of Church, and Commonwealth. Matthew 18, 29. *Have patience, and I will pay thee all.* Printed at London for Francis Coules 1642. 4°, 4 leaves.

GREENE, ROBERT.
The Pleasant and Delightful History of Dorastus and Favnia. . . . By Robert Green, Master of Arts in Cambridge. London : Printed by W. O. for G. Conyers at the Ring in Little Britain, 1700. Price 6d. 4°, black letter, B—F in fours, and the title, on which is a woodcut.
> On the back of the title occurs : *Dorastus his Love-passion* . . . in verse.

GREGORY, JAMES, *of Aberdeen.*
Geometriæ Pars Vniversalis, Inserviens Quantitatum Curvarum transmutationi & mensuræ. Patavii, MDCLXVIII. . . . 4°. †, 6 leaves : A—T in fours. With diagrams.

GRUMBLETONIAN.
The Character of a Grumbletonian, Or, The New Malecontent. London, Printed and are to be Sold by Richard Janeway . . . MDCLXXXIX. A folio leaf.

GUEZ, JEAN LOUIS, *Sieur de Balzac.*
Aristippvs, Or, Monsr de Balzac's Masterpiece. Being A Discourse Concerning the Court. With an Exact Table of the principall Matter. Englished by R. W. London, Printed by Tho. Newcomb, for Nat. Eakins at the Gun, and Tho. Johnson, at the Golden Key in Pauls-Church Yard, 1659. Sm. 8°. A, 8 leaves : B—H in twelves : I, 4. *B. M.*

GUALDO PRIORATO, GALEAZZO.
The History of the Managements of Cardinall Julio Mazarine, Chief Minister of State of the Crown of France. Written in Italian by Count Galeazzo Gualdo Priorato. And Translated according to the Original. In the which are Related the Principal Successes Happened from the Beginning of His Management of Affairs till His Death. Tom 1. Part 1. London : Printed by H. L. and R. B. in the Year 1671. Sm. 8°, A—Y 10 in twelves, A 1 with *Imprimatur* and Y 10 with *Errata :* Tom. 1. Part 11. dated 1672, B—S 3 in twelves and the title. With a portrait. *B. M.*
> The author's dedication to the Duke and Duchess Regent of Modena and Reggio is retained.

Reprinted, 12°, 1691.

GUILD, WILLIAM, *Minister at King-Edward.*
Isaachars Asse, Braying, Vnder a double Burden. Or, The Vniting of Churches. [Quotations.] Aberdene, Imprinted by Edward Raban. Cvm Privilegio. 1621. 4°, A—C in fours. With some verses at the end. Dedicated to John Urquhart of Craighous, &c., and his wife Elizabeth Seton.

H. A., *Scoto-Britain.*
A Bitte to stay the Stomacks of good Svbiects. Or A suddaine and short Vindication of the Scots Commissioners Papers Intitvled The Answer of the Commissioners . . . Printed Anno Dom. 1647. 4°, A—B 2 in fours.

H. I., *M.D.*
Scelera aquarum : Or, A Supplement to Mr. Graunt On the Bills of Mortality. Shewing As well the Causes, as Encrease,

of the London, Parisian, and Amsterdam Scorbute : With all its Attendants. Demonstrating the Locality, of the said Causes, and how they result from Morbifick Salts, which abound in the Strata of the Earth, and Stagnate Waters, round those three Cities. [Quot. from Pliny, Nat. Hist. Lib. 25. cap. 3.] London : Printed for the Author, and Sold by Du Chemin, at the Sign of Abraham Sacrificing Isaac, over against Somerset-House in the Strand, . . . 1701. 4°, A—E 2 in fours. *B. M.*

HA, JO., *of the Inner Temple, Esquire.*
Nahash Redivivus In a Letter from the Parliament of Scotland, Directed to the Honorable William Lenthal, Speaker of the House of Commons. Examined and Answered. . . . London, Printed for Thomas Brewster, and are to be sold at the three Bibles in Creed-Lane, near the West-End of Pauls. 1649. 4°, A—C in fours.

HACKET, JOHN, *late Lord Bishop of Lichfield and Coventry.*
Scrinia Reserata : A Memorial Offer'd to the Great Deservings of John Williams, D.D. who some time held the Places of Ld Keeper of the Great Seal of England, Ld Bishop of Lincoln, and Ld Archbishop of York. Containing A Series of the Most Remarkable Occurrences and Transactions of His Life, in Relation both to Church and State . . . In the Savoy : . . . Printed by Edw. Jones, for Samuel Lowndes over-against Exeter-Exchange in the Strand. M.DC.XCIII. Folio, B—Ff in fours, besides the title, portrait by White, and *Errata*.

HAINES, RICHARD.
A Method of Government for such Publick Working Alms-Houses as may be Erected in every Country for bringing all idle hands to Industry. As the best known Expedient for restoring and advancing the Woollen Manufacture. . . . With Allowance. London, Printed for Langley Curtis on Ludgate-hill. 1679. 4°, 4 leaves.

England's Weal & Prosperity Proposed : Or, Reasons for Erecting Publick Work Houses in every County, For the speedy promoting of Industry and the Woollen Manufacture, shewing how the Wealth of the Nation may be encreased, many Hundred thousand pounds *per Annum*. . . . To which is added a Model of Government for such Work-Houses prepared by the same Author, . . . pur-

suant to a *Breviate of P*. merly published. Lon Langley Curtis, in Goa gate-hill. 1681. 4°,
The Method, with a ne Dedicated by Haines Ward, Lord Mayor of L

HALL, JOSEPH, *Bisho*
The Honor of the Maintayned against the lenges of C. E. Masse Apologie written some y marriage of persons Ecc good against the Canils Catholike Priest. In T Ios. Hall, D. of Diuin. London Printed by W. 1620. 8°. A, 8 leaves leaves : B—Z in eight George, Archbishop of C
The Museum copy pur for H. Feth[erstone].

HALLEY, GEORGE, *A. Ripon.*
A Sermon Preach'd in t Metropolitical Church York : On Friday, the ber, 1697. Being the . . . With a Postscript which clearly discov Designs against the Eng Nation. London : Pri by Tho. Baxter, Book Gate, York. 1698. 4°, Dedicated to the Archbi
The two letters at end Laud and Bramhall, when Bramhall was Bisl

HAMILTON, JAMES,
[A Declaration as to the 1638, and his share in High Commissioner of t is no title ; but the first imprint :] Imprinted a Robert Young, Printer t Excellent Majestie . . . A in fours = 8 leaves.

HARE, JOHN.
St Edwards Ghost : O isme : Being a pathetica Motion in the behalfe Nation against her goo Grievance, Normanisme *lism) est ista voluntaria* in orat. Phil. 1. Lond Richard Wodenothe at t Peter's Church in Corn B—D in fours, besides ti
The date at the end and in his Address to

states that the tract had lain some time by him.

HARRINGTON, SIR JAMES.
Horæ consecrataɔ, or Spiritual Pastime. Concerning Divine Meditation upon the great mysteries of our faith and salvation. Occasional meditations and gratulatory reflexions upon particular providences and deliverances, vouchsafed to the Author and his family. Also a Scripture-Catechisme dedicated to the service of his wife and children. And now published, together with other treatises mentioned in the following page for common use . . . London, printed for the Author. 1682. Folio. Two leaves, then A—Zzzzz in twos, not counting the portraits of Sir James and Lady Katherine Harrington. *Bodleian.*

HARRIS, BENJAMIN.
A Short but Just Account of the Tryal of Benjamin Harris upon an Information brought against him for Printing and Vending a late Seditious Book called *An Appeal from the Country to the City*. . . . Printed in the Year 1679. Folio, A—B, 2 leaves each. *B. M.*

HAY, JAMES.
Collonel James Hays Speech to the Parliament Upon the Debate concerning Toleration. As it was taken by Anonimus A Member of the House, and sent to the Press with this Epigram on the Author
Fælix fisa suis cœlebrata Catonibus Eheu /
Clodius in miseros furit, & Catalina Britannos.
Printed in the Year 1655. 4°, A—D in fours, and a leaf after D 4 with " An Epistle to the Reader."

HENRY VIII. TUDOR, *King of England.*
Le traicte de la paix perpetuelle du roy treschrestiē nostre souuerain seigñr et madame sa mere / regente en France en son absence. Auec treshault & trespuissant prince Henry huytiesme de ce nom/ par la grace de dieu roy Dangleterre/ leurs heirs et successeurs. publie a Lyon le .xxij. de septēbre. Lan Mil. ccccc.xxv. [A crowned shield with the fleurs de lys.] Auec priuilege. [Paris, 1525.] 4°, 4 leaves, including one with the device on the title repeated on a larger scale and enclosed in a frame of ornamental design.

HERBERT, EDWARD, *Lord Herbert of Cherbury.*
De Veritate, . . . Exc. Lvtetiae Parisiorvm. cIɔ Iɔc xxiv. Iam denuo sed auctius & emendatius recud. Londini per Avgvstinvm Matthævm. cIɔ Iɔc xxxiii. 4°. a, 3 leaves : A—Hh 2 in fours.

De Veritate, . . . Cui Operi additi sunt duo alii tractatus ; Primus, De Cavsis Errorvm ; Alter, De Religione Laici ; Vna cum Appendice . . . Londini, 1645. 4°. a, 4 leaves : A—Ii 2 in fours : *De Causis Errorvm,* &c., A—X 2 in fours : *Præcepta et Consilia,* directed to his heirs and nephews, A—B in fours, B 4 blank : *De Vita Humana Philosophica Disquisitio,* 4 leaves—both the last in verse.

De la Verité Entant Qvelle est distincte de la Renelation, du Vray-semblable, du Possible & du Faux. . . . Reneu & augmenté par le mesme Auteur. Troisieme Edition. M.DC.XXXIII. 4°. ã, 4 leaves : A—Rr in fours : *Errata,* 2 leaves.

HEYWOOD, JOHN.
John Heywoodes woorkes. A dialogue conteynyng the number of the effectuall prouerbes in the English tonge compact in a matter concernynge two maner of Mariages. With one hundred of Epigrammes : and three hundred of Epigrammes vpō three hundred Prouerbes : and a fifth hundred of Epigrams. Whereunto are now newly added a sixth hundred of Epigrams by the sayde John Heywood. Londini. 1566. [Col.] Imprinted at London in Fleetstrete by Henry Wykes. Cum priuilegio. 4°. black letter, A—Ee 2 in fours. Ee 2 blank. *B. M., Bodl., Capel Coll.,* &c.

On sign. Q 1 verso is a page-woodcut with the full-length portrait of the author, as in the *Spider and the Flie,* 1556.

HICKERINGILL, EDMUND.
Gregory, Father-Greybeard, With his Vizard off ; Or, News from the Cabal in some Reflexions Upon a late Pamphlet Entituled, The Rehearsal Transpros'd. (After the fashion that now obtains) In a Letter to our old Friend, R. L. from E. H. London, Printed by Robin Hood, at the Sign of the He-Cow I. O. if it be not a Bull, on the South-west and by West end of Lake-lemans and sold by Nath. Brooke at the Angel in Cornhil, 1673. 8°, A—X in eights.

HIDES.
The generall Greeuance of all England, Man, Woman, and Child : to the High and Honourable Court of Parliament. [In reference to the transportation or export of raw hides. About 1625.] A broadside.

This document more particularly bears upon the injury sustained by curriers, shoemakers, and cobblers. Sotheby's, Feb. 4, 1889, in Lot 216.

[HILDYARD, CHRISTOPHER, of York.]
A List, Or Catalogve of all the Mayors, and Bayliffs, Lord Mayors, and Sheriffs, of the most Ancient. Honourable, Noble, and Loyall City of Yorke, From the time of King Edward the First; untill this present year, 1664. being the 16th year of the most happy Reign of our most gratious Soveraign Lord King Charles the Second. Together with many, and sundry Remarkable Passages, which happened in their severall Yeers. Published by a true Lover of Antiquity, and a Well-wisher to the Prosperity of the City; Together with his Hearty Desire of the Restoration of its former Glory, Splendor, and Magnificence: York, Printed by Stephen Bulkley, 1664. 4°, A—I 2 in fours, besides the title and frontispiece. *B. M.*

> This is the copy noticed by Mr. Davies (*Memoir of the York Press*, 1868, p. 16) as being preserved in Harl. MS. 6115; it is interleaved, so as to form a thick volume, and is enriched, perhaps by Hildyard himself, with MSS. notes and illustrations throughout.

HODGES or HODGE, JAMES.
A Just and Modest Vindication of the Scots' Design, For the having Establish'd a Colony at Darien. With A Brief Display, how much it is their Interest, to apply themselves to Trade, and particularly to that which is Foreign.... Printed in the Year, 1699. 8°. A, 8 leaves: a, 8 leaves: B—P 4 in eights, P 4 blank.

> A 3 seems to be omitted in the signatures.

Considerations and Proposals, For Supplying the present Scarcity of Money, and advancing Trade. By James Hodges Gent. Edinburgh, Printed; and are to be sold at Mrs. Ogston's Shop in the Parliament-Close, 1705. 4°, A—C in fours, C 4 blank.

HODGES, RICHARD.
Enchiridion Arithmeticon. Or A Manvel of Millions Containing therein Mens Accompts Compvted, or Made vp. Whereby they may Svddenly know the true value of any commodity, at any price whatsoever.... For Ease and Expedition the like hath not bin published. The Time is short 1 Cor. 7. 29. Redeem the Time. Ephes. 5. 16. London, Printed by M. Flesher, and are to be sold in Southwark, within the Closse, neare St. Mary Overies Church, at the house of Richard Hodges a School-master, the Authour thereof. 1631. 8°, A—L 4 in eights. *B. M.*

> The date has been altered to 1634, and the same was the case wi sold at Sotheby's, Feb. 12,

HODGES, WILLIAM.
Great Britain's Groans: C of the Oppression, Ruin, a of the Loyal Seamen of E Fatal Loss of their Pay Lives, and Dreadful Ruin lies... Printed in the A—D in fours. D 4 with t

HOLME, THOMAS, AN FULLER.
A Brief Relation of some ferings of the True Christi of God (in Scorn called Q land, For these last Elea from 1660 until 1671... Year, 1672. 4°, A—K in

HOMER.
Homer Alamode, The Se English Burlesque: Or, upon the Ninth Book of I tion from Statius with an lation.] Invented for th Cambridge, where the P elevated by several degr Printed by S. Roycroft, for man at the Kings Arms i 1681. 8°.

> The copy employed ended im

HOUGHTON, THOMAS, *Gentleman.*
A Book of Funds: Or, able Projections and Propo Three Millions of Money Supplies, to be Granted t By such Ways and Meth least Burthensome to the the War... London: I Authour. 1696. 4°, A—

HOWELL, JAMES.
A Modern Account of Sc An Exact Description of And a True Character of t their Manners. Written f an English Gentleman. Year, 1679. 4°, A—C 2 i

HUGHES, WILLIAM, La *Esquire.*
Hughes's Queries, Or, Cl Moots, Containing several not resolved in the Books. Printed for George Dawe 12°. A, 12 leaves, A 1 wi signed *Fra North:* [a], 6 in twelves: G, 8. Dedicate of Gray's Inn.

HUMOUR.
The Humour of the Age

As it is Acted at the Theatre-Royal in Drury-Lane By His Majesty's Servants. —*Pictoribus atque Poetis* . . . Hor. de Art. Poet. London, Printed for R. Wellington . . . 1701. 4°. List of Plays, title, and unsigned dedication to Charles, Lord Halifax, 6 leaves ; B—K 2 in fours.

> The anonymous writer in his Epistle states that he was only twenty-one years of age, and that this was his maiden effort.

IYMNI.

Hymni canori cum iubilo secundum morem vsum͡q5 prestātissime ac nominatissime ecclesie Eboracēsis emendati at͡q5 correcti recentissime iuxta exemplar ipsius prefate ecclesie. Impensia Johannis Gachet mercatoris librorum benemeriti juxta ptaxatā ecclesiā degētǫ. [Col.] Opusculū psens hymnorum sec͡m cōsuetudin͡e metropolitane ecc'lie Eboracē-is. Exaratū Rothomagi ī officina M. P. Oliuier / cōpletū est die quīta Februarii Anno salut͡e xtiane decimo-septimo supra millesim͡u & quig͡etissim͡u. O͡ipotēti deo virgini͡q5 matri sctō guillermo toti quo͡q5 curie celesti laudes immensas exorat. Impressor erratorum veniam deprecans. 4°. Title and 3 following leaves with anthem to the Virgin, &c. : A—H in eights : I, 6. *B. M.*

> The volume consists of a series of hymns set to music ; some of the leaves are printed on one side only.

MBER, MATTHEW, *Gentleman.*

The Case, Or, An Abstract of the Customs of the Mannor of Merdon, in the Parish of Hursely in the County of Southampton, which are to be Observed and Performed by the Lord and the Customary Tenants of the said Mannor, their Heirs and Successors for Ever. As they were taken out of a Decree Made and Inrolled in the Honourable Court of Chancery, for Ratifying and Confirming the same Customs. Together with some remarkable Passages, Suits at Law and in Equity, and the Great Differences and Expences therein. London, Printed Anno Dom. 1707. 8°, A—F in eights, A 1 and F 8 blank. *B. M.*

> The dedication by the author to certain customary tenants of Merdon is dated from Winchester, June 21, 1707.

NDIA.

A Description of a voyage made by certaine Ships of Holland into the East Indies. With their aduentures and successe ; Together with the Description of the Countries, Townes, and Inhabitants of the same : Who set forth on the second of Aprill. 1595 and returned on the 14. of August. 1597. Translated out of Dutch into English by W. P. London Imprinted by Iohn Wolfe. 1598. 4°, A—L in fours. With woodcuts, including a representation of the copper and lead money current in Java (the former Chinese). Dedicated to Sir James Scudamore, Knight, by W. Phillip.

> In the dedication Phillip states that the Dutch narrative had fallen into his hands, and appeared to him equally important with the discoveries of his own countrymen in the same region, namely, those of Captain Raimoud in the *Penelope*, Master Foxcroft in the *Merchant-Royal*, and Master James Lancaster in the *Edward Bonaventure* in 1591, as well as Master John Newbery and Richard Fich overland through Syria, &c.— and of Fich himself to Bengal, &c.—as described by Hakluyt.

(ii.) An Addition to the Sea Iovrnal Or nauigation of the Hollanders vnto Iaua, contayning the appearances, shewes, or resemblances of the Cape of Bona Speranza, of the road of S. Bras, of the Promontorie of S. Iustus, and of the Cape of S. Augusta, with the true shapes of the wastes of Madagascar, Sumatra, and Iaua : and also a Mappe and description of the Kingdome and Island of Bally : Together with the exposition of certain words of the people of Madagascar : and with a dictionary of the language of Malacca : compiled by Cornelius Gerardson of Zuidland. Whereunto are annexed the true portraitures of the naturall inhabitants of the Cape of Bona Speranza, of the King & people of Antongil, of the Gouernour and people of Sumatra, of the inhabitants and ships of Iaua, of the people of China, and of the King of Bally and his stately traine. London Imprinted by Iohn Wolfe. 1598. 4°, A—E in fours, besides the dedication by the Printer to the worshipful and wellminded Mathias Rutten, citizen of London, and the map of Bally. C 4 is occupied by woodcuts. *B. M.*

> A sequel to the narrative by Phillip.

The Petition and Remonstrance of the Governovr and Company of Merchants of London trading to the East Indies, exhibited to the Right Honourable the Lords and Commons, in the High Court of Parliament assembled. London Printed for Nicholas Bourne. 1641. 4°, A—E in fours.

A Discourse concerning Trade, And that in particular of the East Indies. Wherein several weighty Propositions are fully discussed, and the State of the East-India-

K

Company is faithfully stated. [Col.] London, Printed and Sold by Andrew Sowle at the Crooked-Billet in Holloway-Lane in Shoreditch; And at the Three Keys in Nags-Head-Court, in Grace-Church-Street, over against the Conduit, 1689. 4°, A—B 2 in fours. Without any regular title.

The East-India Trade. A true Narration of divers Ports in East-India; of the Commodities, and Trade one Kingdome holdeth with another; whereby it appeareth, how much profit this Nation is deprived by restraint of Trade to those parts, which is farre greater then all the trade of Europe. [London, about 1689.] 4°, A—B in fours. Without a regular title.

IRELAND.

A Gun-Powder Plot in Ireland For the blowing up of the chiefest Church in Dublin, when the Lords and others were at Sermon, on Sunday, October, 31. 1641. Which Conspiracie was plotted to bee done by the Papists and Priests in Dublin. With a further Discovery of their bloody intention for the Massacring of the English Protestants in Ireland. By the Information of Thomas Creamor of Grayes-Inne Gentleman, . . . London, Printed for John Thomas. 1641. 4°, 4 leaves.

A Perfect Relation of the Beginning and Continuation of the Irish-Rebellion, From May last, to this present 12th of January, 1641. With the Place where, and Persons who, did Plot, Contrive, and put in Execution that Romish damnable Designe. As also their inhumane Cruelties which they have, and still execute, with devillish hatred upon the Protestants. Written by a worthy Gentleman, and sent over by a Merchant now dwelling in Dublin. Whereunto is annexed the Merchants letter who sent the Copy of this Relation: With another letter wherein is truely related, The Battell fought betwixt our English, and the Rebels, on the tenth of January, at a Town called Swords, eight Miles from Dublin. London, Printed by J. R. 1641. 4°, A—B in fours.

A Declaration of the Commons assembled in Parliament; Concerning the Rise, and Progresse of the Grand Rebellion in Ireland. Together with a multitude of Examinations of persons of quality, whereby it may easily appear to all the World, who were and still are the Promoters of that cruell and unheard of Rebellion.

With some Letters and Papers of g consequence of the Earl of Antr which were intercepted. Also some ters of Mart, . . . London, Printed Edw. Husbands, . . . Iuly 25. 1643. A—H in fours.

Censvra Propositionvm Qvarvmdam, ex Hibernia delatarvm, Tùm ex du libris, Angliæ Sermone conscriptis Latinum bonâ fide conuersis excerptar per Sacram Facultatem Theologiæ Pa ensis facta. Iussu Cleri denuò in lu edita. Parisiis, Excudebat Antonivs tray, . . . M DC.XLIII. Cvm Privil Regis. 4°, A—K in fours.

The Case of the Irish Protestants Relation to Recognising, Or Swea Allegiance to, and Praying for I William and Queen Mary, Stated Resolved. London, Printed for Ro Clavel, at the Peacock in S. P Church-Yard. MDCXCI. 4°. A, 2 lea B—D in fours: E, 2, E 2 with Ad tisements.

The Report made to the Honour House of Commons, Decemb. 15. 1 By the Commissioners appointed to quire into the Forfeited Estates of land. London; Printed in the MDCC. 4°, A—G in fours, A 1 with title.

A Short View of Both Reports, In I tion to the Irish Forfeitures. In a F liar Dialogue between A. and B. Humbly Offer'd to the Consideratio Both Houses of Parliament. Lon Printed in the Year, 1701. 4°, B—I fours, and the title.

The edition of the Report itself, noticed, differs from that in the Huth (logue, and this explains the meaning o reference to two Reports.

IRETON, HENRY, Lord Deputy of land.

A Letter from The Lord Deputy-Ge of Ireland, Unto the Honorable Wil Lenthal Esq; . . . Concerning the dition of the City of Limerick: . London, Printed by John Field, Pri to the Parliament of England, 1651. A—B in fours.

JACOBITE.

The Character of a Jacobite, By Name or Title soever Dignifyed or tinguish'd,——Written by a Perso Quality. . . . London, Printed for Author. 1690. 4°, A—E 2 in fours blank.

JART, *King of Scots.*
:ing to the Restoration of
of Scotland.

hs were mingled in his Book,
itness fail'd, the Prophet spoke.
                    DRYDEN.

ted for W. Jones, at the
in the Poultrey. 1716.
A—D in fours.

UART THE FIRST

Thanksgiving to be vsed
s Maiesties louing Subiects,
deliuerance of his Maiestie,
he] Prince, and States, of
t, [from] the most Traite-
y int[ent to] Massacre by
e fif[th day of] Nouember.
orth by authority. Im-
don by Ro[bert Barker,]
And by the A[ssignes] of
Anno 1606.] 4°, black
in fours, title on A 2.
iployed was mutilated.

ART THE SECOND

odest Vindication of His
is the Duke of York: In
pon a late Revived Pam-
, A Word without Doors.
teasons and Arguments of
are Considered and Ex-
lon, Printed for Thomas
reen's Rents, near Fleet-
xxx. 4°, A—B in fours.

ı: Being Choice Collec-
Principal Matters in King
gn: Which may serve to
ancy betwixt Mr. Town-
r. Rushworth's Historical
London, Printed for W.
    Green Dragon without
1681. 8°. A, 4 leaves:
. With a portrait of Sir
iry, and a print at p. 91
ll full-lengths of the Earl
f Somerset. *B. M.*

tion of James II.] Lon-
by the Assignes of John
. . 1684 [-5, 7 Feb.] A
M.

f the Ceremonial at the
Their Most Excellent Ma-
mes II. and Queen Mary,
, the 23 of April 1685.
r of His Majesties Reign.
)rder of the Duke of Nor-
hal of England. Printed
by Thomas Newcomb in the Savoy, 1685.
A large broadside. *B. M.*

[A Proclamation by James II. respecting
the landing of the Duke of Monmouth
and others at Lyme in Dorsetshire, 13
June, 1685.] God Save the King. London, Printed by the Assignes of John Bill
deceased: and by Henry Hill, and Thomas
Newcomb, . . . 1685. A broadside.
B. M.

A Poem Occasioned by His Majesties
Most Gracious Resolution Declar'd in
His Most Honourable Privy Council,
March 18. 168⁷⁄₆. For Liberty of Con-
science. London, Printed by George Lar-
kin, at the Coach and Horses without
Bishopsgate. 1687. A broadside. *B. M.*

By the King, A Proclamation [for further
liberty of conscience in Scotland, 21 July,
1687.] Edinburgh, Printed by Andrew
Anderson, . . . and Reprinted by Thomas
Newcomb for P. Forrester, in Kings-
street Westminster, 1687. A broadside.
B. M.

Reason and Authority: Or, The Motives
of a Late Protestants Reconciliation to
the Catholic Church. Together with
Remarks upon some late Discourses
against Transubstantiation. Publisht
with Allowance. London, Printed by
Henry Hills, Printer to the King's Most
Excellent Majesty, For his Household
and Chappel, 1687. 4°, A—R 2 in fours.

An Answer to a Book, Entituled, Reason
and Authority: . . . Together with a
brief Account of Augustine the Monk,
and Conversion of the English. In a
Letter to a Friend. London, Printed by
J. H. for Brabazon Aylmer, . . . 1687.
4°. Title and *Imprimatur,* 2 leaves:
B—N in fours.

Observations Upon a late Libel, Called
A Letter from a Person of Quality to his
Friend, concerning the Kings Declaration, &c. [London, 1687.] 4°, A—B 2 in
fours. Without any title-page.

By the King. A Proclamation [confirm-
ing his Declaration of Liberty of Conscience in Scotland, 28 May, 1688.] Edinburgh, Printed by the Heir of Andrew
Anderson . . . 1688. A broadside.
B. M.

The Kings Letter to the Great Council
of Peers. London, Printed for W. Thomson, 1688. A small broadsheet. *B. M.*

The Princess Anne of Denmark's Letter
to the Queen. [Nov. 1688.] A broadsheet. *B. M.*

By the King. A Proclamation [against a threatened invasion from Holland.] London, Printed by Charles Bill . . . 1688. A large broadsheet. *B. M.*

A Declaration of His Most Sacred Majesty King James II. To all his Loving Subjects in the Kingdom of England. [Dublin, 8 May, 1689.] A small broadsheet. *B. M.*

The Anatomy of an Arbitrary Prince ; Or, King James the II. Set forth in his Proper Colours, and what England may expect from such a one. Written . . . by a Son of the Church of England. Printed for R. Baldwin, near the Black-Bull in the Old-Baily, 1689. A folio leaf.

The Abdicated Prince: Or, The Adventures of Four Years. A Tragi-Comedy, As it was lately Acted at the Court of Alba-Regalis, By several Persons of Great Quality. *Nec Lex est justior ulla* . . . London, Printed for John Carterson, 1690. 4°. A, 2 leaves, with the title and Actors' names : B—I 2 in fours.

> A political piece referring to the transactions of the English Court and Government at this time. See Halliwell's *Dictionary of Old Plays*, 1860, in v.

A View of the Court of St. Germain, From the Year 1690, to 1695. With an Account of the Entertainment Protestants meet with there. Directed to the Malecontents Protestants of England. London, Printed for R. Baldwin, near Oxford-Arms-Inn in Warwick-lane, MDCXCVI. 4°. A, 2 leaves : B—E 2 in fours.

An Elegy on the Death of King James the Second, Late King of England, Who departed this Mortal Life, on Wednesday the 3d of Septemb. at St. Germains en Lay, at 3 a Clock in the Morning in the Sixty Eight Year of His Age, 1701. London, Printed by H. H. in Black-Fryers. 1701. Large folio, surmounted by royal arms and funeral emblems. *B. M.*

JENKINS, DAVID.
The Vindication of Judge Jenkins Prisoner in the Tower, the 29. of Aprill, 1647. 4°, 4 leaves. Without a titlepage.

The Cordiall of Iudge Ienkins For the good People of London : In reply to a Thing, called, An Answer to the poysonous seditious Paper of Mr. David Jenkins ; By H. P. Barister of Lincolns-Inne. Printed in the Yeere 1647. 4°, A—B in fours.

JOHANNES DE BURGO.
Pupilla oculi õibus presbyteris precipue Anglicanis summe necessaria : per sapientissimũ dinini cultus moderatori Johannem de burgo quondã alme vniuersitatis Cantabrigien. cancellariũ : . . Venũdatur Londoñ. apud bibliopolas in cimiterio sancti Pauli : sub intersignic sancte ac indiuidue trinitatis. [Col.] . . in alma Parisiorum academia opera Wolfgãgi hopylii impressa Anno nostre redemptiõis Millesimo quingentesimo-decimo. vij. kalendas Julij. Folio, a—r in eights : s, 9 leaves. In two columns.

JOHANNES DE MEDIOLANO.
Regimen Sanitatis Salerni. The Schoole of Salernes most learned and inditious Directorie, . . . Perused, and corrected . . London, Imprinted by Barnard Alsop, and are to be sold by Iohn Barnes, at his shop in Hosier Lane. 1617. 4°, A—Ff 2 in fours. Dedicated in this impression by ANONYMUS to Master Joseph Fenton Esquire, "a Gentleman skillfully experienced both in Physicke and Chirurgery."

JOHNSON, SAMUEL, M.A.
Purgatory Prov'd by Miracles : Collected out of Roman-Catholick Authors. With some Remarkable Histories Relating to British, English, and Irish Saints. With a Preface concerning the Miracles [Quot. from Card. Allen's *Defence of th Doctrine of Purgatory*.] London : Printed for Richard Baldwin. MDCLXXXVIII. 4° B—B in fours, besides title and preface, 3 leaves. *B. M.*

JOHNSON, THOMAS, *Merchant*.
A Plea for Free-Mens Liberties : Or The Monopoly of the Eastland Marchants anatomized by divers arguments (wch wil also serve to set forth the unjustnesse o the Marchant-Adventurers Monopoly, and proved illegal, unnaturall, irrationall against the honour of the Nation, tending to its ruine and vassalage, . . . Penned for the publique good, by Thomas Johnson Merchant. [Quotations.] Printed Anno 1646. And are to be sold in London, at every Stationers shop, that loves liberty, and hates Monopolies. 4°, leaves. *B. M.*

JONES, JOHN.
Judges judged out of their own mouthes Or The Question resolved by Magna Charta &c. Who have been Englands Enemies Kings Seducers, and Peoples Destroyers from Hen. 3. to Hen. 8. and before and since Stated by Sr. Edward Coke, Knt late L. Chief Justice of England. Ex-

postulated, and put to the Vote of the People, by J. Jones, Gent. Whereunto is added Eight Observable Points of Law, Executable by Justices of Peace. . . . London, Printed by W. Bently, and are to be sold by E. Dod, and N. Ekins, . . . MDCL. 12°. A, 2 leaves, with title and dedication to the Parliament and People: B—F in twelves, F 11-12 blank. *B. M.*

Jurors Judges of Law and Fact: Or certain Observations of certain differences in points of Law between a certain reverend Judg, called, Andr. Horn, and an uncertain Author of a certain Paper, printed by one Francis Neale this year 1650, styled, A Letter of due Censure and Redargution to Lievt-Col. John Lilburn, touching his Tryall at Guild-Hall, . . . London, Printed by W. D. for T. B. and G. M. [1650.] 12°, A—E in twelves, A 1 and E 12 blank. Dedicated by Jones to the Army of England "From my Lodging at Mr. Mundays hous in Clarkenwel, this 29. of July, 1650." *B. M.*

ONES, MICHAEL.

Lieut: General Jones's Letter To the Councel of State, of a Great Victory which it hath pleased God to give the Forces in the City of Dublin under his Command, on the Second of this instant August, against the Earl of Ormond and the Lord Inchiquin's Forces before that City. Together with the list of all the Prisoners. . . . London, Printed for Edward Husband, . . . August 11. 1649. 4°, A—B 2 in fours.

ONSTON, ARTHUR.

Paraphrasis Poetica Psalmorvm Davidis. Anctore Artvro Ionstono, Scoto. Accesserunt ejusdem
    Cantica Evangelica
    Symbolvm Apostolicvm,
    Oratio Dominica,
    Decalogvs.
Aberdoniæ, Imprimebat Edwardus Rabanus, Anno 1637. Sm. 8°. Title, dedication, and to the Reader, 3 leaves: A—M in eights.

URIEN, PIERRE.

The Reflections of the Reverend and Learned Monsieur Jurien Upon the strange and Miraculous Exstasies of Isabel Vincent, The Shepherdess of Saov in Dauphiné; Who ever since February last hath sung Psalms, Prayed, Preached, and Prophesied about the present Times, in her Trances. As also Upon the Wonderful and Portentous Trumpetings and Singing of Psalms that were heard by Thousands in the Air (in many parts of France) in the Year 1686: . . . To which is added, A Letter of a Gentleman in Dauphiné, To a Friend of his in Geneva, containing the Discourses and Prophesies of the Shepherdess. All Faithfully Translated out of the French Copies, for Publick Information. . . . London, Printed for Richard Baldwin in the Old-Baily, 1689. 4°, B—K2 in fours and the title. *B. M.*

JURY-MAN.

The Grand-Jury-Man's Oath and Office Explained: And the Rights of English-Men Asserted. A Dialogue between a Barrister at Law, and A Grand-Jury-Man. London, Printed for Langley Curtis, near Fleet-Bridge upon Ludgate-Hill. 1680. 4°, B—D in fours and the title.

JUVENAL AND PERSIUS.

Ivnii Ivvenalis Et Avli Persii Flacci Satyræ: Cum Annotationibus ad marginem, quæ obscurissima quæ que dilucidare possunt. Londini Excudebat Richardus Field impensis Guilielmi Welby. 1612. Sm. 8°, A—L in eights, L 8 blank. Dedicated by the Editor, Thomas Farnaby, to Prince Henry. *B. M.*

KEN, THOMAS, *Bishop of Winchester.*

A Manual of Prayers For the Use of the Scholars of Winchester College. And all other Devout Christians. To which is added three Hymns for Morning, Evening, and Midnight; not in the former Editions: By the same Author. Newly Revised. London, Printed for Charles Brome . . . 1700. 12°, A—F in twelves, A 1 with the Arms of the College.

KENNET, WHITE, *D.D., Bishop of Peterborough.*

Memoirs of the Family of Cavendish. By White Kennet, D.D. Archdeac. of Huntingdon, and Chaplain in Ordinary to Her Majesty. London, Printed and Sold by H. Hills, . . . For the Benefit of the Poor, 1708. 8°, A—F in fours.

KENT.

A baudie song of a maide of Kent. [1568.]
    Mentioned by Gosson (*Plaies Confuted*, repr. Hazlitt, p. 189) as having formed part of some dramatic performance about this time; he probably refers to the snatch in Wager's *The longer thou livest, the more fool thou art*, 1568, and doubtless the author quoted from a production under his eyes in the shape of a broadsheet. See Chappell's *Popular Music*, i. 348.

KIRBY, RICHARD, AND JOHN BI-
SHOP, *Students in the Celestial Science.*
The Marrow of Astrology In two Books.
Wherein is contained the Natures of the
Signes and Planets, with their several
Governing Angels, . . . Also a new
Table of Houses, exactly calculated for
the Latitude of London, . . . London:
Printed by Joseph Streater, near Paul's-
Wharf in Thames-street, for the Authors,
and are to be Sold by John Southby at
the Harrow in Cornhill. 1687. 4°, A—P
in fours, and a leaf of Q: Part 2, A—O
in fours, and a, 4 leaves.

L. M., *D.D.*
Proposals to the King and Parliament, Or
a Large Model of a Bank, Shewing how a
Fund of a Bank may be made without
much charge, or any hazard, that may
give out Bills of Credit to a vast extent,
that all Europe will accept of, rather than
Money. . . . London, Printed for Henry
Million at the sign of the Bible in Fleet-
Street, 1678. 4°, A—F in fours.

LADY.
The Lady's New-years Gift: . . . . The
Second Edition Corrected by the Original.
London, Printed by Matt. Gillyflower in
Westminster-Hall, and James Partridge
at Charing-Cross. 1688. Sm. 8°, B—
H 10 in twelves, beside the frontispiece,
title, and an Advertisement.

> In the Advertisement the publishers in-
> form us that the original MS. had been
> sent to a scrivener to be copied out, and
> that he had made a large number of mis-
> takes, which disfigure the first edition, and
> that the true copy may be distinguished by
> the engraving before the title.

LA FONTAINE.
Miscellaneous Poetical Novels or Tales,
Relating Many pleasing and instructive
Instances of Wit and Gallantry in Both
Sexes: Suited to the Belle-Humeur of
the Present Age. Adorn'd with Sculptures. London; Printed for John Nutt,
near Stationers-Hall. MDCCV. Folio, B
—F, 2 leaves each and the title: G, 1
leaf: *Second Collection,* B—F, 2 leaves
each and the title.

LAING, JAMES, *Scotus, Doctor of the
Sorbonne.*
De Vita et Moribvs atqve Rebvs Gestis
Hæreticorvm nostri Temporis &c. Tra-
ductis ex sermone Gallico in Latinum,
quibus multa addita sunt, . . . Parisiis,
Apud Michaelem de Roigny . . . 1584.
. . . 8°. ã, 8 leaves : ẽ, 4 leaves: I, 8
leaves, last blank: A—P 6 in eights.
Dedicated to Mary, Queen of Scots.

LAW.
Humble Proposals to the P
Assembled. Whereby th
the Civil Law may be u
Cases, to the great ease an
People, without looking t
pacy, or any thing that i
making any use of the P
monly called The Canon
away any thing from the
and in a perfect compli
present Government. L
by E. C. for R. Royston a
Ivie-lane, 1656. 4°, A—
B 2 blank.

LEAGUE.
The Necessarie Leagve.
of Septemb. 1625. Sm.
eights, B 8 blank. Engl.

LEAGUE AND COVEN.
Generall Demands Conce
Covenant: Propounded b
and Professors of Divinit
to some Reverend Breth
thither to recommend the
to them, . . . Edinburg
Robert Young, Anno 163
legio. 4°. A—E in fours.

The Answeres of some
Ministerie, To the Reply
sters and Professours of Di
deene: Concerning the
2 : Chron. 15. 15. *And al*
. . . Printed the yeare of
A—I, 2 leaves each.

A Phenix, Or, The Soler
Covenant. Whereunto
The Form and manner o
Coronation in Scotland.
then preached on that occ
Douglas of Edenburgh.
tion of the Kings Majesty
Subjects of the Kingdo
&c. in the Yeare 1650.
Danger of Covenant-break
the substance of a Serm
Edm. Calamy the 14. of J
the then Lord Mayor of
don, Sir Tho. Adams, to
Sheriffs, Aldermen, and C
of the said City : being t
taking the Solemn Leagu
at Michael Basenshaw,
burgh, Printed in the ye
breaking. Sm. 8vo, A—
besides the frontispiece, ti
3 leaves more.

LE CLERC, M.
The Life and Character

Locke, Author of the Essay concerning Humane Understanding . . . done into English by T. F. P. Gent. London: Printed for John Clark at the Bible and Crown in the Old Change near St. Pauls . . . 1706. 4°. Title and Translator's Preface, 2 leaves: B—E in fours.

LE FEVRE, RAOUL.

The Recuyles or Gaderīge to gyder of ȳ Hystoryes of Troye. Wynkyn de Worde, 1503. Folio.

> Mr. Quaritch informs me that he has examined his copy of this book, formerly in the Enschede Collection in Holland, since in two American collections successively, and now in Mr. Quaritch's possession, and that there is no doubt of the true date being 1503, not 1502, as in the Pepys example. The copy at King's College, Cambridge, according to Dr. Aldis Wright, who referred to it for me some years ago, has had the additional numeral inserted in MS.

LEICESTERSHIRE.

The Late Barbarous and Inhumane Cruelties Inflicted upon certain Persons Called Quakers for their Peaceable Religious Meetings, in the County of Leicester, by the Instigation of Thomas Cotten Priest, and divers Officers of the Parish of Broughton, . . . London, Printed for Benjamin Clark . . . 1682. 4°, A—B 2 in fours.

LE STRANGE, SIR ROGER.

The Case Put. Concerning the Succession of His Royal Highness the Duke of York . . . The Second Edition Enlarged. London: Printed by M. C. for Henry Brome . . . 1679. 4°, A—E 2 in fours.

The Reformed Catholique: Or, The True Protestant. [Matth. 24. 26 . . .] London, Printed for Henry Brome, . . . 1679. 4°. Title preceded by a blank, 2 leaves: B—F 2 in fours.

The Casuist Uncas'd. In a Dialogue betwixt Richard and Baxter, With a Moderator Between them, For Quietnesse Sake. By Roger L'Estrange. London, Printed for Henry Brome . . . 1681. 4°, A—L in fours.

An Answer to a Letter to a Dissenter, Upon Occasion of His Majesties Late Gracious Declaration of Indulgence. London, Printed for R. Sare at Grays-Inn-Gate in Holborn, 1687. 4°, A—G 2 in fours.

LETTER.

A Letter to Monsieur B - - - de M - - - at Amsterdam, written Anno . 1676. No place, &c. 4°, 4 leaves.

A Letter from a Soldier, Being some Remarks Upon a Late Scandalous Pamphlet: Entituled, An Address of some Irish Folks to the House of Commons. Printed in the Year, 1702. 4°, A—D, 2 leaves each.

A Letter to the Author of the *Memorial of the Church of England*. London, Printed in the Year 1705. 4°, A—D in fours, and a leaf of E.

LETTER, PRINTER'S.

Specimen of the Several Sorts of Letter Given to the University by Dr John Fell Sometime Lord Bishop of Oxford. To which is Added The Letter Given by Mr F. Junius. Oxford, Printed at the Theater A.D. 1695. 4°, a—f 2 in fours. *B. M.*

> The two last leaves are occupied by a List of the Matrices given by Bishop Fell. The whole of the text is a reproduction of the several founts.

LINDEWOODE OR LYNDEWODE, WILLIAM.

[Provinciale seu Constitutiones Provinciales Angliæ. Oxford, Theodore Rood, about 1485.] Large folio. In two columns. With signatures and headlines, the latter having the appearance of having been separately worked, and without catchwords and foliation. a—c in eights, a 1 being blank on *recto*, and occupied on *verso* by a woodcut: d, 6: e—g in eights: h, 6: i, 8: k—l omitted: m—o in eights: p, 6: q—s in eights: t, 6: v—y in eights: z, 6: A—D in eights: E, 6: F—N in eights: O, 6: P—R in eights: S, 10 leaves, the 10th blank: the *Table*, aa—cc in eights, aa i blank: dd, 9 leaves. On the 9th leaf of S occurs the colophon, but no imprint. *B. M.*

De summa trinitate & fide catholica [This is the whole title on A 1 *recto* as a head-line; on A 1 *verso* occurs as a running title:] Liber primus De cōstitutiōibus. [Col.] Expliciunt constitutiones Legatum cum Johanne Othone. Impressum per me Richardum Pynson. [About 1495.] 8°, a—g in eights: h, 9, followed by two blank: Constitutiones Othonis, a—e 4 in eights. With the colophon on E 2 *verso* and the mark on E 4 *verso*. Without catchwords and pagination, and with the signatures (except h) marked only on first leaf of sheet. *B. M.*

Prouinciale seu Constitutiones Anglie Cum summariis atqʒ iustis annotationibus: honestis characteribus: summaqʒ accuratione rursum impresse. [Col.] Explicitū est opus . . . in inclyta parisiana academia. Anno salutis nostre Millesimo quingentesimo primo. Maii vero die xxviij. Folio. In two columns. a⁸: b⁶: c⁸: d⁸: e⁸: f⁸: g⁸: h⁶: i—q:⁸ r⁶: s—z in eights: one sheet of eight and one of six under irregular signatures: A—B in sixes: C, 7. *B. M.*

From the press of A. Bocard.

Prouinciale seu Cōstitutiones Anglie: cū summarijs / atq3 iustis annotationibus / politissimis caracteribus / summaq3 accurationæ rursum reuise atq3 impresse. [Col.] Explicit preclarū opus Willhelmi Lindwoode eruditissimi viri super constitutiones prouinciales Anglie: summa cura atq3 diligentia Christophori Endouien. Antwerpie impressum. vna cū annotationibus debitis... Impensis vero Francisci Brickman honesti mercatoris Anno salutis nostre millesimo quingentesimo vicesimo quinto. xx. die Decembris. Folio, printed in two columns, with copious marginal glosses. A (with verses and woodcuts enclosed in a border, Table, &c.)—D 4 in eights, D 4 blank: A (repeated) — X in eights: AA—KK in eights: LL, 10.

LISTER, MARTIN, *F.R.S.*
Martini Lister E Societate Regia Londini Hystoriæ Animalium Angliæ Tres Tractatus: Unus de Araneis. Alter de Cochleis Tum Terrestribus tum Fluviatilibus. Tertius de Cochleis Marinis. Quibus adjectus est Quartus de Lapidibus ejusdem Insulæ ad Cochlearum quandam imaginem figuratis. *Memoriæ & R ttiomi.* Londini, Apud Joh. Martyn... 1678. 4° A—Kk in fours, A 1 with *Imprimatur* and Kk 8 with *Errata.* With folded plates in D, P, X, Z, Cc, Dd, Ee, Ff, and Ii.

LLOYD, DAVID, *Dean of St. Asaph.*
The Legend of Captaine Jones: Relating His adventure to Sea: His first landing, and strange combate with a mighty Bear. His furious battell with his sixe and thirty men Against the Army of eleven Kings, with their overthrow and deaths. His relieving of Kemper Castle. His strange and admirable Sea-fight with sixe huge Gallies of Spaine, and nine thousand Souldiers... London, Printed by M. F. for Richard Marriot, and are to be sold at his Shop under the Kings Head Tavern in Fleet-street, neere Chancery lane end. 1648. 4°, A—C in fours and A—F in fours, including a frontispiece by W. Marshall to the first portion. *B. M.*

LONDON.
Another Cry of the Innocent & Oppressed, For Justice: Or, A Second Relation of the unjust proceedings at the Sessions held a Hicks's Hall for the County of Middlesex and at the Old-Baily, London, the 6th an the 14th dayes of the 10th Month or December, 1664. With and against 32 mor of the People called Quakers. ... Vnt which also is now Added, A Brief, Shor Summary of the Sentencing of 36 mor of the aforesaid people, in scorn called Quakers ... at the two places abov mentioned, ... where they were all Sen tenced for to be Transported to the Islanc of Jamaica ... London, Printed in the Year, 1664. 4°, A—D in fours.

Another Cry of the Innocent and Oppressed for Justice. Or a third Relation of the unjust proceedings at the Sessions held at Hicks's Hall ... Upon the 18th and 27th dayes of the twelfth Month called February, in the year 1664. ... Unto which is added a Short Postscript. ... Printed in the Year 1665. 4°, A—B in fours.

Many of these were also shipped to "Gamaica," as it is spelled on the title, for seven years.

The Second Part of the Peoples { Antient and Just }
Liberties Asserted in the Proceedings against, and Tryals of Tho. Rudyard, Francis Moor, Rich. Mew, ... At the Sessions begun and held at the Old-Bailey in London the last day of the 6th Month, ... Printed in the Year, 1670. 4°, A—1 2 in fours.

Here is a full and true Relation of one Mr. Rich. Langly, a Glazier, Living overagainst the Sign of the Golden-Wheat-Sheaf in Ratcliff Highway, London. that lay in a Trance for Two Days and One Night. He also saw the Joys of Heaven, and the Terrors of Hell ... Licensed according to Order. London: Printed for T. Bland near Fleetstreet. 1708. 8°, 4 leaves. *B. M.*

LYNDSAY, SIR DAVID.
The Workes of the Famovs and Worthy Knight, Sir Dauid Lindesay, of the Mount, alias, Lyon, King of Armes: Newlie corrected and vindicate from the former errours, ... Edinbvrgh, printed by Andrew Hart. 1634. 8°, black letter, A—Y in eights. With the fictitious portrait of the author on the title. *B. M.*

As Andrew or Andro Hart was dead some time prior to 1634, the imprint appears to be inaccurate. Other books of this date purport to be printed by Hart's heirs.

The Works of the Famous and Worthy Knight, Sir David Lindesay, ... Edinbvrgh, Printed by Andrew Anderson, and are to be sold at his House, on the Nornh [sic] side of the Cross, Anno Dom. 1670. Small 8vo, black letter, A—L in twelves: M 8, the last leaf blank. *B. M.*

The Works of the Famous and Worthy Knight, Sir David Lindesay of the Mount, alias Lyon, King of Armes. . . Glasgow, Printed by Robert Sanders, one of His Majesties Printers, 1696. 12°, A—L in twelves. Black letter. *B. M.*

Puttick's, Jan. 31, 1889, No. 664, misdated in catalogue 1656. I suspect this to be the identical copy which occurred at a previous auction, and was then erroneously described as of 1636. The third figure of the date is a broken or partly-erased letter; and the same is the case in that in the British Museum. Sanders was not a printer or publisher at Glasgow till after the Restoration; nor was there printing there before 1638.

The Works of . . . Sir David Lindsay . . . Edinburgh, Printed by the Heirs and Successors of Andrew Anderson, . . . 1709. 12°, black letter, A—L in twelves. *B. M.*

The Works of Sir David Lindsay . . . Belfast, Printed by James Blow, and are to be sold at his Shop 1714. 12°, A—P in twelves. *B. M.*

MACARIA.

A Description of the Famous Kingdome of Macaria; Shewing its Excellent Government: Wherein the Inhabitants live in great Prosperity, Health, and Happinesse; the King obeyed, the Nobles honoured, and all good men respected, Vice punished, and vertue rewarded. An Example to other Nations. London, Printed for Francis Constable, Anno 1641. 4°, A—C 2 in fours. *B. M.*

MACE, RICHARD, *one of the Clerks of Trinity College Chapel, Cambridge.*
Profit, Conveniency, and Pleasure, to the whole Nation. Being a short Rational Discourse, lately presented to His Majesty, Concerning the High-ways of England: Their Badness, the Causes thereof, ... Printed for a Publick good in the Year 1675. 4°, A—D 2 in fours.

MACKENZIE, SIR GEORGE.
Religio Stoici. Acts 1. 11. *Ye men of Galilee,* . . . Edinbvrgh, Printed for Robert Brown, and are to be sold at his Shop, at the Sign of the Sun, over against the Cross, 1663. Sm. 8°. A, 8 leaves, first blank: B, 4: B (repeated)—E in eights: F, 7 leaves, no pp. 79, 80: G—L in eights. *B. M.*

MACKWORTH, SIR HUMPHREY, *M.P.*
England's Glory: Or, The Great Improvement of Trade in General, By a Royal Bank, Or Office of Credit, To be Erected in London; Wherein many Great Advantages that will hereby accrue to the Nation, to the Crown, and to the People, are mentioned; With Answers to the Objections that may be made against this Bank. . . . By H. M. . . . London, Printed by T. W. for Tho. Bever, at the Hand and Star, within Temple-Bar, 1694. 8°. A, 4 leaves: B—G in eights, G 8 blank. Dedicated to Sir William Ashurst. *B. M.*

Peace at Home: Or, A Vindication of the Proceedings of the Honourable the House of Commons, On the Bill for Preventing Danger from Occasional Conformity. Shewing the Reasonableness and even Necessity of such a Bill, for the better Security of the Established Government, for Preserving the Publick Peace both in Church and State, and for Quieting the Minds of Her Majesty's Subjects. London: Printed by Freeman Collins, . . . 1703. Folio, A—E, 2 leaves each.

A Bill for the Better Relief, Imployment, and Settlement of the Poor, As the same was Reported from the Committee of the Honourable House of Commons; In order that (by Reason of the great Importance and Universal Concern of the said Bill) the same be farther Consider'd against the Next Session of Parliament. London; Printed by the Direction of Sir Humphry Mackworth, By Fr. Collins in the Old-Baily, for George Strahan, at the Golden-Ball, near the Royal Exchange . . . 1704. Folio, A—E, 2 leaves each, and the title.

An advertisement at end is dated by Mackworth from his house in Park Street, Westminster, April 24, 1704.

MAN.
The Man in the Moon, Discovering a World of Knavery under the Sunne; Both in the Parliament, the Counsell of State, the Army, the City, and the Country. With Intelligence from all parts of England, Scotland, and Ireland. [1649.] 4°, A—I in fours(?).

The present is No. 9, from June 5 to June 13, 1649, and is under sign. I. Whether there were more than nine numbers, I do not yet know.

MANLEY, THOMAS.
A Discourse; Shewing That the Exportation of Wooll is destructive to this Kingdom: Wherein is also shewed the

necessity of promoting our woollen Manufacture, and moderating the Importation of some Commodities, and Prohibiting others; with some easie Expedients touching thereunto. By Thomas Manly Esquire. London. Printed for Samuel Crouch, 1677. 4°, A—B in fours.

MARKHAM, GERVASE.
The Complete Farriar, Or The Kings High-Way to Horsmanship. Experimentally unfolding
1. The dyeting and governing of the Running Horse.
2. How to order, feed, and keep any Horse for War, Pleasure, Hunting, or Travell.
Lastly, Certaine rare and approved secrets for the Cure of the worst infirmities in Horses. By G. Markham. London, Printed by J. D. for R. Young, and are sold by P. Nevill in Ivie-lane, 1639. 8°, A—M 6 in eights. *B. M.*

MARTIN, JAMES, *of Dunkeld, Professor of Philosophy at Turin.*
Iacobi Martini Scoti Dvnkeldensis: . . . de prima simplicium, & concretorum corporum generatione . . . . Avgvstae Tavrinorvm Apud hæredes Nicolai Beuilaquæ. M.D.LXXVII. 4°, A—T in fours. Dedicated to the Archbishop of Turin, Chancellor of the University. *B. M.*

Iacobi Martini . . . de prima simplicium . . . generatione disputatio. . . . Cantabrigiae, Ex officina Thomæ Thomæ celeberrimæ Academiæ Cantabrigiensis Typographi. 1584. 8°. ¶, 8 leaves: A—M in eights. *B. M.* and *Bodl.*

Iacobi Martini . . . De prima simplicium . . . generatione . . . . Francofvrdi Apud Ioannem Wechelum. MDLXXXIX. 8°, A—I 4 in eights. *B. M.*

MARTIN, RICHARD, *of the Middle Temple.*
A Speech Delivered to the Kings most Excellent Majesty, in the name of the Sheriffs of London and Middlesex. Printed at Oxford for William Webb, And reprinted for Anthony Vinson, 1643. 4°, 4 leaves.
Originally published in 1603.

[MAY, THOMAS.]
Arbitrary Government Displayed to the Life, In The Tyrannical Usurpation of a Junto of Men called the Rump Parliament. And More especially in that of the Tyrant and Usurper, Oliver Cromwell. . . . With the Characters and Lives of several of those Usurpers, . . . Illustrated with several Brass-Cutts, representing the Chief Persons, and Passages therein. London, Printed for Charles Leigh in the Year, 1682. 12°, A—D in twelves: *, 2 leaves: E—I in twelves. With a frontispiece and plates in compartments in signatures B, C, D, and I.

MERCURIUS.
Numb. 1. Of the Parliament's second Purge. Mercvrjvs Militaris, Or The People's Scout. Discovering the Designes Interests and Humors of the Civil and Martial Conventicles
Of ⎧ Westminster,
⎨ Darby-House
⎩ and White-Hall, &c.

The English Frenchmen are quite gone,
The English Scots past Tweed,
And the English Jews got in the Throne,
Next (sure) the true English speed.

. . . Printed in the Yeer 1649. 4°, A—B in fours.
This number is for the week from Tuesday, April 17, to Tuesday, April 24, 1649.

MISSALE.
Missale Ad vsum celeberrime ecclesie Eboracensis optimis caracteribus recēter Impressum cura peruigili maximaq5 lucubratione mendis q̄ pluribus emendatum. Sumptibus & expensis Johannis gachet mercatoris librarii bene meriti iuxta prefatum ecclesiam commorantis. Anno dñi decimo sexto supra millesimum et quingētesimū. Die vero quinta Februarii completum atq5 perfectum. Folio. *B. M.*
This copy is very incomplete.

MONEY.
The mistaken Advantage by Raising of Money, discovered in a Letter to a Friend. [Col.] Edinburgh, Printed by John Reid, . . . 1695. 4°, A—D 2 in fours, D 2 blank.

MONIPENNIE, JOHN.
An Abridgement or Summary of the Scots Chronicles. . . . Newly inlarged, corrected, and amended. Glasgow, By Robert Sanders, Printer to the Town, and are to be sold at his shop. 1671. Sm. 8°, A—K in twelves. With a folded Table of the Kings of Scotland.

MONK, GEORGE, *Duke of Albemarle.*
The true state of the Transactions of Colonel George Monk with Owen-Roe-Mac-Art-O-Neal; As it was Reported to The Parliament by the Councel of State. Together with the Votes & Resolutions of the Parliament thereupon. . . . London, Printed for Edward Husband, . . . August 15. 1649. 4°, A—B in fours.

The Northern Qveries from the Lord Gen: Monck His Qvarters, Sounding an Allarum, to all Loyal Hearts, and Free-born English-men. Arms, Arms, Arms, In Defence of our Lives, Laws, liberties, and Parliaments; Against the Tyrannical Power, and Domination of the Sword. Printed in the Year of Englands Confusions, and are to be sold at the Sign of Wallingford House, right against A Free Parliament. 4°, 4 leaves.

MOORE, ADAM.
Bread for the Poor. And Advancement of the English Nation. Promised by Enclosure of the Wastes and Common Grounds of England. London: Printed by R. & W. Leybourn, for Nicholas Bourn, . . . 1653. 4°, B—G in fours: a, 4 leaves, and the title.

MORGAN, SYLVANUS.
Peplvm Heroum. A Tretise of Honor and Honorable men. Wherein the nature, Antiquity, necessity, effects of Armes and honor is fully demonstrated. Exemplified in divers remuneration an[d] signall Armoriall Remembrances. . . . By Silvanus Morgan 1642. 4°, 85 leaves. With a few arms in trick, &c.

Unpublished MS. sold at Sotheby's, March 29, 1889, No. 942.

MORLAND, SIR S.
Tuba Stenoro-Phonica, An Instrument of Excellent Use, As well at Sea, as at Land; Invented and variously Experimented in the Year 1670. And Humbly Presented to the Kings Most Excellent Majesty Charles II. In the Year, 1671. The Instruments (or Speaking-Trumpets) of all Sizes and Dimensions are Made and Sold by Mr. Simon Beal, one of His Majesties Trump[s]: in Suffolk-street. London, Printed by W. Godbid, and are to be sold by M. Pitt at the White-Hart in Little-Britain. 1672. Folio, A—D, 2 leaves each. With a series of engravings printed with the letterpress.

The Poor Man's Dyal With an Instrument to Set it. Made applicable to any place in England, Scotland, Ireland, &c. By Sir Samuel Morland Knight and Baronet. 1689. And are to be Sold at all the Button-Sellers, Cutlers, and Toy-Shops about the Town. And will be shortly publisht in several other Sizes and Dimensions, for the Good of the publick, and for the consumption of the manufacture of our Nation. 4°, 4 leaves. With a Diagram of the Dial on A 2. *Lambeth.*

Reprinted by Mr. Prosser of the Patent Office, 4°, 1886.

MOSCHINI, CARLO.
Brutes Turn'd Criticks, Or Mankind Moraliz'd by Beasts. In Sixty Satyrical Letters Upon the Vices and Follies of our Age . . . now done into English with some Improvements. . . . London, Printed for Daniel Dring at the Harrow and Crown at the Corner of Cliffords-Inn-Lane in Fleetstreet, 1695. 8°. A, 8 leaves: a—b 6 in twelves: B—H in twelves, H 12 with Advertisements.

Dedicated by John Savage, the translator, to Thomas Coke of Melbourn in Derbyshire. With several sets of commendatory verses, including some in English by A. Boyer, J. Drake, E. Hart, and Alexander Oldis.

MUN, THOMAS.
England's Benefit and Advantage By Foreign Trade, Plainly Demonstrated. Dedicated to the Merchant-Adventurers of England. By Tho. Mun, Merchant. London: Printed by E. J. for Tho. Horne . . . 1698. 8°. A, 4 leaves: B—M in eights.

MUSÆUM MINERVÆ.
The Second Lecture Being an Introduction to Cosmographie: Read Publiquely at Sr Balthazar Gerbiers Academy on Bednall Greene. Rom. cap. 1. ver. 20. . . . London Printed for Robert Ibbitson in Smithfield near the Queenshead Tavern, 1649. 4°. A—C in fours. Dedicated by Gerbier D'Ouvilly to the President of the Council of State, from Bethnal Green, Nov. 5. 1649.

NAPIER, JOHN, *Lord Napier of Merchistoun.*
Logarithmorvm Canonis Descriptio, Sev Arithmeticarvm Svppvtationvm Mirabilis Abbreviatio. . . . Lvgdvni, Apud Barth. Vincentium. M.DC.XX. . . . 4°, A—M 2 in fours. Dedicated to James I.

Mirifici Logarithmorvm Constrvctio. Et Eorvm ad Natvrales ipsorum numeros habitudines; . . . Lvgdvni, . . . M.DC.XX. 4°. . . . A—H in fours, H 4 with Priviledge. With a preface by Robert Napier, the writer's son.

Napiers Narration: Or, An Epitome of his Booke of the Revelations . . . London, Printed by R. O. and G. D. for Giles Calvert. 1641. 4°, A—C in fours. *B. M.*

NETHERLANDS.
A Proclamation Given by the Discreet Lords and States, against the slanders laid vpon the Euangelicall and Reformed Religion, by the Arminians and Separatists: Containing all the Points, Accusa-

tions, Declarations and Confessions, taken out of the last Prouinciall Synode holden at Arnhem, the 15. day of September last past. 1618. Together with the seuerall Examinations and Confessions (at Vtrecht and the Haghe) . . . Printed according to the Dutch Originals, At London By G. E. for Th: Th: and Richard Chambers, and are to be solde at the signe of the blacke Beare in Paules Church-yard. 1618. 4°, A—C in fours, C 4 blank. *B. M.*

A Letter from the Synod of Zeland, To the Commissioners of the Generall Assembly of the Kirk of Scotland : Written by them in Latin, and now faithfully translate into English : Expressing, 1. Their fellow-feeling of the present condition of the Kirks of Ireland and England, & exciting us to the like . . . Printed at Edinburgh by Evan Tyler, . . . 1643. 4°, A—C 2 in fours.

A Relation of the Defeating Card. Mazarine & Oliv. Cromwel's Design to have taken Ostend by Treachery, in the Year, 1658. Written in Spanish by a Person of Quality (who was a chief Actor in the preventing of it) by way of Letter to a friend of his presently after the business. Since Printed in that Language, and now Translated into English. *Fallere falentem* [sic] *non est fraus.* London, Printed for Hen. Herringman, . . . 1666. Sm. 8°. A, 6 leaves, title on A 2 : B—F in twelves : G, 6. *B. M.*

A Journal of the late Notions and Actions of the Confederate Forces Against the French, in the United Provinces and the Spanish Netherlands With Curious Remarks on the Situation, Strength and Rarities of the most considerable Cities, Towns and Fortifications in those Countreys. Together with an exact List of the Army. Written by an English Officer, who was there during the last Campaign. London, Printed, and are to be sold by Richard Baldwin, near the Black Bull in the Old-Baily, 1690. 4°. A, 2 leaves : B—E in fours. *B. M.*

NEVILE, ALEXANDER.

Norfolkes Fvries, Or A View of Ketts Campe : Necessary for the Malecontentes of our Time, for their instruction, or terror ; and profitable for euery good svbject, to incourage him vpon the vndoubted hope of the Victorie, to stand faithfully to maintayne his Prince and Covntrey, his Wife and Children, goods, and Inheritance. With a Table of the Maiors and Sheriffes of the Worshipfull City of Norwich, euer since the first grant by Henry the Fourth ; Together with the Bishops of that See, and other Accidents there. Set forth first in Latin by Alexander Nevil, Translated into English, for the vse of the common People, by R. W. Minister of Frettenham in Norfolke, and a Citizen borne, who beheld part of these things with his yong Eyes. [Quot. from Rom. 13. 5.] London, Printed by William Stansby for Henry Fetherstone, and are to be sold at his shop in Pauls Churchyard, at the signe of the Rose. 1615. 4°, A—L in fours. Dedicated to Sir Thomas Hiren, Knight, Mayor of Norwich. *B. M.*

NEW ENGLAND.

Newes from New-England : Of A most strange and prodigious Birth, brought to Boston in New-Englaud, October the 17. being a true and exact Relation, brought over April 19. 1642. by a gentleman of good worth, now resident in London. Also other Relations of strange and prodigious Births in these Countries following. The 1. from New-England. The 2. from Ouieres. The 3d. in Ravena. The 4. in Paris. The 5. in St. Andwes Church in Paris. The 6. in the Forrest Biera. [Col.] London : Printed for John G. Smith [sic], 1642. 4°, 4 leaves. With cuts on the title and at end. *B. M.*

Good news from New-England : With An exact Relation of the first planting that Countrey : A description of the profits accruing by the Worke. Together with a briefe, but true discovery of their Order both in Church and Commonwealth, and maintenance allowed the painfull Labourers in that Vineyard of the Lord. With The names of the severall Towns, and who be Preachers to Them. London ; Printed by Matthew Simmons, 1648 [March 10, 1647-8.] 4°, A—C in fours, a leaf of D, and the title. Chiefly in verse. *B. M.*

New-England's Present Sufferings under their Cruel Neighbouring Indians ; Represented in two Letters, lately Written from Boston to London. London, Printed in the Year 1675. 4°, 4 leaves.

News from New-England, Being A True and last Account of the present Bloody Wars, carried on betwixt the Infidels, Natives, and the English Christians, and Converted Indians of New-England, declaring the many Dreadful Battles fought betwixt them : As also the many Towns and Villages burnt by the merciless Heathens. . . . London, Printed for J.

Coniers at the Sign of the Black-Raven in Duck-Lane, 1676. 4°, 4 leaves. *B. M.*

A Brief Relation of the State of New England, from the Beginning of the Plantation to the Present Year, 1689. In a letter to a Person of Quality. London, Printed for Richard Baldwin, near the Black Bull in the Old-Baily, 1689. 4°, A—C 2 in fours, C 2 with *Advertisements. B. M.*

A Trip to New-England. With a Character of the Country and People, Both English and Indians. London, Printed in the Year, 1699. Folio, A—D, 2 leaves each.

Probably written by William Fuller.

NEWNHAM, JOHN.

Newnams Nightcrowe. A Bird that breedeth braules in many Families and Housholdes. Wherein is remembred that kindely and prouident regard which Fathers ought to haue towards their Sonnes. Together with a disciphring of the innurious dealinges of some younger sorte of stepdames. *Vnicuique secundum opera eius.* Cor. 2. *Vix reijcis florem qui dulcem præbet odorem.* London, Printed by Iohn Wolfe. 1590. 4°, A—H in fours. Dedicated to Thomas Owen, Esquire, Serjeant-at-law. In prose, except some verses at the end to and by the writer, and "The Bookes purpose" on the back of the title. *B. M.*

NEWTON, JOHN, *A.M., sometime Fellow of Clare Hall, Cambridge, and now Vicar of St. Martins, Leicester.*

The Penitent Recognition of Joseph's Brethren. A Sermon Occasion'd by Elizabeth Ridgeway, who for the Petit Treason of Poysoning Her Husband, Was, on March 24. 168¾, according to the Sentence of the Right Honourable Sir Thomas Street, one of His Majesties Judges of Assize for the Midland Circuit, Burnt at Leicester: When and where were also Executed William Tannessy and Edward Orton, for Burglary; Sons of one Woman. To which is prefixed a full Relation of the Woman's Fact, Tryal, Carriage, and Death. *Ornari res ipsa negat, contenta doceri.* London, Printed for Richard Chiswell, and sold by William Atkins, Bookseller in Leicester. 1684. 4°, A—F 2 in fours, A 1-2 and F 2 blank. Dedicated to Andrew Freeman, Esq., Mayor of Leicester. *B. M.*

NICCOLS, RICHARD.

Monodia Or Walthams Complaint, Vpon the death of that most Vertuous and Noble Ladie, late deceased, the Lady Honor Hay, sole Daughter and Heire to the Right Honorable Edward, Lord Dennie, Baron of Waltham, and wife to the Right Honourable Iames Lord Hay. *Virtus post funera vinit.* By R. N. Oxon. London, Printed by W. S. for Richard Meighen and Thomas Iones, and are to be sold at their shop without Templebarre vnder S. Clements Church. 1615. Small 8°. *Bodleian.*

Collation:—A—B in eights, title on A 4, A 1-3 having been probably blank, as was B 8. Printed within head and tail pieces, only the first leaf of B signed.
Dedicated by Niccols in verse "To the same right Honorable Lords, the Lord Dennie, and the Lord Hay;" on the back of which leaf is a curious woodcut. There is a second on B 7 *verso*. Communicated by the Rev. F. Madan, of the Bodleian Library.

NORFOLK.

Good Counsel and Advice unto the Magistrates and People of Norwich: With a brief Relation of some of the Sufferings of the People of God, called, Quakers in the said City. Printed in the Year 1676. 4°, 4 leaves.

NOTTINGHAMSHIRE.

The Cry of Oppression Continued & Encreased in Nottingham-Shire Being A brief Relation of some of the late Cruel Sufferings of the People of God, called, Quakers in the said County; ... Printed in the Year, 1676. 4°, A— in fours.

The copy employed ended imperfectly on A 4.

OBSERVATOR.

The Observator Defended in A modest Reply to the late Animadversions upon those Notes the Observator published upon the new Doctrines and Positions which the King by way of Recapitulation layes open so offensive. [About 1643.] 4°, 6 leaves.

ORIGEN.

Origen against Celsus: Translated from the Original into English. By James Bellamy, Gent. ... London, Printed for R. Mills, and Sold by J. Robinson at the Golden Lyon in St. Paul's Church-Yard 8°, A—Dd 6 in eights, A 1 with half-title.

OTWAY, THOMAS, *of Trotton, Sussex.*

Don Carlos Prince of Spain: A Tragedy: ... The Second Edition Corrected. London, Printed by E. Flesher, for R. Tonson, ... 1679. 4°, A—I in fours. Dedicated to the Duke of York.

The History and Fall of Caius Marius.

A Tragedy. As it is Acted at the Dukes Theatre. By Thomas Otway.
Qui color Albus erat nunc est contrarius Albo. London, Printed for Tho. Flesher, at the Angel and Crown in S. Paul's Churchyard. 1680. 4°, A—K 2 in fours. Dedicated to Viscount Falkland.

The Orphan Or the Unhappy Marriage: A Tragedy As it is Acted at His Royal Highness the Duke's Theatre. Written by Tho. Otway. [Quot. from Petronius.] London. Printed for R. Bentley and S. Magnes, ... 1685. 4°, A—I in fours. Dedicated to the Duchess of York.

OVIDIUS NASO, PUBLIUS.
The Poet Banter'd: Or, Ovid in a Vizor. A Burlesque Poem on His Art of Love. ... The Second Edition with Additions. London, Printed for A. Baldwin, in Warwick-Lane, 1702. 8°, A—F in fours. *B. M.*

P. D.
A Letter from a Jesuit at Paris, to his Correspondent in London; Shewing the most effectual way to ruine the Government and Protestant Religion. London, Printed, and are to be sold by Jonathan Edwin, at the Three Roses in Ludgate-street. 1679. 4°, A—B 2 in fours.
> The initials D. P. occur at the end as those of the writer, who dates from Paris, 12 Feb. 167$\frac{8}{9}$.

PAINTING AND VARNISHING.
A Short Introduction to the Art of Painting and Varnishing. London, Printed for George Dawes, over against Lincolns-Inne-Gate, in Chancery-Lane, 1685. Sm. 8°, A in eights. *B. M.*
> Probably by John Smith, author of *The Art of Painting*, 1676, with which it is bound up at the British Museum.

PAIOLI, ALFONSO, *Ferrarese.*
Vite del Cardinale Givlio Mazarini, e di Oliviero Cromvele. In Venetia, Et in Bologna. 1675. ... 8°, A—G 10 in twelves.

PALATINATE.
His Majesties Manifest, Touching the Palatine Cavse: And Act of Parliament concerning the same. Published by His Majesties Command. Edinbvrgh, Printed by Robert and James Bryson, Anno Dom. 1641. 4°, A—B in fours.

PALMER, ROGER, *Earl of Castlemaine.*
An Account of What past on Monday the 28th of October, 1689 In the House of Commons, And since at the Kings-Bench-Bar at Westminster, In Relation to the Earle of Castlemaine. London, Printed for Matthew Granger, 1690. 4°, A—C 2 in fours.

PANKE, JOHN.
The Fal of Babel. By the confusion of tongues, directly proving against the Papists of this, and former ages; that ... it cannot be discerned by any man living, what they would say, or how be vnderstoode, ... Printed at Oxford by Ioseph Barnes. 1608. 4°, A—D 3 in fours. *B. M.*
> There is in the Museum a reissue, 4°, Oxford, 1623.

PARADISE.
The Paradyse of daynty denyses ... 1576.
> Sotheby's, Feb. 14, 1889, No. 659, a copy wanting A 4, and having other leaves slightly defective. It was misdescribed as "probably unique," although the owner might have known that it was not so, and the auctioneers ought certainly to have been aware that such a statement was erroneous and misleading, since at the Heber sale George Ellis's copy sold for £16. The latter is now, I believe, at Britwell, and I personally informed the artist who executed the facsimile of the missing leaf, that there was a duplicate of this volume in existence.
> Herbert, in his edition of Ames, describes "the next earliest edition," that of 1577, from a copy then belonging to Sir John Hawkins; but that impression, so far as I know, is not in the British Museum, which only possesses the issue of 1596. This appears to be a second serious error in the catalogue. Nor do I see the validity of the farther assertion that "every possible search has been made for it in both public and private libraries without success." Nor do I believe that it was "bound by F. Bedford." I know that Bedford's private library was sold *after his death* in 1884. However, under the auspices of these romantic allurements, the item realised a large sum.
> I challenge every alleged fact published respecting it:—1. That it was probably unique. 2. That every possible search had been made for a second copy. 3. That the missing leaf was supplied in facsimile from the next earliest edition in the British Museum. 4. That it was bound by F. Bedford.

PARKER, SAMUEL.
[Insolence and Impudence triumphant; Envy and Fury enthron'd. The Mirrour of Malice and Madness, In a late Treatise, Entituled, *A Discourse of Ecclesiastical Polity, &c.*. Or, The lively Portraiture of Mr. S. P. Limn'd and drawn by his own hand: And a brief View of his Tame and Softly, *Alias*, Wild and Savage Humour: As also, some account of his cold & frigid, *i.e.* fiery Complexion. ...

Printed in the Year 1669. 4°, A—C 2 in fours.]

PARLIAMENT.
Englands Prosperity in the Priviledges of Parliament, Set forth in a briefe Collection of their most Memorable services for the honour and safety of this Kingdome, since the Conquest, till these present times. London, Printed for Nicholas Iones. 4°, 4 leaves.

The Petition of Rights, Exhibited to His Majestie, By the Lords Spiritvall and Temporall, and Commons in Parliament assembled, concerning Divers Rights and Liberties of the Subjects: with the Kings Majesties severall Answers thereunto. With his Majesties Declaration upon the same. London, Printed for M. Walbancke and L. Chapman. 1642. 4°, 4 leaves.
    The date has been altered with a pen to 1648.

A Declaration of the Parliament of England. Written to the High and Mighty Lords, the Lords States Generall of the Vnited Provinces of the Low-Countreys: Concerning their Last Embassie Extraordinary into England. London, Printed for Laurence Blaiklock, at the Signe of the Mearmaid at the Middle-Temple Gate, 1645 [August 5.] 4°, Title and *Imprimatur*, 2 leaves: B—E in fours: F, 2 leaves.

A Second Declaration of the Lords and Commons Assembled in Parliament; Of The whole Proceedings with the late Extraordinary Ambassador from the High and Mighty Lords, the States Generall of the United Provinces; Concerning Restitution of Ships, and the Course of Trade. London: Printed for Edward Husband, ... Sept. 18. 1645. 4°, A—D in fours, A 1 with *Imprimatur*.

By the Parliament. A Proclamation for the Discovery and Apprehending of Charls Stvart, and other Traytors his Adherents and Abettors. London, Printed by John Field, Printer to the Parliament of England. 1651. A broadside. *B. M.*

A Declaration of the Parliament of the Commonwealth of England, Relating to the Affairs and Proceedings between this Commonwealth and the States General of the United Provinces of the Low-Countreys, and the present Differences occasioned on the States part. And the Answer of the Parliament to Those Papers from the Ambassadors Extraordinary of the States General, upon occasion of the late Fight between the Fleets. With a Narrative of the late Engagement between the English and Holland Fleet. As also A Collection of the Proceedings in the Treaty between the Lord Pauw, Ambassador Extraordinary from the States General of the United Provinces, and the Parliament of the Commonwealth of England. ... London, Printed by Iohn Field, Printer to the Parliament of England, 1652. 4°, A—I in fours, I 4 blank.

Instructions Lately agreed upon by the Lords and Commons Assembled in Parliament, For the Commissioners sent by them to the Hague, unto the Kings most Excellent Majesty. Together with the Speech made thereupon by the Honorable Denzell Holles Esq; one of the Commissioners, on Wednesday the 16th day of May, 1660. Now Published for the taking off and disproving those false Reports raised by some malicious Persons, as if he had gone beyond his Commission, and the said Instructions. *Sit Liber Judex*. London, Printed for Robert Clavel ... [1660.] 4°, A—B in fours, A 1 with the Royal Arms.

A Present Answer to the late Complaint Vnto the House of Commons. By divers Members of the said House. Printed in the Yeare M.DC.XLII. 4°, 4 leaves.

PARTRIDGE, JOHN.
The Treasurie of hidden Secrets. ... At London, Printed by I. W. for Edward White, ... 1608. 4°, black letter, A—I in fours.

PASTOR.
The Faithfull Pastor His Sad Lamentation Over, heart-rending challenge and dreadful thunders against, Sharp reproof of, and seasonable warning to his Apostat-Flock. In a letter written by a French Minister, ... Now carefully translated ... Printed in the Year, 1687. 4°, A—G in fours. *B. M.*

PATERSON, WILLIAM, *Founder of the Bank of England.*
Proposals & Reasons for Constituting a Council of Trade. Edinburgh, Printed in the Year, 1701. 8°. *, 4 leaves: **, 4 leaves: A—Bb in fours.

PENN, WILLIAM.
The Frame of the Government of the Province of Pennsylvania in America: Together with certain Laws Agreed upon in England by the Governour and Divers Free-Men of the aforesaid Province. To be further Explained and Confirmed there by the first Provincial Council and Gene-

ral Assembly that shall be held, if they see meet. Printed in the Year MDCLXXXII. Folio, A—D, 2 leaves each, B 2 misprinted A 2.

The Preface is subscribed by Penn.

PETER, CHARLES, *Chirurgeon.*
New Observations on the Venereal Disease, With the True Way of Curing the same. The Second Edition Corrected and Enlarged. . . . London, Printed by S. D. and D. N. and are to be Sold by the Author, at his House in St. Martin's-Lane near Long-Acre, four doors from Newport-street, 1695. Price bound one Shilling. Sm. 8°, A—M in sixes.

PETITIONS.
The severall Humble Petitions of D. Bastwicke, M. Burton, M. Prynne. And of Nath. Wickins, Servant to the said Mr. Prynne. To the Honourable House of Parliament. Whereto is added the humble petitions of severall Friends of the said Mr. Prynne, and the acknowledgment prescrib'd to be made by Calvin Bruen, and the rest, in the Cathedrall Church of Chester, and Town-Hall thereof, for visiting the said Mr. Prynne. Printed in the Yeere, 1641. 4°, A—F 2 in fours.

PETRUCCI, LODOVICO.
Raccolta D'Alcvne Rime, Del Cavaliere Lodovico Petrvcci, Nobile Toscano, . . . Farrago Poematvm, Eqvitis Lvdovcci, Nobilis Tuscani, diversis locis et temporibus conscriptorum, & ad diversos Principes dedicatorum ; vna cum sylva, suarum Persecutionum. Oxoniæ, Excudebat Josephus Barnesius. 1613. 4°, A—Q in fours, Q 4 with *Errata*, besides a leaf of arms, &c , before the title. Dedicated to James I. *B. M.*

Some of the pieces are addressed to Oxonians ; others refer to Queen Elizabeth, Sir Thomas Bodley, Prince Charles, the Elector Palatine, &c. The text is in Latin and Italian on opposite pages.

Apologia Eqvitis Lodovici Petrvcci contra Calvmniatores svos Vna cvm Responsione ad libellum à Jesuitis contra Serenissimum Leonardum Donatvm Ducem Venetvm promulgatum. Excusum Londini. 1619. 4°. Title, 1 leaf : Dedication to James I., 1 leaf : a leaf accompanied by an emblem, containing verses on one side directed to Archbishop Abbot, Sir F. Bacon, &c, and on the other an attestation by the Bishop of Salisbury, dated 25 Oct. 1617 : engraved portrait of the author, with 4 lines of verse beneath, 1 leaf : To the Reader, a preface in Italian, dated by Petrucci from the Fleet prison, 10 July 1619 : A, with verses and emblems in copper, 4 leaves : A (repeated)—B in fours : C, 1 leaf : ¶, 3 leaves : D 2—F 2 in fours. *B. M.*

The book ends imperfectly on F 2 with the catchword *Ad re.* Petrucci was at one time a sergeant-major in the Venetian service in Crete.

PETYT, WILLIAM, *of the Inner Temple, Esquire.*
Miscellanea Parliamentaria : Containing Presidents 1. Of Freedom from Arrests. 2. Of Censures. . . . London, Printed for T. Basset . . . and J. Wickins . . . 1680. Sm. 8°. Title, preface, and contents, 3 leaves : A—S in twelves : T, 8 : besides a, 4 leaves.

PEYTON, SIR EDWARD.
The Divine Catastrophe of the Kingly Family of the House of Stuarts : . . . London : Printed for T. Warner, . . . MDCCXXXI. Price One Shilling. 8°. A, 2 leaves : B—I in fours : K, 2.

PHILIPPS, FABIAN.
Regale Necessarium : Or The Legality, Reason and Necessity of the Rights and Priviledges Justly Claimed by the Kings Servants, And which ought to be allowed unto them. . . . London, Printed for Christopher Wilkinson and are to be Sold at his Shop at the Sign of the Black-Boy in Fleet-street, . . . 1671. 4°. a—c in fours : *, 4 leaves, the last with the *Errata* : B—4 L in fours. Dedicated to the Duke of Ormond.

PIEDMONT.
Matchlesse Cruelte. . . . 1655.

The Narrative has a separate title as follows :—

A Collection or Narrative Sent to his Highness the Lord Protector of the Common-Wealth . . . Concerning The Bloody and Barbarous Massacres, Murthers, and other Cruelties, committed on many thousands of Reformed, or Protestants dwelling in the Vallies of Piedmont, by the Duke of Savoy's Forces, joyned therein with the French Army, and severall Irish Regiments. Published by Command of his Highness. Printed for H. Robinson, at the three Pigeons in St. Paul's Church-Yard, 1655.

PIERCY, HENRY.
Master Henry Piercies Letter to the Earle of Northumberland, and presented to the Parliament, June, 16. 1641. 1. Concerning the Bishops functions and votes. . . . Printed in the yeare, 1641. 4°, 4 leaves.

PLOUGH.
God Speede the Plovgh.
Genes. 26. 12.
Serens Iitzchak in terra illa, adeptus est, in eodem anno centuplas mensuras.

London Printed by Iohn Harison, dwelling in Pater noster row, at the signe of the Gray-hound, and are there to be solde. 1601. 4°, A—B in fours.

POOLEY, WILLIAM.
Part of the Sufferings of Leicestershire & Northamptonshire, By Informers and Priests. Also, God's Mercies Testified Unto, And Mans Cruelty Bore Witness against .... As it hath of late been manifested, and notoriously acted by the Priest and People of the Town of Farthinstone, in the County of North-hampton, ... London, Printed in the Year 1683. 4°, A—B 2 in fours.

POPERY.
A Pill to Pvrge ovt Popery : Or A Catechisme for Romish Catholikes ; Shewing, That Popery is contrary to the grounds of the Catholike Religion, and that therefore Papists cannot bee good Catholikes. London Printed for Beniamin Fisher, and are to be sold at his shop in Pater-noster-Rowe, at the Signe of the Talbot. 1624. Cum Priuilegio. 8°, A—C in eights. *B. M.*

> In the *Ordinary*, by W. Cartwright, written in 1634 (Hazlitt's *Dodsley*, xii. 272), Vicar Catchmey says to Christopher—
>> "I shall live to see thee stand in a play-house door with thy long box,
>> Thy half-crown library, and cry small books.
>> *Buy a good godly sermon, gentlemen—*
>> *A judgment shown upon a knot of drunkards :*
>> *A pill to purge out popery——*"
> I had not seen, when I edited Dodsley, a copy of this little volume.

A Blowe for the Pope. Touching the Popes prerogatiues. Extracted word for word out of the Booke of Martyres. Edinbvrgh, Printed by Iohn Wreittonne. 1631. 4°, A—F 3 in fours and the title. *B. M.*

The Popes Brief : Or Romes Inquiry after the death of their Catholiques here in England, during these Times of Warre : Discovered by two Commissions, ... Together with a Catalogue of the Vicars Generall, and Archdeacons under the Bishop of Chalcedon, ... With divers Letters concerning the same. Also severall Letters and Papers of the Lord Inchiquines in Ireland, ... London, Printed for Edw : Husbands. Decem. 7. 1643. 4°, A—E in fours.

The Unreasonableness and Impiety of Popery: In a Second Letter Written upon the Discovery of the Late Plot. London,
Printed for R. Chiswell, ... 1678. 4°, A—E in fours, E 4 blank.

The Creed of Pope Pius the IV. Or A Prospect of Popery taken from that Authentick Record. With short Notes. London, Printed for L. Meredith at the Angel in Amen Corner. 1687. 4°, A—B 2 in fours.

POVERTY.
The Prevention of Poverty ; Or, New Proposals Humbly Offered, For Enriching the Nation, Advancing His Majesties Revenue, and Great Advantage both of the City of London and Country ; By Increase of Trade from our own Manufactures, ... London, Printed for H. H. in the Year 1677. 4°, 4 leaves.

PRESBYTERY.
A Modell of the Government of the Church under the Gospel, by Presbyters. Proved out of the holy Scriptures, to be that one, onely uniform Government of the universall visible Church, and of all Nationall, Provinciall, Classicall and Congregationall Churches : which is according to the will and appointment of Jesus Christ. ... Composed by a Presbyterian Minister of the City of London, and approved by divers of his learned Brethren, and at their request Published. London, Printed for Tho. Vnderhill, ... 1646. 4°, A—E 2 in fours. Dedicated to the City and Inhabitants of London.

> "This is with deference the best Treatise on Church government that we have in the English language."—JAS. SUTCLIFFE.—*MS. note on back of title in an eighteenth-century hand.*

PRICE, DANIEL, *M.A. of Exeter College, Oxford.*
The Marchant. A Sermon Preached at Pavles Crosse Sunday the 24. of August, being the day before Bartholomew faire. 1607. At Oxford, Printed by Ioseph Barnes. 1608. 4°, A—E 2 in fours, besides the title and dedication "To the Honourable Companie of Merchants of the Cittie of London." *B. M.*

PRIESTS.
Historia Del Glorioso Martirio di Sedici Sacerdoti Martirizati in Inghilterra per la confessione, e difesa della fede Catolica, l'anno 1581, 1582, & 1583. Con vna prefatione, che dichiara la loro innocenza ; composta par quelli, che cõ essi praticauano mentre erano viui, ... Tradotta di lingua Inglese ... S'e aggiunto il martirio di due altri Sacerdoti, & vno secolare Inglesi [*sic*], martirizati l'anno 1577. & 1578. In

L

Macerata, ... 1583. 8°, A—O 4 in eights.

I am not at present aware of any English original of this narrative.

PRIMER.
The Primer in English and Latin after Salisburye vse, set out at length with manye Godly prayers. Newly imprinted by the assignes of John Wayland this presente yeare. An. 1558. Cum priuilegio ad Imprimendum solum. Sm. 8°, printed in red and black, with the Latin in Roman type in the margin. Title, Calendar, and first leaf with Paternoster. 8 leaves: ¶, 8 leaves: A—Kk in eights, Kk 7 with the colophon and last leaf blank. [Col.] Imprinted at London by the assines of John Wailand, forbiddyng all other to print or cause it to be printed this primer, or anye other. An. 1558 The . xxii of August.

PROTESTANT.
A Præfatory Discourse to A late Pamphlet, Entituled, A Memento for English Protestants, &c. Being An Answer to that Part of the Compendium, which reflects upon the Bishop of Lincoln's Book. Together with some Occasional Reflections on Mr. L'Estrange's Writings. London, Printed by Tho. Dawks, for the Author. 1681. 4°. A, 6 leaves, including an Advertisement to the Reader with the *Errata* on back and a dedication to Thomas Lord Bishop of Lincoln: B—C in fours: D, 5. *B. M.*

A Protestant of the Church of England, No Donatist. Or, Some Short Notes on *Lucilla and Elizabeth*. London, Printed for T. Basset, ... 1686. 4°, 4 leaves.

PSALMS.
The Book of Psalmes, Collected into English Meeter, by Thomas Sternhold, ... London: Printed by M. B. for the Company of Stationers, 1647. Cum Priuilegio. 4°, A—H in eights. In two columns. With the music.

PUGET DE LA SERRE, JEAN, *Historiographer of France*.
Histoire de l'Entree de la Reyne Mere dv Roy Tres-Chrestien, dans la Grande-Bretaigne. Enrichie de Planches. A Londres, Par Jean Raworth, pour George Thomason, & Octauian Pullen, a la Rose, au Cimetiere de Sainct Pavl. M.DC.XXXIX. Folio. Title, frontispiece, and dedication, 8 leaves: A—O, 2 leaves each. With plates accompanying the text, except the folding one of the procession through Cheapside and three others in B, D, and L.

PYM, JOHN, *M.P.*
A Letter Written out of the Country to Mr Iohn Pym Esquire, one of the Worthy Members of the House of Commons, February 1. Printed for W. Webb. M.DC.XLII 4°, 4 leaves.

R. R.
A Blast blown out of the North And Eechoing up towards the South, to mee the Cry of their Oppressed Brethren Being a Relation of some of the Suffering and other Exercises of several of the . . Quakers in and about Richmond, Massam Coverdale, Wensleydale and Swaledale and some others of the adjacent Part and Places in the North Riding of the County of York, since the beginning o the year 1660. ... Printed in the Yea 1680. 4°, A— in fours.

The copy employed ended imperfectly on F 3. The preface is signed *R. R.*, and informs us that portions of the narrative had been prepared some years prior to the date of publication.

RAGUENET, F.
Histoire D'Olivier Cromwel. A Paris Chez Claude Barbin, au Palais, . . M.DC.XCI. Avec Privilege Du Roy. Larg 4°, ã—I in fours: A—3 L in fours. With portrait of the Protector by C. Vermeulen Dedicated to Bossuet, Bishop of Meaux *B. M.*

Three editions the same year, two at Paris and one at Cologne (?).

RALEIGH, SIR WALTER.
Sir Walter Raleigh's Observations, Touching Trade & Commerce with the Hollander, and other Nations, as it was presented to K. James. Wherein is proved that our Sea and Land Commodities serve to inrich and strengthen other Countries against our owne. With other Passages of high Concernment. London, Printed by T. H. and are to be sold by William Sheeres. ... 1653. 12°. A, 6: B—I in twelves: E, 6. With a portrait by Vaughan. A 1-2 and E 5-6 are blank.

RANDOLPH, THOMAS.
Poems With the Muses Looking-Glass and Amyntas: Whereunto is added, The Jealous Lovers. By Tho. Randolph, M.A. ... The Fifth Edition ... Oxford Printed [by Henry Hall] for F. Bowman and are to be sold by John Crosley, Bookseller in Oxford. 1668. Sm. 8°, A—F in eights, A 1 with a half-title *Randolph Poems*.

This is an entirely distinct impression from that previously noticed (*Coll.* and

Notes, 1876, p. 351), although it has the same collation. The *Muses' Looking-Glass* has a London imprint. On the top of the title in this copy occurs: "Anglesey. March. 9. 1670. 2ˢʰ· 6." and the sides of the original calf binding have a crowned P in gold.

REGE SINCERA.
Observations both Historical and Morol upon the Burning of London, September 1666. With an Account of the Losses. And a most remarkable Parallel between London and Mosco, both as to the Plague and Fire. Also an Essay touching the Easterly-Winds . . . . London Printed by Thomas Ratcliffe, and are to be sold by Robert Pawlet at the Bible in Chancery-lane. 1667. 4°. A, 2 leaves : B—F 2 in fours.

REGICIDES.
An Exact and Impartial Accompt of the Indictment, Arraignment, Trial, and Judgment (according to Law) of Twenty nine Regicides, The Murtherers of His Late Sacred Majesty . . . London, Printed for Andrew Crook at the Green Dragon in St. Paul's Church-yard, and Edward Powel at the White-Swan in Little-Britain. 1660. 4°.

The copy employed ended imperfectly on B 4, containing B in fours and the title.

RELATION.
A True Relation of the Inhumane and Unparallel'd Actions, and Barbarous Murders of Negroes or Moors : Committed on three English-men in Old Calabar in Guinny. Of the Wonderful Deliverance of the Fourth Person, after he had endured Horrid Cruelties and Sufferings : who lately arrived in England, and is now in his Majesties Fleet. Together with a short, but true Account of the Customs and Manners and Growth of the Country, which is very Pleasant. London, Printed for Thomas Passinger . . . and Benjamin Hurlock . . . 1672. 4°, B—D 2 in fours, no A. *B. M.*

A true and Perfect Relation of the Great Fight Fought the fourth of Decem. 1676 between the Danish and Swedish Armies. London Printed in the Year 1676. 4°, 4 leaves. *B. M.*

REYNOLDS, JOHN, *of the Tower Mint, Assay-Master.*
A Brief and Easie way by Tables, To cast up Silver to the Standerd of XI. Ounces ij. Penny-weight. And Gold to the Standerd of XXII. Ounces. With Questions wrought by the Golden-Rule. Also by Decimall Tables. Calculated by John Reynolds of the Mynt in the Tower. London, Printed by Thomas Fawcet. 1651. Sm. 8°. Title and following leaf, 2 leaves : A—I in fours : Aa, 1 leaf : B—K 2 in fours. *B. M.*

In this copy at the end occurs in the author's autograph : "12 August 1653 Exᵈ by me John Reynolds." The same was the case with the only other copy which I have seen, if indeed this be not the same rebound.

RHEAD, ALEXANDER.
Description of the Body of Man. With the Practise of Chirurgery, and the use of three and fifty Instruments. By Artificiall Figures representing the members, and fit termes expressing the same. Set forth either to pleasure or to profit those who are addicted to this Study. Printed by Tho. Cotes, and are to be sold by Michael Sparke at the blew bible in Greene Arbor 1634. 4°, A—Y in fours, besides the extra leaves with the engravings : X—Ee in eights.

RIDLEY, MARK, *M.D., late Physician to the Duke of Moscow or Muscory.*
A Short Treatise of Magneticall Bodies and Motions. London. Printed by Nicholas Okes. 1613. 4°. A, 4 leaves, A 1 blank : a, 4 leaves : A—X in fours, X 4 blank. With the title engraved by Elstrack, a portrait of the author on the back of a 4, Eta : 34, An : 1594, and diagrams. *B. M.*

Magneticall Animadversions. Made by Marke Ridley, Doctor in Physicke. Vpon certaine Magneticall Advertisements, lately published, From Maister William Barlow. London, Printed by Nicholas Okes. 1617. 4°, A—F in fours. *B. M.*

R[OBINS] T[HOMAS.]
The Amazement of Future Ages : Or, The Swaggering World Turn'd Up-side down. By which means the Astonishing Curiosities, the Charming Varieties, the Pleasant Remarks, the Ingenious Devices, the Unspeakable Miracles, the Merry Journeys and Voyages, the Roaring Practices, the strange Prodigies, the Delightful Experiments, the Pretty Customs, Humours, Laws, Governments, Dwellings, Inhabitants of the World

> Under our Feet,
> Of the World on which we tread,
> And of the World in the Moon,

Are Faithfully Described, to the Satisfaction of every Curious Palate. Written by T. R. on purpose to make Delightful Sport and Pastime these Winter Nights. London, Printed for John Dunton, . . .

1684. Sm. 8°. A, 2 leaves: B—G in twelves. *B. M.*

ROTHMANN, JOHN, *M.D.*
Keiromantia: Or, The Art of Divining by the Lines and Signatures Engraven in the Hand of Man, By the Hand of Nature, Theorically, Practically. . . . Together With A Learned Philosophicall Discourse of the Soule of the World, and the Vniversall Spirit thereof. A Matchlesse Piece. Written Originally in Latine . . . now Faithfully Englished, By Geo: Wharton Esq. *Manus membrum Hominis loquacissimum.* London, Printed by J. G. for Nathaniel Brooke, at the Angell in Corne-Hill, 1652. 8°, A—N 4 in eights, A 1 occupied by a woodcut frontispiece. Dedicated to Elias Ashmole, Esq.

S. R.
The Counter-Scuffle. Whereunto is added The Counter-Rat. Written by R. S. London: Printed by J. C. for Andrew Crook. 1670. 4°, A—G in fours, G 4 blank. With a woodcut on title and a second at D 4.

SALMON, JAMES.
Blovdy Newes from Ireland, Or, The barbarous Crueltie By the Papists acted in that Kingdome. By putting men to the sword, deflowring Women, and dragging them up and downe the Streets, and cruelly murdering them, and thrusting their Speeres through their little Infants before their eyes, and carrying them up and downe on Pike-points, in great reproach, and hanging mens Quarters on their Gates in the Street at Armagh . . . and other Places in Ireland. As also, the Bloudy Acts of Lord Mack-queere their Ring-leader, and Cousin to that Arch-Rebell Mack-queere Generall to Tyron, in the time of Queene Elizabeth of never dying memory. Related by James Salmon, lately come from thence, who hath lived there with his wife and children, these 10 yeeres last past, and now to escape the Blond-thirsty Rebels, made an escape away by night; who is here resident in this City, Decemb. the 1. 1641. London, Printed for Marke Rookes, and are to be sold in Grubstreet, neere to the Flying Horse. 1641. 4°, 4 leaves. With a cut on the last page.

SANDERSON, WILLIAM, *Esquire.*
Graphice. The use of the Pen and Pencil. Or, The Most Excellent Art of Painting: In Two Parts. London, Printed for Robert Crofts, at the signe of the Crown in Chancery-Lane, under Serjeant's Folio. Title and verses by 2 leaves: a—b, 2 leaves title, verses by G. M. on the Charles I., 2 leaves: B—Z, With portrait of the auth(and of Charles I. by Faitho

SAVOY.
An Admonition giuen by on of Sauoyes Councel to his H ing to disswade him from against France. Translated by E. A. London Printed b 1589. 4°, A—C 2 in fours.

SCHOOL.
A School for Princes. Reflections upon three Co1 ceding the Death of Alexan Translated out of French b don, Printed for Thomas I Bible in St. Pauls Churcl 12°. A, 4 leaves, A 1 bla twelves.

SCOTLAND.
Decermina Qvaedam Phil Theses, Problemata, & Logicae, . . . Edinbvr[Ioannes Wreittoun. 1629. fours, and a leaf of F.
A series of academical th and argued at St. Andrews which the president was Jol Gibson-Craig, part 3, No cation copy to John, Lord I velvet, with initials in gold

From Scotland. Two copy The one sent from his Ma[to the Lord Keeper, . . Sept. 1. from a Gentleman concerning the proceedings ment in Scotland. Printed 1641. 4°, 4 leaves.

Good Counsell come from A Solemn and Seasonable \ Estates and Degrees of Per out the Land: For holding f and Covenant with England every thing that may prov tentation to the breach th Commissioners of the Gene . . . Edinbvrgh, Printed b . . . 1646. 4°, 4 leaves.

An humble Remonstrance c of Edinburgh to the Conv Estates of Scotland Concern Majestie, and the Kingdom With A Declaration touchi nant of the Kingdome, an for Peace. March 1. 1648. E. T. for the use of the Inh(

City of Edinburgh. 4°. A, 2 leaves: B—F in fours: G, 2.

A Necessary and Seasonable Testimony against Toleration and the present proceedings of Sectaries and their Abettors in England in reference to Religion and Government, with an Admonition and Exhortation unto their Brethren there, from the Commissioners of the Kirk of Scotland. As also The return of the Estates of the Parliament of Scotland thereupon, concurring with the said Testimony, and manifesting, that all the Members of Parliament have upon their solemn oath disclaimed the knowledge of or accession to the proceedings of the English Army, against his Majesty or the Members of Parliament in England, Jan. 18. 164⁸⁄₉. Together also with a letter from the said Commissioners to the Ministers in the Province of London, of the same date. Allowed of and entred according to Order. London, Printed by A. M. for Tho. Vnderhill at the Bible in Woodstreet. 1649. 4°, A—C in fours.

A Proclamation for calling together the Militia on this side of Tay, and the Fencible Men in some Shires. Edinburgh, the Thirtieth day of March, 1689. [Col.] Edinburgh, Printed in the Year, 1689. Folio, 4 leaves.

An Account of the Affairs of Scotland, In Answer to a Letter Written upon the occasion of the Address lately Presented to His Majesty by some Members of the Parliament of that Kingdom. [January, 1689-90.] 4°, A—F in fours, F 4 blank. Without a regular title.

This narrative is dated at the end from London, Dec. 1, 1689.

Overtures Offered to the Parliament, in which this Proposition is Advanced, That a small Summe Impos'd on the Nation, for Reforming Our Standard, and for Repairing the Losses of the African and Indian Company, &c. bestowed on the Method propos'd, will be of ten times more value to the Nation in General, &c. To almost the whole individual Persons in the Kingdom, than the samen Summ will be, it Retained in each Particulers Hand. Edinburgh, Printed by John Reid, in the Year MDCC. 4°. Title and preface, 2 leaves: A, 4 leaves.

A Further Explication of the Proposal relating to the Coyne. [1700.] 4°, A—C, 2 leaves each, and a leaf of D.

The Circumstances of Scotland Considered, With Respect to the present Scarcity of Money: Together with some Proposals for supplying the Defect thereof, and rectifying the Ballance of Trade. Edinburgh, Printed by James Watson in the year 1705. 4°, A—D 2 in fours.

The Actis of Parliament of the maist hie, maist excellent and michtie Prince, and our Souerane Lord Iames the sext, be the grace of God, King of Scottis, begun and haldin at Edinburgh, the xv. day of Decemb. The ʒeir of God ane thousand, fyue hunderth lxvii. ʒeir. Be our said Souerane Lord his derrest cousing & Uncle Iames Erle of Murray, Lord Abirnethie, &c. Regēt to our Souerane Lord, his Realme and Leigis. Togidder with the Prelatis, Erlis, Barronis, Commissioneris of Burrowis, specialie comperand in the said Parliament, as the thre estatis of this Realme. The saidis actis being oppinlie red, concludit, and votit in the said Parliament, to remane as perpetuall lawis to the subjectis of this Realme in all tymes cuming. [The rest of the page is occupied by a large and fine shield of arms with supporters, &c. Col.] Imprentit at Edinburgh be Robert Lekpreuik, Prentar to the kingis Maiestie, the vi. day of Aprill, the ʒeir of God ane thousand fyue hundreth thre scoir aucht ʒeiris. Folio, A—F in fours. B. M.

Of the two copies in the British Museum, one has the title slightly mutilated, and the other is titleless. The Gibsou-Craig copy had no title.

The Actis of the Parliament of the Maist hie, maist Excellent and Michtie Prince, and our Souerane Lord Iames the sext . . . . begune and haldin at Edinburgh, the xv. day of december. The ʒeir of God ane thousand, fiue hundreth lxvij. ʒeiris. Be our said Souerane Lordis derrest cousing . . . Imprentit at Edinburgh be Iohne Ros. M.D.LXXV. Cum Priuilegio Regali. Folio, A—F in fours. B. M.

In the Parliament of the richt Excellent, richt heich, and michtie Prince, James the Sext, . . . begonne at Striuiling, the xxviij. day of August, the ʒeir of God ane thousand fyue hundreth three scoir and ellouin ʒeirs, and in the Fyft ʒeir of his hienes Regne. Be his Maiesties derrest Gudschir vmquhile Mathew Erle of Lennox Lord Dernelie . . . The Actis, and Constitutiounis. . . . Imprentit at Sanctandrois be Robert Lekpreuik. Anno Do. M.D.LXXIII. Folio, A—C in fours. B. M.

In the Parliament of the Richt Excellent . . . Iames the sext, our Soueraue Lord, begune at Striuiling, the xxviij. day of August, the 3eir of God ane thousand fiue hundreth thre scoir and ellenin 3eiris, and in the Fyft 3eir of his hienes Regne. Be his Majesteis derrest Gudschir vmquhile Mathew Erle of Lennox, Lord Dernelie, &c. Regent to his hienes, his Realme, and leigis : And thre Estatis of this Realme. And endit, and concludit vpon the seuint day of September nixt thairefter following, be vmquhile Johne Erle of Mar. Lord Erskine &c. being Regent . . . The Actis and Constitutiounis following war concludit to be obscruit as Lawis in time cumming. Imprentit at Edinburgh be me Iohne Ros. M.D.LXXV. Cum Priuilegio Regali. Folio, A—D in fours. *B. M.*

In the Parliament Haldin at Striviling the xxv. day of Iulii, the zeir of God, ane thousand, fyue hundreth, thre scoir and auchtene zeiris. The Lawis, statutis and Constitutiounis ar denysit, ordanit, and concludit be the richt Excellent, . . . Iames the Sext, . . . Imprentit at Edinbrugh be Iohne Ros. Anno Do. 1579. Cum Priuilegio Regali. Folio, A—G 2 in fours : H, with the Proclamation for publishing these Acts and the colophon, 2 leaves. *B. M.*

In the Cvrrent Parliament Haldin at Edinburgh the xxii day of Maii, the zeir of God ane thousand, fyue hundreth, fourscoir zeiris, Thir Lawis, Statutis, & Constitutionis ar denisit, ordinit, and concludit be the richt excellent, . . . James the Sext, . . . ¶ Imprentit at Edinburgh be Alexander Arbuthnet, Printer to the Kingis Maiestie. Folio, A—D in fours. *B. M.*

In the Parliament Haldin and begun at Edinburgh the xxiiii. day of October, The Zeir of God, ane thousand, fyue hundreth, four scoir, ane Zeiris. Thir Lawis, Statutis, and Constitutiounis, ar dinisit, ordanit, and concludit, be the richt Excellent . . . Iames the Sext, . . . Imprentit at Edinburgh, be Henrie Charteris. Anno. M.D.LXXXII. Cum Priuilegio Regali. Folio, A—E in fours : F, 5. *B. M.*

An Assertion of the Government of the Church of Scotland, in the points of Ruling-Elders, and of the Authority of Presbyteries and Synods. With a Postscript . . . . Edinburgh, Printed for Iames Bryson, 1641. 4°. ¶ and ¶¶, 4 leaves each ; A—Dd in fours, Dd 4 blank : *Postscript*, B—F in fours.

Propositions Concerning Church-Government and Ordination of Ministers . . . Reprinted at London for Robert Bostock . . . 1647. 4°, A—F in fours.

Some Questions Resolved Concerning Episcopal and Presbyterian Governmen in Scotland. . . . London, Printed fo the Author, and are to be Sold by Randal Taylor, . . . 1690. 4°, B—D ii fours, besides the title and preface.

The Psalms of David in Meeter : Newl Translated, ... Allowed by the au thority of the General Assembly of th Kirk of Scotland, . . . Edinburgh, Printe by Thomas Brown, one of His Majestie Printers : 1675. Cvm Priuilegio. Smal obl. 12°, A—K in twelves.

Delitiæ Poetarvm Scotorvm hujus æv Illvstrivm. [Pars Prior et altera.] Am sterdami, . . . CIƆ. IƆ CXXXVII. Sm. 8° *Pars Prior*, pp. 699, including title an dedication to Sir John Scot of Scotstarvet *Pars altera*, pp. 573.

Edited by Arthur Jonston.

SEDGWICK, WILLIAM.
The Leaves of the Tree of Life : For th healing of the Nations. Opening all th wounds of this Kingdome, and of ever party, and applying a remedy to them By which we come to a right understand ing between King and Parliament. . . By the light of God shining upon Willia Sedgwick. Do you not know that th Saints shall judge the World ? Londo Printed by H. [*sic*] for Giles Calvert . . 1648. 4°. Title, 1 leaf : Preface, leaves : *Errata*, &c., 1 leaf : B—Q i fours.

SEDLEY, SIR CHARLES, *Baronet.*
Antony and Cleopatra : A Tragedy. A it is Acted at the Dukes Theatre. Wri ten by the Honourable Sir Charles Sedley Baronet. . . . London, Printed for Richar Tonson. . . . MDCLXXVII. 4°. A, 2 leaves B—I in fours.

SELLER, JOHN, *Hydrographer in Ord nary to the King.*
The Coasting Pilot. Describing the Se Coasts, Channels, Soundings, Sand Shoals, Rocks, & dangers: The Baye Roads, Harbours, Rivers, Ports, Buoye Beacons, and Sea-marks, upon the Coast of England Flanders and Holland Wit directions to bring a Shipp into any Ha bour on the said Coasts. Being furnishe

with new Draughts, Charts, and Descriptions, gathered from ȳ experience and practise of diverse Able and Expert Navigators of our English Nation. Collected and Published by John Seller. . . . And are to be sold at his Shopps at the Hermitage in Wapping : And in Exchange-Alley in Corne-Hill. . . . Cum Privilegio. [About 1680.] Folio, A—N, 2 leaves each : O, 1 leaf, besides the engraved title and ten maps engraved by F. Lamb, &c. *B. M.*

> Under the same press-mark (1804, b.) occurs a set of 27 volumes of Seller's publications, in which he was partly concerned as author.

SETTLE, DIONYSE.

A true reporte of the laste voyage into the West and Northwest regions, &c. 1577. worthily atchieued by Captaine Frobisher of the sayde voyage the first finder and Generall. With a description of the people there inhabiting, and other circumstances notable. Written by Dionyse Settle, one of the companie in the sayde voyage, and seruant to the right Honourable the Earle of Cumberland. *Nil mortalibus arduum est.* ¶ Imprinted at London by Henrie Middleton. Anno. 1577. Sm. 8°, 32 leaves or A—H in eights. Dedicated to George Clifford, Earl of Cumberland. With verses on the back of the title by Abraham Fleming.

> Fifty copies reprinted at New York, 4°, 1868, by Mr. Bartlett, probably from the Carter-Brown copy.

La Navigation dv Capitaine Martin Forbisher Anglois, és regions de west & Nordwest, en l'année M.D.LXXVII. Contenant les mœurs & façons de viure des Peuples, & habitans d'icelles, auec le portraict de leurs habits & armes, & autres choses memorables & singulieres, du tout incognues par deça. M.D.LXXVIII. Pour Anthoine Chuppin. 8°, A—E in eights, besides the folded plate headed : *Le Portraict des trois Sauuages admenez en Angleterre, leurs habits, armes, tentes & bateaux.* Dedicated by Nicholas Pithou, Sieur de Cham-Gobert, the translator, to M. de Hault, &c. *Grenv. Coll.*

> The "discription of the purtrayture and shape of those strange kinde of people," &c., was separately licensed to John Allde, to be printed in English, Jan. 30, 1577-8, but it does not seem to be known.

SHADWELL, THOMAS.

A True Widow, Acted by the Duke's Servants. Written by Tho. Shadwell. *Odi profanum* . . . London, Printed for Benjamin Tooke, . . . 1679. 4°, A—L in fours, besides the *Dramatis Personæ.* Dedicated by the Author to Sir Charles Sedley, from London, Feb. 16, 167⅞.

SHAKESPEAR, WILLIAM.

Venus and Adonis. *Vilia* [sic]. . . . London, Printed by Elizabeth Hodgkinsonne. For F. Coles, T. Vere, I. Wright, and J. Clark. 1675. Sm. 8°, A—D 4 in eights, D 4 blank.

> Putticks, April 12, 1889 ; badly folded and cut.
> This is a roughly printed chapman's edition, but curious as being the latest appearance of the poem in a separate shape. The dedication to the Earl of Southampton is preserved.

SHAW, JOHN.

The Blessednes of Marie the Mother of Iesvs. [Quot. from Luke i. 28, 45, 48.] London, Printed by Richard Field dwelling in Great Woodstreete. 1618. Sm. 8°, A—K 2 in eights. Dedicated to Lady Dorothy Zouch, wife of Sir Edward Zouch of Oking. With two sets of verses at the end : "The Comfort of a Christian" and "The Complaints of a Sinner." *B. M.*

SHEPHERDS.

The Shepherd's Kalender : Or, The Citizens & Country Man's Daily Companion : Treating of many Things that are Useful and Profitable to Man-kind, with above Two Hundred wonderful Curiosities, never before Published. Also, A Discourse of the Eclipses . . . An Account of the Luckey and Unluckey Days throughout the Year. The Mosaick Wand to find out Hidden Treasure. The Calculation of Nativities, and to Resolve all Lawful Questions. To which is Added, The Country Man's Almanack, . . . Being above Forty Years Study and Experience of a Learned Shepherd. The Second Edition, with Additions. Printed by C. [and ?] A. Milbourn, for Tho. Norris, at the Looking-Glass on London-Bridge. Price Bound One Shilling. 12°, A—G in twelves. With a frontispiece and cuts.

> The Preface is signed J. S., *i.e.*, John Shirley, author of this abridgment.

SHERINGHAM, ROBERT, *M.A., late Fellow of Gonvill College, Cambridge.*

The King's Supremacy Asserted : . . . The Third Edition Corrected, Amended and Enlarged, by Robert Sheringham, . . . The Author of *Codex Ionu & Disceptatio de gentis Anglorum Origine.* London, Printed for Jonas Hart and Charles Morden in Cambridge. 1682. 4°, A—Q in fours. Q 4 blank, and b, 4 leaves. Dedicated to Charles II.

SHERLOCK, WILLIAM, D.D., *Master of the Temple.*
The Case of the Allegiance due to Soveraign Princes, Stated and Resolved, According to Scripture and Reason, And the Principles of the Church of England, With a more particular Respect to the Oath lately enjoyned, of Allegiance to their Present Majesties, K. William and Q. Mary. London: Printed for W. Rogers, ... 1691. 4°, A—K 2 in fours, besides title and *Imprimatur.*

The Case of the Allegiance due to Soveraign Princes, Further Consider'd, and Defended: With a more particular Respect to the Doctrine of Non-Resistance and Passive-Obedience. Together with a Seasonable Persuasive to our New Dissenters. London, Printed for W. Rogers, ... 1691. 4°. Title and half-title, 2 leaves: B—E 2 in fours.

SINCLAIR, GEORGE, *sometime Professor of Philosophy in the University of Glasgow.*
The Principles of Astronomy and Navigation: Or, A Clear, Short, yet Full Explanation, of all Circles of the Celestial, and Terrestrial Globes, and of their Uses, ... To which is Added A Discovery of the Secrets of Nature, which are found in the Mercurial Weather-Glass, &c. As also A New Proposal for Buoying up a Ship of any Burden from the Bottom of the Sea. Edinburgh, Printed by the Heir of Andrew Anderson ... 1688. 8°. A, 4 leaves: B—L 4 in eights, L 4 blank. Dedicated to Magnus Prince, Lord Provost of Edinburgh.

SMITH, GEORGE, *Gentleman.*
Great Britains Miserie, With the Causes and Cure ... The second edition, corrected and enlarged by the Author ... London Printed by E. P. for Lawrence Chapman and Francis Coles, ... 1645. 4°, A—H in fours: I, 5.

SMITH, J., *Gentleman.*
Profit and Pleasure United: Or, The Husbandman's Magazine. Being A most Exact Treatise of Bulls, Oxen, Cows, Calves, Horses, ... Together with Easie and Plain Rules for improving Arrable and Pasture-Lands, ... The Manner of ordering Flax, Hemp, Saffron and Licoresh: With Directions for the Encreasing and Preserving of Bees, ... To which is Added, The Art of Hawking, Hunting, Angling, and the Noble Recreation of Ringing. London: Printed for J. Blare, ... 1704. 12°, A—G in twelves: A 1 blank or with a frontispiece.
Published at 1s.

SMITH, JOHN, *Clock-Maker.*
The Art of Painting. Wherein is included The whole Art of Vulgar Painting, according to the best and most approved Rules for preparing, and laying on of Oyl Colours. The whole Treatise being so Full, Compleat, and so Exactly fitted to the meanest Capacity, that all Persons whatsoever may by the Directions contained therein be sufficiently able to Paint in Oyl Colours not only Sun-Dials, but also all manner of Timber Work, whether Poles, Pales, Pallisades, Gates, Doors, Windows, Wainscotting, Border Boards for Gardens, or what ever else requires either Use, Beauty, or Preservation from the Violence or Injury or Weather. Composed by John Smith Philomath. London, Printed for Samuel Crouch ... 1676. Sm. 8°, A—G 2 in eights. *B. M.*

The Art of Painting in Oyl .... The second Impression, with some Alterations, and many useful Additions. London: Printed for Samuel Crouch, ... 1687. Sm. 8°. A, 6 leaves: B—H 2 in eights. *B. M.*

The Art of Painting in Oyl. Wherein is included each particular Circumstance relating to the best and most approved Rules for Preparing, mixing, and working of Oyl Colours. ... The Fourth Impression with some Alterations, and many Matters added, ... To which is now added, The whole Art and Mystery of Colouring Maps, and other Prints, with Water Colours. London: Printed for Samuel Crouch, ... 1705. Sm. 8°. A, 4 leaves: B—H in eights. *B. M.*

SMITH, THOMAS.
The Armies Last Propositions to the Commons of England: Wherein they declare, Their further Resolution, touching the Confines of London, and their marching on towards the said City; for the Seizing of His Majesty in his Royall Palace at Westminster, and securing of the Rights, Liberties, and Peace of the Kingdome. June 28. 1647. ... London: Printed for Edward Simpson . 1647. 4°, 4 leaves.
This is a letter subscribed *Tho. Smith,* and dated from St. Albans, June 26, 1647.

SPAIN.
The Succession of Spain Discuss'd. With a Project of reconciling all the present Pretensions to that Crown, for the Advantage of Europe, And England in particular; And the Necessity of a War, In case an Accommodation be rejected. Dublin Re-Printed by John Brocas in School-House-Lane, for John Ware, over

against Michaels Church in High-street, Bookseller, 1701. 4°, A—B in fours. *B. M.*

SPECULUM.
Speculum spiritualiū: in quo nō solum de vita actiua et cōtemplatiua: verum etiā de vitiis / quibus humana mens inquinatur / ac virtutibus quibus in deū accēditur: ppulchre tractatur. cū varijs exemplis... Additur insuper et opusculum Ricardi Hampole de emēdatione vite: ac de regula bene viuendi. Venale habet Londonie apud bibliopolas in cimiterio Seti Pauli ad signū stissime ac Idinidue trinitatis. 4°. Title, &c., 10 leaves: a—z in eights, followed by two sheets of eight irregularly signed: A, 10 leaves. In two columns. [Col.] Opera predicta in alma Parisioř academia p wollſgangū hopyliñ sunt impressa: sumptibus et expensis honesti viri Guilhelmi brettoñ ciuis Londoñ. Annodn̄i millesimo quingentesimo decimo.

Sotheby's, March 29, 1889, No. 584, imperfect.

SPOTTISWOOD, JAMES.
The Execvtion of Nesebech and the confyning of his Kinsman Tarbith. Or A Short Discovrse, shewing the difference betwixt damned Usvrie, and that which is Lawfull. Wherevnto there is subioyned an Epistle of that Reuerend and judicious Divine Mr John Calvin, touching that same argument: faithfully translated out of Latine. Edinbvrgh, Printed by Andro Hart, For Christopher Pounder, Stationer in Norwich, and are to be solde at his Shop, at the Signe of the Angell In the Yeere of our Lord 1616. 4°, A—G in fours, G 4 blank. *B. M.*

STANDSFIELD, PHILIP.
The Tryal of Philip Standsfield Son to Sir James Standsfield of New-Milns, For the Murder of his Father, and other Crimes Libel'd against him. Published by Authority. Edinburgh, Printed by the Heir of Andrew Anderson... Anno Dom. 1688. Folio, A—L, 2 leaves each.

STATIONERS' COMPANY.
The Orders, Rules, and Ordinances. Ordained... by the Master... of the Mystery and Art of Stationers.... London: Printed for the Company of Stationers. 1682. 4°, A—B 2 in fours. *B. M.*

STATUTES.
A table to all the Statutes made in the tyme of the most victorious Reigne of kynge Edward the sixte. Londini in ædibus Thomæ Bertheleti. Anno verbi incarnati. M.D.LIII. Cvm priuilegio... Folio. *B. M.*

The Table occupies four leaves; the remainder of the volume consists of the original editions from the press of Grafton bound up together.

A Table to all the Statutes made from the beginning of the raigne of Kyng Edwarde the . vi. vnto this present . xii. yeare of the reigne of oure moste gratious and soueraigne Ladye Queene Elizabeth. In ædibus Richardi Tottelli. Cum priuilegio. Folio. *B. M.*

The Table makes six leaves; the rest of the book is a collection of the separate impressions printed by Grafton, Cawood, &c., of the Statutes within the specified period.

There is no doubt that these year-books were kept in print, and that there was scarcely any of which there are not repeated issues. Large editions were also probably made, and copies are still sufficiently common.

Anno Primo Edwardi Sexti. Statvtes made in the Parlamente begon at Westminster the fowerthe daye of Nouember, in the firste yeare of the reigne of our moste dreade Soueraine lorde Edward the . vi. By the grace of God, kinge of Englande, Fraunce, and Irelande, defendour of the faithe, and of the Churche of Englande, and also of Irelande in earthe the supreme hed: and from thence continued to the xxiiii. daye of December then nexte ensuyng, that is to saye in the first Sesion of the same Parlamente as foloweth. [Col.] God saue the king. ¶ Excusum Londini in ædibus Richardi Graftoni Regii Impressoris. Anno. M.D.xlviii. ¶ Cum priuilegio ad imprimendum solum. Folio, A—E in sixes: F, 8. *B. M.*

Anno Secvndo Et Tertio Edovardi Sexti. Actes made in the Session of this present Parlament, holden vppon prorogation at Westminster, the fourthe daye of Nouembre, in the seconde yeare of... Edwarde the . vi. ... and there continued and kepte to the . xiiii. daye of Marche in the . III. yere of our said soueraigne Lorde, as foloweth. [Col.] Richardvs Graftonvs Typographus Regius excudebat. Anno domini. 1552. Cum priuilegio... Folio, A—G in sixes: H, 4: I—K in sixes: L, 4: M, 6. *B. M.*

Anno III. & IIII. Edwardi Sexti. Actes made in the Session of this present Parlament, holden vpon prorogation at Westmynster, the . iiii. daye of Nouembre, in the thirde yere of... Edward the . vi. ... and there continued and kept to the first daye of Februarye, in the . iiii. yere of the reigne . . . [Col.] ¶ Imprinted at London by Richard Grafton, printer to the Kynges Maiestie. 1553 Cum priuilegio . . . Folio, A—D in sixes: E—F in fours. *B. M.*

Anno Qvinto et Sexto Edvardi Sexti. Actes made in the Session of this preset parlamente, holden vpon prorogation at Westminster, the . xxiii. daye of Jannarye, in the fyueth yeare of . . . Edwarde the . vi. . . . and there continued and kepte tyll the . xv. daye of Apryll, in the vi. yeare of the reygne . . . [Col.] Richardvs Graftonvs typographus Regius excudebat Mense Iunii. Anno. M.D.LII. Cum priuilegio . . . Folio, A—E in sixes: F, 3. *B. M.*

Two editions the same year.

Anno Septimo Edvvardi Sexti. Actes made in the Parliament holden at Westminster, the first daie of Marche, in the . VII. yere of the reigne of . . . Edwarde the . vi. . . . And there continued to the dissolution of the same being the laste daie of the saied moneth of Marche, as foloweth. [Col.] Londini in aedibus Richardi Graftoni typographi Regii excusum. Mense Aprilis. Anno Domini. M.D.LIII. Cum priuilegio . . . Folio, A—F in sixes: G—H in fours. *B. M.*

> Grafton printed this 7th year more than once; and Herbert, p. 1462, notices from a copy in his own possession another from the press of John Oswen at Worcester, printed in folio the same year, with this colophon: At Worcestre [by John Oswen] Printer appointed by the Kinges Maiestie, for the Principalitie of Wales, and Marches of the same. Anno Domini. M.D.LIII. Cum priuilegio [ad imprimendum] solum. I have not seen this issue, and cannot therefore say whether it is an independent impression, or merely one of Grafton's copies with Oswen's imprint inserted.

Anno Mariae Primo. Actes made in the Parlyament begoune and holden at Westminster the seconde daye of Apryll, in the firste yeere of the raygne of oure moste gratious Soueraygne Ladye, Marye by the grace of God . . . and there continued and kepte to the dissolution of the same, beynge the v. daye of Maye then next ensuing as foloweth. Cum priuilegio Regiae Mariae. [Col.] excusum Londini in aedibus Iohannis Cawodi Typohraphi [sic] regiae Maiestatis. Anno. M.D.Liiij. Mense Maio. Cum priuilegio Reginae Mariae. Folio, A—B in sixes: C—D in fours. *B. M.*

> Cawood printed this at least twice; in the present edition he has not done himself much credit as royal typographer. What

is evidently a reimpression is in the British Museum; press-mark, 506. d. 5.

7

Anno Mariae Primo. Actes made in the Parliament begoune and holden at Westminster the . v. daye of October, in the first yere of the reigne of . . . Mary . . . and there continued to the . xxi. day of the same moneth, that is to saye, in the fyrst session of the saide parliament, as foloweth. [Col.] Excvsvm Londini in aedibus Iohannis Cawodi typographi Regiae Maiestatis. Anno M.D.LIIII. Cvm priuilegio. . . . Folio. A, 5 leaves, including first title and the Act repealing certain treasons, &c.: B—D in sixes: E, 4, the last leaf with the colophon only. *B. M.*

Anno primo et secūdo Philippi & Mariae. Actes made at a Parliament begon and holden at Westminster the . vi daye of Nouember in the firste and secōd year of the reigne of our soueraigne Lorde and Lady, Philippe and Marye by the grace of God, kinge and Queen of England, . . . Princes of Spayne, . . . And there contynued and kept, vntyll the dissolution of the same, beynge the xvi. daye of January then next ensuing, were enacted as foloweth. Cum priuilegio. . . . [Col.] excusum Londini in aedibus Iohannis Cawodi Typographi Regiae Maiestatis. Anno. M.D.LV. Folio. A in sixes: B, 4: C—F in sixes. *B. M.*

Anno Secundo et Tertio Philippi & Mariae. Actes made at a Parlyamente begon and holdē at Westmister the . xxi. daye of October, in the seconde and thyrd yeare of . . . Phylyppe and Marye . . . and there continued and kepte vntyl the dissolution of the same, being the . ix. day of December then next ensuing, there enacted as foloweth. Cum priuilegio . . . [Col.] God saue the kyng and the Quene. Excusum Londini in aedibus Iohannis Cawodi Typographi Regiae Maiestatis. Anno. M.D.LV. . . . Folio, A—I in sixes: K, 4. *B. M.*

Anno quarto et quinto Philippi & Mariae. Actes made at a Parliament begoun and holden at Westminster the . xx day of January in the fourthe and fifte yeare of . . . Philippe and Marye . . . And there contynued and kept, vntyll the . vii. day of Marche then next folowing, . . . [Col.] ¶Excusum Londini in AEdibvs Iohannis Cawodi. Tipographi Regiae Maiestatis. Anno. M.D.LVIII. Cum priuilegio . . . Folio, A—G in sixes, G 6 blank. *B. M.*

Anno Qvinto Regine Elizabethe. At the Parliament holden at Westmynster, the . xii. of January, in the fifth yere of . . . Elizabeth . . . To the hygh pleasure of Almyghty God, and the weale publique of this Realme, were enacted as foloweth. Anno. 1563. [Col.] Imprinted at London in Poules Churcheyarde, by Rycharde Jugge, and John Cawood, Prynters to the Queenes Maiestie. Cum priuilegio. . . . Folio, A—M in sixes : the *Act of Subsidy*, A—B in sixes : C, 8. *B. M.*

Anno Quinto Reginæ Elizabethe. ¶ At the Parliament holden at Westminster the . xii. daie of Ianuarie, in the fifth yeare of the raigne of our Soueraigne Lady Elizabeth, . . . 1563. [Col.] Imprinted at London by Richard Iugge, Printer to the Queenes Maiestie. Cum priuilegio. . . . Folio, A—L in sixes : M, 7 : *Act of Subsidy*, A—C in sixes. *B. M.*

¶ Anno octauo Reginæ Elizabethe. At the Parl'ament by prorogation holden at Westminster the last day of September, in the eight yeare. . . . Anno Christi. 1566. [Col.] Imprinted at London by Newgate market next vnto Christes Church, by Richard Iugge, Printer to the Queenes Maiestie. Cum priuilegio. . . . Folio, A—B in sixes : C, 4 : no D—E : F, 4 leaves. *B. M.*

Sign. D—E appear to have been omitted, as the capitulation is consecutive.

Anno. xiij. Reginæ Elizabethe. At the Parliament begunne and holden at Westminster the seconde of April, in the . xiii. yere of the raigne of our most gratious soueraigne Lady Elizabeth, . . . 1571. [Col.] God saue the Queene. No printer's name. [London, R. Jugge, 1571-2.] Folio, A—L in sixes : M, 4. *B. M.*

Anno. xviij. Reginæ Elizabethe. At this present Session of Parliament by prorogation holden at Westminster the . VIII. day of February, in the . xviii. yeare of the raigne of our most gratious soueraigne Lady Elizabeth, . . . 1572. [Col.] Imprinted at London by Richarde Iugge, printer to the Queenes Maiestie. . . . Folio, A—I in sixes : K, 8. *B. M.*

STEERE, RICHARD.
The History of the Babylonish Cabal : Or The { Intrigues, Progression, Opposition, Defeat, and Destruction } of the Daniel-Catchers ; In a Poem.
—*Nec Lex est justior ulla, Quam Necis Artifices arte perire sua.*—Ovid.

London, Printed for Richard Baldwin in the Old-Bayley. 1682. 4°. Dedicated to Anthony, Earl of Shaftesbury.

The copy used ended imperfectly on B 4. The author speaks of having produced a similar piece in prose.

STRUTHER, WILLIAM, *Preacher at Edinburgh.*
A Looking Glasse For Princes and People. Delivered in a Sermon of Thanksgiving for the Birth of the hopefull Prince Charles. . . . Printed at Edinburgh, by the Heires of Andro Hart. 1632. 4°. *, 4 leaves : A—O in fours.

A Looking Glasse for Princes and Popes, Or A Vindication of the sacred Authoritie of Princes, from the Antichristian vsurpation of the Popes. By the same Authour M. William Struther . . . Edinburgh, Printed by the Heires of Andro Hart. 1632. 4°. Title and Table, 2 leaves : ¶, 4 leaves : ¶¶, 2 leaves : A—Z 2 in fours, Z 2 blank.

These two books appear to have been issued together.

STUBBE or STUBBS, HENRY, *of Christ Church, Oxford.*
Horæ Subsecivæ : Seu Propheticæ Jonæ et Historiæ Svsannæ Paraphrasis Græca Versibus Heroicis. [Quot from Pliny Jun. *Ep. ad Fuscum.*] Londini, Typis Du-Gardianis. Anno Dom. 1651. Sm. 8°. A, 4 leaves : B. 8 : C, 8 : D, 4. Dedicated to Dr. Busby. A 1 is occupied on the *recto* by the arms of the Commonwealth and on the reverse by an encomium in Greek by W. James of Westminster School. Lat. and Gr. *B. M.*

SURREY.
The Division of the County of Surrey into Six Classicall Presbyteries. Together with the Names of the Ministers and others fit to be of that Classis. Approved of by the Committee appointed thereunto by both Houses of Parliament. London, Printed by A. M. for Christopher Meredith. . . . 1648 [March 6, 1647-8.] 4°, 4 leaves. *B. M.*

TAYLOR, JOHN, *the Water-Poet.*
The Vnnaturall Father : Or, The cruell Murther committed by Iohn Rowse of the Towne of Ewell, ten miles from London, in the County of Surrey, vppon two of his owne Children. With his Prayer and Repentance in Prison, his Arraignement and Iudgement at the Sessions, and his Execution for the said fact at Croydon, on Munday the second of Iuly. 1621. London printed for I. T. and H.G. 1621.

4°, A—C in fours. With a large cut on the title. In prose, except some curious verses at the end. *B. M.*

> Licensed to John Trundle and Henry Gosson, 10th July 1621.

The Water-Cormorant His Complaint: Against a Brood of Land-Cormorants. Diuided into fourteene Satyres. By Iohn Taylor. London, Printed by George Eld. 1622. 4°, A—F in fours, title on A 2. With a curious woodcut Diagram on the title exhibiting the fourteen kinds of land-cormorants. In verse. *B. M.*

TESTAMENT.
Testament Newydd Ein Harlwydd A'Nhiachawdr Jesv Grist. Rhvf. 1. 16.... Printiedig yn Llundain gan Matthew Symmons ... 1647. 12°, A—Kk in twelves. *B. M.*

TENTZEL, ANDREAS.
Medicina Diastatica Or Sympatheticall Mumie: Containing, Many mysterious and hidden Secrets in Philosophy and Physick.

By the { Construction, Extraction, Transplantation, and Application } of Microcosmicall & Spirituall Mumie.

Teaching the Magneticall cure of Diseases at Distance, &c. Abstracted from the Works of Dr Theophr. Paracelsus: By the labour and industry of Andrea Tentzelius, Phil. & Med. Translated out of the Latine By Ferdinando Parkhurst, Gent. [Quot.] London, Printed by T. Newcomb for T. Heath, ... 1653. 8°, A—T in eights, and (a) 4 leaves, (a 2) apparently misprinted (a 3). Dedicated by Parkhurst to Basil, Earl of Denbigh. With commendatory verses by Roger Ellis, Esq., and others, and a prose address by W. Lilly to the translator. *B. M.*

> On the title-page of a second copy before me occurs, "E Libris Joannis Reynoldi Medicinæ, Astrologiæ, &c. studiosi. 1715."
> The original Latin appeared at Jena, 4°, 1629.

TINDALL, MATTHEW, *LL.D.*
An Essay Concerning the Laws of Nations, and the Rights of Soveraigns. With an Account of what was said at the Council-Board by the Civilians upon the Question, Whether their Majesties Subjects taken at Sea acting by the late King's Commission, might not be looked on as Pirates? With Reflections upon the Arguments of Sir T. P. and Dr. Ol. London, Printed for Richard Baldwin ... 1694. 4°, B—E in fours: F, 1 leaf: and the title.

TITHES.
An Item against Sacriledge: Or Sundry Queries Concerning Tithes. Wherein is held forth, The Propriety and Title that Ministers have to them.... Collected and composed by one that hath no Propriety in Tithes.... London, Printed by Abraham Miller for Thomas Vnderhill ... 1653. 4°, 4 leaves.

TORRIANO, GIOVANNI.
Select Italian Proverbs: The most significant, very usefull for Travellers, and such as desire that Language. The same newly made to speak English, and the obscurest places with Notes illustrated, usefull for such as happily aim not at the Language, yet would see the genius of the Nation. By Gio. Torriano, ... Sen. *Etiam in pusillis rebus est sua gratia.* Printed by R. D. Printer to the Vniversitie of Cambridge, and are to be sold by J. Martin and J. Ridley, at the Castle in Fleet-street by Ram-ally. 1649. Sm. 8°, A—E 6 in twelves, E 6 blank. Dedicated to Mildmay, Earl of Westmoreland. *B. M.*

Della Lingua Toscana-Romana. Or, An Introduction to the Italian Tongve. Containing such grounds as are most immediately useful, and necessary for the speedy and easie attaining of the same. As also A new store House of proper and choice Dialogues Most Useful for such as desire the speaking part, and intend to travel into Italy, or the Levant.... By Gio: Torriano, ... London: Printed for J. Martin, and J. Allestrye, ... 1657. 8°, A—V in eights: the Dialogues, A—Q in eights: R, 4 leaves. *Trin. Coll. Camb.*

The Italian Reviv'd: Or, the Introdvction to the Italian Tongve ... London, Printed by T. R. for J. Martyn, ... 1673. 8°. A, 4 leaves: B—Z in eights. *B. M.*

Mescolanza Dolce di Varie Historiette, Favole Morali & Politiche, Facetie, Motti & Burli ... Da Gio. Torriano, Mastro di Lingue. Con Givnta di Dialoghi novi, non più stampati, & tradotti in Lingua Inglese dal medesimo. Stampata in Londra, Appresso Tomaso Roycroft, ad istanza di Giovanni Martino, ... 1673. 8°, A—K in eights. Without prefixes. *B. M.*

> Bound up with the Turner copy of Torriano's *Italian Revived*, 1673, and it doubtless forms part of the book, as in the later edition of 1689.

The Italian Reviv'd: Or, The Introduction to the Italian Tongue. Containing such Grounds as are most immediately useful and necessary for the speedy and easie attaining of the same. As also a new Store-House of Proper and Choice Dialogues, ... Together with the Modern Way of Addressing Letters ... With Alterations and Additions. By Gio. Torriano, an Italian, And Professor of the Italian Tongue, &c. in London. London, Printed for R. Chiswell, T. Sawbridge and R. Bentley, 1689. 8°, A—Z in eights: The *Mescolanza*, as in the edit. of 1673, with a new title, dated 1688, A—K 4 in eights. *B. M.*

TRANSACTIONEER.
The Transactioneer. With some of his Philosophical Fancies: In Two Dialogues. London; Printed for the Booksellers of London and Westminster. 1700. 8°, A—M in fours.

> A satire on the compiler of the *Philosophical Transactions*. The first dialogue is between a Gentleman and a Virtuoso, the second between a Gentleman and a Transactioneer.

TREATISE.
A Godly Newe short treatyse instructyng euery parson, howe they shulde trade [sic] theyr lyues in ȳ Imytacyon of vertu / and ȳ shewyng of vyce, ... Imprited At London by me Robert Stoughton, Dwelling with in Ludgate, at the sygne of the Bysshoppes Myter: [At the end is added:] Anno. 1548. the . 23. October. Sm. 8°, A—B in eights: c, 1 leaf.

A briefe treatise contayning many proper Tables and easie Rules: verie necessarie and needefull, for the vse and commoditie of all people, collected out of certaine learned mens workes. Perused, corrected, and augmented by W. W. The contents whereof, the leafe that followeth doth expresse. Newely set forth and allowed according to the Queenes maiesties iniunctions. At London, Printed by Iohn Charlwood, for Thomas Adams. 1591. 8°, black letter. Title and three other leaves: A—H 4[?] in eights.

> The present copy ended imperfectly on H 3.
> This curious volume, of which there were several editions, comprises a Calendar, lists of counties and towns, a table of the tides, the fairs and highways, the wards and churches of the City of London, and other information.

TURNER, ROBERT, *of Barnstaple.*
Roberti Tvrneri Devonii Oratio & Epistola de Vita & Morte Reverendissimi et Illvstrissimi Dn. Martini A Schavmberg, Principis & Episcopi Evstadiani: ... hæc scripta Romam ad Reuerendissimū & Illustrissimum Dn. Gvlielmvm Alanvm S.R.E. Cardinalem ... Ingoldstadii, ... Anno cIɔ.Iɔ.xxc. 8°, A—E 4 in eights, E 2 omitted, besides title, dedication, &c., 8 leaves. *B. M.*

Roberti Turneri Deuonij Oratoris et Philosophi Ingoldstadiensis Panegyrici Dvo, de Dvobvs Trivmphis clarissimis, illo Romæ de translatione Gregorij Nazianzeni; hoc Leodii in inauguratione Ernesti Ducis Bauariæ, ... Eiusdem Orationes xvi. Et Tres Commentationes in loca Scripturae, ... Additæ sunt eiusdem Epistolæ. Editio Secvnda melior & auctior. ... Ingoldstadii, ... Anno M.D.XCIX. 8°, A—O in eights: a—z in eights: Aa, 7 leaves.

Roberti Tvrneri Devonii Angli, Professoris Ingoldstadiensis, Posthuma. Orationes Septendecim, Tractatus Septem, Epistolarum centuriæ duæ. nusquam vnquam antehac edita ... Ingoldstadij, Typis Ederianis ... Anno M.DC II. 8°, A—Z in eights: a—z in eights: Aa, 8 leaves: Bb, 4: Campion's *Literary Remains*, A —F 4 in eights, F 4 blank. *B. M.*

Roberti Turneri Devonii Oratoris et Philosophi In Academia Ingoldstadiensi Epistolæ, Qvae reperiri potvere, additis centuriis duabus Posthumis Antehac nusquam coniunctim editæ. Coloniæ Agrippinæ ... M.DC.XV. 8°, A—Ee 4 in eights, besides the title: Index, &c. 4 leaves. *B. M.*

Roberti Tvrneri Viri Doctissimi Professoris in Academia Ingoldstadiensi Orationvm Volvmen Secvndvm, Recens in lucem editum. Accesservnt Edmvndi Campiani Societatis Iesv Martyris in Anglia, Orationes, Epistolæ, Tractatus de imitatione Rhetorica. à Roberto Tvrnero Campiani Discipvlo Collecta. Omnia nunc primum è M.S. edita, cum reliquis opusculis quotquot reperiri potuere. Coloniae Agrippinae ... Anno M.DC.XXV. 8°. A, 8 leaves: a—t 6 in eights. *B. M.*

TURNER, ROBERT, *of Holshot, Philomathos.*
Microkosmos. A Description of the Little-World. Being a Discovery of the Body of Man, exactly delineating all the Members, Bones, Veins, Sinews, ... Hereunto is added the maner of reducing, and curing dislocated, and fractured Bones. The Cure of Wounds made with Gunshot, ... Select Receipts for all manner of Diseases. ... The Judgement of Urine, and of Bathings ... London, Printed for

John Harrison, and are to be sold at the Holy Lamb, at the East end of Pauls. 1654. 8°, A—M in eights, A 1 and M 7-8 blank. Dedicated to the wife of Sir John Thorowgood, Knight, of Kensington. *B. M.*

Botanologia. The British Physician: Or, The Nature and Vertue of English Plants. Exactly describing such Plants as grow Naturally in our Land, with their correct Names, Greek, Latine, or English, Natures, Places where they grow, Times when they flourish, ... By means whereof People may gather their own Physick under every Hedge, or in their own Gardens, ... London, Printed by R. Wood for Nath. Brook at the Angel in Cornhill. 1664. 8°, A—Bb in eights, A 2 with the title. Dedicated to Sir Richard Chaworth, &c. *B. M.*

Botanologia. The British Physician: ... London, Printed for Obadiah Blagrave, ... 1687. 8°. Title, 1 leaf: a, 5 leaves: B—Bb in eights. With a curious portrait of the author. *B. M.*

TURNER, WILLIAM, *M.A., Vicar of Walberton, Sussex.*

An Essay upon the Works of Creation and Providence: Being an Introductory Discourse to the History of Remarkable Providences, Now preparing for the Press. To which is added a Further Specimen of the said Work: As also Meditations upon the Beauty of Holiness. ... London, Printed for John Dunton, ... and are also sold by Edm. Richardson near the Poultry Church. 1695. 8°, A—N 4 in eights, N 2-4 with Advertisements. Dedicated to the Worshipful James Butler, of Patcham, Sussex, and his virtuous consort. *B. M.*

> The *Meditations* have a separate title and a dedication "To my Dear Friends and Acquaintances in Flintshire, Shropshire, and Sussex, &c."

TUTCHIN, JOHN.

An Heroick Poem upon the Late Expedition of His Majesty, to rescue England from Popery, Tyranny, and Arbitrary Government. London: Printed, and are to be sold by R. Janeway, 1689. Folio, A—C, 2 leaves each.

TYSON, EDWARD, *M.D.*

Orang-Outang, sive Homo Sylvestris: Or, The Anatomy of a Pygmie Compared with that of a Monkey, an Ape, and a Man. To which is added, A Philological Essay Concerning the Pygmies, the Cynocephali, the Satyrs, and Sphinges of the Ancients. Wherein it will appear that they are all either Apes or Monkeys, and not Men, as formerly pretended. By Edward Tyson M.D. Fellow of the Colledge of Physicians, and the Royal Society: Physician to the Hospital of Bethlem, and Reader of Anatomy at Chirurgeons-Hall. London: Printed for Thomas Bennet ... and Daniel Brown ... and are to be had of Mr. Hunt at the Repository in Gresham-Colledge. MDCXCIX. 4°. *Imprimatur* by John Hoskins, V.P.R.S., 1 leaf: title, 1 leaf: dedication to Lord Chancellor Somers, 2 leaves: A, 2 leaves: B—O in fours: P, 2 leaves: *The Essay*, with a new bastard title, A—H in fours: I, 2 leaves, the second blank. With 17 figures on 8 plates.

> An anti-Darwinian book, demonstrating the improbability of man having evolved from the monkey by reason of the organic differences in the bones and muscles.

UBALDINO, PETRUCCIO, *Citizen of Florence.*

La Vita di Carlo Magno Imperadore. Londra Appresso Giouanni Wolfio Inghilese. 1581. 4°, A—D in fours, D 4 blank. Dedicated (in Italian) to the Knights and other Gentlemen of the English Nation. *B. M.*

> Said to be the earliest Italian book printed in London.

La Vita di Carlo Magno Imperadore: Scritta in lingua Italiana, & di nuouo corretta e reformata da Petruccio Vbaldino Cittadin Fiorentino. [No place and printer's name.] 1599. 4°, A—P in fours, P 4 blank. *B. M.*

> The Museum Catalogue ascribes this edition to the Oxford press.

Expeditionis Hispanorvm in Angliam vera descriptio Anno: M D LXXXVIII. [London, A. Ryther Sculpsit, 1588.] Large folio, eleven maps and the engraved title. *B. M.*

Militia Del Gran Dvca di Toscana. Capitoli, ordini, & priuilegij della Militia, ... 1597. 4°, A—I 2 in fours. Dedicated by Ubaldino to Queen Elizabeth. *B. M.*

> Lord Lumley's copy, with his autograph at foot of title as usual. This tract, which gives an account of the ordinances of Cosmo I. de Medici and his successors, as well as those of Sienna down to the year 1566, is ascribed by the Museum Catalogue to the English press. I confess that I am very doubtful.

URINES.

Here begynneth the seynge of Urynes of all the couloures that Urynes be of with the medycines annexed to euery Uryne / & euery Uryne his Urynall muche profitable for euery man to knowe. [Col.] Here endeth the boke of seynge of Waters Imprynted at London in Foster lane by me John Waley. 8°, A—F in eights. With the printer's mark below the colophon.

USHER, JAMES, *Archbishop of Armagh*. Strange and Remarkable prophesies and predictions of . . . James Usher. . . . Printed Anno 1681. 4°, 4 leaves. *B. M.*

USURY.
A Tract against Vsvrie. Presented to the High Court of Parliament. London, Printed by W. I. for Walter Burre, . . . 1621. 4°, A—C in fours.

V. J.
The danger of Treaties with Popish-Spirits. Or, A reasonable Caveat, and Premonition to our present most renowned Parliament, touching the frail trust in the Vowes and Protestations of Popishly-Affected Princes, for Peace and Reconcilement with their Protestant Subjects. *Abundans Cautela non nocet.* [Col.] London, Printed for I. Rothwell. 1644. 4°, 4 leaves.

VANE, SIR HENRY.
A Healing Motion From abroad to the Parliament of the Commonwealth of England, Scotland, and Ireland, &c. 8°. A, 4 leaves: B—E in eights.

The preface is dated September 1656, and purports to have been sent to the publisher "from some part of Germany."

VAUDOIS.
The History of the Negotiation of the Ambassadors sent to the Duke of Savoy, By the Protestant Cantons of Switzerland, concerning the Vaudois. Translated from the Original Copy printed in Switzerland. London : Printed for Richard Baldwin, . . . MDCXC. 4°, B—I in fours, besides title and *List of Books*.

VICARS, JOHN.
Coleman-street Conclave Visited. And, That Grand Impostor, the Schismaticks Cheater in Chief (who hath long, slily lurked therein) truly and duly discovered. . . . By John Vicars. . . . London : Printed for Nathanael Webb, and William Grantham, . . . 1648. 4°, A—G in fours, A 1 and G 4 blank, and B misprinted C. With a portrait of John Goodwin, beneath which are two copies of engraved verses.

VILLEGAS, ALPHONSO, *of the Order of St. Dominic*.
The Lives of Saints. Written in Spanish by the reuerend and learned father, . . . Translated out of Italian into English, and diligentlie compared with the Spanish. Whereunto are added the liues of sundry other Saints of the vniuersall Church. Extracted out of F. Ribadeniera, Surius, and out of other approued Authors. The Third edition, set forth by Iohn Heigham. [Quot. from Sap. 5. 4. *Wee senecles* . . .] With Priuiledge for ten yeares. Anno 1630. 4°. *, 4 leaves: A—6 U in fours, 6 U 4 with the *Priuilege : The Appendix*, A—L in fours, L 4 blank.

VIRGIL AND HOMER.
Verdicts of the Learned Concerning Virgil and Homer's Heroic Poems. *Nihil potest placere quod non decet.* Quintil. London : Printed for J. Hartley, next Middle-Row in Holbourn. 1697. 4°, A—D in fours.

VITIS.
Vitis Degeneris : Or, The Degenerate-Plant. Being a Treatise of Antient Ceremonies. Containing An Historical Account of their Rise and Growth, their first Entrance into the Church, and their gradual Advancement to Superstition therein. Written originally in French, but now, for general information and benefit, faithfully translated into English [by Thomas Douglas.] . . . London, Printed in the Year, 1668. 8°, A—O in eights, O 8 presumably blank.

VOX.
Vox Populi, Expressed in xxxv. Motions to this present Parliament. Being the generall voyce and the humble and earnest request of the people of God in England to our most Honorable and Religious Assembly, For reforming the present corrupt State of the Church. Published by Irenæus Philadelphus. Printed in the Yeare, 1641. 4°, A—B in fours, B 4 blank.

W. T.
A Second Letter to a Dissenter, Upon Occasion of His Majesties Late Gracious Declaration of Indulgence. London : Printed for John Harris, at the Harrow against the Church in the Poultrey. 1687. 4°, A—C 2 in fours.

WALES.
The Petition of Six Counties of South-Wales, and the County of Monmouth, Presented to the Parliament of the Com-

mon-wealth of England, for a supply of Ministers, in lieu of those that have been Ejected. Printed in the Year, 1652. 4°, A—D in fours.

Animadversions upon A Letter and Paper, first sent to His Highness by certain Gentlemen and others in Wales: And since printed, and published to the world by some of the Subscribers. By One whose Desire and Endeavor is, to Preserve Peace and Safety, By removing Offence and Enmity. Printed in the year 1656. 4°, A—O in fours.

WALLACE, SIR WILLIAM.
The Life and Acts of ... Sr William Wallace, ... With a Preface containing a short summe of the Historie of that time. Printed at Edinburgh by Iames Bryson, and are to be sold at his shop a litile aboue the Kirk Style at the signe of the golden Angell, Anno Dom. 1640. 8°. Title, Preface, and Table, 12 leaves: A—Aa in eights. Black letter. *B. M.*

> The *Bruce*, announced in the Preface, does not occur at the end; perhaps it was not actually issued.

WATSON, WILLIAM, *Student in Law.*
A Lawyer's Advice to the Devil's Agents: Or, Some Strokes at the Unfruitful Works of Darkness, Tending to their Destruction. Made with a Weapon taken out of the Armory of the Most High ... London, Printed for J. P. Bookseller at the Corner of Bread-street, in Cheap-side. 1693. 8°, A—E 4 in eights. *B. M.*

WEDLOCK.
Wedlock a Paradice: Or, A Defence of Woman's Liberty against Man's Tyranny. In Opposition to a Poem, Entituled, *The Pleasures of a Single Life*, &c. London, Printed, and are to be Sold by J. Nutt, ... 1701. Folio, A—D, 2 leaves each. In verse.

WEEMES, JOHN, *of Lathoquar in Scotland, Preacher of Christ's Gospel.*
The Povrtraitvre of the Image of God in Man. In his three Estates, of

{ Creation.
{ Restauration.
{ Glorification.

Digested into two parts. ... London, Printed for Iohn Bellamie, and are to be sold at his shop, at the signe of the three Golden Lions, in Cornhill, neere the Royall Exchange. 1627. 4°, A—Vv in fours, Vv 4 blank, besides (a)—(c 2) in fours. De licated to Sir David Fowlis, Knight and Baronet, one of the Councill of the North.

WERMYLIERUS, OTHO.
A Spirituall, and most precious Pearle, ... ¶ Printed at London for William Leake. 1560. Very small 8° or 12°, A—Z 3 in eights.

> Sotheby's, April 25, 1889, No. 191.

WESTMINSTER SCHOOL.
Institutio Græcæ Grammatices Compendiaria, In usum Regiæ Scholæ Westmonasteriensis. Editio prioribus emendatior. In usum studiosæ juventutis adduntur etiam quidam literarum nexus & scripturæ compendia, quæ partim elegantiæ, partim Brevitatis causâ usurpari solent. *Scientiarum janitriæ Grammatica.* Londini, Excudit Rogerus Nortonus Regius in Latinis, Græcis & Hebraicis Typographus. 1662. 8°, A—M in eights, first leaf blank. *B. M.*

Institutio ... Londini, Excudit Rogerus Nortonus. ... 1667. 8°, A—M in eights, first and last leaves blank. *B. M.*

Institutio Græcæ Grammatices Compendiaria, In Usum Regiæ Scholæ Westmonasteriensis. ... Londini, Excudit Rogerus Nortonus, Regius in Latinis, Græcis & Hebraicis Typographus. 1679. Cum Privilegio. 8°, A—M in eights.

> There is a long series of editions of this Manual, of which the inception is ascribed to William Camden.

WHISTON, JAMES.
England's Calamities Discover'd: With the Proper Remedy to Restore Her Ancient Grandeur and Policy. Humbly Presented By James Whiston. .... London: Printed for the Author, and are to be sold by Joseph Fox ... 1696. 4°, A—E in fours.

Englands State-Distempers, Trac'd from their Originals: With Proper Remedies and Means to make her Vertuous and Prosperous. Humbly Presented by James Whiston .... (ii.) The Mismanagement in Trade Discovered, and adapt Methods to Preserve and Improve it. ... 1704. 4°, A—F 2 in fours: A—E 2 in fours.

WHITBOURNE, RICHARD, *of Exmouth.*
A Discovrse Containing A Loving Invitation both Honourable, and profitable to all such as shall be Aduenturers, either in person, or purse, for the aduancement of his Maiesties most hopefull Plantation in the New-Fovnd-Land, lately vndertaken. Written by Captaine Richard Whitbovrne of Exmouth, in the County of Deuon. Imprinted at London by Felix Kyngston, Dwelling in Pater-noster-Row. 1622.

4°, A—G in fours, G 4 blank. Dedicated to Henry, Viscount Falkland.
This is a sequel to the first narrative.

WHITE, JOHN.
A Rich Cabinet, With Variety of Inventions: ... The fourth Edition, with many Additions. London, Printed for William Whitwood, at the sign of the Golden Lion in Duck-Lane next Smith-field. 1668. 8°, A—N in eights, including the frontispiece by T. Cross and *The Authour to his Book* in verse. With cuts.

WHITEHALL, ROBERT.
The Coronation. A Poem. By Ro: Whitehall, Fellow of Merton College, Oxon. *Divisum Imperium cum Jove Cæsar habet.* By R. W. London, Printed for John Playford, at his Shop in the Temple, near the Church-door. 1661. Folio, 4 leaves.
The copy in the British Museum, from which I was obliged to take my former account, is cropped, and has the imprint mutilated. I have since met with an uncut one. But, like Whitehall's other publications, it is a pamphlet of remarkable rarity.

The English Rechabite, Or, A Defyance to Bacchvs and all his Works. A Poem in LXVII. Hexastichs: Wherein is rendered a plenary and full Account how Wines are pejorated, (or reduced from better to worse.) And by Admixture of what heterogeneous bodies they become corrupted and marr'd. ... By R. W. a Wellwisher to the Body natural as well as politick. London, Printed by M. Flesher, for Henry Clements, Booksellers in Oxon. Folio, A—D, 2 leaves each. In verse.

WILLIAM III. *of Orange, King of Great Britain* [1688-1702.]
A Memorial from the English Protestants, For their Highnesses the Prince and Princess of Orange. [1688.] Folio, A—G in twos.

A Letter to a Gentleman at Brussels, Containing An Account of the Cavses of the Peoples Revolt from the Crown. London, Printed in the Year MDCLXXXIX. 4°, A—B in fours.

An Answer to the Paper Delivered by Mr. Ashton at his Execution to Sir Francis Child; Sheriff of London, &c. Together with the Paper it self. London: Printed for Robert Clavel, at the Peacock in S. Paul's Church-Yard. 1690. 4°, A—Q in fours, A 1 with the *Imprimatur* signed by Viscount Sydney, and dated March 17, 1690.

A Second Modest Enquiry into the Causes of the Present Disasters in England. And who they are that brought the French Fleet into the English Channel, Described. Being a farther Discovery of the Jacobite Plot. Together with a List of those Noble-men, Gentlemen, and others now in Custody. London, Printed for John Dunton ... and John Harris ... MDCXC. 4°, A—E 2 in fours.
Among the persons in custody occurs the name of Secretary Pepys, who was confined to the Gatehouse.

Their Present Majesties Government Proved to be Throughly Settled, And that we may Submit to it, without Asserting the Principles of Mr. Hobbs. Shewing also, That Allegiance was not Due to the Usurpers of the late Civil War. Occasion'd by some Late Pamphlets against the Reverend Dr. Sherlock. London, Printed for Robert Clavel, and are to be sold by John North in Dublin, 1691. 4°, A—E 2, in fours.

A Letter to a Lord, In Answer to a Late Pamphlet, Intituled, *The Causes of the present Fears* ... In a Discourse between a Lord-Lieutenant and One of his Deputies. London: Printed for Tho. Bennet, ... 1692. 4°, B—E in fours, E 4 blank, and the title.

A Letter [and a second letter] to a Friend, Concerning a French Invasion, To Restore the Late King James to the Throne. And What may be expected from him, should he be Successful in it. Published by Authority. Printed at London, and Re-Printed at Edinburgh, by the Heir of Andrew Anderson, ... 1692. 4°, A—D in fours.

The Present Aspect of our Times, And of the Extraordinary Conjunction of Things therein. In a Rational View and Prospect of the same. As it respects the Publick Hazard and Safety of Britain in this Day. London, Printed for Thomas Parkhurst ... 1694. 4°, A—D in fours.

Observations upon the Papers which Mr. Rookwood and Mr. Lowick deliver'd to the Sheriffs, at the time of their Execution, April 29. 1696. Together with Remarks upon some part of Mr. Cranburn's Discourse with the Sheriffs at the same time. Published by Authority. London, Printed for R. Clavel, ... 1696. 4°, A—C 2 in fours.

The Arraignment, Tryal, and Condemnation of Peter Cooke, Gent. For High-Treason, In Endeavouring to procure Forces from France to invade this Kingdom, and Conspiring to Levy War ... in order to the Deposing of His Sacred

M

Majesty, King William, and Restoring the Late King . . . Penned by the Lord Chief Justice Treby, and the Council present at the Tryal. London, Printed for Benjamin Tooke . . . MDCXCVI. Folio, A—T, 2 leaves each, A 1 occupied by the *Imprimatur* signed Geo. *Treby.*

Limitations for the Next Foreign Successor, Or New Saxon Race. Debated in a Conference betwixt two Gentlemen. Sent in a Letter to a Member of Parliament. *Auctoritate suadendi magis quam jubendi Potestate.* Tacitus *de moribus Germanorum.* London, Printed in the Year 1701. 4°, B—E in fours, E 4 blank, and the title.

WIT.

Wits Academy : Or, The Muses Delight. Being the Newest Academy of Complements. Consisting of Merry Dialogues upon Various Occasions, Composed of Mirth, Wit, and Eloquence. . . . The Ninth Edition, with Additions. London : Printed by R. Janeway, for Eben. Tracy, . . . 1704. Sm. 8°, A—M in twelves, including the woodcut frontispiece.

[WITHER, GEORGE.]

The Speech without Doore. Delivered July 9. 1644. in the absence of the Speaker, and in the hearing of above 000003 persons, then present ; who unanimously consented to all Propositions therein contained, and voted the same fit to be further divulged, as very pertinent to the publike welfare. [London, 1644.] 4°, A—B in fours, B 4 blank. Without a title-page. *B. M.*

WITTIE, ROBERT, M.D.

Gout Raptures. Astromakia. Or An Historical Fiction of a War among the Stars : Wherein are mentioned the 7 Planets, the 12 Signs of the Zodiack, and the 50 Constellations of Heaven mentioned by the Ancients. Also several eminent Stars, and the most principal parts and lines of the Celestial Globe with their Natures and Uses are pointed out. Useful for such as apply themselves to the Study of Astronomy, and the Celestial Globe. Cambridge. Printed by John Hayes, Printer to the University : and are to be sold by John Creed, Bookseller. 1677. 8", A—D in eights, A 1 blank and D 8 with *Errata.* In Greek, Latin, and English verse.

> The author informs us in his preface, that the work originated in a fit of the gout, which happened to himself, and disabled him from reading, &c.

WONDER.

The Worlds Wonder, Or, Joyful Newes from Scotland and Ireland. Comprized in the ensuing Predictions, and Monethly Observations, for this pr[e]sent year, 1651. Foreshewing the great things that will come to pass in England, Ireland, and Scotland. the several fights that will happen between the Lord Gen. Cromwel and the Scots, and the Lord Gen. Deputy Ireton, and the Irish ; . . . joyful tydings for the London Merchants, and exceeding good news for the countrey Farmers, . . . Extracted out of the Original. Licensed according to Order. London, Printed by John Clowes, 1651. 4°, 4 leaves. With a cut on title.

WOODHOUSE, JOHN, *Surveyor.*

A Map for Strangers in the Kingdome of Ireland. Wherein The High-Wayes and Roads from all the Sea-Townes, Market Parishes, great or small, is truely set down, throughout every Province, and the whole Kingdom, by a Surveyor therof John Woodhouse. As also a Map of Ireland, and the Townes thereof Alphabetically Printed, that by the Longitude and Latitude, you may set your finger on the Towne you desire to finde. The use thereof, as also of the mappe, to finde all distances from any places, are in this Book. As also, A True Relation of the Bloody Massacres, tortures, cruelties, and abominable outrages committed upon the Protestants proved upon Oath, and [by] eye-Witnesses. London, Printed for Iohn Rothwell, at the signe of the Sun & Fountain, in Pauls Church yard 1647. 8°, *B. M.*

> This copy wants the map, alphabetical list of towns, &c., and has only A in eights.

The Map of Ireland, With the exact Dimensions of the Provinces therein contained, and those againe divided into their severall Counties. With the names of all the Townes and places great and small alphabetically set downe. . . . As also the High-wayes and Roads from all the Sea-Towns, Parishes, . . . London, Printed by M. Simmons for Tho : Jenner, . . . 1653. 4", A—C in fours : no D : E, 2 leaves. *B. M.*

> This copy presumably wants the map, if not sign. D.

WOOL.

A Treatise of Wool and Cattel. In a Letter written to a Friend, Occasion'd upon a Discourse Concerning the great Abatements of Rents, and Low Value of Lands. Wherein is shewed how their Worth and Value may be advanced by the Improvement of the Manufacture of our English Wool, and the Spending of our Cattel. London : Printed by J. C. for Will. Crook, . . . 1677. 4°, A—E 2 in fours.

A Treatise of Wool, And the Manufacture of it : In a Letter to a Friend Occasion'd upon a Discourse . . . Together with the Presentment of the Grand Jury of the County of Somerset, at the General Quarter Sessions begun at Brewton the Thirteenth Day of January 1684. London, Printed for William Crooke. . . . 1685. 4°, A—C in fours : the Presentment, 4 leaves (from another book).

An Essay on Wool, and Woollen Manufacture, For the Improvement of Trade, To the Benefit of Landlords, Feeders of Sheep, Clothiers, and Merchants. In a Letter to a Member of Parliament. London : Printed for Henry Bonwicke, . . . 1693. Price 3d. 4°, B—C in fours, a leaf of D, and the title.

Some Thoughts on the Bill Depending before the Right Honourable the House of Lords, For Prohibiting the Exportation of the Woollen Manufactures of Ireland to Foreign Parts. Humbly offer'd to their Lordships. Dublin, Printed by J. Ray in Skinner Row, over against the Thalsel for Eliphal Dobson, Bookseller in Castle street, 1698. 4°, A—B 3 in fours.

The Interest of England, In Relation to the Woollen Manufacture, Briefly Consider'd : In a Dialogue between Sir Thomas Flourishing, a Merchant, and Timothy Castdown, a Clothier. . . . London, Printed for J. Nut neer Stationers-Hall, 1701. 4°, A—D in fours.

WORSHIP.
The Great Question Concerning Things Indifferent in Religious Worship, Briefly stated ; and tendred to the Consideration of all Sober and Impartial men. [Quot. from Chillingworth, Præf. s. 34.] London, Printed in the Year, 1660. 4°. A, 2 leaves : B—C in fours.

WYCHERLEY, WILLIAM.
The Gentleman Dancing-Master. A Comedy, Acted at the Duke's Theatre. By Mr. Wycherley. Horat. ——*Non satis est risu* . . . London, Printed by J. M. for Henry Herringman and Thomas Dring, . . . 1673. 4°. A, 2 leaves : B—O 2 in fours. *B. M.*

The Gentleman Dancing-Master. . . . London, Printed for Richard Wellington at the Dolphin and Crown at the West-End of St. Paul's Church-yard. 1702. . . . 4°, A—I in fours. *B. M.*

The Plain-Dealer. A Comedy. As it is Acted at the Theatre Royal. Written by Mr. Wycherley. Horat.—*Ridiculum acri* . . . London, Printed by T. N. for James Magnes and Rich. Bentley. . . . M.DC.LXXVII. 4°, B—N in fours, besides title, dedication "To my Lady B——," Prologue and Epilogue, 6 leaves. *B. M.*

Three editions the same year.

The Plain-Dealer. . . . The Sixth Edition. London, Printed for R. Bentley, . . . MDCXCIV. 4°, A—M 2 in fours, and a, 2 leaves. *B. M.*

The Country-Wife, A Comedy, Acted at the Theatre-Royal. Written by Mr. Wycherley. [Quot. from Horat.] London : Printed for T. Dring, and sold by R. Bentley, . . . 1688. 4°. A, 2 leaves : B—K in fours. *B. M.*

The Country-Wife, A Comedy, Acted at the Theatre-Royal. Written by Mr. Wycherley. [Quot. from Horace—*Indignor quicquam reprehendi*. London, Printed for Samuel Briscoe in Russel-street Covent-Garden. and David Dring at the Harrow in Fleet-street. 1695. 4°. A, 2 leaves : B—I in fours.

Love in a Wood, Or, St. James's Park. A Comedy. As it is Acted By Their Majesties Servants. Written by Mr. Wycherley.
—*Excludit sanos Helicone poetas Democritus ;*—Horat.
London, Printed by T. Warren for Henry Herringman, . . . 1694. 4°, A—I in fours. Dedicated to the Duchess of Cleveland. *B. M.*

Miscellany Poems : As Satyrs, Epistles, Love-Verses, Songs, Sonnets, &c. By W. Wycherley, Esq ;
—*Et precor integra* . . .
Hor. lib. 1. Ode 31.
London : Printed for C. Brome, J. Taylor, and B. Tooke ; . . . MDCCIV. Folio, [a]—[m], 2 leaves each : A—3 I in fours. With a portrait of the author. *B. M.*

This is called the first volume at the end ; but no more is known to have appeared. Copies were printed on large paper ; one occurred at the Surrenden sale, which had been presented by Wycherley "to the fairest lady in Kent," Mistress Jane Twysden.

YOUNG, THOMAS, *of Staple Inn.*
Englands Bane : Or, The Description of Drunkennesse. . . . London, Printed by W. I. for Thomas Bayly, . . . 1634. Sm. 8°, A—F in eights, first and last leaves blank. Dedicated to Sir Francis Dowse, Knight. *B. M.*

ADDENDUM.

CERTANI, GIACOMO, *L'Abbate.*
Il Mosè Dell' Ibernia Vita Del Glorioso S. Patrizio Canonico Regolare Lateranense, Apostolo, e Primate dell' Ibernia . . . In Bologna, ... MDCLXXXVI. 4". Prefixes, 10 leaves, including half-title : a plate of the Saint exorcising demons : A—3 Y in fours : *Errata*, 1 leaf.

FANATICS.
A True and Exact Copy of a Treasonable and Bloody Paper, Called, The Fanaticks New-Covenant : Which was taken from Mr. Donald Cargill, at Queens-Ferry, the Third Day of June, Anno Dom. 1680. One of their Field-Preachers, a declared Rebel and Traytor. Together with their Execrable Declaration . . . Reprinted at London by T. N. according to the Copy Printed at Edenburgh ; and are to be sold by Andrew Forrester in King-street Westminster. 1680. Folio, A—C, 2 leaves each.

FULKE, W.
A Most pleasant Prospect, Into the Garden of Naturall Contemplation, . . . The third Edition corrected and amended. London, Printed by E. G. for William Leake, . . . 1640. 8", black letter. ¶, 4 leaves, the first blank : A—I in eights, I 8 blank.
    The date has been altered with the pen to 1646 in this copy.

GIBBON, JOHN.
Day-Fatality : Or, Some Observation of Days Lucky and Unlucky, Concluding with Some Remarques upon the Fourteenth of October, the Avspicious Birthday of His Royal Highness, James Duke of York. *Ataris qui Regibus editus* . . . Num. XVII. 8, 9. . . . . [London, 1678.] Folio, 4 leaves.
    The date is given on the authority of Aubrey.

GYFFORD, GEORGE.
A Catechisme conteining the summe of Christian Religion, giuing a most exellent light to all those that seeke to enter the path-way to saluation : Newlie set foorth by G. G. Preacher of Gods worde at Malden in Essex . . . Imprinted at London at the three Cranes in the Vintree by Thomas Dawson. 1583. 8°. *, 2 leaves : A—L 4 in eights.

NAUDÆUS, GABRIEL.
News from France. Or, A Description of the Library of Cardinall Mazarini : before it was utterly ruined. Sent in a Letter from Monsieur G. Naudæus, Keeper of the publick Library. London, Printed for Timothy Garthwait, at the little Northdoor of Pauls, 1652. 4°, 4 leaves.

PATRICK, ST.
Histoire De la Vie et dv Pvrgatoire de Saint Patrice Archevesqve, & Primat d'Hybernie Mise en François par le R. P. François Bovillon, . . . A Paris, Chez Iean dv Pvis, ... M.DC.LXV. Auec Approbation. 8°. ã, 4 leaves : ẽ, 2 : A—T in eights : V, 4 : X, 8 : Y, 4 : Z, 8 : Aa, 1. Dedicated to Mme Charlot.

RECORDE, ROBERT, *of Tenby.*
Record's Arithmetick, Or, The Ground of Arts ; . . . . now diligently perused, corrected, illustrated and inlarged : . . . . London, Printed by James Flesher, and are to be sold by Robert Boulter, . . . 1668. 8°, A—M in eights.
    This book in its present form exhibits the additions of several editors, including Robert Hartwill and Thomas Willsford.

SCOTLAND.
A True and Impartial Account of the Examinations and Confessions of several Execrable Conspirators Against the King & His Government in Scotland. Together with the Proclamation Issued upon that Occasion by the Lords of His Majesties Privy-Council of that Kingdom. Published by Authority. London: Printed for Andrew Forrester, near the Mitre-Tavern in King-street Westminster. MDCLXXXI. Folio, A—E, 2 leaves each.

SPARKE, THOMAS, AND JOHN SEDDON.
A Catechisme, Or Short Kind of Instrvction, Whereby to teach Children and the Ignoranter Sort, the Christian Religion. Whereunto is prefixed a learned Treatise of the necessity and vse of Catechising; Together with Godly praiers most fit for al estates at al times. At Oxford, Printed by Ioseph Barnes, & are to bee sold in Paules Church-yard at the Signe of the Tygers head, 1588. 4°, A—Ff in fours, Ff 4 blank. Dedicated by Sparke and Seddon to Arthur, Lord Grey of Wilton.

WESTMINSTER.
Several Orders Made and agreed upon By the Iustices of the Peace for the City and Liberty of Westminster, Vpon Monday the 10. day of March, 1655. Concerning the future Licensing of all Inn-keepers, Victualers, & Alehouse-keepers, within the said City and Liberty. Putting in execution the Laws and Ordinances for the better Observation of the Lord's-day; And the Laws and Statutes concerning the Punishment and Conveyance of Rogues, Sturdy Beggers, and Vagrants, to the place of their births. With a declaration of such persons as are accounted Rogues by the several Statutes; and the penalties of several persons, both Officers and private persons neglecting their duty concerning them. Setting forth what will be for the time to come expected from the Church-wardens, Overseers of the Poor, Constables and others, Inhabitants within the said City and Liberty. London, Printed by W. G. [1655-6.] Folio, 6 leaves unpaged and unsigned.

The first meeting of the Middlesex justices here recorded was held at the Half-Moon in the Strand on the 29th of March, 1649.

A SELECT LIST

OF

Works or Editions

BY

WILLIAM CAREW HAZLITT

OF THE INNER TEMPLE

CHRONOLOGICALLY ARRANGED

1860—1889.

---

1. **History of the Venetian Republic**; Its Rise, its Greatness, and its Civilization. With Maps and Illustrations. 4 vols. 8vo. *Smith, Elder, & Co.* 1860.
   A new edition, entirely recast, with important additions, in 3 vols. crown 8vo, is in readiness for the press.

2. **Old English Jest-Books, 1525-1639.** Edited with Introductions and Notes. *Facsimiles.* 3 vols. 12mo. 1864.

3. **Remains of the Early Popular Poetry of England.** With Introductions and Notes. 4 vols. 12mo. *Woodcuts.* 1864-66.

4. **Handbook to the Early Popular, Poetical, and Dramatic Literature** of Great Britain. Demy 8vo. 1867. Pp. 714 in two columns.

5. **Bibliographical Collections and Notes.** 1867-76. Medium 8vo. 1876.
   This volume comprises a full description of about 6000 Early English books from the books themselves. It is a sequel and companion to No. 4. See also Nos. 6-9 *infrà*.

   "There never was a more accurate and painstaking bibliographer than Mr. Hazlitt, nor is there any bibliography of English literature which can compete with his works. I have found from personal experience that they are absolutely necessary to the English collector."— BERNARD QUARITCH.
   These and the three following items are the result of more than thirty years' continuous labour, during which the author doubtless has had submitted to his notice more English book-rarities than any other bibliophile in Europe. There are several thousand of articles in this work, which may be regarded as an appendix to the bibliographical account of Early English Literature.

6. **Bibliographical Collections and Notes.** SECOND SERIES. 1876-82. Medium 8vo. 1882.
   Uniform with First Series. About 10,000 titles on the same principle as before.

   "I very respectfully, yet with cordial pleasure, submit to such sections of the educated and reading English community in the United Queendom, the States of America, and elsewhere, as feel an interest in that early literature, which ought to be dear to the entire English-speaking race, a *Third* and *Final* Series of my *Bibliographical Collections and Notes*, forming (with my Handbook), the fourth volume of my achievement in this province of re-earch.
   "The objection to the multiplication of alphabets by the sectional treatment, which I have adopted since the appearance of the Handbook in 1867, is a very valid objection indeed from the point of view of the consulter. But as this has been, and remains, a labour of love, and as the cost of production was a grave problem, I simply had no alternative; and to the suggestion which I offered in a prior Introduction, that, after all, these serial volumes might be regarded in the same light as so many catalogues of public or private collections, I have now the gratifying announcement to add, that a complete Index to the Handbook and the three Series of Collections and Notes is in preparation by Mr. Gray of Cambridge, who has most generously volunteered to do the work, and will form a separate volume, to be published by Mr. Quaritch, when it is completed.
   "I have incorporated (generally with additions and corrections) in my volumes by degrees nearly the whole of the Bibliotheca Anglo-Poetica, Corser's Collectanea (excepting, of course, the lengthy and elaborate extracts and annotations), the British Museum Catalogue of Early English Books to 1640, the Typographical Antiquities of Ames, Herbert, and Dibdin, the Chatsworth, Huth, Ashburnham, and other private cabinets, and the various publications of Haslewood, Park, Utterston, and Collier.
   "Since the Second Series came from the press in 1882, several large private libraries have been dispersed under the hammer, and all the articles previously overlooked by me have been duly taken

up into my pages. I may enumerate, for example's sake, the celebrated collections of the Earl of Jersey, the Earl of Gosford, Mr. James Crossley of Manchester, Mr. Payne Collier, the Duke of Marlborough, Mr. Hartley, Mr. N. P. Simes of Horsham, Sir Richard Colt Hoare, Mr. Michael Wodhull, Sir Thomas Phillipps of Middle-Hill, the Rev. J. Fuller Russell, Mr. Henry Pyne, and Professor Solly."—*Preface to Second Series.*

"Mr. W. C. Hazlitt's second series of *Bibliographical Collections and Notes* (Quaritch) is the result of many years' searches among rare books, tracts, ballads, and broadsides by a man whose speciality is bibliography, and who has thus produced a volume of high value. If any one will read through the fifty-four closely-printed columns relating to Charles I., or the ten and a half columns given to 'London' from 1541 to 1794, and recollect that these are only a supplement to twelve columns in Hazlitt's *Handbook* and five and a half in his first *Collections*, he will get an idea of the work involved in this book. Other like entries are 'James I.,' 'Ireland,' 'France,' 'England,' 'Eliza eth,' 'Scotland' (which has twenty-one and a half columns), and so on. As to the curiosity and rarity of the works that Mr. Hazlitt has catalogued, any one who has been for even twenty or thirty years among old books will acknowledge that the strangers to him are far more numerous than the acquaintances and friends. This second series of *Collections* will add to Mr. Hazlitt's well-earned reputation as a bibliographer, and should be in every real library through the English-speaking world. The only thing we desiderate in it is more of his welcome marks and names, B.M., Britwell, Lambeth, &c., to show where all the books approaching rarity are. The service that these have done in Mr. Hazlitt's former books to editors for the Early-English Text, New Shakespere, Spenser, Hunterian, and other societies, has been so great that we hope he will always say where he has seen the rare books that he makes entries of."—*Academy, August 26, 1882.*

7. **Bibliographical Collections and Notes.** A Third and Final Series. 1886. 8vo.

Uniform with the First and Second Series. This volume contains upwards of 3000 Articles.

"Mr. Hazlitt has done much work during the last thirty years, and some of it has been bitterly attacked; but we venture to think that the debt of gratitude which all students of Old English literature owe to him for his bibliographical collections must remain in the most enduring opinion of his labours. We would bid all readers who care for the books of the past read the practical, manly, and comprehensive introduction prefixed to this volume. It forms one of the best pleas for the study of English literature which we know; and coming close upon the important speech of Mr. John Morley, it takes up a phase of the subject not yet adequately recognised. The academic side has been put by Mr. Morley, the practical by Mr. Hazlitt: 'The England in which we dwell is one with the England which lies behind us. So far as the period which I comprehend goes, it is one country and one race; and I do not think that we should precipitately and unkindly spurn the literature which our foregoers left to us and to our descendants for ever, because it may at first sight strike us as irrelevant to our present wants and feelings. . . . The considerer of modern opinions and customs is too little addicted to retrospection. He seems to be too shy of profiting on the one hand by the counsels or suggestions, on the other by the mistakes of the men who have crossed the unrepassable line, who have dealt with the topics and problems with which we have to deal.' These are stirring and sensible words, and we should much like to see them more widely distributed than the limited issue of this volume will allow.

"It is impossible, in a short notice such as we can only give, to do justice to the contents of this work. The titles of every book or tract are given in full, having been transcribed by Mr. Hazlitt himself; and there is often appended to the entry interesting information about the condition, history, and, above all things, the present locale of the book. Such work as this requires labour, and skill, and knowledge of no ordinary kind. Now that Mr. Bradshaw is dead, there are few indeed who possess these qualities, and apparently only one who puts them at the service of his fellows. It has been often said of late that the bibliographer and indexer are more needed than the book-writer; and if this is true, as we are inclined to think it, Mr. Hazlitt's work must, in relation to the age in which it is produced, be awarded a very high place. It enables us to ascertain what has been done in English literature, and therefore ought to enable us to do our work so much the better. Almost all departments of study are now occupied as much with a reconsideration of old facts as with the discovery of new, and for this purpose such books as Mr. Hazlitt's are indispensable. We are happy to say that a competent Cambridge student has undertaken to compile an index to the four volumes of bibliography issued by Mr. Hazlitt, and that this will be published by Mr. Quaritch as soon as it is ready."—*The Antiquary,* April 1887.

8. **Bibliographical Collections and Notes.** Supplements to the Third and Final Series. Medium 8vo. 1889. Pp. 181 + 8.

9. **A General Index to Hazlitt's Bibliographical Works** (1867-89). By G. J. Gray. Medium 8vo. 1889. About 400 pp.

This invaluable volume will assist the student and collector in using the several volumes of which the Series now consists, and will enable him to ascertain at a glance whether and where a book, tract, or broadside is to be found. It is a labour which Mr. Gray has undertaken *con amore,* and reflects the highest honour on his industry, discernment, and literary zeal.

. All these books are now on sale by Mr. Quaritch.

10. **Memoirs of William Hazlitt.** With Portions of his Correspondence. Portraits after miniatures by John Hazlitt. 2 vols. 8vo. 1867.

During the last twenty years the author has been indefatigable in collecting additional information for the *Life of Hazlitt,* 1867, in correcting errors, and in securing all the unpublished letters which have come into the market, some of great interest, with a view to a new and improved edition.

11. **Inedited Tracts.** Illustrating the Manners, Opinions, and Occupations of Englishmen during the 16th and 17th Centuries. 1586-1618. With an Introduction and Notes. *Facsimiles.* 4to. 1868.

12. **The Works of Charles Lamb.** Now first collected, and entirely rearranged. With Notes. 4 vols. 8vo. *E. Moxon & Co.* 1868-69.

13. **Letters of Charles Lamb.** With some Account of the Writer, his Friends and Correspondents, and Explanatory Notes. By the late Sir Thomas Noon Talfourd, D.C.L., one of his Executors. An entirely new edition, carefully revised and greatly enlarged by W. Carew Hazlitt. 2 vols. 1886. Post 8vo.

13a. **Mary and Charles Lamb.** New Facts and Inedited Remains. 8vo. *Woodcuts and Facsimiles.* 1874.
    The groundwork of this volume was an Essay by the writer in *Macmillan's Magazine.*

14. **English Proverbs and Proverbial Phrases.** Arranged alphabetically and annotated. Medium 8vo. 1869. Second Edition, corrected and greatly enlarged, crown 8vo. 1882.

15. **Narrative of the Journey of an Irish Gentleman through England** in 1751. From a MS. With Notes. 8vo. 1869.

16. **The English Drama and Stage, under the Tudor and Stuart Princes.** 1547-1664. With an Introduction and Notes. 4to. 1869.
    A series of Reprinted Documents and Treatises.

17. **Popular Antiquities of Great Britain.** I. The Calendar. II. Customs and Ceremonies. III. Superstitions. 3 vols. Medium 8vo. 1870.
    Brand's *Popular Antiquities*, by Ellis, 1813, taken to pieces, recast, and enormously augmented.

18. **Inedited Poetical Miscellanies.** 1584-1700. Thick 8vo. With Notes and Facsimiles. 50 copies privately printed. 1870.

19. **Warton's History of English Poetry.** An entirely new edition, with Notes by Sir F. Madden, T. Wright, F. J. Furnivall, R. Morris, and others, and by the Editor. 4 vols. Medium 8vo. 1871.

20. **The Feudal Period.** Illustrated by a Series of Tales (from Le Grand). 12mo. 1874.

21. **Prefaces, Dedications, and Epistles.** Prefixed to Early English Books. 1540-1701. 8vo. 1874.
    50 copies privately printed.

22. **Blount's Jocular Tenures.** Tenures of Land and Customs of Manors. Originally published by Thomas Blount of the Inner Temple in 1679. An entirely new and greatly enlarged edition by W. Carew Hazlitt, of that Ilk. Medium 8vo. 1874.

23. **Dodsley's Select Collection of Old Plays.** A new edition, greatly enlarged, corrected throughout, and entirely rearranged. With a Glossary by Dr. Richard Morris. 15 vols. 8vo. 1874-76.

24. **Fairy Tales, Legends, and Romances.** Illustrating Shakespear and other Early English Writers. 12mo. 1875.

25. **Shakespear's Library:** A Collection of the Novels, Plays, and other Material supposed to have been used by Shakespear. An entirely new edition. 6 vols. 12mo. 1875.

26. **Fugitive Tracts (written in verse) which illustrate the Condition** of Religious and Political Feeling in England, and the State of Society there, during two centuries. 1493-1700. 2 vols. 4to. 50 copies privately printed. 1875.

27. **Poetical Recreations.** By W. C. Hazlitt. 50 copies printed. 12mo. 1877.
    A new edition, revised and very greatly enlarged, is in preparation.

28. **The Baron's Daughter.** A Ballad. 75 copies printed. 4to. 1877.

29. **The Essays of Montaigne.** Translated by C. Cotton. An entirely new edition, collated with the best French text. With a Memoir, and all the extant Letters. *Portrait and Illustrations.* 3 vols. 8vo. 1877.
    The only library edition.

30. **Catalogue of the Huth Library.** [English portion.] 5 vols. Large 8vo. 1880. 200 copies printed.

31. **Offspring of Thought in Solitude.** Modern Essays. 1884. 8vo, pp. 384.
    Some of these Papers were originally contributed to *All the Year Round*, &c.

32. **Old Cookery Books and Ancient Cuisine.** 12mo. 1886.

"Full of curious information, this work can fairly claim to be a philosophical history of our national cookery."—*Morning Post.*

33. **An Address to the Electors of Mid-Surrey, among whom I live.** In Rejoinder to Mr. Gladstone's Manifesto. 1886. 8vo, pp. 32.

"Who would not grieve, if such a man there be?
Who would not weep, if Atticus were he?"—POPE.

34. **Gleanings in Old Garden Literature.** 12mo. 1887.

35. **Schools, Schoolbooks, and Schoolmasters.** A Contribution to the History of Educational Development. 12mo. *J. W. Jarvis & Son.* 1888. Pp. 300 + vi.

Survey of the old system of teaching—Dr. Busby—Early Dictionaries—Colloquies in the Tenth, Twelfth, and Thirteenth Centuries—Earliest printed works of instruction. Donatus and others—Stanbridge—Robert Whittington—Guarini of Verona—Vulgaria of Terence—School Classics—Erasmus and More—Dean Colet—Foundation of St. Paul's—Thomas Linacre—Wolsey's Edition of Lily's Grammar—Merchant Taylors' School—Old Mode of Advertising Private Establishments—Museum Minervæ at *Bethnal Green*—Manchester Old School—Shakespeare, Sir Hugh Evans, and Holofernes—Educational Condition of Scotland—Female Education—Shakespeare's Daughters—Goldsmith—Ascham and Mulcaster—Ben Jonson and Shirley, writers of Grammars—Foreigners' English—Phonography—Bullokar—Charles Butler—Dr. Jones.

SELECTIONS FROM PRESS OPINIONS:—

"A perusal of Mr. W. Carew Hazlitt's book is calculated to make both parents and boys thankful that they live in an age of comparative enlightenment. The work does not profess to be an exhaustive one, the object being 'to trace the sources and rise of our educational system, and to present a general view of the principles on which the groundwork of this system was laid.' In pursuing this plan the writer has succeeded in producing a book, which, though dealing with what some readers may consider rather a dry subject, is full of curious and interesting information, judiciously arranged and pleasantly conveyed."—*Morning Post.*

"This book contains a great deal of very curious information. After an introductory chapter on the system of teaching in the good old times when holidays were unknown and stick ointment laid the basis of all culture, an account is given of the various vocabularies, glossaries, and colloquies in use in mediæval times. Some interesting and amusing details are also given of sixteenth century school-books, and Mr. Hazlitt sketches the scholastic work done by Erasmus, Colet, Linacre, Lily, Ruddiman, and others, and gives us an insight into the methods followed in such schools as St. Paul's and the Merchant Taylors' Institution. . . . One of the most interesting chapters in the volume is that on female education."—*Glasgow Herald.*

". . . Mr. Hazlitt knows his subject, and he also knows how to write. No small praise."—*St. Stephen's Review.*

". . . Some of Mr. Hazlitt's pages are occupied with the humorous side of school life; and as he tells a story well, these portions of the book come upon one with singular pleasure."—*Antiquary.*

"Mr. Hazlitt has evidently a favourite speciality in school-books. He has collected them, we should judge, with a good deal of zeal, and has acquired a really considerable amount of knowledge about them, &c."—*Spectator.*

FROM THE PREFACE.—

"My main object has been to trace the sources and rise of our educational system, and to present a general view of the principles on which the groundwork of this system was laid. So far as I am capable of judging, the narrative will be found to embody a good deal that is new and a good deal that ought to be interesting.

"The bias of the volume is literary, not bibliographical; but its production has involved a very considerable amount of research, not only among books which proved serviceable, but among those which yielded me no contribution to my object.

"When we regard a History of English Literature, and the works which either constitute its principal strength and glory, or even such as, rather from the circumstances connected with them than their own intrinsic importance, lend to it a certain incidental or special value, it becomes natural to inquire by what process or course of training the men and women whose names compose the roll of fame became, or were aided at least in becoming, what they were and remain."